Ethnic Identity and Power

SUNY series,
Power, Social Identity, and Education
Lois Weis, editor

Edited by Yali Zou and Enrique T. Trueba

Ethnic Identity and Power

Cultural Contexts of Political Action in School and Society

STATE UNIVERSITY OF NEW YORK PRESS

Production by Ruth Fisher
Marketing by Anne M. Valentine

Published by
State University of New York Press, Albany

Printed in the United States of America

For information, address the State University of New York Press, State University Plaza, Albany, NY 12246

Library of Congress Cataloging-in-Publication Data

Ethnic identity and power : cultural contexts of political action in school and society / edited by Yali Zou and Enrique (Henry) T. Trueba.
p. cm.
Includes bibliographical references and index.
ISBN 0-7914-3753-1 (alk. paper). — ISBN 0-7914-3754-X (pbk. : alk. paper)
1. Minorities—Education—Cross-cultural education. 2. Ethnicity—Cross-cultural studies. 3. Critical pedagogy—Cross-cultural studies. 4. Politics and education—Cross-cultural studies.
I. Zou, Yali. II. Trueba, Henry T.
LC3719.E85 1998
371.829—DC21 97-31489
CIP

10 9 8 7 6 5 4 3 2 1

Dedication

The editors and contributors want to dedicate this volume to Louise Schaubel Spindler in gratitude for an entire life of dedication to educational anthropology, equity in education, and the future of American society. Her work with Native Americans, especially her study of Menominee women in Wisconsin and their acculturation, her research on cultural psychology and change, on modernization, and together with George Spindler on many other topics, more recently on cultural therapy with teachers and students, has become an inspiration for many educators and social scientists.

Louise, as a small token of our love and appreciation we offer you this volume. Thank you for your encouragement, your honesty and your presence. Your memory, kind smile and words of wisdom will always live in our hearts and carry us to higher levels of academic excellence and educational equity.

On behalf of the contributors,

Enrique (Henry) T. Trueba, Ph.D.

Yali Zou, Ph.D.

Contents

Foreword ix
Acknowledgments xiii
Introduction • *Enrique (Henry) T. Trueba and Yali Zou* 1

1. Cultural Politics of the White Ethniclass in the Mid-Nineties • *George and Louise Spindler* 27
2. Leadership, Education, and Political Action: The Emergence of New Latino Ethnic Identities • *Cirenio Rodríguez and Enrique (Henry) T. Trueba* 43
3. Power and Learning in a Multi-Ethnic High School: Dilemmas of Policy and Practice • *Jon Wagner* 67
4. Teaching Against the Grain in Bilingual Education: Resistance in the Classroom Underlife • *Rebecca Constantino and Christian Faltis* 113
5. Affirmative Action in Engineering Education: A Case Study • *James F. Shackelford, Penelope L. Shackelford, and Enrique (Henry) T. Trueba* 133
6. The Policy of Modernization of Education: A Challenge to Democracy in Mexico • *Beatriz Calvo* 159

7. Indigenous Images and Identity in Pluricultural Mexico: Media as Official Apologist and Catalyst for Democratic Action • *Robert DeVillar* 187

8. The Role of Media in Armed and Peaceful Struggles for Identity: Indigenous Self-Expression in Mexico • *Robert DeVillar and Victor Franco* 221

9. Mixed Messages: Moroccan Children in the Netherlands Living in Two Worlds • *Lotty Eldering* 259

10. State Terrors: Immigrants and Refugees in the Post-National Space • *Marcelo M. Suárez–Orozco* 283

11. Identity, Cultural Diversity, and Education: Notes Toward a Pedagogy of the Excluded • *Elvira S. Lima and Marcelo G. Lima* 321

12. Dancing with Bigotry: The Poisoning of Racial and Ethnic Identities • *Donaldo Macedo and Lilia I. Bartolomé* 345

13. Aspects of the Cultural Politics of Alaskan Education • *David M. Smith* 369

14. Dilemmas Faced by Critical Ethnographers in China • *Yali Zou* 389

15. Afterword: ¡Ya Basta! • *Peter McLaren* 411

Contributors 433
Index 439

Foreword

In our politics and policy analyses we have profoundly ambivalent approaches to the idea of culture. Our national myth has been that we are a uniquely open and successful blending of cultures into a modern continental society with a shared culture, a shared language, and a common "civic religion." The myth persists in spite of a history in which our land was taken from those considered to have inferior or pagan cultures and in spite of the fact that the powerful systems of slavery, which dominated a large sector of our society for nearly two and a half centuries, and legal apartheid, which dominated seventeen states until the 1960s, are absolutely formative realities of American life. We have a society in which color is assumed to be connected to culture and in which racial and ethnic discrimination persists with great intensity but where whites claim that there is equal opportunity and the judicial and political institutions are dismantling key protections for minority rights.

In the United States it has been apparent to minority group leaders and close observers for many years that neither assimilation nor successful integration into a pluralistic society are working for millions of people concentrated in continually growing African American and Latino communities as well as smaller groups of American Indians and refugee Asians. Nor has isolation in impoverished communities abandoned by the middle class and by employers been a workable alternative. Politics has been dominated by those who strongly oppose any serious use of governmental power to attack discrimination or to transfer resources for internal development. The dominant conservative movement, in fact, often claims that these policies are responsible for or seriously exacerbate the social divisions and inequalities which are rooted in the divergent and inferior values of the minority communities and the lack of the right market incentives (dire personal need) to force divergent cultural groups to conform to America's individualistic market orientation. The kind of prescription embedded in the radical alteration of welfare policy includes the assumption that the market is fairly open to all and that any group experiencing severe economic problems is deficient or lazy. Political leaders who would never speak of genetic inferiority often speak of cultural inferiority.

In its most cynical form, the racial politics of the conservative movement recognizes that the racial fears of the dominant racial group or groups can be exploited to make many voters in those groups forget that their economic and social needs and interests are much closer to those of the minorities. The tactic can also deflect accountability for lackluster or incompetent leadership by shifting the blame to racial and ethnic scapegoats. Historically, such tactics enabled conservatives whose policies hurt working-class whites to defeat progressives whose policies were denounced as threats to the social order. The long history of race-baiting demagogic politics moved north with the civil rights revolution and the urban riots in the 1960s and a virulent anti-immigration streak which has episodically erupted over the generations has come to focus on the supposed threat to American culture posed by a huge Latino immigration. These tactics may be particularly effective in times of economic troubles and rapid demographic transitions, situations like California in the early 1990s.

Such tactics do not directly threaten the state and the social order if the order is one of almost total domination and subordination, like much of the pre-1960s South. When the groups have their own increasingly powerful base, however, such tactics risk opening Pandora's box and creating out-of-control racial and ethnic earthquakes tearing apart societies. Although many societies have experienced such problems in the twentieth century, it seems that the possibility is usually discounted until it is irreversibly under way.

One day in the mid-1980s, a senior scholar from the Soviet Academy of Sciences came to visit me in my office at the University of Chicago. The new liberalism of the Gorbachov era meant that a few Soviet bloc scholars were exploring the social science of the

West. When I discussed with him the work I was doing on civil rights and social policies in metropolitan America he told me that no one in the Soviet Union had ever been allowed to carry out such research though the divisions within the USSR were obviously important to the future of the society. He hoped that such work could be done within a decade or so. Another scholar from Warsaw showed me calculations he had made of segregation indices like those we compute about housing and education in the United States. The residential segregation level was much like that of blacks and whites in the United States but it was the segregation of public employees (Communist Party members) from the rest of the population. Well before the nascent social science enterprise could begin to describe and create public debate about the divisions within the society, the society and the state—one of the two greatest powers in the history of the world—had simply ceased to exist. As soon as the state no longer had legitimacy and will to maintain itself by force, it split into many countries along ethnic, cultural, and historical lines. As soon as the Communist Party permitted a choice, it was gone as a major force in most countries. No political scientist or statesman had predicted anything like what occurred. The immense effort of the Soviet Union to project and expand its power in the world turned out to be meaningless. One has only to look at the recent history of such once successful multiethnic cities as Sarajevo and Beirut to understand the terrible importance of understanding and dealing with the substructures of politics.

The vast demographic transformation that the United States is now experiencing greatly raises the stakes. Many more forms of either polarization or cross-cutting ties are possible in a multiracial society. In a country where the two largest states already have a non-white majority among young people and the whole country will experience this change in about a quarter century, the issues cannot be controlled at the margins and they cannot be resolved successfully until we add to our repertoire a much more sophisticated understanding of the various cultures involved, including what is still the majority culture.

It is extremely important to have the best possible understanding of all dimensions of social and economic inequality of groups—psychological, cultural, sociological, political, and legal—if we are to understand how societies work and to craft and implement policies to successfully address the problems. Understanding these issues at only one level blinds the observer to the dynamics that can produce surprisingly rapid change on very salient and explosive issues. Typically those concerned with law and policy take the relationships among observable variables in relatively recent time periods to be functional and stable and see their problem in making small adjustments or considering the potential unanticipated consequences of other policies. Ethnographers, social psychologists, and anthropologists, on the other hand, often brilliantly describe underlying values, institutions, and practices without considering how they are shaped by external forces or assessing the political, legal, and other levers that might be used to create and support policies that could more sensitively deal with cultural differences. The scholars in this volume who have tried to cross those lines deserve special respect as do those who have tried to explain and give voice to groups and cultures that are relatively powerless. I hope that these and other scholars will continue to develop their insights and to apply them to the search for policies and practices that can increase the chance that in the United States and other multicultural societies we will develop both the understanding and the will to respect and cherish our cultures while finding the language, the understanding, and the core public values that permit us to solve our common problems.

Gary Orfield
Harvard University

Acknowledgments

Our intellectual debts extend far beyond our current endeavors and the zig-zaging paths of our ideas in this book. The work of Lev S. Vygotsky, George and Louise Spindler, George Peter Murdock, Paulo Freire, George DeVos, Courtney Cazden, and other outstanding scholars whose work has extended for several generations will be recognized in these pages. Along with seminal work of those giants, the reader will find the intellectual tracks of Dell Hymes, Roy D'Andrade, Jim Wertsch, John Ogbu, Michael Cole, F. Erickson, and those more recent scholars such as Suárez-Orozco, Michelle Fine, Margaret Gibson, Diego Vigil, Peter McLaren, Henry Giroux, Michael Apple, Ruben Donato, Donaldo Macedo, Lilia Bartolomé, Kris Gutierrez, Mike Rose, Jeannie Oaks, Gloria Ladson-Billings, Concha Delgado-Gaitan, and many more whose writings and lectures have impacted us profoundly. We express our gratitude to all of the above, our professors and colleagues, and our students who stimulated many of the ideas presented in this volume. We want to thank all and each of the persons who assisted the editors along the long journey of putting together this volume, particularly Priscilla C. Ross, Jennie Dolling, Anne Valentine and Ruth Fisher, and their wonderful team at SUNY Press. Their insightful comments, excellent suggestions and continued support improved significantly the quality of this volume. For the editing of early versions of several chapters we are deeply grateful to Jackie Captain; and for the typing and assistance in the preparation of portions of this manuscript we want to thank Diane Jerome and Trang Phan. We are also truly grateful to those students who gave us feedback on early drafts of some chapters, especially to Mariela Páez and Norma Jiménez from Harvard University.

Enrique (Henry) T. Trueba and Yali Zou

Introduction

> One of the tasks of the progressive educator, through a serious correct political analysis, is to unveil opportunities for hope, no matter what the obstacles may be. After all, without hope there is little we can do. It will be hard to struggle on, and when we fight as hopeless or despairing persons, our struggle will be suicidal . . . (Freire, 1995:9)

The relationship between ethnic identity and power has important consequences in a modern world that is changing rapidly through global immigration trends. Over a hundred million people have left their countries of origin to seek the satisfaction of the important needs of safety (away from physical and mental violence) and assured sustenance, as well as in search of a better life (better education and higher standards of living). As ethnic groups abandon their home countries and towns of origin, they carry with them a worldview, a lifestyle, a language and a family structure that they try to maintain in the host country. For as long as they maintain their cultural markers and other symbolic components of their identity, they seem to muster the energy and courage needed to adapt and survive. In fact, as immigrants and ethnic groups reaffirm and redefine their identities in contrast with other groups as well as mainstream peoples, they seem to hold power, to control their destiny, and to succeed in their risky ventures as immigrants. To a certain extent, internal migrations within a country that allow ethnic groups to maintain their sense of peoplehood and togetherness seem to provide them with the power to face the psychological challenges of change. But a second and third generation of children must also adapt and reconstruct their identities, and must compromise their efforts to retain their ethnic identity without becoming marginalized and stereotyped by the mainstream society. The studies of conflict of ethnic identity become necessarily studies of political power, social status, school achievement, and allocation of resources. The recognition of power by an ethnic group, however, creates competition for control and rivalry for power over public arenas. It is in this context that the present volume provides interesting insights into the dilemmas faced by immigrants, members of ethnic groups, school personnel, and policymakers.

> The First World has indeed always been an example of scandals of every sort, always a model of wickedness, of exploitation. We need only think of colonialism—of the massacres of invaded, subjugated, colonized peoples; of the wars of this century, of shameful, cheapening racial discrimination, and the rapine [sic] that colonialism has perpetrated. No, we have no monopoly on the dishonorable . . . *Pedagogy of Hope* . . . is written in rage and love, without which there is no hope. It is meant as a defense of tolerance—not to be confused with connivance—and radicalness. It is meant as a criticism of sectarianism. It attempts to explain and defend progressive postmodernity and it will reject conservative, neo-liberal postmodernity. (Freire, 1995:9–10)

Scope and Content of Volume

The "hegemony of violence" or "cultural war" (alluded to by Donaldo Macedo and Lilia I. Bartolomé in this volume) that perpetuates a climate of racism and xenophobia in American and other Western societies, is intended to kill any hope for empowerment among the oppressed. Using Paulo Freire's metaphors and philosophy, this book weaves a beautiful and powerful tapestry of important contributions by researchers from different cultures, ethnic groups, and disciplinary traditions in North America, Europe, Mexico, Brazil, and China. Through different academic voices and intensity, a single powerful message emerges from this volume, which invites reflection about self-identification processes, and allows a deeper understanding of the empowering consequences of a clear and strong personal, cultural, ethnic, and social identity. These pages offer a keen grasp of the undeniable political contexts of education and how it metamorphisizes into political action or *praxis* in schools and society.

As with any other intellectual endeavor in the educational arena, research takes place in a highly sensitive climate of tempestuous unexpected storms of righteousness and moral debate. More than ever our modern world critically examines the role of researchers and demands a new integration of ethical principles associated with the generation and acquisition of new knowledge. A group of outstanding scholars from multiple generations and disciplinary backgrounds (anthropology, sociology, art, critical theory, communications, applied pedagogy, cultural psychology, and educational ethnography), have given us honest, profound, and stimulating accounts of their struggles to decipher self-identification processes in various political contexts, as well as their personal reflections on the study of ethnicity. Ethnic identity, ethic loyalty, and political action are inseparable in the context of oppression, conflict, and fight over scarce resources in daily human interaction.

Many of the international crises the Western world experienced during the twentieth century are related to power control and cultural purity, about the rejection of ethnic groups (and even their systematic destruction through genocidal long–term planning), as well as, in the end, the emancipation and resiliency of oppressed human populations. If we had to identify the single most important departure from traditional research canons and practices at the turn of the twentieth century (a century of incredible violence and unexpected global change), we probably would have to say that researchers can no longer retain political neutrality or hide their political values behind the pretense of objectivity or the shield of methodological or theoretical purity. Social science researchers cannot be indifferent to genocide, slavery, child labor, or child exploitation through pedophilia, racism, xenophobia, homophobia, gender inequities, and other abuses of persons by their fellow humans; there is no possible objectivity in the study of human exploitation because the abuse of any human being is an offense against all human beings.

Many social scientists aim at doing a better job in documenting their biases in the study of human conflict and in pursuing the implications of their research to reach adequate solutions. Critical theory (the heart of critical pedagogy) offers a great deal of hope to social scientists attempting to do quality advocacy research. Some critical theorists, however, seem to stay away from empirical research and genuine grounded research in schools and communities. Consequently, much of their time and energy is spent in sharpening their discourse and criticizing each other, rather than in engaging in substantive data collection and analysis. This volume offers precisely the opposite; it is based on a new trend among critical theorists, a new trend characterized by three unique features: (1) research grounded in specific geographical settings and clearly focused theoretical issues about the power struggle of ethnic groups, (2) theoretical claims which are modest but clearly organized to open new horizons for further research and development, and (3) a pragmatic and unambiguous recognition of the need to pursue cross-cultural research on issues of race, ethnicity, power, and equity.

Ethnic identification processes are today a main preoccupation of many social scientists. Concepts of the self are a moving target in a world of rapid change and hectic interpersonal interactions with diverse audiences. We seem to develop and maintain multiple identities *vis-à-vis* the people with whom we interact in specific domains; we redefine ourselves as we change from one cultural world to another, from one linguistic group to another, from one crisis to another. This book takes us to different places and settings in search for answers. The first part of the book consists of specific studies of ethnic identity. Chapter 1, by George and Louise Spindler, confronts America's most controversial drama of the "White Ethniclass." In direct and specific language the Spindlers share their profound psychoanalytical views of the traumatic experiences faced by white males in a world that is turning brown and that is culturally different. Their response seems to take form in radical militias, angry anti-immigrant groups, and an anxious nostalgic search for the America they knew when they thought they had control of their lives and could display their cultural capital at times in contradictory fashion as hard work, individualism, freedom, conformity, sociability, achievement, and collective success. This theme is revisited in a more detailed theoretical statement by

Marcelo M. Suárez-Orozco in Chapter 10, in the following section. The first chapter offers a predominant view of the people who are in power but begin to see the conspicuous presence and rising power of ethnic minority groups, especially African Americans and Latinos. Chapters 2 and 9 are dedicated to culturally and linguistically diverse groups in the United States and abroad. Chapter 2, by Cirenio Rodríguez and Enrique T. Trueba, offers the perspective of the Latinos who are discovering their political power and beginning to articulate their determination to become an integral part of American society, while demanding political representation and the benefits of belonging to mainstream society. Chicanos struggling for liberation are also struggling for a new identity. Their marginalization during years of struggle is reflected in their somewhat contradictory views of themselves collectively, and their debates over the appropriate course of action needed to succeed in the academic, political, and academic world of high achievers.

Chapters 3, 4, and 5 are examples of how educators in the United States perceive the challenges of educating culturally and linguistically diverse students, and what strategies are designed in order to create more effective instructional practices and policies. Chapters 6, 7, and 8 illustrate political and pedagogical movements in Mexico, and Chapter 9 is a special case study of Moroccan children in Holland and their socialization within the family. All these studies provide both the historical and political contexts that affect ethnic identification of children and the pedagogical approaches used to educate them.

Chapter 3, by Jon Wagner, brings us directly into the arena of school socialization where the struggle for self-identification is intense and decisive. The needs of culturally and linguistically diverse students require new approaches that cannot be taught at the university and must be learned as part of on-the-job training. This chapter, in a very detailed and clear fashion, shows how high school teachers and administrators design and implement specific reform policies and programs in a multiethnic setting. A number of teaching strategies are discussed, including heterogeneous groups with the intent of detracking students, interdisciplinary teaching teams to assist or resocialize teachers, and a number of collaborative school-wide decision-making groups of teachers and administrators. The combination of politics and pedagogy, the goals set forth in the school and efforts at creating interdisciplinary teaching teams and curricula, are a symbolic expression of the value placed by the school on cultural and linguistic diversity. The experimental approaches and new pedagogical initiatives enhanced students' commitment to learn, and transformed the role of teachers and the essence of schooling. Indeed, new educational goals and a new relationship between teachers and administrators, teachers and students, and students with each other, created a strong sense of community and a high level of enthusiasm. The reaffirmation of ethnic identities in students empowered them to achieve academically. In a clear and precise way Wagner spells out the way school empowers students, the role of ethnicity in this process, the role and primary responsibilities of teachers, the role of students, the role of administrators, the functions of the curriculum and of extracurricular activities, how teachers and administrator view the community, and finally, the meaning of success. This chapter is an extraordinary and rare example of a well–documented study of educational change in contemporary American schools, with clear analytical statements of the process of empowerment and the factors of success. The significant implications of this study for educational reform policies in the country cannot be overemphasized.

Based on the premises established by critical theorists and researchers who focused on hegemonic discourses in the classroom, Rebecca Constantino and Christian Faltis present, in Chapter 4, another concrete example of self–initiated response by teachers seeking change. Deeply committed to the education of all children, the teachers under study insisted on finding more effective pedagogies for culturally and linguistically diverse students. Some teachers' courage in opposing conformist pedagogies that ignore the linguistic and cultural capital which children bring to school was demonstrated in how the teachers confronted political decisions on a daily basis, in their use of nonstandard discourse and the Spanish language when deemed appropriate, in their choice of curriculum materials, and in other efforts to resist hegemonic discourse in school. These teachers publicly opposed the transitional bilingual education policies of federal agencies and boycotted the National Association of Bilingual Education for accepting such policies. They also refused to use commercial assessment instruments in English that they perceived as unfairly used and applied to children who spoke other languages, thus measuring English proficiency rather than intellectual or academic abilities. Perhaps one of the most important contributions of these teachers was in the day-to-day organization of their instruction in conformity to their own high standards of an adequate pedagogy that takes into consideration children's sociocultural capital and other assets.

Chapter 5, by James and Penelope Shackelford and Enrique Trueba, describes programs at the University of California, Davis, that were established in various engineering and science units in partnership with other institutions. These efforts, based on affirmative action policies which existed until recently, have been abandoned as a result of California Proposition 209. The authors discuss the political context of affirmative action in California with Proposition 209 and the resulting discontinuation of some of their efforts. The future of activities such as those described in this chapter is extremely uncertain, and the absence of these activities will have significant negative consequences for culturally and linguistically diverse students (particularly Latinos and Blacks). Affirmative action continues to be debated on many campuses, and it is under serious revision by legal experts, philosophers and educators.

Chapter 6, by Beatriz Calvo, the first of three chapters dealing with education in Mexico, provides the reader with a general historical background that explains the governmental modernization movement and resource allocation policies constituting a symbolic gesture toward the creation of a new and genuine democratic climate. The chief goal of this modernization is to decentralize programs, fund them adequately, and give momentum to regional planning to meet the needs of specific students. There are clear tensions between a rhetoric of modernization and the conspicuous lack of resources to train professionals in some regions. In this environment of highly diversified populations, the ideal of democratization in Mexico takes on a new political character in the context of Indian education. The author discusses the contrast between official discourse (government rhetoric) of the democratic nature of education and the practical daily discourse of selective access to education and differential quality. Public education in Mexico advocates three values: (1) solidarity with and social participation of those who have less, who are marginalized in the poorer regions of the country; (2) political independence and cultural autonomy; and

(3) equity of opportunity for all. The author alludes to the impact of *maquiladoras* and the economic development of border cities, such as Ciudad Juárez, that attract thousands of potential employees. The proximity with the United States also creates high expectations for many undocumented groups of immigrants in search of employment. The schools in the border cities of Mexico have become highly diversified with children of families from different parts of the country and different ethnic traditions. The implications of these rapid sociopolitical and economic changes require new approaches and philosophies, and new teachers who understand children from such diverse backgrounds. The parallel between problems in the United States Southwest and in the northern Mexican border towns reflects a reality of a binational existence with two entirely different educational and political systems. Coordination and dialogue are urgently needed between the two sides of the border.

Chapter 7, by Robert DeVillar, provides a sociopolitical and historical context for Indian education as a result of the Mexican Revolution that gave voice to the poor and enslaved peasants. The revolution showed that the submissive and patient behavior of the Indian soul did not completely repress the Mexican potential for violence. The rhetoric of democracy is in clear contrast with electoral fraud, corruption, patronage, and paternalism. The frustration of many Mexicans is fueled by their conviction that the profound inequities between the poor and the rich cannot be resolved by state or municipal governments, because the federal government is in total control. The conflict in Chiapas with the *Zapatistas* is but one example of the central control. The towns controlled by the *Zapatistas* in Chiapas in their revolt of desperation and hunger were taken back by the *federales* with a conspicuous display of force and cruelty. The author discusses in great and rich detail the multiple indigenous images and identities of Indian groups and the role of the media in the process of democratization. DeVillar presents a forceful picture of the restrictive and selective policies of acculturation that curtail channels of education for indigenous peoples. The contexts in which the media point to these selectivity are: (1) the brutal examples of Chiapas' Zapatista National Liberation Front and the killings of Mayan Indians by the *federales*, (2) the new policies of the North American Free Trade Agreement (NAFTA), and (3) the persistent economic crises in the Mexican economy. The extremely important role of the media as apologist and catalyst is captured and eloquently presented by DeVillar. Public discourse and government rhetoric continues to blame the Indians for their poverty and isolation without alluding to historical systematic exploitation and isolation policies. Thousands of Indians died of hunger and curable diseases in Chiapas in 1944 during the *Zapatistas'* struggle with the federal government. The dramatic effects of domination and control, the creation of hegemonic structures to exploit Indian groups, the consequences for ethnic identity, and the precarious present condition of these groups, is discussed with forceful clarity by DeVillar.

As a followup, Chapter 8, by Robert DeVillar and Victor Franco, describes the role of the media during the armed and peaceful struggles for identity on the part of various ethnolinguistic groups in Mexico. The oppressed peoples from Chiapas, ignored by Mexican authorities, are brought to an international audience by TV cameras, and this fact instantly changes the attitude of the Mexican government. This phenomenon is what the authors call the "demarginalization" of indigenous causes. Without the power of the media, this demarginalization would never be possible. Indians in Mexico found their voice in the stormy encounters between the *federales* and the *Zapatistas* documented by international TV cameras. Their pronouncements essentially unveiled the lack of democracy, the lack of freedom, and the lack of respect for human rights. Furthermore, it was the *Zapatistas* who exposed the practice institutionalized in Mexico of enlisting reporters on the government's payroll and paying the newspaper to publish propaganda. Video images as cultural expressions giving legitimacy to various ethnic identities have become very important in Mexico.

The video study of the Ñahñu Indians from the State of Hidalgo gave their cause a voice and an image that could no longer be avoided and forgotten by the government. Their way out of their economic and cultural isolation was handled by the Indians themselves by taking over the control of initiatives to make their lifestyles public via video. The dilemmas of cultural assimilation and self-determination in the maintenance of their ethnic identity is discussed by the authors. With support from government organizations and a research center, this Indian group organized a video project to document their alphabet and writing, their life as shepherds (with the modernized production of caprine and ovine livestock), their family life, and their migration to urban centers in Mexico and the United States. The results of this project are analyzed by the authors as an outstanding example of the Ñahñu Indians' determination to promote their self-identity and to fight marginalization. This chapter brings back the notions of Freire's critical pedagogy about the inherent relationship between politics and education, political actions as praxis, and the struggle for liberation. It documents a powerful example of how media, in the hands of the oppressed, can alter history. A unique combination of self-determination and international media attention shows the vision of modern Indians in Mexico. They are creating drastic changes in their mode of negotiation with the Mexican Government because they know that the credibility of Mexico as a civilized country—one in which humans rights must be respected in order to keep foreign investments—is of paramount importance.

The last chapter of this section, Chapter 9, by Lotty Eldering, offers by contrast and comparison the study of Moroccan children in the Netherlands. The author takes the theoretical position that identity formation does not occur in a vacuum, but in the specific sociocultural context of family and society where values and norms are internalized. Minority children, however, get messages at home that are contradicted by messages in the larger society. Using a socioecological model, the author describes the Moroccans' subordinate status in society, their different cultural background, and the mechanisms of socialization. Moroccans, the third-largest ethnic group in the Netherlands, number 165,000 people. The author, having learned a Moroccan-Arab dialect, worked intensively with a sample of 45 Moroccan families in a small Dutch town. She describes the formation of ethnic networks and communities that function to reconstruct cultural life and provide mutual support and solidarity to the families. The visits to Morocco by these families facilitated their biculturalism and reinforced the cultural and religious values of the family. Afraid that the more permissive lie of Dutch society may ruin the children (get them into drugs and delinquency), parents arrange marriages for their children at a young age. Traditional values of virginity in women and the submissiveness of women to men is stressed in the socialization of children. The author describes the crises of women who are forced to seek divorce and protect themselves and their children against their husbands' violence. The problems in the socialization of children are different from those in two-parent families. The author explores the biculturalism of these children "living in two worlds" and their adjustment process to the Netherlands. This is an important chapter because it underlines the similarities and differences between culturally and linguistically diverse students in the United States and those in Europe facing similar lower status and oppressive circumstances. This chapter is an appropriate transition to the following chapters which have a clear theoretical focus because it explores the relative validity of the cultural ecological model and the peculiar ways in which Moroccan families in the Netherlands socialize children. The use of ethnic networks and community institutions (with their stratified structures) is brought to the Netherlands from Morocco and used, along with the religious belief system, by immigrant families in the socialization of young children. Moroccan women in this context are most instrumental and clearly involved in assisting children to adapt to the Netherlands and to succeed academically.

The second part of this book focuses directly on some of the lessons learned from social science research on ethnic identification and the critical study of equity, with its implications for pedagogy. Chapter 10, by Marcelo M. Suárez–Orozco, entitled *State Terrors: Immigrants and Refugees in the Post-National Space*, addresses the cultural malaise pervasive in postindustrial democracies replete with contradictions and conflictive positions. The fear of losing control of the forces around us, the vacuum of legitimacy leading to a collective paranoia, and our irrational rage over a world we cannot recognize as "ours" has targeted immigrants as culprits responsible for all our problems. Suárez–Orozco takes us through a subtle and profound psychoanalysis of American personality at the turn of this tumultuous century, suffering *dis-locations*, downsizing, economic threats, and massive influxes of "new" immigrants (immigrants of color from Latin America, and the Caribbean, with very diverse cultures). The author feels that as the old concepts of "nation," "community," and "home" fall apart during crises of lost jobs, homes, and communities, and lost faith in our nation, "we find ourselves struggling to create a new language to imagine new 'postnational' communities" with conflicting positions regarding immigration. At times we view immigrants as sharing our values and qualities, and we display confidence that their children are tough, brave and smart enough to face the challenges of our nation. But soon we turn around and view immigrants as the enemy—"illegal, criminal and alien—attempting to take over our country. The struggle then is to control our borders and stop the "torrent of people flooding" our land with terrorists and criminals. These polar positions, according to the author, intimately relate to serious problems in "our" own identity and our sense that we are losing control of "our" land. In a cross–cultural comparison with similar crises in Europe, with rich details of current events, public opinion, and federal policies in the United States, Suárez–Orozco discusses the global context for the crisis that has resulted in the current xenophobia, antiimmigrant violence, and the high level of anxiety among mainstream populations of Western democracies. This chapter is a powerful statement with profound psychoanalytical observations based on systematic and serious reflections of the crises affecting members of postindustrial democracies entering a new age of transnational collectivities.

Chapter 11, by Elvira and Marcelo Lima, focuses on the pedagogical implications of the crises described in the previous chapters. The common denominator of the oppressed populations of immigrants, or other groups with unique ethnolinguistic, racial, socioeconomic or gender characteristics, is that they all are excluded from adequate instructional pedagogies in schools. Based on the research by L. S. Vygotsky and the Neo-Vygotskians, Elvira S. Lima and Marcelo G. Lima analyze the concepts of cultural diversity and identity, multiculturalism, group affiliation and the structure of social relationships defining a person's symbolic membership in a group. The authors ask questions about the basic need for social identification and the need we all have for creating adequate pedagogical environments in which teachers and students co-construct knowledge. Toward the end of this introduction I will discuss some of the theoretical foundations of the position taken here by the Limas. The important issue in this chapter is the recognition that a sound pedagogy must consider the cultural experiences of students and acknowledge the critical role of language and culture in the acquisition of knowledge for individuals who belong to different cultural groups.

In Chapter 12, Donaldo Macedo and Lilia Bartolomé focus on the roots of faulty pedagogies that result in the academic failure of oppressed groups. Racism, ethnic violence, the prevalence of hegemonic discourse in schools and other educational institutions, all have a similar ideological basis that explains attacks against immigrants. This chapter unveils in clear analytical terms the impact of prejudice among educators working with children of immigrants. Symbolic violence, sexism, racism, and cultural war are different labels to characterize the crises alluded to in previous chapters by the Spindlers, Rodríguez and Trueba, Constantino and Faltis, Suárez–Orozco, the Limas, and later on by David M. Smith and Peter McLaren.

Chapter 13, by David Smith, carries further the implications of prejudice in the context of Alaska's educational system. The history of the education of Native Alaskans reflects policies and practices that illustrate the politics of exclusion in contrast with the norms of sound pedagogy. Critical pedagogy and the need for "cultural therapy" link this chapter to Chapter 1 by the Spindlers and to other chapters alluding to the embedded conflict in conducting research among oppressed peoples (for example, Chapter 14, by Yali Zou). We will discuss more about the relationship of critical pedagogy to cultural therapy at the end of the introduction.

The chapter on critical ethnography, by Yali Zou, brings home the serious conflicts that exist for the ethnic researcher in doing a study of ethnic identity and power. This conflict exists for all researchers, but in a special way it affects the changes in personal identity taken by ethnic researchers studying their own country's equity problems and pedagogical exclusions. In a very insightful and provocative fashion, Zou raises issues about the authenticity and consistency of ethnic researchers as advocates for the oppressed and as judges of equity in highly explosive and risky research environments, as China is today. Can the researcher (a Han Chinese woman educated in this country as an immigrant since 1988), ask questions to minority students in China without imposing her own hegemonic notions? What is the role of a critical ethnographer who is at the same time a member of the most powerful group in China? Zou attempts to answer these questions.

Chapter 14, by Peter McLaren, describes the precarious conditions of confrontation and uncertainty for ethnic groups who negotiate their ethnic identities in the current historical juncture of racism, white supremacist growth and political right radicalism. The author's Afterword statement on the entire volume shows his commitment to eliminate racism and promote critical ethnography. He also comments on the various chapters and warns us about the problems associated with the use of terms such as *race* in an environment of culturally marked distinctions and usages that turn these terms into "a racialized category" when, in fact, racial groups are not monolithic categories of existing human beings. McLaren recommends that we move to a discussion of racial relations and practices, exploitation and resistance. He also comments on the multiple identities of the contributors to this volume as educators, researchers, intellectuals, social agents, and members of various ethnic groups. He discusses, in passing the important issue of *essentialized identities* and the need to understand the *denationalized, de-Mexicanized, and trans-Chicanized, and pseudo–internationalized* identities of Latinos. In a time of rapid mobility and rapid hybridization of all human groups, especially those in this hemisphere, multiculturalism is the point of departure for critical pedagogy.

Theoretical Contributions of This Volume

Traditional disciplinary barriers are often crossed at some risk, even when the complementarity of approaches seems to be clear and productive. For years a number of scholars from anthropological, sociological, and psychological traditions have used critical pedagogy concepts that eclectically combine their own main disciplines with genuinely new epistemological and methodological inquiries related to issues of equity, curriculum reform, institutional racism, effective teaching strategies, and the role of the ethnic community in the development of adequate pedagogies (Apple, 1989, 1993; Freire and Macedo, 1987; Freire and Macedo, 1996; Macedo, 1991, 1993; Gutierrez, Larson and Kreuter, 1995; Gutierrez, Rymes, and Larson, 1995; McLaren, 1989, 1995; McLaren and da Silva, 1993; Bartolomé, 1996; Moll, 1986, 1990). Since the mid-1970s until today, various contributions from anthropology in the study of cultural adaptation and academic success (vis-à-vis the cultural and linguistic continuities and discontinuities faced by immigrants and refugees) often focused on the differential performance of immigrant children. Those classified as "caste-like" (Ogbu, 1974, 1978, 1982, 1987, 1992; Gibson and Ogbu, 1991) seem to display permanent characteristics that prevented them from adapting to mainstream schools and society. The unsettling features behind the rigidity of this model are that, (1) by creating the appearance of providing a full explanation of the failure of those "others" who are not like us—that is, the "caste-like" ethnics—we are taking away their voices and denying them an opportunity to respond to our "theories" of failure; and (2) we stopped our inquiry without getting into the complex and difficult area of knowledge acquisition, and the role of the home language and culture in that process. Effectively, a rigid explanation based on structural theories that argues the individual "caste-like" or their teachers cannot do anything to bring about academic success, thus offering a culturally deterministic explanation of success or failure in the United States. Social scientists have developed parallel trends of resistance to ethnocentric and rigid explanatory models of differential success and failure across ethnic, racial, socioeconomic and "other" nonmainstream groups, by developing emancipating discourses such as critical pedagogy. Until recently, however, critical discourse was dominated by mainstream scholars, some of whom appeared to be less interested in gathering empirical data on emancipation in field-based settings (actual schools and communities), than in debating each other and dissecting each other's discourse. The actual development of alternative, creative, and constructive pedagogies based on genuinely interdisciplinary and cross-cultural approaches is a recent development. The fact is that we know of many successes, many exceptions to the rule of caste-like performance—children who everybody expected to see fail in school, yet who managed to succeed, individually and collectively.

In order to explain differential achievement within the same ethnic group and in those in similar socioeconomic and political contexts, we can use Paulo Freire's critical pedagogy and Vygotsky's theory of human development. Each provides a very useful perspective, and both have been highly instrumental in helping educators implement effective pedagogical approaches. Scaffolding, or joint construction of new knowledge in a collaborative relationship between teacher and students, is best analyzed using Vygotsky's theories of human development. One of the most important contributions of Vygotsky to our understanding of immigrant children's intellectual development and school achievement, especially of those undergoing rapid sociocultural change, was his theory about the relationship between cognitive and social phenomena (Vygotsky, 1962, 1978; Moll, 1986, 1990; Cole, 1985, 1990; Wertsch, 1981, 1985, 1991; Scribner and cole, 1981; Trueba, 1991). Vygotsky states that the development of uniquely human higher-level mental functions, such as consciousness and the creation of taxonomic cognitive structures (required for academic learning), find their origin in day-to-day social interaction. According to Moll, if teachers follow Vygotskian principles, they will see literacy as "the understanding and communication of meaning" and will make efforts "to make classrooms literate environments in which many language experiences can take place and different types of literacies can be developed and learned" (1990:8). Indeed, Moll stresses the idea that "teachers who follow this approach reject rote instruction or reducing reading and writing into skill sequences taught in isolation or a successive, stagelike manner. Rather, they emphasize the creation of social contexts in which children actively learn to use, try, and manipulate language in the service of making sense or creating meaning" (Moll, 1990:8).

Effective teachers who understand the process of internalization that permits students the transition from interpsychological experience to intrapsychological cognitive categories adopt culturally and linguistically meaningful teaching strategies (D'Andrade, 1984; Cole, 1985; Vygotsky, 1962, 1978); that is, strategies occurring within the zone of proximal development of children. The zone of proximal development was defined by Vygotsky as the distance between a child's "actual developmental level as determined by independent problem solving" and the higher level of "potential development as determined through problem solving under adult guidance or in collaboration with more capable peers" (1978:86). Furthermore, if we accept the intimate relationship between language and thought proposed by Vygotsky (who sees language as a symbolic system mediating all social and cognitive functions), we must link the lower intellectual development and school achievement of some immigrant children with the abrupt transition from a familiar to an unfamiliar sociocultural environment, and therefore, the lack of both linguistic and cultural knowledge to interact meaningfully with adults and peers. Consequently, no suitable zones of proximal development are opened up for them by adults or more informed peers, and the discourse and cognitive categories required to function in school are not readily available to them (Brown, Campione, Cole, Griffin, Mehan, and Riel, 1982; Trueba, 1991). In other words, it is impossible to create appropriate zones of proximal development in oppressive and unfamiliar learning environments without the symbolic tools that allow a child to make sense of social transactions and translate them into intrapsychological phenomena. A bilingual and bicultural teacher who understands the predicament of immigrant children, however, can create appropriate zones of proximal development. The use of these zones of proximal development requires not only awareness of the relationship between language, thought, and culture, but also of the principles of critical pedagogy. A teacher's own experience as an immigrant child of a farmworker sensitizes him or her to the traumas of immigrant children of farmworkers.

The book will present contextual information gathered in various interactions between teachers and students, parents and children, to help the reader understand the significance of culturally appropriate pedagogies based on critical consciousness, on efforts to resist domestication and oppression by creating liberating learning environments. Mexican working families in central California (Trueba, 1997) represent the quintessence of resistance to oppression. The conspicuous display of Mexican culture in their daily lives, their civil and religious ceremonies and life events, their family networks, and frequent communication with their hometowns in Mexico, offer children the cultural foundation to reaffirm their identity and refuse to be treated as an underclass by teachers and the surrounding English-speaking society. Bilingualism is the rule, and academic excellence in both languages is the mechanism to earn respect from teachers. These families articulate a vision for their children's economic future through academic hard work. It is a vision of resistance to oppression to show the oppressors that Mexicans are smart and can achieve. It is not an oppositional self-identity in the Ogbuan sense of resigning themselves not to excel in the arenas where the mainstream population is successful, but to do better than the whites in their own arenas, in school and in various careers and professions. The key role in the socialization of Mexican children for academic success is played by women, the mothers who keep a close watch on their children's schooling.

The efforts of immigrant women in central California demonstrate an underlying collective organization through networks, and long-term economic planning necessary to counteract the inherent instability of farm labor and its meager pay. Economic survival is as important as cultural survival. The integrity of the family life both in the United States and the Mexican hometowns requires very careful use of family resources. Many of these families had originally planned to return to Mexico and used about half of their income in various investments in their hometowns (purchase of land, new businesses, construction of homes, and so on). Three factors have forced them to change their long-term plans: (1) new economic crises in Mexico, (2) the backlash against immigrants in the United States (see Suárez–Orozco in this volume), and (3) the academic aspirations of the children who are now well adjusted in the United States. The plan to go back has been placed on the back burner, if not abandoned. Instead, massive requests for citizenship have occurred among the various generations of the families (including retired members of the family now in Mexico, who worked in this country most of their lives). The intergenerational efforts to support children's education in a culturally and linguistically familiar environment among migrant families seen to have been more effective than the rapid loss of the home language and cultures among Mexican youth in neighboring larger cities now infested by marginalized teenagers preyed on by gangs and drug addiction. The use of critical pedagogy (and of critical ethnography, based on Freire's philosophy) focuses not only on the oppression of a given population, but on their strategies for reaching empowerment; that is, it focuses on schooling, on the actions of a teacher who paves the way for the children of an oppressed population to escape the trap of underachievement and marginalization. School children learn that one's own low economic status, clearly resulting from oppressive working conditions, should not destroy their ethnic identity, their aspirations for a better life, and their self-confidence. Classroom instruction provides the home language and culture with a legitimacy and high status that enhances the strong affiliation of families to their home language and culture, as well as personal confidence to acquire English as a second language and the academic skills necessary to function in American society. Instructional style and its effectiveness in the teaching of mathematics are only the beginning of their empowerment and their successful adaptation to this country. Mexican immigrant women, in particular, express in powerful terms their commitment to the academic success of their children as the cornerstone for cultural and economic survival.

The complementary approaches of critical ethnography and learning theories that recognize the importance of children's home language and culture is considered today part a powerful theoretical and methodological tool to be used in lieu of broad rigid models based on social stratification. Critical ethnography (see Carspecken, 1996) is linked to the work of Paul Willis (1977) and Bowles and Gintis (1976); but its quintessential roots are in the seminal work of the early educational ethnographers such as George Spindler, Margaret Mead, Jules Henry and others (Spindler, 1955). The ideological relationship of critical ethnography to Paulo Freire's pedagogy (1973, 1995) however, is extremely important because it was Paulo Freire who established the fundamental principle that all educational endeavors are inherently political, and that without conscientization (reflective awareness) of oppression, there is no way we can escape it. He urged social science researchers to integrate theory and praxis and demonstrate their commitment to oppose oppression and search for adequate means to liberate people through the acquisition of knowledge. I see critical ethnography in education focused on discussing cultural themes that constitute the essence of oppression in the form of a hidden curriculum and other mechanisms intended to reproduce the social order and exclude the underclass. As McLaren states, students often feel that "they are denied a voice with which to be present in the world; they are made invisible to history and rendered powerless to shape it (1989:233). McLaren and da Silva feel that "emancipatory knowledge is never realized fully, but is continually dreamed, continually revived, and continually transformed in the heart of our memories, the flames of our longing and the passion of our struggle" (1993:59). Critical ethnography permits us to get into the emancipatory knowledge that motivates students' resistance to the dominant culture in the United States. By retaining their ethnic identity they feel empowered to resist racial and ethnic prejudicial policies and practices. Critical ethnography also permits us to re-examine cultural hegemony and the nature of cultural conflict as a drama taking place right in the classroom via reflection on historical factors of ethnic and racial legitimacy, reproduction of the social order, and the right to a voice in one's own language (Leistyna, Woodrum and Sherblom, 1996:334). In the end, a few reflections from the ethnographer will be presented. Critical ethnography is risky and painful. Carspecken offers the following penetrating remarks:

> Any identity that depends on negating the worth of others is ultimately limited and ultimately falls short of human potentiality. Most people gain a sense of worth through cultural systems that pit them against other groups of humans. This is why many people enjoyed a privileged position in society feel threatened by the plight of the poor. They do not want to know too many of the details. They want to explain social inequality by blaming the victims or in any other way that leaves their accustomed identities intact. They are afraid of being wounded (Carspecken, 1996:170–171).

Because critical ethnography is committed to praxis, discourse alone is not sufficient. To explain why relatively powerless immigrant families can create their own systems of resistance to dominant beliefs, values, norms, and practices, may seem irrational or even frightening to some people, especially if heroes of the emancipation movement are the mothers (uneducated, low-income immigrant women who defend at any cost their cultural integrity in all arenas, especially in their home and schools).

In brief, the compatibility and complementarity of critical ethnography and Vygotskian development psychology can help explain differential success among children expected to fail, and may help teachers develop appropriate pedagogical approaches to effectively teach children who are culturally and linguistically different. We need to offer pedagogical solutions and role models to teachers and teacher educators. The purpose is to gain a clear understanding of the instructional requirements for empowering all children (especially those who are different culturally, socially, racially, or economically) to achieve academically in schools by creating appropriate learning environments. Teachers can understand Vygotskian principles of scaffolding and adequate pedagogies that capitalize on children's assets and the support of their families; they also understand the role of the collaborative relationship between teacher and parents in order to create culturally and linguistically appropriate leaving environments. What educators and social scientists have some difficulty in grasping are the principles of the culture of therapy (as discussed by George and Louise Spindler, see discussion in this volume, and Spindler, 1994). A fundamental position of the Spindlers is that the point of departure in any interethnic and cross–cultural venture, and a *sine qua non* for understanding multiculturalism as it exists in this country, is to understand one's own cultural background in a historical perspective. The very roots of our ethnocentrism and its potential conflicts in interacting with people from other backgrounds are inculcated early in life with the formation of the self concept and are re-enforced or changed as we adapt to different circumstances. The formation of the "enduring-self" (or the original self as formed in the earliest socialization during the formative years) is modified as we grow and undergo various rites of passage (adolescence, adulthood, changes in status, language and culture, and so on). Any major adjustment comes with a new "situated self," which allows us to redefine our self-identity and to behave in different ways to cope with changes in the environment. The discontinuities resulting from drastic cultural, linguistic, social, educational, religious, and economic changes, affect our own self-definitions and personal identity. Over the most critical periods of our life, however, we continue to use as a point of reference our "enduring self." We resolve conflicts and adjust by linking the situated selves with the enduring self and thus we recognize some intrinsic continuities that permit us to retain some measure of personality integration. When the changes are drastic and we can no longer recognize ourselves or reconcile the differences between our situated selves and our enduring self, then we arrive at a "endangered self," a crisis in personal identity. At a deeper level of the personality, the multiple interactional settings in which we participate, the multiple identities we carry as we selectively function in different networks (even in different languages and cultures) is ultimately integrated by understanding how we move from one situated self to another, and what the relationship is between each of them and the enduring self. This connection is intimately structured as part of our self-concept and our ability to codeswitch and communicate with different audiences about different subjects. There is nothing strange about it in modern life. What is more difficult is to recognize the cultural lenses we carry and the biases, mis–expectations and assumptions that contextualize our interactions in daily life, especially if our daily life exposes us to deal with people very different from us. Everybody, especially teachers, needs to be reflectively aware of their cultural lenses in order to be effective instructors with all children. Cultural therapy can provide some help and assistance in guiding educators to understand their cultural, social, economic, religious, genre, racial, and class biases. This book shows some of the ways cultural healing is taking place.

References

Apple, M. W. (1989). *Teachers and Texts: A Political Economy of Class and Gender Relations in Education*. New York: Routledge. (First published in 1986).

———. (1993). *Official Knowledge: Democratic Education in a Conservative Age*. New York and London: Routledge.

Aronowitz, S., & H. Giroux (1991). *Postmodern Education: Politics, Culture and Social Criticism*. Minneapolis: University of Minnesota Press.

Bartolom, L. (1996). Beyond the Methods Fetish: Toward a Humanizing Pedagogy. In P. Leistyna, A. Woodrum & S. Sherblom (eds.), *Breaking Free: The Transformative Power of Critical Pedagogy, Harvard Education Review, Reprint Series No. 27*, pp. 229–252.

Bowles, S., & H. Gintis (1976). *Schooling in Capitalist American: Educational Reform and the Contradictions of Economic Life*. New York: Basic Books.

Brown, A., E. Campione, M. Cole, P. Griffin, H. Mehan, & M. Riel (1982). A Model System for the Study of Learning Difficulties. *The Quarterly Newsletter of the Laboratory of Comparative Human Cognition*, 4(3):39–55.

Carspecken, P. F. (1996). *Critical Ethnography in Educational Research: A Theoretical and Practical Guide*. New York: Routledge.

Cole, M. (1985). The Zone of Proximal Development: Where Culture and Cognition Create Each Other. In J. V. Wertsch (ed.) *Culture, Communication and Cognition: Vygotskian Perspectives* (pp. 146–161). New York: Cambridge University Press.

———. (1990). Cognitive Development and Formal Schooling: The Evidence from Cross–Cultural Research. In L. Moll (ed.) *Vygotsky and Education: Instructional Implications and Applications of Sociohistorical Psychology* (pp. 89–110). New York: Cambridge University Press.

Cole, M., & R. D'Andrade (1982). The Influence of Schooling on Concept Formation: Some Preliminary Conclusions. *The Quarterly Newsletter of the Laboratory of Comparative Human Cognition*, 4(2):19–26.

D'Andrade, R. (1984). Cultural Meaning Systems. In R. A. Shweder & R. A. Levine (eds.), *Culture Theory* (pp. 88–119). New York: Cambridge University Press.

Freire, P. (1973). *Pedagogy of the Oppressed*. New York: Seabury.

———. (1995). *Pedagogy of Hope: Reliving Pedagogy of the Oppressed.* Translated by Robert R. Barr. New York: Continuum.

Friere, P., & D. Macedo (1996). A Dialogue: Culture, Language, and Race. In P. Leistyna, A. Woodrum & S. Sherblom (eds.), *Breaking Free: The Transformative Power of Critical Pedagogy. Harvard Education Review, Reprint Series No. 27*, pp. 199–228.

———. (1987). *Literacy: Reading the Word and Reading the World.* Critical Studies in Education Series. Massachusetts: Bergin & Garvey Publishers, Inc.

Gibson, M., & J. Ogbu (eds.) (1991). *Minority Status and Schooling: A Comparative Study of Immigrant and Involuntary Minorities*. New York & London: Garland Publishing Inc.

Gutierrez, K., J. Larson, & B. Kreuter (1995). Cultural Tensions in the Scripted Classroom: The Value of the Subjugated Perspective. *Urban Education* 29(4):410–442.

Gutierrez, K., B. Rymes, & J. Larson (1995). Script Counterscript, and Underlife in the Classroom: James Brown versus Brown v. Board of Education. *Harvard Educational Review*, 65(3):445–471.

Leistyna, Pepi, A. Woodrum, & S. A. Sherblom (eds.) (1996). Breaking Free: The Transformative Power of Critical Pedagogy. *Harvard Educational Review, Reprint Series No. 27.*

Macedo, D. (1991). English Only: The Tongue–Tying of America. *Journal of Education*, 173(2):9–20.

———. (1993). Literacy for Stupidification: The Pedagogy of Big Lies. *Harvard Educational Review*, 63(2):183–206.

McLaren, P. (1989). *Life in Schools: An Introduction to Critical Pedagogy in the Social Foundations of Education*. White Plains, NY: Longman.

———. (1995). *Critical Pedagogy and Predatory Culture*. New York and London: Routledge.

McLaren, P., & T. da Silva (1993). *Decentering Pedagogy: Critical Literacy, Resistance and the Politics of Memory*. In P. McLaren & P. Leonard (eds.) Paulo Freire: A Critical Encounter (pp. 47–89). New York: Routledge.

Moll, L. (1986). Writing as Communication: Creating Strategic Learning Environments for Students. *Theory to Practice*, 26(2):102–108.

———. (1990). Introduction. In L. Moll (ed.) *Vygotsky and Education: Instructional Implications and Applications of Sociohistorical Psychology* (pp. 1–27). New York: Cambridge University Press.

Ogbu, J. (1974). *The Next Generation: An Ethnography of Education in an Urban Neighborhood*. New York: Academic Press.

———. (1978). *Minority Education and Caste: The American System in Cross–Cultural Perspective*. New York: Academic Press.

———. (1982). Cultural Discontinuities and Schooling. *Anthropology and Education Quarterly*, 13(4):290–307.

———. (1987). Variability in Minority School Performance: A Problem in Search of an Explanation. *Anthropology and Education Quarterly*, 18(4):312–334.

———. (1992). Understanding Cultural Diversity. *Educational Research*, 21(8):5–24.

Scribner, S., & M. Cole (1981). *The Psychology of Literacy*. Cambridge, MA: Harvard University Press.

Spindler, G. D. (ed.) (1955). *Anthropology and Education*. Stanford, CA: Stanford University Press.

Spindler, G., & L. Spindler (1994). *Pathways to Cultural Awareness: Cultural Therapy with Teachers and Students*. Thousand Oaks, CA: Corwin Press.

Suárez–Orozco, M. M. (1996). California Dreaming: Proposition 187 and the Cultural Psychology of Racial and Ethnic Exclusion. *Anthropology and Education Quarterly*, 27(2):151–167.

Trueba, H. T. (1991). Linkages of Macro–Micro Analytical Levels. *Journal of Psychohistory*, 18(4):457–468.

Vygotsky, L. S. (1962). *Thought and Language*. Cambridge, MA: MIT Press.

———. (1978). Interaction between Learning and Development. In L. Vygotsky (1978). *Mind in Society: The Development of Higher Psychological Processes* (pp. 79–91). M. Cole, V. John-Teiner, S. Scribner, & E. Souberman (eds.). Cambridge, MA: Harvard University Press.

Wertsch, J. (1981). *The Concept of Activity in Soviet Psychology*. New York: M. E. Sharpe, Inc.

———. (1991). Beyond Vygotsky: Bakhtin's Contribution. In J. Wertsch, *Voices of the Mind: A Sociocultural Approach to Mediated Action* (pp. 46–66). Cambridge, MA: Harvard University Press.

———. (ed.) (1985b). *Culture, Communication, and Cognition: Vygotskian Perspectives*. New York: Cambridge University Press.

Willis, Paul (1977). *Learning to Labor: How Working Class Kids Get Working Class Jobs*. London: Grower.

George and Louise Spindler

1

Cultural Politics of the White Ethniclass in the Mid-Nineties

Our purpose in this essay is to explore the applicability of four concepts we have found useful in our recent analyses of dynamic processes in American culture to the analysis of recent radical rhetoric and action as they affect education. The concepts are: the American cultural dialogue; types of adaptation to disruptive culture change; white ethniclass; and cultural therapy (G. and L. Spindler, 1989, 1990, 1992, 1994). *The American Cultural Dialogue* we will discuss shortly; *types of adaptation* refer to such processes as synthesis of opposing cultural elements, withdrawal, and reaffirmation, engaged in by populations experiencing radical culture change; *white ethni-class* refers to the European-American majority and its ethnicity, and *cultural therapy* has to do with a process of reflection on one's own cultural biases. We will put recent ideological and political turmoil, particularly the attacks on established institutions issuing from sources ranging from fringe groups such as the Montana militia to respectable Republicans, into a broad but integrated sociocultural perspective using these concepts as the framework for analysis. We will conclude by discussing the implications of the turmoil for school programs utilizing cultural therapy. This is a biased paper written from a liberal point of view.

The American Cultural Dialogue

We have used the term "American cultural dialogue" to stand for a process that has been, we believe, central to communication in

America about virtually everything that matters for a long time (G. and L. Spindler, 1990). We posit certain values, such as honesty, hard work, individualism, freedom, sociability, success and achievement gained by hard work, equality, time, and conformity, as pivotal in the dialogue, but as pivotal in the sense that they are centers of opposition as well as agreement. They constitute norms for one's own behavior and expectations for behavior from others, but they are subject to argument, criticism, debate. That is, they are when the dialogue is working. When the dialogue is working the oppositions as well as the agreements verify the active presence of the pivotal value. For example, arguments about the value of honesty acknowledge the virtue of honesty if it were practical, or possible, or if there were not so many dishonest people about. Or the individual is important but only as a member of the group or as a contributor to the welfare of the community. Or hard work is the way to become successful but a lot of people get ahead by luck, cheating, or "kissing ass."

There are certain of these pivotal values that are changing more rapidly than others. Our extensive sample of responses to an open-ended values projective technique, collected from Stanford students (and some others) since 1952, indicates that attitudes toward artists, intellectuals, nudity, concepts of personal success, and sociability, have undergone substantial change. We are more tolerant of the kinds of deviance suggested by artists and intellectuals, we accept nudity as natural, if not always appropriate, we think that success is not merely material but a matter of personal balance and self-recognition, we balance sociability with listening to the inner self. (It is important to remember that a substantial minority has held on to the more traditional value orientations.) With the partial exception of the values of success, however, these values were never central to the dialogue. Certain central values have undergone changes as well. For example, the future is no longer seen with unguarded American optimism, but is more often seen as "bleak" or "uncertain." Success and achievement are perceived more guardedly, with reservations that were not heard, or rarely so, even ten years ago. We still think equality is a basic ideal, but we are more cynical about its attainment. There is more questioning of the right of the individual to act in his or her own behalf without regard for the welfare of others but individuals and their rights still stand supreme for the majority. In general, there is more dispersion of responses, so that the modalities are not quite so large.

For example, although from 40 to 60 percent of respondents complete the open-ended sentence, "Honesty is," with "the best policy" or words to that effect, such frequent responses as "useful sometimes," "not always best," or "very rare," rob the majority response of its clear dominance. But note that these dispersive responses acknowledge the adage, "Honesty is the best policy," so the dialogue retains its integrity.

We hypothesize that the American cultural dialogue is in a tender state at present. We acknowledge that the Stanford sample is special. After all, Stanford students are selected from the "Top Three Percent" (though we do have small samples from other institutions and even some high school students), but if the "cream of the crop" exhibits some deterioration of the stability of core values, the effect must be more pronounced among people who have suffered a decline in real wages for the past ten years and whose employability is even more in question. The core values are not as core as they were only a short time ago, though it is true that the fifties were challenged by the sixties and early seventies, that the eighties re-established the traditional profile (with some modifications), and that the nineties again challenge the temporary stability of the eighties. We will make something of this "tender state" later on. For now we want to turn to the second concept, typologies of adaptations to radical or disruptive culture change, that we are integrating into this essay.

Types of Adaptation to Disruptive Culture Change

In our field work with the Menominee Indians of Northeast Central Wisconsin we discovered that not all Menominee were the same (Spindler and Spindler, 1984). There were "native-oriented," peyotists, several kinds of transitionals, in-betweeners, laboring-class acculturated, and elite acculturated. After several seasons of field work we came to regard these types of response as constructions of adaptations to the transformative culture change the

Menominee had experienced since the coming of Europeans to their area. Of course it was not merely culture change they experienced. It was sweeping changes in the economy by which they made their living, the political struggles by which they were governed, and the very environment they inhabited. We can say that the result of all of these varieties of change was cultural, since we regard culture as the primary adaptation that humans make to changing conditions of survival. Be that as it may, there is no doubt that there were dramatic differences between these groups of Menominee. The elite-acculturated appeared to be middle-class white in their culture, the "native-oriented" appeared (to us) to be quite traditional in their way of life. The peyotists appeared somewhat mixed, ranging from native-oriented to poor mainstream in culture but with a clear ideology and a workable sysnthesis of Christian and native religious belief. There were several kinds of transitionals—people who were culturally suspended, vegetating, vacillating between being white and being Indian; people who were trying hard to make sense of their lives, and experimenting with various kinds of cultural solutions; people who had withdrawn into alcohol and apathy; people who were marginal, some of them constructively and some destructively. And there were the two major types of acculturated: those who earned their living doing unskilled or semiskilled labor, and those who were in managerial positions in the lumber mill or in the administration of the Menominee reservation. They were equally culturally American mainstream in its Wisconsin form. There were also a few individuals who were bicultural, apparently at home in both the Menominee and mainstream cultures. Of these various alternatives we will focus on the native oriented for the purposes of our analysis.

We came to perceive the members of the native-oriented group as active, not passive, in their adaptation to disruptive change. We saw them as actively constructing and maintaining a way of life that asserted the old values and patterns of culture. They worked hard to carry on the rituals they understood as representing the "old way," such as the Dream Dance (Nemehetwen), Medicine Lodge (Mitåwin), Chief's Dance (Oketshetaweshemon). They held "song services" several nights a week, using the "big drum" and singing songs from traditional repertoires. They buried their dead with spirit offerings and grave houses erected over the grave. They offered prayers and exhortations in the Menominee language. They lived well off the highway intersecting the reservation in shacks and Quonset huts they constructed themselves.

At first we thought this group consisted solely of survivors from the past. It was true that most of the old people who were truly Menominee in culture were members of this group. They monitored the rituals and were advisors for the traditional cultural content. But as we came to know the group better, we discovered that all of the people under 50 had been out in the world, going to school or earning a living away from the reservation. They had tired of life in the mainstream and had come back to "get hold of the old ways," They were actively acquiring their own culture from the old people who knew it because they had never stopped living it. Eventually we described this group as "reaffirmative."

What we mean by "reaffirmative" is that the members of this nativeoriented group were trying to reaffirm their traditional way of life as they understood it. Actually the religious organizations that they were reaffirming, such as the Dream Dance and the Medicine Lodge were not ancient ritual organizations. They had both been brought into and had been modified to fit the Menominee culture since their contact with Europeans. In fact both of them were parts of revitalization, or "nativistic" movements that were set in motion by the impact of European invaders. But from the point of view of the members of the present-day nativeoriented group they were traditional organizations and rituals. And it is true that they did express Menominee concepts and values. In any event, these organizations and their associated beliefs and practices were what the people wanted to reaffirm. To do this they had to attempt as "pure" a form of cultural practice as they could under modern circumstances and they had to exclude as much as they could of practices flowing from the outside world. Of course they were only partially successful on either count. Their practice was not pure, and their exclusion was far from perfect—they did use pickup trucks, transistor radios, Western medicine and hospitals, and a myriad of other things and practices that were never a part of the traditional culture. But their reaffirmation was impressive.

When we were well back in the woods, crowded into a Quonset type hut made of scrap lumber, bent saplings for a frame, covered by tarpaper, with six to ten men pounding a drum the size of a washtub and everyone singing in Indian style, the twentieth-century mainstream culture from which we came seemed to be in another dimension. We lived as they did for months at a time, traveled with them, picked cherries with them, became quasi-members of their ceremonial organizations. To us, their reaffirmation seemed eminently successful.

What has this reaffirmation process to do with the intent of this essay, which is to attend to the cultural politics of the white ethniclass? We think that this ethniclass, or at least a significant portion of it, is engaged in a reaffirmative movement. What they are saying and doing, particularly some of those persons who are charged with speaking for the rest of us (in short, elected representatives), fit well the characteristic features of such movements. The resemblance to the Menominee situation seems quite clear.

White Ethniclass Behavior

Why do we say "white ethniclass"? We say it because the phenomena we believe denote *reaffirmation* appear to be almost exclusively engaged in by European Americans, "white" people. In fact, given the most visible actors on the current scene, one could say that much of the activity is engaged in by *referent white ethniclass* persons. This may be too subtle a distinction for our purposes. It is explained in some detail in *The American Cultural Dialogue and Its Transmission* (Spindler and Spindler, with Trueba and Williams, 1990). What this designation distinguishes is a "core" class of white ethnics, mostly upper middle class, who have historically had overweening influence on the manners and morals of American culture and by whom substantial power is wielded. There are some dangers in comparing white mainstream behaviors to those of the Menominee traditionalists. The differences in power are substantial. The Menominee engaged in reaffirmation were virtually powerless. The Gingriches, Doles, Bennets, and Limbaughs and others spearheading current reaffirmation could be seen as essentially manipulating what they recognize as a swelling of sentiment among voters. Although there are doubtless elements of this in the action, we think it is too cynical a view to be an accurate interpretation of the movement as a whole. So too is the "conspiracy" interpretation offered by most of our sociological or politically minded colleagues who have read this paper in draft. The vocalists in Washington, they say, are "looking out for their friends" by introducing and supporting legislation to loosen or eliminate controls on water and air pollution, or tobacco advertising, and eliminating agencies, such as the Department of Commerce, that get in the way of "free enterprise." This seems to us to be a "top-down" interpretation taking into account only the motivations of some of the elite. The internal consistency of reaffirmative statements and expression of sentiment by ordinary people as well as the leaders of the movement would be difficult to contrive, and even if contrived at some level, the mass of expressed sentiments taken together seems decidedly real.

By using the terms "white ethnics" or "white ethniclass" we are denoting our perception of all white Americans as having ethnicity, not just those of Italian, Polish, or Irish (among others) descent, so there is a cultural unity that is often overlooked in interpretations of white American behavior and attitudes that may or no reflect itself in political choices, but that is a decisive factor in supplying the energy for a reaffirmative movement.

? such as what?

There is ample evidence of reaffirmative behavior on the part of white Americans. A wide range of behaviors can be included in this category. When William Bennett visited Stanford in 1988 (I was there), just as the faculty was engaged in a heated debate about proposed changes in the core curriculum for undergraduate study, he publicly excoriated them, likening the responsible Stanford faculty to the agents of Vichy France—sellouts to a foreign power. The changes were mostly in the direction of including minorities and women authors on the required list of readings, and inserting multiculturalism into the curriculum, with a corresponding diminution of the classics from the Western heritage. His recent book, *The Book of Virtues*, a volume extolling traditional values, confirms his reaffirmative position. His interview in *Modern Maturity* (1995) extends it. The enormous popularity of his book suggests that he is far from alone in his reaffirmation. Newt Gringrich has given us many examples of reaffirmative opinions, ranging over a wide variety of subjects, including health care, welfare, warfare, women, and the Clintons. Perhaps one of his most revealing remarks was directed at the President, whom he characterized as "countercultural."

Various members of the Republican Party have recently made negative pronouncements on support for public broadcasting, the national geological survey, the Department of Commerce, the Department of Education, children's support and care programs, school lunches, welfare, health programs, controls on the tobacco industry, gun control, environmental regulation, aid to underfunded college aspirants, and affirmative action, many of which seem to have a reaffirmative flavor. They call for a return to the past, when government was simpler, and we, the mainstream, didn't have all those minorities to worry about, or at least while we might have had them, we didn't have to think about them and when poor people were somebody else's concern and besides, they were poor because they didn't work hard or weren't ambitious. Pete Wilson, governor of California and Presidential aspirant (until his withdrawal) rides the reaffirmative bandwagon when he talks about affirmative action and immigration.

The recent activism in the western states where all forms of governmental regulation of grazing on public land, timber cutting, and water rights are being contested, is more evidence of a reaffirmative movement under way. No interference with individual property rights. The least government is the best government. There are, of course other than reaffirmative elements imbedded in these actions and pronouncements.

There has recently been an outburst of extreme statements directed at the federal government and particularly at the attempts of its agents (the Federal Bureau of Investigation or FBI, and the Bureau of Alcohol, Tobacco and Firearms or ATF) to control the stockpiling of assault weaponry. The invective is expressed not only by extreme fringe elements such as the Montana Militia, and by the "Patriots," as well as the Freemen, who at this writing were holed up in their Montana stronghold, surrounded by the FBI, but also by "respectable" organizations such as the National Rifle Association (NRA), and by elected representatives such as Helen Chenowith of Idaho. Though such sentiments have been smoldering in the United States for a long time, the Randall Weaver and Waco incidents seem to have ignited the fire. Weaver's wife and 14-year-old son were killed during a siege by the FBI, and in the Waco incident 78 people, including 24 children, died in a holocaust after a 51 day siege. To make matters worse, Weaver's wife was killed by an FBI sniper as she stood in the doorway of their cabin, holding her baby. (Her killing is held to be an accident by the FBI.) The penultimate expression of these sentiments took the form of the bombing of the federal building in Oklahoma City. Some interpreters of these events disavow any possible connection of the bombing to the invective and the defense is beginning to make a case for foreign terrorism (for McVeigh, the alleged perpetrator of the bombing) but the distance between word and deed is not untraversable.

The underlying tension seems to be fear and anger about changes that have taken place in our culture during the past few decades, and a desire to return to a simpler, clearcut, mythically moral, past. Pat Buchanan, the gadfly in the Republican ointment, is a perfect example, in his isolationism and protectionism. In this and other ways the white ethniclass movement is like the "native-oriented" Menominee. The Menominee reaffirmative movement rejected a whole way of life and celebrated the return to a version of traditional culture. The white ethniclass movement rejects mainstream developments of the period since the New Deal of FDR and celebrates a return to a version of traditional values. The central value appears to be a combination of individualism, success, and freedom—the individual person is not to be hampered in the pursuit of success by regulations, taxes, or concern for the common good, or the fate of the "down and out," single mothers, new immigrants, poor minorities, or anyone who isn't playing the mainstream games successfully. This is the core value configuration, as well, that all federal regulations are seen as eroding. It is a "white ethniclass" movement. There are virtually no minority persons making any such pronouncements or engaging in any such actions. There are, of course, a few, but they are exceptions. Nor, with a few exceptions, are there women so engaged though many appear to give tacit support to the movement. The activists seem to be mostly male and white. This is precisely where we would expect the energy for a movement of this kind to come from. White ethniclass males have the greatest stake in traditional values. Their values seem to be eroding (remember "tender state"?) and this population has been hit with corporate "downsizing," new technologies, and sudden obsolescence. One is not so sure that hard work and competence will pay off. Likewise, the eroding small towns of the Middle and Far West that are losing population, business, and life styles supply personnel for the militias now operating in at least 25 states (*Klanwatch*, Feb., p. 1) and the energy for virulent anti–government rhetoric.

The ostensible purpose of the militias is to defend against enemies of the Republic, and an enemy is anyone who represents an alien culture, especially immigrants, or anyone who might be a communist or even a "liberal," or anyone who might represent or be affiliated with the federal government. Paranoid statements provide the agenda for these organizations.

The ideas advanced by the extreme fringes as well as by the mainstream antagonists (such as the NRA) include the notions that Bill Clinton is an illegitimate President; liberals are the enemies of normal Americans; gun control is a conspiracy to tyrannize, or render helpless the populace; and a New World Order is being put into place by foreign bankers (Adam Grobnik, p. 8). The radical extremists themselves go further: the United States is secretly building concentration camps to house resisters to the New World Order; microchips are being implanted in the bodies of people to monitor their movements; road signs contain secret codes to direct foreign invaders; armed conflict with the federal government is inevitable (*U.S. News and World Report*, May 8).

Whether these expressed sentiments can legitimately be regarded as "reaffirmative" is moot. They go too far, one would think, to be included, if the reaffirmation is about the reaffirming of traditional values such as individual rights, and yet, they are a logical extension of such reaffirmations taken beyond the boundaries of sanity into what Michael Kelly describes as "fusion paranoia" (Kelly, 1995) melding the left and right extremes of opinion in America.

The life expectancy of reaffirmative movements may not be long, and American opinions and superficial value shifts tend to cycle through rather short time periods. The major phases of value shifts in our more than 40 years of data collection at Stanford (supplemented by other sources as well) seem to have lasted about a decade each. The present situation is extreme, however, and such extremity does not, probably, last as long as a decade. It is true that reaffirmative movements eventually tend to assume conventional forms, they are *institutionalized* and lose much of their radical character. As of this writing, this is already beginning to happen at the political level as Congress and its Republican majority attempts to cope with swings in public opinion. The long-term results, however, may last much longer than the movement itself.

It is our position that William Bennett, Newt Gringrich, the New Republicans, the N.R.A., the militias, the "Patriots," the Oklahoma City bombing, and western activism, are all expressions of a reaffirmative movement, an attempt to revitalize a white American that has been increasingly threatened by massive political and social change (as seen by white America) and by an overwhelming increase in minorities that will eventually make white Americans a minority group. Many readers will resist putting all of these (and many more) groups and actions into a sweeping characterization as a reaffirmative movement. They will point out, for instance, that the new Republicans are not against government, they are just against the government the Democrats have constructed. This interpretation ignores the fact that the Republican attacks have been directed at almost every governmental agency from the Department of Education to the National Geological Survey. They are aimed at dismantling government as it has operated since FDR's New Deal. The consequences are unclear. It remains to be seen whether dismantling antipollution regulations, for example, would not kill more Americans than the Oklahoma City bombing.

The Relevance to Education

What does this have to do with education? Education has been hit directly by reaffirmative trends. The antagonism to bilingual programs, second-language programs and any other program that departs from the Eurocentric center of cultural transmission, has been active for some time. All moves, such as English as the official language of America, can be considered reaffirmative, and are supported by the white ethniclass. The antagonism extends well beyond the language arena. Lately there have been attacks on multicultural education, efforts in the schools to raise the self esteem of minority children, any hint of an Afrocentric or Latinocentric curriculum, and in fact any addition of materials about the cultures of immigrants or minority children into the curriculum, or any "multicultural" emphasis. Teachers are embattled, subject to extra stress, for most of the younger ones at least, have been enculturated into a more or less liberal point of view concerning all of these matters in their professional education training. Coming at the same time as a general crunch on expenditures for education, and calls for elimination of the National Department of Education and many of the programs supported under its aegis, the situation of teachers must be considered rather desperate.

It remains for us to bring together with the elements of our argument one last segment, and that is *cultural therapy*. Cultural therapy has been one of our preoccupations for the last decade or so, though we did our first publication on it in the fifties.

Cultural Therapy

What is cultural therapy? In its most straightforward form it is the process of getting to know one's cultural biases, particularly as they influence one's perceptions of others representing cultures different from one's own. Our most recent publication on it is *Pathways to Cultural Awareness; Cultural Therapy with Teachers and Students* (Spindlers, 1994). Our favorite example of a successful cultural therapy is Roger Harker, a fifth grade teacher with whom George Spindler worked in the 1950s. The lessons learned in this extended case study have lasted for a career. Roger was a good teacher, well thought of by the administration of the school and school system where he taught. In fact he was one of the favorite young teachers. And he was a good teacher by our standards as well. But he was a good teacher for only a minority of the students in his class—those who were culturally like him—upper middle white ethniclass. This is understandable but intolerable in schools with diverse cultural elements.

George did a thorough ethnographic study of his classroom, focussing, after a sterile introductory period, on Roger's interaction with every student in his class. He collected ample evidence of

Roger's selective bias in favor of those children culturally like himself. He was not mean or hostile to those unlike himself, but he knew little about them and didn't interact with them in the supportive manner that he did with those who were culturally like him.

His cultural therapy consisted of a series of sessions devoted to holding up a mirror of his behavior. Together we went over the details of his interaction—both his statements about and to students, and his behaviors, such as frowns, winks, a friendly hand on the shoulder, or facial expressions when he was listening to them give reports. At first Roger was deeply resistant toward any data that displayed his cultural biases. In fact he bolted from the first interview in anger, but he returned for the next session and for many after that. He came to accept his biases as "natural" and to see that something could be done about it to make him a better professional. He could regard his "culture" as something from which he, himself, had a certain emotional distance. His cultural therapy did not change his personality but it changed his culture or at least his expression of it in the classroom. His therapy made his culture more open and gave him cultural knowledge about students from cultures other than his own that he found useful and that influenced his behavior toward them.

Roger's cultural therapy has served as a model for our work. It seems so clearcut and so sensible. The model works and serves us well. There are however, complications. Teachers are not alone in their biases. Students bring to their classrooms profound cultural biases that directly affect their ability to succeed in school. Some regard education as the channel to success in life, and they are not all middle-class white ethnic. Others regard school as anathema, and as irrelevant or in opposition to their projected way of life. We can do cultural therapy with the teacher but if the students remain untouched by this process it is much less effective than it can be.

Consequently we are moving into therapy of selected groups of students and teachers, sometimes mixing them, in whole classrooms, and even in whole schools. Our colleagues, as they report in *Pathways*, have taken cultural therapy in these modes further than we have. Our most successful effort to date has been the Schønhausen/Roseville project (Spindlers, 1989, 1992). This project did not start out as cultural therapy, but as our work progressed in the two schools, one in Germany and one in the United States, it became evident that it was functioning as cultural therapy.

The essential feature of group, classroom, or schoolwide cultural therapy is that a feasible means be employed to cause participants to reflect on issues about cultural relations with each other. This can be done, as we did in Schønhausen/Roseville, by using video exposures of critical interactions and working through the interpretations of these with individuals and groups. It can also be done with discussion of relationships and issues without video exposure. Most of the workers reporting on their field experience in *Pathways* did it this way. We found that whatever method is used, a comparative analysis was critical in stimulating useful reflection. We termed our method a "comparative cross-cultural, reflective interview." Comparison need not be between schools in different countries, as in our case, but may be made between schools in a single community, or even within schools, between classes.

Given the radical extremism and paranoid quality of much social and political action today it seems doubtful that cultural therapy could be applied successfully to the leaders of radical elements. In fact, trying to do it with them seems like a good way to get into a lot of trouble. But schools are not all battlegrounds, at least not yet, and it appears possible to carry on cultural therapy in some of them.

Paradoxically, just when cultural therapy seems most needed as a way to get culturally engendered issues out in the open, the forces of reaffirmation are most likely to avert or dampen, or wholly suppress, such efforts. Latent biases among teachers are reinforced. Open intercultural communication is blocked. Experimentation with multicultural programs becomes unpopular, even dangerous to professional survival. Teachers and students need help understanding the failures at communication that characterize schooling today, and help in dealing with mounting feelings of frustration and futility. They are unlikely to get either kind of help if the reaffirmative movement becomes the dominant reality.

If our analysis is even only partially correct, the very people who need cultural therapy the most are the ones most likely to resist, and with the support of reaffirmation, most likely in fact, to scourge it, for themselves, and others. Cultural therapy itself will become regarded as subversive. We think that we are in for some hard times; but in the long run the imperative forced upon us by real, not mythical, conditions will prevail.

References

Bennett, William J. (19••). *The Book of Virtues.*

———. (1995). Interview by Peter Ross Range. *Modern Maturity* March–April: pp. 26–30, 78, 80, 82.

Gropnik, Adam (1995). "Violence as Style," *New Yorker* May: pp. 60–70.

Klanwatch, SPLC Report, (1994). 24 (55) (Dec.) pp. 1 and 5.

Kelly, Michael (1995). "The Road to Paranoia" *New Yorker* June 19, pp. 60–70.

Spindler, George, & Louise Spindler (1984). *Dreamers With Power: The Menominee Indians.* Prospect Hts. IL: Waveland Press.

———. (1989). Instrumental Competence, Self–Efficacy, Linguistic Minorities, Schooling and Cultural Therapy: A Preliminary Attempt at Integration. *Anthropology and Education Quarterly.* 20. pp. 36–50.

———. (1992). Crosscultural, Comparative, Reflective Interviewing in Schønhausen and Roseville. In M. Schratz, ed. *Qualitative Voices in Educational Research.* London and Bristol, PA: Falmer Press.

———. (1994). *Pathways to Cultural Awareness: Cultural Therapy with Teachers and Students.* Thousand Oaks, CA: Corwin Press.

Spindler, George D., & Louise Spindler with Henry Trueba & Melvin Williams (1990). *The American Cultural Dialogue and Its Transmission.* London and Bristol PA: Falmer Press.

U.S. News and World Report (1995). May 8, p. 38.

Cirenio Rodríguez and Enrique (Henry) T. Trueba

2

Leadership, Education, and Political Action

The Emergence of New Latino Ethnic Identities

> To be Chicanas in the myriad and infinite ways there are of being, to come as we are, poses a threat to integrated schools and to mainstream society. In the absence of collectivity in my graduate seminar, I could not be true to my vision of a Chicana. . . . As I look back, describe, and theorize about my seminar experience, I can articulate the elements that constituted my marginalization and my complicity in the discourses of difference and "othering." The power of the dominant discourse of "other," the objectification of my experiences as the "other" through detached, rational argumentation, and the severing of a collective vision and memory that disabled me and rendered me voiceless, all constituted marginalization and complicity. . . . My dilemma of being a Chicana and a researcher became problematic in ways similar to my experiences in the seminar, that is, as an accomplice to the marginalization and objectification of my identity and experiences as a Chicana, which became embedded in the power structure of the dominant and the disenfranchised. (Villenas, 1996:718–19)

Wrestling with ethnic identity is a daily event that takes many forms. If we carry the language and ideology from one setting (our home) to another (school, or work), we are in trouble. We readily see ourselves as unable to function and communicate. If we keep these worlds separate, we feel marginalized in all of these worlds, and not really belonging to any; worse, we feel that we are betraying one culture any time we switch. Writing this chapter and editing this book has been a struggle similar to the one described above so eloquently by Sofia Villenas.

Brief Historical Perspective

The United States, Mexico, and Latin America are inextricably intertwined by a complex history of several hundred years of, at times, stormy relationships. Through personal sacrifice, at times working in subhuman conditions, millions of Latinos and Latinas, the single fastest growing ethnic group in America, have made significant contributions to this country's economy, cultural life, and democracy. In the Southwest they built the most powerful agricultural industry in the world. The Latino people are racially, socially, and economically highly diversified; but they share cultures, language, history, values, a world view, and ideals. Some lived in the Southwest before it belonged to the United States. In dealing with Latinos, we cannot forget the ethnic, social, racial, and economic differences of Latino subgroups. Caribbean, Puerto Rican, and Cuban Latinos have experiences that may polarize them racially and economically. Their upward mobility varies a great deal and their literacy levels, bilingualism, and educational needs differ. Latinos from Mexico tend to be represented more by the rural and Indian subgroups than by the European and *mestizo* subgroups. They come from diverse ethnolinguistic communities whose Indian roots, home languages, and cultures may be very distant from those of Mexicans from middle and upper classes living in large cities. Their religious practices, community social organization, home and village lifestyles may be shockingly different, and their reactions to urban violence and poverty also differ a great deal. We know that early experience in urban centers tends to marginalize Mexican youth in the United States and destroys their family unit, often resulting in gang activity (see C. Suárez–Orozco and M. Suárez–Orozco, 1995; Vigil, 1983, 1988, 1989; Moore, Vigil and Garcia, 1983).

Many Latinos were in the Southwest prior to the annexation of Mexican territory by the Guadalupe Hidalgo Treaty of 1848, and many more came later. According to the Black Legend, this annexation was justified on the basis of Manifest Destiny, that is, the presumed will of God to have Anglo–Saxon people Christianize the savage Mexican folks deemed unworthy of keeping their land. T. J. Farnham, for example, wrote in his travel journal of 1855:

> Californians [Mexicans] are an imbecile, pusillanimous race of men, and unfit to control the destinies of that beautiful country. . . . The Old Saxon blood must stride the continent, must command all its northern shores . . . and in their own unaided might, erect the altar of civil and religious freedom on the plains of the Californias (cited by Menchaca and Valencia, 1990:229).

The exploitation of "inferior" people and the accepted practice of depriving them of certain rights was a common practice last century. The Civil Practice Act of 1850 which excluded the Chinese and Indians from testifying against whites, was extended to Mexicans because they were part Indian. The residential segregation of Mexicans firmly established on the West coast at the turn of the century, became the foundation for the widespread segregation of the 1920s and 1930s; they were not allowed in public facilities such as schools, restaurants, swimming pools, and theaters (Menchaca and Valencia, 1990:230). Mexicans had been coming to the United States to work in increasing numbers from the beginning of this century. In 1900 the U.S. Census estimate of Mexican immigrants was 103,393. By 1910, there were 221,915; by 1920, 486,418, and by December 31, 1926 the official count was 890,746 (Gamio, 1930:2).

To paraphrase Suárez–Orozco, the anxiety generated by the immigration waves of the end of the 20th century, intimately related to the worldwide restructuring of the economy, ethnic identities, and symbolic space, has created a mirror of our own dislocation and a sense of homelessness. In the face of drastic global sociopolitical and economic change, we tend to blame immigrants for all our sufferings, demonizing them as criminals who break our laws, abuse our services, and deprive us of employment. These Latinos and Latinas are no "guest" workers but *ghost* workers who are needed to do the jobs no one else wants to do, but must remain voiceless and invisible (Suárez–Orozco, Chapter 10, this volume).

Consequently, police officers, vigilantes, coyotes, and racist citizens commit repugnant acts of violence against undocumented immigrants. According to Suárez–Orozco, even Border Patrol supervisors seem to encourage beatings of suspects who run away from agents: "Thump'em" and "Catch as many tonks as you guys can. Safely. An alien is not worth busting a leg." Tonk, the sound made as an agent's flashlight strikes the head of a suspect, is now used to refer to an "undocumented worker." Paranoid and hateful law enforcement officers portray undocumented workers as terrorizing gangs of aliens who invade our country and break our laws. Nothing is farther from the truth. In fact, Mexican workers seek only a chance to work and survive; and they are the true victims, as Suárez–Orozco has amply documented (cited by Suárez–Orozco in this volume).

Redefinition of the Self and New Leadership

The formation of ethnic identity is an ongoing process that responds to the new personal experiences of individuals as they undergo continuous social, political, and educational change. George and Louise Spindler (1989, 1994) have described this process when they speak of an *enduring self* constructed during the formative years in which the most fundamental human relationships are established and the basic norms of human interaction are internalized. As we grow and mature, we form a new self-concept, the *situated self* (or *situated selves*) that reflects successive and sequential adaptations of the person to the changing environment. New human experiences require changes in behavior and a "new" presentation of the self. Physical and mental growth, rites of passage, changes in lifestyle and personal relationships, and changes in language and culture, are often associated with modern mobility and worldwide political and economic instability. Adequate coping with these changes demand a reconceptualization of the self. However, when the contrast between our enduring self and our situated self becomes conflictive and overwhelming to the point that we no longer recognize ourselves and cannot reconcile our present behavior with our original values, then we face and "*endangered self*," or a state of turmoil and confusion that can result in "multiple incompatible selves" reflected in changing patterns of behavior as we interact with different groups of people. Multiple identities, a common phenomenon observable in multicultural modern Western societies, do not reflect pathology but adaptive strategies to a changing world, a fast changing world that creates bizarre and complex interactional settings among people from diverse cultural, linguistic, ethnic, social, economic, and educational backgrounds. Are these interactive arenas becoming closer to a pathological pattern of "multiple personalities" in conflict? Are they resulting in a lack of cohesive value systems and clear personal identities? Are Latinos falling into this pattern? No, in fact, they are creating a new common identity on the basis of common cultural values and the increasing advantages of political alliances for action presumed to benefit the diverse Latino ethnic subgroups. In some real sense, political action seems to play an instrumental role in forming a new ethnic identity with new cultural ties and values among Latinos who had been marginalized and isolated. What is the nature of this process of individual and collective redefinition of the self, and what is the role of new leaders in promoting a new collective self-identity?

First, this chapter provides a general description of the diverse Latino populations in the United States, with their own socioeconomic, historical, racial, and ethnic characteristics; second, it presents an example of how political action has contributed to a new ethnic identity of Chicanos in northern California as they have successfully obtained political power; third, observations regarding leadership and representation of Chicanas and Chicanos will bring us back to essential factors in the redefinition of collective ethnic identities. Thus, Chicanos, one of the largest Latino groups in this country, are shown to have found a new sense of self-esteem and collective political power through successful participation in political action. The emergence of Chicano leaders involved in political action is politically significant at the end of a century that has been marked by a drastic departure from traditional racial, class, and ethnic roles in American democracy. The formation of a middle class of Chicanos who are well educated, understand the American political system well, and function effectively within that system has significant consequences for the future of America in both domestic and foreign affairs. Thus, the emergence of a new ethnic leadership is linked with the education and mainstreaming of a large group of new immigrants of color. To use Freire's concepts in critical pedagogy, education and politics are not only inseparable in the context of political action, but the necessary and sufficient condition for creating a genuine democracy. This means that political action has educated both Chicanos and the rest of society, has redefined them ethnically within the lager society, and has facilitated their own survival, as well as the survival of American democratic structures in schools and society. The making of ethnicity, as it occurred in the example given here, brings together the fundamental role of culture in politics, of use of community resources for purposes of self-identification precisely during political action. Most importantly, this example brings up issues of how new ethnic leadership is exercised by educated persons who not only understand well (through their personal experiences) the nature of hegemonic structures, poverty, oppression and ignorance, but who know the importance of education as the key requirement for conscientization, participation in the democratic process, and, ultimately, empowerment. Political action is presented as culturally and linguistically congruent with the new Latino self-definitions (the situated selves) by leaders who exemplify successful adaptation without loss of their cultural identity. Political socialization is clearly embedded in the educational process, in teaching and learning. Attitudes about the social system, ethnic, cultural, and economic diversity, about exploitation and multicultural curricula, are all an integral part of teaching. As Freire has pointed out:

> There has never been, nor could there ever be, education without content, unless human beings were to be so transformed that the processes we know today as processes of knowing and formation were to lose their current meaning. The act of teaching and learning—which are dimensions of the larger process of knowing—are part of the nature of the educational process. There is no education without teaching, systematic or not, of a certain content. . . . The fundamental problem—a problem of a political nature, and colored by ideological hues—is who choses the content, and in behalf of which persons and things the "chooser's" teaching will be performed—

> in favor of whom, against whom, in favor of what, against what. (Freire, 1995:109).

Many of the processes associated with the formation of one's own self-identity are related to the acquisition of knowledge. But we are less aware of who chooses what is taught and why. Political action, especially as it develops in the context of educational institutions, is highly instrumental in making us aware of the real purpose and nature of schooling.

One of the most reasonable explanations for the formation of a new ethnic identity among Latinas and Latinos through political action—which often begins in schools—is based on the common experience that such action is inherently empowering, invites profound reflection and is transformative, demands immediate change. Political action, if it is meaningful (congruent with the appropriate sociocultural codes), can indeed impact and change dramatically the self-perception of members of an ethnic group by leading the group into a new understanding of the interrelationships between ideology, power, and culture. If Latinos view their lives in the United States as representing experiences of unequal distribution of power on the basis of race, cultural origin, social class, or gender, they can logically search for a common culture, based on a similar historical tradition, and try to break the hegemony (or ideological domination) of mainstream American society by importing cultural traditions from their places of origin. Trueba cites a clear example in California:

> The organization of the *Comité Pro-Fiestas*, the *Comité de Guadalupanas* (originally a religious organization), and the Mexican cowboy (*charro*) associations, such as the *La Regional, Los Caporales*, and the folkloric dance groups function as the larger umbrellas within which Mexican families found the moral support and appropriate climated to maintain their cultural values, rituals, and the activities that enhanced their identity. The splendor and pleasure that cultural activities produced were the cement that bonded ethnic pride and a sense of belonging within the community. Under this general umbrella, newcomers found an opportunity to share important information about the resources available from the various members

> of the Mexican community, valuable in both practical terms to resolve daily problems, and symbolically to restore the psychological wellbeing often threatened by degrading experiences (racial prejudice, economic exploitation, exclusion from services, and opportunities available to other citizens) (Trueba, 1993:134).

In the context of these and other cultural activities, new networks are formed, for example through the informal organization of *compadrazgo*, a civil and religious binding relationship between godparents and godchildren was established through baptism or confirmation whereby a child's spiritual welfare is ritually and officially entrusted to a close friend or relative, the godfather or godmother. In the end, the organization of this network grows into viable political organizations that sponsor celebrations and foster a sense of ethnic community. Through the relationships and networks a number of reciprocal services are exchanged in the form of partnerships, collaborative efforts, loans, information and referral services, recommendations, and so on. A number of major celebrations are used to retain cohesive clusters of Latinos: *Fiestas Patrias* such as *Día de la Raza* on October 12; *Cinco de Mayo* on May 5; *Día de la Independencia* September 16; *Fiesta de la Virgen de Guadalupe,* celebrating the Patron Saint of Latin America on December 12; and on November 2, *Día de los Muertos*, a traditional celebration with pre-Hispanic cultural meaning, and many others. The transition from merely social and cultural activities to political organizational meetings is quite natural. In the case of Woodland, for example, (Trueba, Rodríguez, Zou and Cintrón, 1993), in a single generation a number of political groups were formed, such as the Mexican American Political Action, the *Movimiento Estudiantil Chicano de Aztlán*, the Brown Berets, and the *Latinos Unidos para Mejor Educación*.

According to Camarillo, Latino organizations have been the result of a dramatic increase in immigration that required fraternal organizations, mutual aid and insurance benefits, protection of their rights and privileges as Mexicans, and promotion of cultural and recreational activities (1979:148). The emerging new leadership of Latinos, with an increased political participation in American democracy, is a very significant development of the last decade

(Garcia, 1989). Latinos pursued their goals of participation in the political process in order to obtain a higher quality of life and greater dignity in our society, without compromising their ethnic identity. The matter is still of great preoccupation in recent immigrants from Mexico and Latin America (Trueba, in press). The training grounds for political organization in Latino communities was the Civil Rights movement of the 1960s and 1970s. A clear example of this process was the organization of Chicano militant groups at California's university campuses. The *Movimiento Estudiantil Chicano de Aztlán* (MECHA) was one of the most important because of its large membership and significant accomplishments throughout the entire state. Other important national organizations were the Association of Mexican American Educators (AMAE), and the United Farm Workers Union. Without these organizations the political victories of Latinos in the west coast struggle for equity in schools, in the agricultural fields, or in city government positions, would have not been possible.

Socioeconomic, Ethnic, and Educational Diversity of Latinos

In 1980, the Latino population was 14.5 million, 6.4 percent of the total United States population of 228 million. Within a decade the Latino population had increased 5.6 million to a total of 20.1 million in 1990 (or 8.7 percent of the entire United States population of 248 million that year). It grew at a rate four times faster than the rest of country (Valencia, 1991:15). This growth was felt primarily in California, Texas, New York, and Florida—the states that account for 75 percent of the total Latino population. California alone has 34 percent of all Latinos (6.8 million, mostly of Mexican ancestry); Texas has 21 percent of Latinos (4.3 million, also mostly of Mexican ancestry); New York has 10 percent (2 million, mostly Puerto Rican), and Florida has 8 percent (1.6 million, mostly Cuban). About 1.7 million Latinos live in Arizona, Colorado, and New Mexico (mostly of Mexican origin). In New Jersey there are some 640,000 Latinos, mostly Puerto Ricans. The remaining Latino population is scattered throughout the other states. It is expected that sometime in the middle of the next century, the Latino population will be near 55 million and become larger than the African American population (Valencia, 1991:15). Naturally, some states will change more rapidly (Valencia, 1991:3–16; C. Suárez–Orozco and M. M. Suárez–Orozco, 1995:48–81). According to Hayes–Bautista, Schink and Chapa:

> A state-by-state breakdown of the 1980 data gives a clue to possible future trends. At that time California had 4.5 million Latinos (or 30.8 percent of the total), Texas 2.9 million (19.8 percent), New York 1.7 million (11.4 percent), Florida 0.8 million (5.8 percent), and Illinois 0.6 million (4.1 percent) . . . Mexicans are by far the largest Latino subgroup in the United States, numbering 8.7 million in 1980, or 60 percent of all Latinos. Since it is widely agreed that undocumented people were severely undercounted in the census, this figure may be well off the mark. . . . Some 83 percent resided in California, Arizona, New Mexico, Texas and Colorado in 1980. The only other state with a significant Mexican population is Illinois (Hayes–Bautista, Schink and Chapa, 1988:129–130).

In 1980, the Puerto Ricans formed the second largest Latino subgroup, about two million in 1980, concentrated in New York and New Jersey (61 percent) and Illinois (20 percent). The Cuban subgroup numbered 803,226 in 1980, concentrated in Florida (59 percent). The three subgroups, Mexicans, Puerto Ricans, and Cubans account for 11.6 million of the 14.7 million counted in the 1980 census (Hayes–Bautista, Schink and chapa, 1988:131). To understand the long-term population trends and impact of the Latinos, we must examine what we know about Latino immigrants from the last three decades. According to Rumbaut (1995:16–69), in 1990 there were 19.7 million immigrants (defined as Latinos born outside the United States territory) in the United States (or 6.8 percent of the United States population), of which 8,416,924 were Latinos (including Caribbean), from Cuba, Colombia, Jamaica, Nicaragua, Haiti, Dominican Republic, Guatemala, El Salvador and Mexico; of them 4,298,014 were from Mexico. Of all Latino immigrants, 78 percent came between 1970 and 1989 (6.5 million, one-third of all immigrants), and 50 percent came in the 1980s; only 27 percent of the Latinos have become U.S. citizens, which is understandable, given the recency of their arrival, type of work, rural background, and limited assistance. Sixty percent of Mexican immigrants live in California. The vast differences of these diverse Latino and Caribbean populations of recent immigrants are summarized in Tables 2.1 and 2.2 (see following pages). The Cuban, Colombian, Jamaican, and Nicaraguan immigrants have an education comparable to those of mainstream Americans, and have the highest numbers of workers in the upper-white-collar jobs, with the highest percentage of homeowners. A person's educational level seems to predict economic level and employment. The highest rates of poverty are found among the populations with the least education Mexicans, Salvadorians, Guatemalans, Dominican Republicans, and Haitians. The only exceptions are the Nicaraguans who, holding a higher educational level, show a poverty level comparable to the less educated populations. There is not a correlation between higher levels of education (percentage of college degrees) and the use of public assistance. The Cubans have the highest educational level and the second highest use of public assistance.

There are other important differences among these recent immigrants. As you can see in Table 2.2, although the most educated populations tend to be older, have lower fertility rates, and larger percentages of families with both parents, there is no clear correlation between the dominant language (Spanish) in the homes and their income, fertility, and college degrees. The largest, youngest, and least educated populations seem to have highest levels of fertility. This fact has significant implications for the future generations of Latinos, and helps us understand the clusters of enduring poverty among them, especially among the farm workers. It also suggests a lack of education and employment opportunities for women.

Latinos have benefited the least from the economic recovery of the 1980s and 90s. High rates of Latino poverty have continued in the Latino community. In 1979, 21.8 percent of Latinos were poor; in 1988, the rate was 26.8 percent. In 1979, 28 percent of Latino children lived in poverty; in 1988, 37.9 percent lived in poverty. Latino families living in poverty in 1979 were 13.1 percent; in 1988, 16.1 percent. In 1978, 12.5 percent of Latino families with householders who had completed four years of high school lived in

Table 2.1 1990 Latino and Caribbean immigrant population by country of origin, ranked by percentage of college graduates, and by labor force distribution

	POPUL. #S	COLLEGE GRAD. %	LABOR FORCE %	SELF EMPLOY. %	UPPER WHITE COLLAR %	LOWER BLUE COLLAR %	POV. RATE %	PUBL. ASST. %	OWN HOME %
Cuba	736,971	15.1	64.1	7.3	23	18	14.7	16.2	56
Colombia	286,124	15.5	73.7	6.6	17	22	15.3	7.5	38
Jamaica	334,140	14.9	77.4	4.0	22	11	12.1	7.8	44
Nicaragua	168,659	14.6	73.1	4.7	11	24	24.4	8.4	26
Haiti	225,393	11.8	77.7	3.5	14	21	21.7	9.3	37
Dom. Rep.	347,858	07.5	63.8	5.1	11	31	30.0	27.8	16
Guatemala	225,739	05.8	75.7	5.2	07	28	25.8	8.3	20
El Salvador	485,433	04.6	76.3	4.7	06	27	24.9	7.1	19
Mexico	4,298,014	03.5	69.7	4.5	06	32	29.7	11.3	36

Source: Adapted from Rumbaut, 1995:23–26. (Based on the U.S. Bureau of the Census, *The Foreign Born Population in the United States*, CP–3–1, July 1992, tables 3–5; *Persons of Hispanic Origin in the United States*. CP–3–3, August 1993, tables 3–5; and data drawn from a 5% Public Use Microdata Sample, PUMPS, of the 1990 U.S. Census).

Table 2.2 1990 Latino/Caribbean immigrant population by country of origin (ranked by percentage of college graduates), median age, fertility, percentage of females household heads, of families with both parents, and of English proficiency

	MEDIAN AGE	FERTILITY # OF BIRTHS PER WOMAN 35–44 YRS.	FEM. HEAD %	BOTH PARENTS %	ENGLISH ONLY %	SOME/NO ENGLISH %
Cuba	49	1.8	16.5	72	5	40
Colombia	35	1.8	21.5	65	5	34
Jamaica	36	2.2	34.6	53	94	00
Nicaragua	30	2.5	21.0	66	4	34
Haiti	35	2.4	27.6	56	6	23
Dom. Rep.	34	2.5	41.3	47	4	45
Guatemala	30	2.6	19.5	66	3	45
El Salvador	29	2.7	21.4	61	3	49
Mexico	30	3.3	14.1	73	4	41

Source: Adapted from Rumbaut, 1995:23–26. (Based on the U.S. Bureau of the Census, *The Foreign Born Population in the United States*, CP–3–1, July 1992, tables 3–5; *Persons of Hispanic Origin in the United States*. CP–3–3, August 1993, tables 3–5; and data drawn from a 5% Public Use Microdata Sample, PUMPS, of the 1990 U.S. Census).

poverty. In 1988, this figure rose to 16 percent. While Latinas saw a small increase in the annual earnings from 1979 to 1988 (from $13,759 to $14,845), male Latinos saw a decrease (from $20,626 to $17,851), (Valencia, 1991:19–20). In 1993, out of the 16 million children living in poverty (one-fourth of all children under six years of age), 3.9 million (40.9 percent) were Latinos (Rodgers, 1996:11–12). Between 1981 and 1993, the number of poor Latino families with children under 18 years of age headed by the mother only, almost doubled, from 374,000 to 706,000, about 60 percent of all Latino families (Rodgers, 1996:40).

Farm workers constitute the most enduring underclass of the twentieth century in California, in spite of the fact that they are an extremely hard working group. In some counties (such as McFarland, Madera, Santa Barbara, and San Luis Obispo) there are clusters of Mexican farm workers in poverty working for very low wages and in subhuman conditions (working long hours, without appropriate clothing or protection, and living in deplorable housing). The population in these countries increased rapidly in response to demands for manual labor for cultivation of specialized crops. Specialized crops (which saved California's economy in the 1960s and 1970s) have always required intensive handlabor. As Palerm points out, in the last three decades we did not see the mechanization, but the Mexicanization of commercial agriculture (Palerm, 1994).

The demographic predictions of the 1970s were too conservative. The increased immigration of Latino and Asian populations has rapidly shifted both the total number of children in schools and their racial and ethnic balance *vis-à-vis* the white non-Latino population. California will face radical changes before any other state. In 1970 there were only 30 percent ethnic and racial minority students in K–12 public schools. After 140 years of predominant white enrollment, in 1990, 50 percent of the California public school students belong to ethnic or racial subgroups. There is no longer a numerical majority of whites. By the year 2030, white students will constitute about 30 percent of the total enrollment and Latino students will represent the largest group (44 percent of the total enrollment) (Valencia, 1991:18–19).

The *Chronicle of Higher Education* (*Chronicle of Higher Education Almanac*, September 2, 1996:17–26) published college enrollment and other educational statistics on the educational gains of Latinos. In 1984 there were 535,000 Latinos enrolled in college, and in 1994, 1,046,000 (the actual Latino population more than doubled during this period); in 1994, there were slightly more women than men in college, and more in two-year colleges than in four-year colleges; 968,000 were undergraduates, 64,000 graduate students and 13,000 professionals. The overall educational attainment of Latinos, in 1990, was the lowest in the country, with 30.7 percent of the Latino population having eight or fewer years of education, in contrast with whites (with only 8.9 percent), Asians (12.9 percent), blacks (13.8 percent), and American Indians (14.0 percent). Of the 64,000 graduate students, only 903 obtained doctorates in 1993–94. In 1995, Latinos (U.S. citizens and permanent residents) obtained 1.8 percent of the nation's doctorates in business and management, 2.2 percent of doctorates in the physical sciences, 2.3 percent in engineering, 3.0 percent in the life sciences, 3.1 percent in professional fields, 3.7 percent in arts and humanities, 4.2 percent in the social sciences, and 4.3 percent in education. In 1992, of the 526,222 full-time faculty members with regular instructional duties, Latinos held 12,076 positions. Latino men had 1.7 percent and Latino women 0.8 percent of the total number.

In the late sixties, there were more than three times as many African Americans as Latinos in the school population, and there was one Latino for every 17 white students; 20 years later Latino enrollment is two-thirds of the African American student population, and there is one Latino student for every seven whites. The white student population decreased 17 percent, while the Latino student population increased 103 percent in that period (Orfield, cited by Valencia 1991:18–20). This trend has been accentuated for complex historical reasons in the 1990s (Orfield and Eaton, 1996). Paradoxically the economic and technological future of this country will depend precisely on the educational success of Latinos, African Americans, and Asians as, by the mid-twenty-first century they will constitute half of the total U.S. population. Latino children will be the majority in many of our schools. North America has not prepared for this challenging change. Educators need to be trained to communicate with Latinos effectively and to understand the critical role of Latinos in our future. Latinos will continue to view the family and community as the center of religious, economic, and social life. Latinos clearly occupy the most strategic position among immigrants as we approach the twenty-first century; the success of Latinos can easily become the success of America's democracy, as well as economic, technological, and military survival. The world is increasingly complex and less controllable by the American government and its political institutions. During the twenty-first century, American democratic institutions will struggle for survival in the face of the rising power of other nations.

Latino populations will continue to grow and will remain highly diversified. The education of Latinos will be the most critical challenge to be faced by the next century's educators. The survival of American democracy may well depend on the vision and wisdom of intellectual leaders and teachers who understand Latino communities and families, their values and needs, their exclusion and pain. Latino immigration is likely to continue to be strong, given (1) the economic and political instability of Mexico, Central America, and South America; (2) the increasing need of handlabor in the United States for specialized crop agriculture, as well as in other areas of our economic growth requiring undesirable and strenuous work, and (3) the tendency to reunite families (Hayes–Bautista, Schink and Chapa, 1988:132–134). According to Cornelius, Latino population growth will continue as long as economic development in this country demands low-skill, low-wage jobs, and if the political and economic crises in Mexico and Central America remain acute (Cornelius, 1995:2).

We are persuaded of the extraordinary spiritual strength of Latino families. I know they will continue to amaze us with their capacity to survive the subhuman working conditions of agricultural industries and to plan for the future. Their children and their children's children are learning a tough lesson without losing dignity or hope; a lesson they will never forget. What they need, however, is only a fair opportunity to succeed in schools. Over a decade ago Trueba pointed out:

> The end of the twentieth century is rapidly approaching. The children who will crowd our schools are already among us. Minority children are rapidly becoming, or already have become, the majority in a number of cities and areas of this country. . . . Moral, humanitarian, and economic arguments can be made to motivate us to support minority education in our

schools. The future of this country will be in good hands if we extend our support to minority children today (Trueba, 1989:185–6).

Political action unites Latinos because of the tangible common interests and expectations associated with participation in the democratic process; it does create a new cohesiveness among Chicanos, Mexican-Americans, Latinos (Trueba, in press). The mythical existence of Aztlan, radio broadcasting the binational and bicultural existence of many, and the new and powerful engagement in political activities, and even the celebration of public Latino figures who become ethnic icons, such as Selena, the famous singer who was killed in Texas, all point to this new cohesiveness and collective identity. The formation of a new identity is clearly associated with successful political action and the recognition of the political, social and economic importance of Latinos in this country and abroad. Latino new identity is bringing together individuals from very diverse background: Latinos who are from African ancestry, Latinos from European ancestry, *mestizos*, Indians, Spanish monolinguals, English-Spanish bilinguals, Spanish-Indian language bilinguals, upper-, middle-, and lower-class Latinos, recent arrivals and old timers, religious conservatives, and liberals, and so on. We are witnessing the formation of a new ethnic identity that transcends any previous ethnic definition, and an identity clearly associated with the increasing representation of Latinos in political and economic positions of power. Furthermore, in contrast with previous processes of ethnic identification for political power, Latinos are being recognized not only within the United States (as it became clear in the last presidential and local elections) but are now being recognized in Latin American countries. Mexico has declared that Mexican citizens who acquire United States citizenship will not lose their Mexican citizenship. In fact, Mexico will claim over six million United States citizens of Mexican ancestry as its own in order to enhance that country's political power in the United States. It is a clear recognition of the emergence of Latino political, economic and cultural power across nations.

There are other signs of transnational alliances and the emergence of ethnic linkages across nations. China has continued to make overtures to American citizens and permanent residents from

Chinese ancestry. There are over 100,000 recognized Chinese scholars in American educational, political, and economic institutions. Their ties with mainland China have been severely damaged because of the conspicuous violation of human rights among Chinese scholars and students who are advocates for the modernization and democratization of China. In fact, many of these scholars were not allowed to go back to China for many years. The persistent efforts of Chinese authorities have begun to allow these scholars to make short visits. In the United States, the visible achievement of many Asian Americans in the scientific and economic arenas to attract the political attention of the Federal Government and of selected groups of intellectuals in many educational institutions. The formation of pressure groups of Asian (especially of United States citizens from Chinese, Japanese, Korean and Filipino ancestry) is a clear indication that even in the absence of a common langauge, cultural ties and political expedience can lead to the emergence of a new "Asian" ethnicity that not only provides different individuals with a cohesive political umbrella and access to resources, but a powerful lobbying instrument outside the United States with Asian nations. The emergence of "new" ethnicities is plagued with conflict and struggle for control among rival factions, at times based on racial and ethnic differences; that is the case of both modern Latino and Asian groups in the United States. But the fact that these groups function effectively is in itself more significant that the conflicts they face in their fight for political control. It is precisely in this context of cultural conflict and struggle for emancipation that ethnic persons become socialized into the politics of modern democracies, and it is where they learn their distaste for hegemonic structures and the imposition of hegemonic discourse. The debates in universities over ethnic rights, ethnic recognition, fair representation of ethnic intellectuals among the faculty, and fair representation of cultural and theoretical contributions in the curriculum, become the training ground for democracy among foreign students who link with ethnic students born, or raised in this country, or those who have become permanent citizens or naturalized. What is significant about these encounters and political socialization across ethnic groups and nations is that (1) they take place in a country that is already multicultural, highly diversified and highly tolerant of differences, in contrast with many other nations; (2)

they create cultural, political, and ideological linkages among individuals who speak different home languages, belong to different nations, and have different ethnic identities, different social, and economic groups, and even different purposes in their support of debates and political action.

Over a period of 25 years, the degree of political activism and participation in political debates at various universities has fluctuated among generations of Latino students and faculty in Northern California. We have seen radical students become conservative faculty, and conservative faculty become radical faculty. We have seen activists become university intellectuals and administrators politically conservative, and we have seen intellectuals become radicalized as they defend their faculty rights (or so they argue). Most of all, we have seen cannibalistic, violent and conflictive behaviors divide Latino groups by generation, political ideology, participation in the control of university functions, visibility in the community, and so on. But what we had not seen is the creation of strong new political fronts across the various Latino conflictive groups for the sake of gaining some political power at the state and national levels. This phenomenon is related to the emergence of new leaders who have a keen political vision and substantial following in their local communities.

Concluding Reflections

Latinos are finding a national voice that permits them to create a new self-identity, which is not in conflict with their other identities (ethnic, social, religious, and so on). This new identity is associated with education for political action and participation in the democratic processes of ideological debate and involvement with the political system at all levels. The ideological debate and involvement is guided by new leaders who possess specific qualities of vision, biculturalism, multiple identities and the ability to code-switch, and a profound commitment to the democratic ideal of fair participation in the political and economic arena for all Americans. How do we handle the ideological debate and encourage the political participation of students and faculty in universities? What should be the role of universities *vis-à-vis* "education" or instruction to facilitate the role of leaders in the new multicultural world in which we live. As Macedo has insightfully pointed out:

> Literacy for cultural reproduction uses institutional mechanisms to undermine independent thought, a prerequisite for the Orwellian "manufacture of consent" or "engineering of consent." In this light, schools are seen as ideological institutions designed to prevent the so-called crisis of democracy . . . I analyze how the instrumentalist approach to literacy, even at the highest level of specialism, functions to domesticate the consciousness via a constant disarticulation between the narrow reductionistic reading of one's field of specialization and the reading of the universe within which one's specialism is situated. The inability to link the reading of the word with the world, if not combated, will further exacerbate already feeble democratic institutions and the unjust, asymmetrical power relations that characterize the hypocritical nature of contemporary democracies (Macedo, 1996:35–36).

The development of new Latino identities is linked to the fight against what Macedo has called "literacy for stupidification" that takes place particularly in institutions of higher education when the university ruling elites pretend to offer an education totally divorced from the politics of daily life, the reproduction of the social and economic system, and the struggle for liberation on the part of unrepresented groups. Political action in the educational (university) context has the particular value of presenting intellectual (potential leaders) with the consequences of their ideology for real-life issues and for real people, not as an exercise in futility to debate purely academic content.

One of the main goals of the new Latino leadership in higher education is to open up institutions that have been traditionally closed by increasing the pool of qualified candidates for both student and faculty positions. In fact, Harvard and the Massachusetts Institute of Technology now count hundreds of Latino students who are functioning well and obtaining a very intensive academic socialization in two of the most competitive universities in the world. This is a new phenomenon. But increasing the pool of candidates is only one of the requirements for successfully hiring, promoting and retaining persons from underrepresented racial or ethnic groups. A more serious challenge is to provide these persons with adequate mentoring and guidance. We need to create new support systems, a combination of partnerships, state and federal grants and support from private agencies in order to identify and nurture the new generation of Latino intellectual leaders.

Senior scholars could take under their supervision (with the necessary financial support) young Latino researchers, mentoring them through an extended period (several years), and exposing them to participation in seminars, conferences, and research across institutions. An important part of this process ought to concentrate on providing young Latino intellectuals with an intense socialization in conducting research and writing, in acquiring additional methodological and analytical skills, and in developing a broad network with peers and senior scholars. A followup of these young intellectual leaders must take the form of periodical conferences to provide them with specific professional advice in their professional careers. We believe that the time for seriously investing in Latinos is here. The social and intellectual implications of such a movement toward minority excellence and the development of leadership will certainly have an impact at all levels of education, and it will prepare this country for the challenges of multicultural America in the next century.

There are at least two parallel processes taking place among ethnic communities in the United States. One that affects each individual at a different pace and is primarily a psychological process permits an ethnic person to redefine the self in adaptation to new social, economic, educational, and political surroundings; thus, personal experiences can bring a person to a new understanding of the space he or she occupies, and the need to find a voice in a competitive multicultural world. Another process is political, collective, and public; it strikes groups of individuals with a shared ethnicity with the realization that they can have power through political action, and that this power alters dramatically their collective and personal identities in the public arena. What characterizes a new collective identity is the emergence of leadership and representation of common interests in the political arena.

References

Camarillo, A. (1979). *Chicanos in a Changing Society*. Cambridge, MA: Harvard University Press.

Chronicle of Higher Education (1996). Almanac Issue, *Chronicle of Higher Education* XLIII (1) Sept. 2.

Cornelius, W. (1995). Educating California's Immigrant Children: Introduction and Overview. In R. G. Rumbat & W. A. Cornelius (eds.) *California's Immigrant Children: Theory, Research, and Implications for Educational Policy* (pp. 1–16). University of California, San Diego. San Diego, CA: Center for U.S.–Mexican Studies.

Freire, P. (1995). *Pedagogy of Hope: Reliving Pedagogy of the Oppressed*. New York: Continuum.

Gamio, M. (1930). *Mexican Immigration to the United States: A Study of Human Migration and Adjustment*. Chicago: University of Chicago Press. [The 1971 Dover Publications, Inc. of New York reproduces exactly the 1930 original version].

Garcia, M. (1989). *Mexican Americans*. New Haven: Yale University Press.

Hayes–Bautista, D. E., W. O. Schink, & J. Chapa (1988). *The Burden of Support: Young Latinos in an Aging Society*. Stanford, CA: Stanford University Press.

Macedo, D. (1996). Literacy for Stupidification: The Pedagogy of Big Lies. In P. Leistyna, A. Woodrum & S. A. Sherblom (eds.) *Breaking Free: The Transformative Power of Critical Pedagogy. Harvard Education Review, Reprint Series No. 27*: 31–57.

Menchaca, M., & R. R. Valencia (1990). Anglo–Saxon Ideologies in the 1920s–1930s: Their Impact on the Segregation of Mexican Students in California. *Anthropology and Education Quarterly*, 21(3):222–249.

Miranda, L., & J. T. Quiroz (1989). *The Decade of the Hispanic: A Sobering Economic Retrospective*. Washington, DC, National Council of La Raza.

Moore, J., D. Vigil, & R. Garcia (1983). Residence and Territoriality in Chicano Gangs. *Social Problems,* 31*(2)*:183–194.

Orfield, G., & S. E. Eaton (eds.) (1996). *Dismantling Desegregation: The Quiet Reversal of Brown v. Board of Education*. New York, NY: The New Press.

Palerm, J. V. (1994). *Immigrant and Migrant Farm Workers in the Santa Maria Valley, California*. Center for Chicano Studies and Department of Anthropology. University of California, Santa Barbara. Sponsored by the Center for Survey Methods Research, Bureau of the Census, Washington, D.C.

Rodgers, H., Jr. (1996). *Poor Women, Poor Children: American Poverty in the 1990s*. Third edition. New York: M. E. Sharpe.

Rumbaut, R. (1995). The New Californians: Comparative Research Findings on the Educational Progress of Immigrant Children. In R. G.

Rumbaut & W. A. Cornelius (eds.) *California's Immigrant Children: Theory, Research, and Implications for Educational Policy* (pp. 17–69). University of California, San Diego. San Diego, CA: Center for U.S.–Mexican Studies.

Spindler, G., & L. Spindler (1989). Instrumental Competence, Self-Efficacy, Linguistic Minorities, and Cultural Therapy: A Preliminary Attempt at Integration. *Anthropology and Education Quarterly*, 10(1):36–50.

Spindler, G., & L. Spindler (eds.) (1994). *Pathways to Cultural Awareness: Cultural Therapy with Teachers and Students*. Newbury Park, CA: Corwin Press.

Suárez–Orozco, C., & M. Suárez-Orozco (1995). *Transformations: Immigration, Family Life, and Achievement Motivation Among Latino Adolescents*. Stanford, CA: Stanford University Press.

Suárez–Orozco, M. M. (in press). State Terrors: Immigrants and Refugees in the Post–National Space. In H. T. Trueba & Y. Zou (eds.) *Ethnic Identity and Power: Cultural Contexts of Political Action in School and Society*. Albany, NY: SUNY Press.

Trueba, H. T. (1989). *Raising Silent Voices: Educating Linguistic Minorities for the 21st Century*. New York: Harper and Row.

Trueba, H. T. (1993). Lessons Learned: The Healing of American Society. In H. T. Trueba, C. Rodríguez, Y. Zou, & J. Cintrón, *Healing Multicultural America: Mexican Immigrants Rise to Power in Rural California*. London, England: Falmer Press.

Trueba, H. T., C. Rodríguez, Y. Zou, & J. Cintrón (1993). *Healing Multicultural America: Mexican Immigrants Rise to Power in Rural California*. London, England: Falmer Press.

Trueba, H. T. (in press). *Latinos Unidos: Ethnic Solidarity in Linguistic, Cultural and Social Diversity*. Boulder and New York: Rowman and Littlefield Publishers, Inc.

Valencia, R. R. (1991). The Plight of Chicano Students: An Overview of Schooling Conditions and Outcomes. In R. R. Valencia (ed.) *Chicano School Failure: An Analysis Through Many Windows* (pp. 3–26). London, England: Falmer Press.

Vigil, D. (1983). Chicano Gangs: One Response to Mexican Urban Adaptation in the Los Angeles Area. *Urban Anthropology,* 12(1): 45–75.

Vigil, D. (1988). Group Processes and Street Identity: Adolescent Chicano Gang Members. *Journal for the Society for Psychological Anthropology, ETHOS*, 16(4):421–444.

Vigil, D. (1989). *Barrio Gangs*. Austin: University of Texas Press.

Villenas, S. (1996). The Colonizer/Colonized Chicana Ethnographer: Identity, Marginalization and Co–Optation in the Field. *Harvard Education Review* 66(4):711–731.

Jon Wagner

3

Power and Learning in a Multi-Ethnic High School

Dilemmas of Policy and Practice

Students gain and lose access to different kinds of power as they move through school. In schools serving culturally diverse communities, the pattern of these gains and losses is the focus of moral and political concerns. At the heart of these concerns is the prospect—fueled by substantial empirical evidence—that schools as we know them may be unable to achieve ideals of social justice in educating children from culturally diverse communities.

In this essay, I examine how teachers and administrators have tried to guard against this troubling prospect at Turin High School (a pseudonym). Turin is a relatively new school serving a culturally and ethnically diverse population in a rapidly urbanizing area of California's Central Valley. Like their counterparts at many American schools, teachers and administrators at Turin profess a commitment to providing equal education opportunities. However, because of the reform climate within which the school was founded, they also have developed strategies that deliberately challenge several conventional school practices. Among the most visible of these are provisions at the school for collaborative, school-wide decisionmaking; the deliberate assignment of students with different ability profiles to the same classes (i.e., "heterogeneous grouping" or "detracking"); and support for interdisciplinary teaching teams and curricula. Turin teachers and administrators have also made a deliberate effort to affirm—in a variety of public statements to the school and community—both the distinction and value of the school's cultural and linguistic diversity.

The strategies developed at Turin for trying to achieve social justice are interesting in their own right. However, my focus here will be on how the challenges of developing and implementing these strategies stimulated Turin teachers and administrators to change the way they viewed their school and their students. These changes illustrate a relatively neglected feature of schooling: the learning that school teachers and administrators accomplish through their work in schools. As a prelude to examining how issues of ethnicity and power were defined at Turin High School, let me comment briefly on this kind of on-the-job learning.

Learning from Teaching School

The fact that teachers and administrators learn from their work in schools has been largely neglected in studies of social inequality and schooling. There are no images of active, learning teachers in the milestone analyses of aggregate schooling outcomes (Coleman, 1987; Jencks, Bartless, Corcoran, Crouse, Eaglesfield, Jackson, *et al.*, 1979; Jencks, Smith, Acland, Band, Cohen, Gintis, *et al.*, 1972) nor are such images found in the seminal literature of resistance and social reproduction theory (Bourdieu & Passeron, 1990; Bowles & Gintis, 1976; Willis, 1977).

A more common approach within studies of schooling and inequality is to regard teachers and administrators as the embodiment of schooling structures and to contrast this static representation with the dynamic world of children, families and communities. This portrayal of teachers grants them neither inclination nor agency to learn, and it ignores the prospect of teachers acting thoughtfully and efficaciously within the complex cultural and institutional settings in which they work. This truncated portrayal of teachers limits in turn our understanding of the reproduction and maintenance of social inequality and of ethnicity and power in schools.

The neglect within studies of schooling inequality of teachers' learning and action has its counterpart in other research. With a few notable exceptions (Giroux, 1988; Little, 1982; Little, 1990), studies of school change have presented teachers' learning as a response to organized programs of professional preparation, staff development, skills training and program implementation. In studies focusing directly on teachers, attention to teachers as learners is both meager and extremely limited in scope. As Clark and Peterson (1986, p. 292) note in their thoughtful review essay, "Researchers have tended to focus on relatively discrete and isolated aspects of teachers' thoughts and actions, rather than on the whole process of teaching or on the relationships between, for example, teacher planning and interactive thoughts and action in the classroom." Even within the literature on reflective practice, teacher reflection is typically represented as a transitory, case-by-case response to individual problems and decisionpoints, not as a cumulative program of inquiry involving cognitive and behavioral change.

The relative neglect of how and what teachers learn in school is understandable, as schooling ideology assigns school learning functions exclusively to students. For that matter, child development in general has received much more research attention than adult development. In their efforts to focus on children's phenomenal worlds, some researchers have also restricted their own inquiry into the worlds of adult teachers (Eckert, 1989; Everhart, 1983; McLeod, 1995). From the perspective of a child in school—and his or her parents—adult school teachers and administrators also are closely identified with school organization, regulations, and authority. Indeed, working within what Waller (1965) has called the "perilous equilibrium" of schools, teachers and administrators have a vested interest in presenting their work habits in authoritative terms as commonsense features of a stable schooling structure. Given a variety of teaching circumstances and assignments—and great variation among individual teachers—it is also hard to generalize about what teachers learn from their time in school (though what teachers learn is probably at least as varied as what students learn).

Understandable though it may be, the systematic neglect of what teachers and administrators learn while working in school encourages models of teacher preparation and staff development that are pedagogically unsound. It also can lead administrators, parents, students and other teachers to discourage or trivialize among teachers the very forms of independent and reflective inquiry that teachers need to model for their students. In addition, it supports a distorted conception of school change that in turn emphasizes policy and program implementation as the only path to school reform.

As a partial corrective to this neglect, I begin with the premise that all persons engaged in school—students, teachers, administrators, clerical and support staff, and, in some cases, researchers—are engaged in learning and in working, being trained, and in investigations of school. Let me quickly add, however, that both adults and children are most likely to learn through involvement in schooling when such learning is stimulated, supported and encouraged. Little (1982) has described some school-site circumstances that support and encourage learning among teachers. But what circumstances are most likely to stimulate this kind of learning? And what is teacher learning in school most likely to be about?

The tentative answer I propose to these two questions is organized around the concept of a *perspective*. As described by Becker, Geer, Hughes, & Strauss (1961, p. 34), a perspective is "a coordinated set of ideas and actions a person uses in dealing with some problematic situation." Two aspects of this definition deserve additional attention. First, as a *co-ordinated* set of ideas and actions, questions of causality are left open. As the authors note:

> We avoid specifying either actions or beliefs as prior and causal. In some cases, the person may hold the beliefs and act so as to implement them. In others, he may take some actions and develop the ideas as an after-the-fact justification. In still others, ideas and actions may develop together as the person attempts to build a new approach to an unfamiliar situation (*ibid.*, 34–35).

Second, a perspective helps individuals solve problems of understanding and action. That is, "A person develops and maintains a perspective when he faces a situation calling for action which is not given by his own prior beliefs or by situational imperatives" (*ibid*, 35).

To understand how and what teachers, administrators and others learn by working in school, we can examine how their perspectives change over time. This formulation helps identify not only the content of teacher learning (e.g., perspectives) but also the circumstances in which learning is likely to occur. That is, we should expect to see teachers' perspectives change if and when the problematic situations associated with their work change. These situations might change as teachers move to new or unfamiliar schools or in response to school reorganization, demographic shifts, and changes in the teaching profession as whole. Of particular interest to understanding school reform, school situations that are problematic for teachers might also change as teachers try to make changes in their schools and assess the consequences.

Some changes in school problematics affect more teachers than others. However, even when new problematics affect most teachers at a school, it is unlikely that the teachers' collective perspective will change unless they have opportunities to discuss these problematics with each other (Little, 1982). When the problematics change for most teachers and there are opportunities enough to talk them through, conditions may be ripe for teachers to learn from their efforts and experience and to change their perspectives towards teaching, learning, schools and schooling.

As an illustration of the kinds of workplace problematics that can stimulate teachers or administrators to change their perspectives—that is, to learn from their work in school—consider the following statement from a teacher at Turin High School:

> I believe Turin is one of the most culturally diverse schools in California. So, to say that serving "diverse" populations is a "challenge" would be an understatement—a gross understatement. Like many of my colleagues, I serve on many committees that are a part of collaborative decision-making, plan extra-curricular activities, counsel kids, manage myriad lines and then have to set up daily activities that will educate, excite, enrich and enlighten my students. This is at times too overwhelming. Then to top it all off, I must consider the low skilled, the average skilled, the brightly skilled, the discipline problem child, the second language child, etc. It is a challenge!
>
> In one part of the room we have a bright over achiever that has potential to "fly," but I need to work individually with a student who has difficulty with English (as a first or second language; it doesn't matter). I always have to keep in mind that my 50 minutes are structured so that everyone is

> educated—and can move over to the next step in their daily education. But, again, there is that student who can "fly." How do I get to that person? Will I get there in time? What will I say? What do I do? But, I'm still working with the second language kid and try to look to the class to manage behavior. But the "flyer" is waiting patiently. Luckily for me the student is content. Maybe a little happy that I won't have time or maybe bored or disappointed that my class doesn't hack it . . . Oh, guilt!! I'm not doing my job. I haven't done the right thing for everyone. Will I ever do the right thing for everyone? Am I a good teacher? No? Yes? Do I have time to find out or to reflect? The challenge is being met head on every moment of every day, whether you know it or not.
>
> Then to create lessons that tie into, across, through and beyond my partner's class. Have I made connections? Have I offered opportunities for students to make their own conclusions? Have I offered opportunities for students to make their own conclusions? Have I developed units of study that help the student? Will my partner have the boxes on time? Will I have my folders on time? Can we have our units of study on time?
>
> Can anything be on time? Have I (we) done anything that has worked? Did anyone learn anything? I wonder if the second language English speaker is willing to tell the "flyer" the story of his/her personal oppression? I know they both should be in my class . . . I mean after all this is America and we need to TALK!!

Challenges such as these stimulated Turin teachers and administrators to develop distinctive perspectives that could guide and explain their work with Turin students. As these challenges changed over time, the perspectives of teachers and administrators changed as well. As one example, many Turin teachers initially viewed student ethnicity as a *challenge to effective instruction*, then came to view it as *a resource in engaging students in school*, and finally, for some school members, *as a resource for learning and moral development*. As a complement to these evolving views of ethnicity, the perspective of Turin teachers towards empowering students also shifted. Starting from an initial focus on *traditional forms of academic achievement*, teachers and administrators subsequently affirmed a conception of student empowerment that embraced a wider array of *adult competencies valued in schools and workplaces*, including, for some teachers, *competencies of inter-ethnic communication and moral leadership*.

In the remainder of this essay, I will describe in more detail each of these perspectives, how they developed and the relationships between them. I will then discuss the implications of these observations at Turin High School for rethinking relationships between issues of ethnicity and power in schools and the structure of social and educational policy. But first a word or two about Turin High School as the setting in which I noted these perspectives and watched them change over time.

A Multi-Ethnic High School

Turin first opened its doors in the fall of 1989, enrolling at that time about 1,400 ninth and tenth grade students. As these initial student cohorts advanced to become eleventh and twelfth graders, new ninth graders were added. By fall of 1991, the school was serving over 2,400 students, and in the Spring of 1992, Turin graduated its first senior class.

Most of Turin's students have come from relatively low-income families that reflect great ethnic, linguistic and cultural diversity (see Table 3.1). Almost 25 percent of these students are classified as Limited English Proficient (LEP).

During the spring of 1989—before the school had actually opened—the Deer Park Superintendent described Turin with both hopefulness and pride as "something of an experiment." This perspective was shared by a group of core teachers who had been working with the principal to design the school. As the principal noted, "the intent with Turin was not to just build another high school, but to develop a new *kind* of high school that could work well for a really diverse student population."

The experimentation that administrators and teachers associated with Turin focused on a few key school restructuring principles. In the words of the school's early leaders, these included "collaborative decisionmaking," "interdisciplinary curricula," and "heterogeneous grouping."

Table 3.1 Racial and ethnic composition of students at Turin (1991 and 1994) and other schools in the Deer Park District (1991)

1994	TURIN HIGH SCHOOL	1991	TURIN HIGH SCHOOL	HILLSIDE HIGH SCHOOL	DEER PARK HIGH SCHOOL
American Indian	1	American Indian	2	1	1
Asian	23	Asian	20	13	5
Filipino & Pacific Islander	11	Filipino	7	8	3
Hispanic	12	Hispanic	13	16	9
Black	17	Black	16	27	3
White	36	White	41	34	79
		Pacific Islander	1	1	0
Total Percent	100	Total Percent	100	100	100
Total student enrollment	2378	Total student enrollment	2308	1818	2393

Provisions for collaborative decision-making at Turin were based in part on the effective schools literature and relied heavily on an array of school-wide committees of teachers and administrators, with some participation by students and parents. To support interdisciplinary curricula, Turin was organized around multidisciplinary divisions instead of more traditional departments, and an effort was made to support pairs of teachers working across related but distinct subject areas. The emphasis on heterogeneous grouping of students emerged from criticisms and concerns about the abuses of school tracking policies (Oakes, 1985), including those in place at other high schools in the Deer Park district. As one corrective to this practice Turin teachers and administrators sought to ensure that the ethnic diversity of the school was well represented in all individual school classrooms, regardless of the subject or academic level being taught. As both a means and a moral parallel that could foster this outcome, teachers and administrators also sought to ensure that classrooms enrolled students with a wide range of academic abilities.

In response to efforts by school members to implement these innovative operating principles, Turin received attention from the mass media, from the California Department of Education, and from teachers and administrators working at other schools in California and in other states. However, in trying to make good on principles that seemed both newsworthy and promising when the school began, Turin teachers and administrators also found themselves extending and revising these principles, and, in some cases, replacing them with new guidelines for the school's continuing development. Alterations, revisions and modifications also occurred as the school doubled in size in two short years—from 60 teachers and 1,100 students in 1989 to 115 teachers and 2,400 students in 1992—and as Turin teachers and administrators learned more and more about the students the school was designed to serve.

Studying Turin High School

My own efforts to understand the dilemmas and perspectives of Turin teachers began in 1989, the winter before the school actually opened. I was working at a nearby university at the time, and I'd heard about this "school-to-be" from other teachers in the area. I was also exploring with several school districts the prospect of establishing long-term research and development partnerships with the university. In a meeting with the Deer Park Superintendent to discuss that possibility, he recommended Turin as a good place to start. Acting on the superintendent's suggestion, I met the Turin principal-to-be and some teachers on the school planning team, and our discussions led to a collaborative research and development relationship that has extended over six years.

Initially, the focus of my work with the school was on helping Turin colleagues in their own efforts to document and evaluate specific reform strategies and projects they were undertaking at the school. However, in 1992, as a complement and extension to these collaborative efforts, I began pursuing a personal research interest in relationships at Turin between variables of school organization (e.g., grouping practices, activity schedules, task groups, and so on), the engagement of different school members and patterns of student achievement.

To support these multiple lines of inquiry, I worked with my Turin colleagues to collect and analyze a variety of data about the school. In addition to my own field notes, these included official and unofficial school documents (e.g., the school's mission statement; newsletters, memos and reports to parents; minutes and agenda from different schoolwide committees and meetings; proposals for extramural funding; letters and correspondence with outside foundations). Data for these investigations also included responses to several openended surveys of students, teachers and parents; structured and unstructured interviews with selected students, teachers, parents and administrators; and transcribed audio recordings of school and school community meetings.

As a complement to traditional data sources, I also worked with Turin colleagues to design and support a series of annual Evaluation-Retreats. Most of these were held at the end of the school year and brought together students, teachers, administrators and parents for two days of intense discussion, problemsolving, and data analysis. Evaluation Retreats provided opportunities to share data and research observations with members of the Turin school community, but they generated new data about the school as well. These additional data included tape recorded conversations at the Retreats between students, teachers, parents and administrators. The Retreats were also used to generate written reflections from school members about the Turin's mission, goals and objectives, reform strategies, organizational features, challenges to the school's development, the kinds of assistance required and offered by students and teachers, and so on.

In trying to understand how Turin teachers were responding to the challenges of their work, I examined evidence from across these different data sources. This examination revealed three distinctive perspectives that Turin teachers and administrators have developed towards their school. For purposes of this analysis, I refer to these perspective as *academics first*, *student engagement*, and *moral codevelopment*.

By looking systematically at how these perspectives were represented over time in the data noted above, I determined that they were somewhat cumulative (i.e., the second perspective grew out of the first, and the third out of the second). However, I also noticed that all three perspectives stayed very much alive at Turin, and were contested continually. As cumulative constructions, these perspectives illustrate some of what teachers and administrators learned about ethnicity and power by working at Turin. As contested points of view, they also instantiated continuing debates about the purpose of Turin High School and of schooling in general.

The intensity of these debates at Turin has been augmented by the extraordinary obligation that Turin teachers felt to succeed with all their students. Some of this emerged from visibly experimental aspects of the school's design and the tenuous support these had—at least initially—among Turin parents and among teachers and administrators at the two other Deer Park high schools. But pressure for teachers to succeed was also a by–product of the school's collaborative decisionmaking process. As one teacher put it, "When you have this much input into what the school is going to look like, you're that much more responsible for making it work."

The combination of a diverse student population, ideals of educational equity, and a sense of direct responsibility for the school's design presented Turin teachers with a continuing cycle of cognitive and practical challenges. These challenges—made explicit in the teacher's statement reported earlier (page 4)—stimulated Turin teachers to develop the perspectives noted above. As these perspectives reflect evolving ideals for Turin and for schooling in general, I will describe each of them in more detail.

Academics First

During the school's first year or two, academic achievement appeared to be the primary concern of teachers and administrators in thinking about success for Turin students and the school. This concern had two key components: affirming high academic standards for the school as a whole, and trying to ensure that all Turin students succeed in meeting those standards.

Commitment to high academic standards was made tangible in establishing graduation requirements at Turin that exceeded those of the state and the other two high schools in the Deer Park district. This commitment was also reflected in the school's deliberate effort to eliminate classes that in other schools would serve so-called "remedial" students. Commitment to helping all students succeed—the school motto was, "Make Success and Everyday Experience"—was reflected in a variety of instructional strategies, including strategies of cooperative learning and other forms of classroom-based group work.

The affirmation by Turin teachers and administrators of high standards and high success rates challenged expectations of other teachers in the Deer Park district and of some Turin students and their parents. Some teachers from Keel, the middle school attended by most Turin high school students, thought Turin had "gone too far" and was asking so much of its students that many would be doomed to academic failure. Many students themselves were troubled, at least initially, by the increased academic demands affirmed at Turin. As one Turin teacher noted about an incoming class of ninth graders:

> Some of them go into shock when they get here when they find out that we're not going to let them just sit back in the slow classes and not learn anything the way they've gotten

used to. We're asking them to succeed—we're *demanding* that they succeed—and some of them don't like that at all.

Deficits and Diversity

In affirming both high academic standards and success for all students, Turin teachers and administrators made explicit their own conception of how the school might best empower its students. Their primary interest was to increase the power that Turin graduates could exercise as employees or as college students, especially the later. While teachers and administrators did not expect all Turin graduates to attend college, they did want them all to be able to attend if they so desired, and they were uniformly apprehensive about students forfeiting adult opportunities by falling short of college entrance requirements or failing to develop requisite academic skills. As a Turin mathematics teacher put it, "It is imperative that we learn to teach *all* students mathematics, so that none are predetermined to be college bound versus 'laborer'."

This interest shaped an abiding tension at the school between academic goals and the obstacles and resources relevant to achieving them. Obstacles to achieving the school's academic goals included both deficits and diversity. Among the deficits noted by teachers and administrators were the low academic expectations held by many of the school's incoming students and their families, inadequate preparation of many students for high-school academic work, a lack of fluency in English, and cultural patterns and family arrangements that made effective communication between school employees and parents extremely difficult.

In addition to the challenge of working with these apparent deficits, Turin teachers and administrators also regarded the diversity of Turin students as a challenge in its own right. That is, not only was it hard to teach students who lacked English language skills or prior experiences of academic success, it was also hard to serve these students as well as others with quite different skills, abilities and academic experience in the same school and—as expressed by the teacher quoted earlier in this essay—even in the same classroom.

The challenges to academic success posed by these apparent deficits and by the school's ethnic and social diversity were at odds with the emphasis in school planning discourse on valuing the ethnic and social diversity of Turin students, and contradictions between these two views—diversity as an obstacle and a resource—were never resolved. However, the initial planning for the school focused more on overcoming obstacles to academic success than it did on affirming the value of diversity *per se*.

Detracking

In contrast to their tentative valuation of the *social and ethnic diversity* of Turin students, the administrators and teachers most responsible for Turin's initial design fully acknowledged in their planning efforts the *academic diversity* of Turin students. As one outcome of this planning process, the school adopted from the outset a set of "detracking" policies that mandated the placement of students with mixed academic ability in classes, programs and courses. This policies precluded separate college prep, vocational and remedial pathways through the school, and they even pushed the school towards open-enrollment in its state-funded program for gifted and talented students. The same policies mandated that each class at Turin reflect the full range of abilities and achievement levels that characterized the school as a whole. No separate classes were scheduled for extremely able students, nor were any scheduled to serve exclusively those students typically labeled as "special needs," "remedial," or "high risk."

At face value these detracking policies affirmed the instructional value of heterogeneously grouped students over traditional practices of course-by-course ability grouping. But they also affirmed the unrealized academic potential of low-performing students. As the Turin principal noted early in the school's second year:

> We believe that there is one curriculum for all students and we also believe that you do not have to remediate students; that remediation does not work in high school . . . it actually slows students down. What you have to do is take students

> with low skills and build their self-esteem within the regular program and use teaching strategies that work with low achievers as well as high achievers.

While mixed ability grouping was proposed and developed at Turin for working with students with diverse academic skills and experience, it also had implications for how the school responded to issues of race and ethnicity. As a complement to the academic rationale provided by the principal, some teachers described the school's mixed ability groupings as a valiant effort to discourage the "ghettoization" of students from specific racial and ethnic groups within particular classes and programs. As one Turin teacher noted,

> When I hear "diversity" I not only think of the removal of tracking, but also the removal of classes which are racially homogeneous. It has been my experience that the "GATE" [gifted and talented] classes are predominantly middle class, white/Asian, and the "low" classes are predominantly poor, Mexican American and/or African American.

Similar moral and political concerns were held by most other Turin teachers and administrators, but they did not lead to the same kind of organizational and instructional design work that appeared in addressing concerns about academic diversity. Nor were ethnicity, culture and social estate incorporated into the working theories that teachers and administrators developed to guide their decisionmaking at the school. As a result, cultural and ethnic diversity were regarded as more of a challenge to instruction than as an instructional resource. The prospect of using cultural and ethnic diversity to enrich instruction received little schoolwide design and planning attention.

Teachers and administrators did affirm the value of such diversity in public statements, in encouraging cultural sensitivity in classroom instruction, and in supporting some multi-cultural activities for students and parents. But these affirmations appeared initially as a means to achieving academic success, rather than goals in and of themselves. Indeed, when viewed as a means to broadening academic achievement, respect for cultural diversity was seen by some teachers, administrators and students as a transitional value, one that might no longer be necessary once a school culture was established at Turin that affirmed the value of mutual trust, intergroup understanding, and academic excellence.

Indicators of Success

Within the academics first orientation Turin teachers and administrators made substantial progress during the school's first two years. Teachers noted the increasing comfort that students took with the school's high academic expectations and the admirable academic progress that many students were making in classes and courses. As the principal reported at the end of the school's second year:

> We're really impressed with how the students have taken to the academic challenge, and that really surprised us in some ways because we thought it would be more of a battle than it's been. As you say, we're getting a lot of votes of confidence from the students on this with their enrollments, with their beliefs, with what they're signing up for. We thought we'd have big battles to get kids to take academic classes, and what we're finding is that they're taking more than what we even set out there for them.

The increased academic appetite of Turin students were reflected in the relatively high rates at which they enrolled in high-level academic courses (i.e., advanced courses in mathematics, science and foreign languages) and in student requests for an additional academic period during the day. Preliminary analysis of standardized test scores also showed Turin students performing at or above district expectations and also showed that gains were occurring for all segments of the Turin school student body. Indeed, by the end of the school's second year, teachers were committed enough to mixed-ability grouping to express anxiety that it might be diluted in response to parental pressure or student interest and to sound an alarm when some classes were not as heterogeneous as they should have been. In response to direct requests regarding the latter, school administrators worked with the district data processing unit to use random assignment by CTBS scores as a mechanism for ensuring that all classes enrolled students with a good mix of abilities and achievement levels.

In all these ways, the academics first perspective provided a powerful starting point for teachers and administrators who shaped and managed Turin High School, and it had substantial power in guiding decisions and helping refine school policies. However, despite encouraging signs, there were also indications that some Turin students were not succeeding as they should. This stimulated some Turin teachers and administrators to reconsider the academics first as a perspective for guiding their work at the school.

Academics Reconsidered

One of the first signs that academics first was but a partial account of what was happening at the school came when Turin teachers found that, despite their best efforts, some students were failing their classes. This could be cause for little surprise at other high schools, but Turin teachers found this kind of failure extremely toubling. Not only were they trying hard as individuals to avoid such outcomes, they were also responsible as a group for designing the school to guard explicitly against student failure. As such, teachers viewed the failure of Turin students as a failure of their own and as a threat to their guiding vision of helping all students fully develop their academic powers. This sense of responsibility for the instructional and organization program of the school was a key element of their distinctive workplace problematics.

Another challenge to the academics first perspective came as Turin teachers learned that students valued teachers themselves more for how they cared about students than for their technical expertise in pedagogy or their chosen subject. Evidence of this came from a variety of sources, including student surveys and a series of student-teacher interviews and exercises included in the Evaluation Retreat held at the end of the school's first year. But it took its most powerful from in ongoing face-to-face exchanges between students and teaches. By the end of the school's second year, the message had been made quite clear: What most students valued most about the school's teaching staff was that they cared about the students, a kind of caring that placed greater emphasis on human relations than on academic achievement *per se*.

An additional concern about the academics first orientation emerged when it appeared that an interest in accumulating academic credit was over shadowing, for both students and teachers, attention to skills building and intellectual development. As one example of this, students at the second year Evaluation Retreat described their educational goals entirely in terms of specific courses they hoped to take (we had asked the question: "What would you like to learn more about during the rest of your time at Turin?"). On the one hand faculty and administrators were delighted that students were taking coursework so seriously. On the other hand, they saw this seriousness limited frequently to the mechanics of the course. In contrast to what teachers wanted to see, students were not linking school learning to real-life challenges of their individual and collective futures.

A fourth challenge came from the enthusiasm that Turin student leaders expressed for extra–curricular school activities, including clubs and athletics. This enthusiasm contrasted with lower levels of interest—and outright resistance among some students—in academic tasks *per se*. After struggling to ensure that the Turin curriculum was well-designed to ensure student academic success, student enthusiasm for extra-curricular activities came as an unpleasant surprise for Turin teachers and administrators. As one teacher noted, "Here we are staying up late at night to design these courses so that they really work together, and what students are really most interested in is deciding on the school colors!" Statements of this sort precipitated in turn some disaffection among Turin students. As one student noted.

> I think one of the issues not discussed was the tension between some student activities and how they were treated by teaches. Some teachers took the activities lightly, saying that if it's not part of my curriculum then it's not important, while other teachers respected the activities and didn't make students feel badly for doing activities outside of class.

Statements such as these suggested that academics may have come "first" for some Turin students, but certainly not for all.

Engaging Students

A growing awareness of the issues noted above moved some Turin teachers and administrators away from the academics first perspective to emphasize engaging students more fully in the social and political life of the school. Arguing from within this perspective, teachers made the case that if students were not personally engaged in their classes and in the school, their work on academic tasks would not amount to much. To stimulate the kind of student engagement they desired, Turin teachers and administrators initiated new reforms in classrooms, extra-curricular activities, the organization and culture of the school, and school committees.

Classrooms, Clubs and Clusters

Within individual class sessions, cooperative learning strategies and other forms of group work were put in place by many Turin teachers, first as vehicles for teaching mixed ability classes, and then as vehicles for engaging all students more fully in schooling. For example, in a sophomore social studies class, students were given problems to solve in groups that required the use of atlases and other reference works and that led to in-class presentations and performances. In a freshman English class, the teacher organized desks into two opposing panels, then led the students through a dramatic reading of the *Iliad* in which each panel took on different characters. Students were then asked to offer explanations for what their character said and did. In an algebra class, the teacher circulated around the room assisting students who worked in small groups on problem sets; students who finished early were encouraged to play a variety of mathematical games. In a review session for another social studies class, student teams challenge each other in a game of "jeopardy" that focused on important people, events and ideas of the Renaissance. In none of these classes were teachers implementing rigorous forms of cooperative learning. However, in all of them, teachers were using social interaction strategies to engage students in school activities that involved challenging academic work.

New opportunities for student engagement were also provided through a growing array of extracurricular activities. Indeed, students who attended Turin in its first year or two expressed their dismay over the lack of what they had hoped to find in the way of school social activities, including clubs, varsity sports, and so on. And, as more and more of these were provided, students expressed their approval.

Among the extracurricular activities, ethnic clubs played a special role. Initially, these were seen by both teachers and students as an informal resource for supporting students from specific ethnic groups. Loosely coupled to this social support function was the pedagogic ideal of helping club members know more about their ethnic heritage. Over time, the social and pedagogic value of these clubs was complemented, both for students and for teachers, by their political functions. The school principal's description of two new groups established during the school's second year illustrates a more general effort by school faculty and administrators to broader participation in the school through supporting racial or ethnic groups:

> We said, "We need kids to talk to us a little bit more." [And so] we [now] have an Asian girls group and an Asian boys group and that's interesting. A group of girls that are Asian get together with a couple of counselors and a group of Asian boys get together with myself and a counselor and a conflict manager and we found that they were really disenfranchised. If any group was disenfranchised, they were. They really wanted to be enfranchised. They have this strong value of schooling and yet they feel they're on the outside in terms of sports, student government, and all the things they see other people do. And we didn't realize that was a big part of their behavior problem until we started the group.

In affirming student engagement through ethnic clubs and through discourse about their own ethnic heritage and distinction, the school was moving beyond the academics first perspective in which ethnicity was regarded primarily an obstacle to effective instruction.

Another vehicle for increasing student engagement involved the creation of several student-teacher clusters. Called "houses," "academies" and "programs," each of these linked a group of 100 to 200 students with a set of teachers who taught most of their classes for a period of a year or more. Student-teacher clusters emerged in response to Turin's precipitous increase from 1,400 students to over 2,500 students in its first two years. The teachers and administrators who led the "house" projects thought that students—and teachers—were getting lost within the larger school that Turin had become. The cluster approach enabled teachers to become more familiar with the relatively fewer students whom they saw more frequently and to work more closely with a few other teachers. Students also spent more time within a relatively fixed group and got to know both their teachers and their peers better than they might otherwise.

Yet another effort to engage students more fully involved appeared as a "senior project" requirement. To complete this requirement, students had to initiate and complete—during the course of their senior year—a long-term research, development or service project that they would then report on to a panel of teachers, other students and community leaders. Teachers responsible for instituting the requirement hoped that work on senior projects would give Turin students an opportunity to explore in depth and issue or activity that they really cared about personally. Indeed, many students did become quite engaged in their projects, and even students who were minimally engaged in project activities per se became quite engaged in the drama of their end-of-the year reports to the school-community panels.

Pedagogy and Politics

These varied approaches to increasing student engagement were informed by the assumption that greater student involvement in school was a good thing, but this assumption had pedagogic, interpersonal and political dimensions. The pedagogic dimensions were those noted above—if students were not engaged in their school, then they could not and would not apply themselves or profit from valued schooling tasks. The interpersonal component reflected the growing awareness by teachers, also noted earlier, that students appreciated how much Turin teachers seemed to care for them as persons and as students.

The political dimension of the student engagement perspective was fueled in part by the positive experience of many Turin teachers with the school's collaborative decisionmaking process. A Turin administrator described this process as follows:

> Students and teachers have had opportunities to participate in the decision-making process at Turin High School, to serve on various committees as well as provide direct input on decision that affect them. Teachers and students are invited to serve on one or more of the effective schools committees: School Environment, Curriculum and Instruction, Monitoring and Evaluation, and the Planning Team. Each of these committees has specific tasks to perform that include making policies and developing procedures for the school. Students have opportunities to be involved in student government and the Student Senate. A student from each fourth period class is selected to be a part of the Student Senate that meets monthly and provides ongoing feedback and input on things happening in the school. . . . Many of the students and teachers have taken advantage of these opportunities and others have not. An overall goal would be to get more students and teachers involved in collaborative decisionmaking.

At the time of this statement, about half of the school's teachers were participating in one or more of Turin's school–wide committees. For students, this participation rate was about 1/10th of 1 percent, with another 2 percent involved in the Student Senate. This differential is generated in pat by arithmetic alone: It would be hard to design a formula for collaborative, school-wide decision making that involved equal percentages of 2,400 students and 120 teachers. The collaboration put in place at Turin engaged teachers directly but it engaged students indirectly through a few student representatives. After recounting how much he valued direct participation as a faculty member, one teacher noted the lack of just that among Turin students:

> I have been deeply impressed by our school's commitment to collaborative processes. Some schools give the appearance of collaboration, but the ultimate power rests with a principal or superintendent. Turin really does make its decisions through group processes. This has meant a tremendous amount of meeting time this year, and near burnout for some committed staff, but I think the dividends will continue to show for years, and many of the things that are being decided now won't have to be looked at again for quite a while. We are investing time in this process. Two years from now it will be difficult to complain about mot things because you or a coworker will have been involved in its development. I think this will significantly increase our level of commitment and buy-in. A danger here seems to be that our students don't feel included in any real way. That commitment and buy-in doesn't exist for them. We need to work on that.

Though less involved in collaborative decisionmaking than teachers, some parents also noted how this kind of participation might empower students:

> I haven't been personally involved in this process, nor has my child. However, I do see its value: People who collaborate to address and to resolve problems generally are more committed to implementing the solutions which are developed. That's why I think it should be taken a little further at Turin High: Involve the students. Survey them, bring the problem to them and get their feedback (not just concur or disagree, but their ideas for solution). Perhaps there could be some time once a week/two weeks/month, during Social Science classes when a problem confronting the school is brought before the students, discussed, brainstormed, and responded to. Students could submit their solution/ideas/points of discussion. These responses could be tallied by a volunteer/parent/concerned citizens and evaluated and considered as a whole by the committee appointed to address

> the problem. When resolution has been decided, the input of the students could be referred to and the role that input played in the process could be detailed and commented on. The more often this happens, the stronger the students' commitment to the success of their school and schooling.

Despite the laments of some parents, teachers and administrators, the limited involvement of Turin students in schoolwide committees was not necessarily an issue of great importance to students themselves. Students did not want to be excluded, but they were not enamored of the school's committee structure. As a result, the activities that teachers cited as empowering them in the school, were regarded quite differently by many students. As one student noted:

> The effective schools committees look great on paper. They show that students, staff, administration and parents come together to make decisions. The committees in reality will eventually be beneficial to Turin. . . . But at the present time the committees are holding Turin down from progress. Any activity that student government, or any group wants to put on or install has to go through all the committees, with a complete consensus for each committee. These committees kill everything.

As these comments indicate, Turin's schoolwide decisionmaking process was more "schoolwide" for teachers than it was for students. In addition, reliance on committees to manage the political process of the school did not sit well with many students. Thus, despite the interests and good will of Turin teachers and administrators—and despite the fact that Turin students had more opportunities for school decisionmaking than their peers at other district schools—students were less engaged in the political life of the school than they were in its interpersonal and instructional life.

Engagement Reconsidered

When data showed that Turin was graduating over 90 percent of its students—a figure higher than that of other urban schools serving similar populations—proponents of the school engagement perspective were pleased that their efforts appeared to be working. However, engaging students in school activities had a problematic side as well. As students became more engaged in school, they brought with them more of the conflicts and tensions experienced in their home communities, including racial and ethnic conflicts.

Many students viewed this as both normal and unavoidable. In the words of one student: "As for [some racial tension] . . . on campus, I think it's normal. . . . With all these different races and religions and backgrounds, this should have been expected." But other school members wondered whether encouraging students to identify with particular ethnic groups might make matters worse. As one teacher noted:

> Price in one's own ethnic group is extremely important but sharing with others is equally important. . . . We need more interaction among ethnic groups—discussions, activities, person-to-person. Through these channels people can learn to know one another as people, individuals. Clubs that "segregate"—(Maya, Asian, Afro American, European American)—only drive the wedge of difference deeper. Multicultural clubs draw people together to explore history, art, music, food of all groups. As one of my African-American students said, "No one wants to go to another ethnic group's meetings. We feel out of place, as they do at our meetings." We need more emphasis on sharing cultures and ideas to draw us all closer together.

These concerns were augmented in response to media accounts of racial conflicts at Turin, accounts that both students and teachers felt were an oversimplification of the schools complex racial and ethnic dynamics. In challenging these media representations, one student noted the exceptional diverse population the school was serving:

> Our school is such a big school, multi-cultural and different ethnicity, that's why they emphasize our school has racial problems. At ___ [another school] they have more of a certain race. We're like the big melting pot, we're the big mix. They're going to emphasize us more and not look at the other schools

> because really, not one of the other schools is as big of a melting pot.

In arguing against similar media characterizations, another student defended Turin by noting positive aspects of the school's attention to racial and ethnic diversity:

> I have heard about our racial problem, but there are many positive things such as rallies and food fairs which have brought may cultures together. Which suggests that we are all equal. There are tensions that rise which are problems that could be solved with counseling, parents, and teachers. But there are also very good outcomes such as the maturity of Florin since day one.

Turin teachers and students regarded media reports as an exploitation of their own struggles around ethnicity, power and academics. As another student noted:

> Every time there's a fight between two different nationalities, everybody thinks it's a racial thing. When other people from different schools hear about it, they think that the school is bad. I don't think there's really any racism at this school. Something that I don't see at other schools, is that at Florin, there are kids who are one nationality or race going out with another different race. I don't really care what nationality my friends are. I get along with everybody; so I don't have a problem with racism or hating other nationalities.

Comments by students, parents and teachers that challenged negative characterizations of the school in the local news media expressed a protective orientation towards Turin and a moral identification with the school. However, this kind of identification was not quite what proponents of student engagement were looking for, and it was perplexing to many Turin teachers and administrators. Both students and their parents appeared to become much more engaged in the school in response to these external critiques than from the organizational innovations teachers were working had to implement within the school. The teachers' intent was to draw students and their parents into activities that emphasized academic learning, school administration, and cultural exchange. Increasingly, however, teachers found themselves drawn into community activities in which their school appeared more as a lightning rod for intergroup conflict than as a workplace for students and teachers.

Moral Codevelopment

Competing emphases on academics and student engagement are an abiding ingredient of continuing deliberations among Turin teachers and administrators about curricula, extra-curricular activities, discipline policies, assessment strategies, teacher-student relationships, and almost every other aspect of the school. Some teachers subscribe much more to the academics first orientation and others much more to the student engagement perspective. Most Turin teachers not only fall in between these extremes, but waver in their commitment to one perspective or the other as they move through the complex rounds of course planning, teaching, and exchanges with students and with each other that make up their life in the school.

However, there is yet a third perspective toward power and ethnicity emerging among teachers at Turin High School. This third perspective differs from both the academics and students engagement perspectives in two key respects: First, it acknowledges that Turin students are facing cultural, moral and political challenges that may be much more complex than those faced by Turin teachers and administrators in their own adolescence. Second, it acknowledges the value to adults—including teachers, administrators and parents—of learning with and from students about how to face these challenges constructively. Within this perspective—which I am calling "moral codevelopment"—teachers and administrators are also learners and students are also teachers.

The rewards of this kind of codevelopment were acknowledged by many Turin teachers. As one teacher noted, "As a teacher at Turin High School, I feel the most rewarding aspects have been to work with a completely varied cultural and ethnic background of students. I have learned so much about different races and how people react to others over often controversial subjects."

The rewards of learning from students were coupled, however, with the challenge teachers faced in linking time in school with less civil realities of the world outside the school. An African-American teacher at Turin, recognizing that her students were having an experience of multiculturalism that she had never had as a student, described the dilemma of wanting to make her students aware of racism in the larger culture without creating anger and resentment:

> I think that it is probably true here that our students are further along in multicultural understanding than many of us are. Many of us live in our communities and we don't deal with the students until we come here—and the teachers who do live in integrated neighborhoods are feeling right this minute, why are we doing this? The students are not even aware sometimes of other communities . . . that's my struggle. African-American students are a concern of mine, obviously, and here there's a lot of mixing. . . . How to explain to students that there is discrimination, there is racism. You will not be treated as nicely outside of this school as you get treated here, and yet, not provoke them a certain amount of anger and resentment. For me, it is a very important issue. I don't want my students to fail when they leave here. I don't want them so devastated by the fact that everyone else sees them as black and they see themselves as a human being.

Reciprocal Responsibilities

The perspective of moral codevelopment implicit in these comments affirmed reciprocal responsibilities between Turin students and the adults they encountered in school. Within this perspective, moral development was not something students could achieve on their own. It was not something that teachers could do to or for their students, nor could teachers do it for themselves. And, of special interest to Turin teachers, students and their parents, this kind of reciprocal development was very much at odds with newspaper and media accounts of the school.

An apt illustration of the reciprocal responsibilities emerged in an Evaluation-Retreat discussion about the response at Turin to the not-guilty verdict in the trial of Lost Angeles police officers accused of beating Rodney King.

> **Retreat facilitator**: "What happened here after the Rodney King decision?"
>
> **Several students, teachers and administrators** (in unison): "Nothing."
>
> **Facilitator**: "Did that get a few comments in the media?"
>
> **Several students, teachers and administrators**: "No!" (laughter)
>
> **Administrator**: "I was amazed and astounded that we had a greater level of maturity out of the teenagers I was seeing than we saw in the larger population. They showed a lot of insight, they really tried to calm down and look at it from another perspective, and they had some real good thoughts about how to find other ways to deal with the whole complexity of the issue rather than the black and white thinking that I found in the adult community. It was great. Teachers were very proactive in calling kids in and trying to determine what they needed, talking to them individually and in groups, so I think a lot of work was done to ward off what could have been probably some racial tension. But I agree that the students handled it, absolutely. There was a lot of work behind the scenes that never really was showcased."
>
> **Student**: "At our school, I think what we did was our teachers did take time out to talk about it. Cuz I know I came to school very, very hot–headed. I was real mad. And I have public speaking first period, but she took time to let us talk. Our classroom at first was real loud and disruptive, but after we really sat down and talked about it, everything was fine. I think that was the best thing the teachers could do is like take time out of their curriculum schedule to talk about it so that they had let us talk about it. Because I think if they hadn't let us talk about it, there would have been a lot of action going on at Turin."

As this exchange illustrates, at least some Turin teachers used their classroom authority to create safe places for students to talk through their heartfelt and troubling feelings about racial and ethnic conflict. As a *quid pro quo*, at least some students took advantage of these opportunities to bring to other students—and their teachers—the depth of their concerns about such conflict. Out of these complementary contributions, teachers and students forged new moral and political sensibilities about race and ethnicity, sensibilities in which respect for cultural differences was given greater affirmation. As one teacher noted:

> What I perceived from my students was that there was a fair amount of fear and that the kids were afraid that it was going to come here. You know I mean "it" meaning the violence and the looting. Several of my classes spent a lot of time talking about how it didn't look like . . . that people created destruction. I think I agree that the talking did a lot to defuse . . . [and] students discovered in each other different perspectives.

Varied Ideas of Success

The perspective of moral codevelopment was stimulated in part by the racial and ethnic mix of the school, but it applied to other issues as well. Indeed, the increased respect that students expressed for cultural and ethnic differences was in some cases also expressed towards differences in academic performance. During the school's first year or so, for example, students were very concerned about their academic place among other students in the school. When asked to identify different groups of students, they volunteered the categories of "good students"—those who were succeeding in class—and "students in trouble." However, by the end of the school's third year, the importance of relative academic standing to students themselves had diminished, as illustrated by the following exchange at the 1991 Evaluation–Retreat:

> **Facilitator** (addressing a group of students): "I just noticed . . . that you're not making distinctions between kinds of students in terms of academics. You know, high achievers, low achievers."

> **First Student**: "How do you know if they're really stupid? I mean they might be like no good in academics but they'll be real good in the fine arts. You can't really say that someone's just a good student and someone else isn't. . . . But everything's multicultural and it wouldn't be right to tar the students, this student's an 'A' student. It's just not right to label . . . "
>
> **Second student**: "Because some people may be good at English but sorry at math because they love that subject. Then 'A' students love all their subjects."
>
> **First student**: "You can't do that because if you do that they're going to say that you're stereotyping. And that's what we're trying to get away from is stereotyping. (pause) It's not true, either."

Power as the Will to Succeed

While some educators might be alarmed by thoughts of diversifying academic performance, some Turin students saw this as an essential ingredient of their will to succeed. As one of Turin's first graduates noted, when asked how she and her peers had changed during their time at the school:

> Well the first year it was like all we talked about was education and we never had enough fun. We've caught up a little bit, we've had a little more fun. And now we've come back. I guess that the emphasis on EDUCATION made us the people we are today because if it hadn't been EMPHASIZED, we probably wouldn't have GRADUATED. But if that is the purpose of these teachers, the administration, the counselors, teachers that you didn't even have GAVE ON YOU to graduate and that emphasis on SUCCESS—you can be what you want to be, or do what you want to do, and not just well . . . you're slow so you're goign to be here, you're fast so you're going to be there, not that sort of emphasis on students and made everbody that ONE THING. THAT'S what helped a lot of the students make it through their high school year. And maybe make it to go on forever.

In the analysis of this graduating student, for many Turin students the strength to succeed did not come from high academic expectations alone, nor did it come solely from opportunities to be engaged in a variety of school activities and interpersonal relationships. By themselves, these elements could be discouraging as well as encouraging. Students also needed to know that the school embraced a multidimensional view of students, teachers and of success, a view in which young people shared the development of the school's moral order with adults. Though she did not refer to it directly in her comments, it seems unlikely that this view could be nourished at the school unless both teachers and administrators acknowledged the value of what they were learning from the students they had come to teach. As one teacher put it: "We can all work together and talk through stuff. That's a real strength at Florin and I think we're learning more and more how to tap into and how to give power to our kids. That's one of the majors strengths of the school."

Within this perspective, cultural, ethnic and racial diversity appeared not just as a resource for academic engagement, but as a stimulus to the moral development of teachers, students, administrators, parents and other community members. As a Turin parent noted:

> This decade is the crucial time to be prepared to effectively understand the demographic changes in our community. Many are giving lip service rather than doing something constructive. I recognize that we are expecting a lot from the schools, but I couldn't think of a better place to face the challenge of the future than in our schools today.

In treating their multiethnic school as a stimulus to moral development, teachers expected students to draw on their developing academic skills and sensibilities. Certainly, literacy, oralcy and skills in critical analysis were deemed important to that effort. Teachers also encouraged students to continue their academic studies and to acquire schooling credentials that might open doors to social and economic advancement. However, within the perspective of moral codevelopment, these opportunities for individual advancement were tied to responsibilities for moral leadership, a kind of leadership through which students would be teaching adults for some time to come.

Evolving Ideals for Schooling

Different features of the three perspectives noted above are described in Table 3.2. The developmental relationship between these perspectives is revealed in changes in Turin's mission statement during the school's first six years. The school's first mission statement—drafted in 1989, just before the school opened—began with the following preface: "Our purpose is to enable students to pursue excellence, to be competitive in the workplace and in institutions of higher learning, and to make sound, informed ethical decisions both now and during their future lives." Key elements of this initial 1989–90 mission statement were elaborated in terms of specific expectations for how students would hopefully experience their time at Turin High School. Prefaced by the phrase, "all students will," these included the following:

> Participate in successful academic opportunities which emphasize high expectations, self-esteem and dignity, and cultural diversity.
>
> Experience a curriculum driven by a common academic core, concentrating on communication and thinking skills, with careful deliberation on assuring sufficient instructional time for a balanced program representing the various disciplines.
>
> Benefit in an atmosphere where teachers are also learners. Turin High School emphasizes teacher growth and professionalism.
>
> Engage in instruction that reflects the latest in educational technology. Ongoing partnerships with the business and industrial community reflect our purpose as a center of instructional excellence.
>
> Learn to be responsible, productive citizens of the future with an understanding of the value and nature of our nation's democratic process.

Table 3.2 Three perspectives on power and ethnicity at a multi-ethnic high school

QUESTIONS/ ELEMENTS	ACADEMICS FIRST	SCHOOL ENGAGEMENT	MORAL CO-DEVELOPMENT
How does/should school help empower students?	Individual academic achievement as path to individual social and economic advancement.	Social engagement as path to helping students develop adult competencies necessary to individual and collective success in a variety of social settings.	Social and cultural complexity of schools helps students develop unique moral perspectives that are valued by the larger social order.
What role does ethnicity play in this process?	Challenge to effective instruction. Challenge to equity among ethnic groups of individual academic achievement.	Resource for teachers and administrators to use in engaging students in school.	Resource for students in developing leadership for a new moral order.
What is the primary role that teachers play?	Expert in academic discipline, student of pedagogy, and moral leader. Prepare these students for the future.	Pedagogic expert, student of academic disciplines, moral advisor. Prepare these students for the future.	Observer and coexperimenter with students in school setting. Prepare the future for these students.
What are the primary responsibilities of teachers within this role?	Affirm academic standards and value of academic achievement. Show students that you care about them as students, by: Encouraging high academic expectations. Developing and implementing academically challenging curricula that are also engaging to students.	Affirm students' culture and imagination and value of staying engaged in schooling. Show students that you care about them as persons, by: Listening to what they have to say. Developing and implementing engaging curricula that is also academically challenging.	Affirm school culture as a crucible for forming new social order. Show students that you care about them by participating in school culture and by: Debating key questions of value with students and other school members. Entertaining suggestions for redesigning school curricula.

	Getting students to tie their own self-interest to focusing on academics and avoiding distractions of their personal, interpersonal and cultural affairs. Affirming excellence in evaluating student work on academic tasks. If necessary, showing students that you care about them as persons.	Getting students to make connections between their personal, interpersonal and cultural affairs and academics. Affirming growth in evaluating student work on academic tasks.	Making connections as a person between school activities and the larger social world. Helping students think critically about their core values. Affirming students as experts about their own estate.
What role are students supposed to play?	Here to learn academic skills and become prepared for more advanced academic learning. Make as much academic progress as possible as quickly as possible.	Here to make individual progress on multidimensional social and academic agenda.	Here to develop outlook on life. Here to reflect on experience with teachers in creating new moral order. Here to learn from that process and teach others to learn within it.
What role do administrators play?	Manage ethnicity and diversity so they have a minimal impact on the primary academic purposes of the school. Design program to minimize conflict.	Respect cultural diversity within school, support student activities and organizations, manage conflict within homogeneous ethic of multi-culturalism. Design program to sublimate conflict into socially acceptable forms of group affiliation, competition, affirmation, and so on.	Respect school community, explore diversity and manage conflict within multiple cultures. Design program to reveal conflicts and engage others in examining them constructively.

Table 3.2 Three perspectives on power and ethnicity at a multi-ethnic high school *(continued)*

QUESTIONS/ ELEMENTS	ACADEMICS FIRST	SCHOOL ENGAGEMENT	MORAL CO-DEVELOPMENT
What does the curriculum mean within this perspective?	What individual students should learn. Model of knowledge.	What engages individual students in learning. Model of instruction.	Academic school complement and resource to collective cultural and intellectual development.
What do extra–curricular activities mean within this perspective?	Distractions from curriculum.	What keeps students engaged in school.	Nonacademic school complement and resource to collective cultural and intellectual development.
How do teachers and administrators view the community?	Distraction from curriculum, source of compromise to academic integrity of the school.	Distraction from schooling, source of turmoil and conflict for school social order.	Primary point of reference for examining school programs and activities, source of content for reflection and and moral development.
What constitutes success?	Individual students escape limitations of family and community and increase their academic, social and economic status. Move from provincial to cosmopolitan. Success occurs in one way, irrespective of race and ethnicity.	Individual students survive social and academic trials to mature as reasonably competent adults who value education and schooling and who can make a decent living in the real world. Success occurs in many ways, but transcends race and ethnicity.	Students and teachers use school experience to develop a new moral order that is pluralistic, democratic, well-informed and participatory. Students may or may not value schooling, but they become politically effective adults who lead a fulfilling life in the real world. Success occurs in many ways, some of which are tied closely to race and ethnicity.

Imbedded in this mission statement are affirmations of academic work, the experimental ethos of the school (e.g., teachers as learners), and the preparation of students as able competitors and as citizens of a democratic society. Six years later, in 1995, some of these same elements appeared in a preface prepared by the school's second principal to the school's *Report to the Community*, as follows:

> Turin High School celebrates its sixth anniversary as a school with high academic standards for all students. The entire staff works hard to accomplish the goals outlined in our 5 A's Student achievement Plan in the areas of academics, attendance, attitude, activities, and athletics. To assist us in this process, we develop and implement academic programs and school activities that support our school mission listed below." (Douglas, 1995, p. 1)

These continuing academic elements were not preserved, however, in the school's mission statement itself, the 1995 version of which read as follows: "Our purpose is to enable students to develop a positive vision for themselves, and to become responsible, independent, self-directed learners resulting in informed and ethical decision making both now and in their future lives." Like its 1989 predecessor, the 1995 mission statement was elaborated through an accompanying list. However, in 1989 this list referred to expectations for how students would "experience" the school, while the 1995 list focused on the school's role in preparing students to become the following:

> Effective *communicators* who convey significant messages to others both verbally and in writing, and receive and interpret the messages of others in an effective manner.
>
> Complex *thinkers* who apply complex problem-solving processes and critical thinking to real life scenarios; analyze, interpret and evaluate significant concepts within various contexts, and create images to represent significant concepts.
>
> Quality *producers* who create intellectual, artistic, practical and physical products; reflect originality, high standards and the use of advanced technology; and set, pursue, and accomplish realistic and challenging goals for themselves and their peers.

> Collaborative *workers* who use effective leadership skills to foster, develop and maintain relationships within diverse settings; and establish and accomplish effective goals with others.
>
> Self-directed *learners* who assess their needs and apply appropriate strategies to learn the identified concepts and skills, and use effective goal setting strategies to create a positive vision for themselves and their future in order to set priorities and achievable goals.
>
> Community *contributors* who contribute their time, energies, and talents to improving the quality of life in our schools, communities, nation and world, and demonstrate positive and productive citizenship.

While the clear affirmations of academic work imbedded in the school's first mission statement and expectations were missing from this revised list, the newer version was much more specific about the kinds of tasks and skills that students should develop. The range of tasks affirmed in the 1994 statement also went well beyond the boundaries of academic work, narrowly defined.

As described earlier, broader conceptions of success for students—such as creating "intellectual, artistic, practical and physical products," and "images to represent significant concepts"—emerged directly from the workplace problematics experienced by Turin teachers. Primary among these was the tension between affirming common standards of success for all Turin students and respecting the varied talents, dispositions, knowledge, and abilities of Turin students. After six years of working at the school, Turin teachers also had become much more familiar with the constraints students experienced outside of school and understood better how these helped generate variance among student performance within it.

Coupled to increased knowledge of their students, Turin teachers and administrators also were led to an emerging critique of schooling functions that enforce competition among individual students. This critique went well beyond the concerns about school tracking that informed the school's initial commitment to heterogeneous grouping. Rather than worry about the fact that tracking kept some students from advancing in school, some Turin teachers became concerned that competitive school advancement itself was a misguided ideal. In response this concern, they deemphasized academic achievement and advancement for individual students—the kind of "possessive individualism" critiqued by Popkewitz (1991) and others—to affirm more communitarian ideals and the contributions that students should make to society. As one expression of these sensibilities, the school placed increasing emphasis on the expectation that students engage in community service as a regular feature of their high school education.

These newer concerns were reflected in the 1994 mission statement through explicit connections between learning at Turin and problem-solving with others in the "real world." The world defined by these references was one in which individual academic and social advancement is less relevant than the ability of students to "establish and accomplish effective goals with others" and to "contribute their time, energies, and talents to improving the quality of lie in our schools, communities, nation and world." Consistent with this broader view of the world for which Turin was trying to prepare students, the 1994 mission statement included a postscript affirming the role that representatives from that world needed to play in the school: "Our vision to make these learner outcomes a reality is by continuing to work with our parents/guardians and community members as partners in educating our students."

The complexities of culture, persons, and communities that stimulated Turin teachers and administrators to develop new ways of thinking about classroom teaching also led to new ways of thinking about the social product of their school and the potential contributions of students. In general, teacher and administrator perspectives moved from a somewhat naive view of students as the "lucky recipients" of school reform to regard students as "necessary partners" in implementing educational reform. In some cases, this change in perspective went even further to regard students as "valued co-leaders" in an educational enterprise, the scope and consequences of which go well beyond the academic ethos of the school (Corbett & Wilson, 1995).

Reflecting this evolution, the school's 1994 mission statement made explicit a variety of skills associated with the perspective of moral leadership. It also contrasts with the earlier mission statement in attributing greater agency and responsibility to students themselves. While the 1990 statement affirmed the potential of students to be "productive citizens," the 1995 statement proposed a future in which students–use effective leadership skills to foster, develop, and maintain relationships within diverse settings." In ways that its founders lacked the experience to imagine, Turin teachers, and administrators revised and remodeled even the mots thoughtful of the reform ideals with which the school began.

Dilemmas of Policy and Practice

Issues of ethnicity and power are at the heart of contemporary policy discourse in education. It is very difficult, however, to acknowledge the complexity of these issues within the necessarily dualistic discourse of politics and policymaking. It is unlikely, for example, that lessons from the full range of contradictions, possibilities and problems that teachers have been struggling with at Turin High School can be built into specific proposals of broad application for improving the schools. In particular, the multiple conception of student empowerment they worked around do not lend themselves to a single metric or indicator system. Nor is it likely that large-scale policy and program initiatives can embrace the increasingly complex conceptions of education, learning, schooling and ethnicity that are emerging within the research literature (Au, 1981; Delgado–Gaitan & Trueba, 1991; Delpit, 1986; Health, 1983; Moll & Diaz, 1987; Ogbu, 1992; Spindler, 1982; Spindler & Spindler, 1987; Trueba, 1988).

Tensions between demands for simplicity in educational and social policy and increasingly complex models of ethnicity and power in schools create continuing frustrations for researchers, policymakers, teachers and administrators. To resolve these tensions, some propose ignoring questions about ethnicity and power, narrowing school functions and goals—an "academics first" perspective writ large—and separating schools more clearly from the complexities of community life. Others recommend increasing school-community resources to the point where communities can more fully engage and support families and children—an approach with parallels to the student engagement perspective developed by Turin teachers. Still other reformers seek improvement through increased individual and group responsibility for schooling (through school choice, charters, or decentralization) and for strengthened moral leadership.

One difference between Turin and the state and national policymaking contexts in which these different proposals are being debated is that at Turin, proposals of this sort are tested daily in interactions between students, teachers, administrators and parents. As a result of these tests, proposals are blunted or sharpened, remodeled and revised, extended or withdrawn. In addition to their attractions within reform rhetoric, they must constantly carry the freight of serving the Turin students and of making sense to teachers, administrators and parents.

Within state and national policymaking arenas, the struggles of Turin teachers over issues of ethnicity and power can appear to be inefficient, timeconsuming, and fruitless. In those same arenas, the accommodations made by Turin teachers and administrators in implementing reforms can appear to dilute their intended effects. But these struggles and accommodations occurred at Turin because teachers were trying, among their many tasks and challenges, to serve their students in ways that are just. Progress toward this goal could not come from ignoring complexities of the school's diverse community, nor could it come from abandoning ideals of social justice. With this in mind, both the ideal of a socially just school and the struggle of trying to achieve that ideal were signs of health, even if they also were the source of great frustration for Turin school members and for school reformers working at greater remove.

Turin's approximation of a just school still falls far short of ensuring social justice for the Turin school community. Academically, Turin students from all identified racial and ethnic groups made about the same amount of progress on standardized tests during their time at the school. However, they did not necessarily score at the same levels when beginning and ending their high school studies. Among students who made the most progress and the least progress in the school—both on standardized tests and in terms of grade point increases or decreases—the racial and ethnic composition of the school was fairly and fully represented. On most standardized achievement measures the school also fared reasonably well compared to other schools in the district, even though Turin's student body was substantially more diverse. Deer Park district schools as a whole have done better than schools from most other districts in the region serving equally diverse student populations, but they have done less well than some smaller districts that serve higher SES families who are also mono–lingual in English. Compared to the ideal of serving all is students equally well, the school's academic record is good, but not great. Differentials in achievement that students are bringing to Turin are not getting any worse—which is an accomplishment—but neither are they decreasing enough for Turin teachers and administrators to rejoice.

In terms of other forms of empowerment, much remains to be done inside and outside the school to enfranchise all elements of the school's diverse community, even in matters related to the school itself. Acting on its own, the school lacks resources that could ensure full access to education, health services, housing and employment for community residents. It is also clear, however, that Turin teachers and administrators have taken a culturally inclusive ideal of social justice more seriously than their counterparts at other schools, and that, indeed, some schools have been designed and managed to exclude or reject the same kind of diversity that Turin has tried to include and affirm.

For all these reasons, leaving schools entirely to their own devices just won't do. On the other hand, progress at Turin in understanding and responding to the diversity of the Turin school community owes its greatest debt to self-directed learning by Turin teachers and administrators. This learning was stimulated by changing workplace problematics and supported through extensive opportunities for collaborating, discussion and what Little (1990) has called "joint work." These circumstances helped teachers and administrators both develop and question thoughtful perspectives towards their work. The reform agenda of the school also created opportunities for testing perspectives against empirical realities and for examining planned variations in program design and administration. In all of these ways, the perspectives within which teachers and administrators approached their work also functioned as alternative "programs of study" for investigating the school. These circumstances that stimulated, supported and encouraged Turin teachers to learn from their work are not always present in other schools, but when they are, we might also expect teachers and administrators to learn in similar ways.

Recognizing that teachers and administrators can learn through their work in school grants them the same kind of agency for resistance and social production that has been attributed to students (Willis, 1977). It also discourages us from identifying school structure too closely with adults who work in schools, an approach that simultaneously reifies both adults and school structure. This recognition also challenges the assumptions in some deterministic social and political theories that social structure alone determines the course of action. Workplace problematics such as those experienced by Turin teachers certainly owe a great deal to social structure, but the perspectives that teachers and administrators developed in response to those problematics also helped create or "constitute" (Mehan, 1978) the social structure of the school. As Mehan (1992, p. 11) reminds us, "Our understanding of the reproduction of social inequality will be more complete when we include in our theories the constitutive practices that structure students' educational careers." Teachers and administrators learning from their work were a key feature of these constitutive practices at Turin, the outcomes of which included new forms of school organization (e.g., houses and other student–teacher clusters), new kinds of school work (e.g., senior projects, community service), and new definitions of student success.

These observations of Turin High School argue against placing schooling structures outside the domain of individual and collective action and defining issues of ethnicity and power in isolation of variable school structures. Ethnicity is no more outside school than it is in it, and power is no more inside than it is outside. Action in schools and school structure are described better as the warp and the woof of a common fabric than as two separate cloths. A strong pull on either disturbs the weave of both. The changing perspectives of Turin teachers reveal some of the ways in which this fabric can be gathered, loosened, frayed and gathered again around issues of power and ethnicity in school.

References

Au, K. H. a. J., C. (1981). Teaching Reading to Hawaiian Children: Finding a Culturally Appropriate Solution. In H. Trueba, G. Guthrie, & K. Au (eds.), *Culture and the Bilingual Classroom*. Rawley, MA: Newbury House.

Bourdieu, P., & J.–C. Passeron (1990). *Reproduction in Education, Society and Culture*. Newbury Park, CA: Sage.

Bowles, S., & H. Gintis (1976). *Schooling in Capitalist America: Educational Reform and the Contradiction of Economic Life*. New York: Basic Books.

Coleman, J. (1987). Families and Schools. *Educational Researcher*, 16(6): 32–38.

Corbett, D., & B. Wilson (1995). Make a Difference with, Not for, Students: A Plea to Researchers and Reformers. *Educational Researcher*, 24(5): 12–17.

Delgado–Gaitan, C., & H. Trueba (1991). *Crossing Cultural Borders*. London: Falmer Press.

Delpit, L. D. (1986). Skills and Other Dilemmas of a Progressive Black Educator. *Harvard Educational Review*, 56(4):379–385.

Eckert, P. (1989). *Jocks and Burnouts: Social Categories and Identities in the High School*. New York: Teachers College Press.

Everhart, R. B. (1983). *Reading, Writing and Resistance: Adolescence and Labor in a Junior High School*. Boston: Routledge and Kegan Paul.

Giroux, H. (1988). *Teachers as Intellectuals: Toward a Critical Pedagogy of Learning*. Grandby, MA: Bergin & Garvey.

Heath, S. B. (1983). *Ways with Words: Language, Life and Work in Communities and Classrooms*. Cambridge: Cambridge University Press.

Jencks, C., S. Bartless, M. Corcoran, J. Crouse, D. Eaglesfield, G. Jackson, K. McCelland, P. Mueser, M. Olneck, J. Schwartz, S. Ward, & J. Williams (1979). *Who Gets Ahead*? New York: Basic Books.

Jencks, C., M. Smith, H. Acland, J. J. Band, D. Cohen, H. Gintis, B. Heyns, & S. Michelson (1972). *Inequality*. New York: Basic Books.

Little, J. W. (1982). Norms of Collegiality and Experimentation: Workplace Conditions of School Success. *American Educational Research Journal*, 19(3):325–340.

———. (1990). The Persistence of Privacy: Autonomy and Initiative in Teachers' Professional Relations. *Teachers College Record*, 91(4):509–536.

MeLeod, J. (1995). *Ain't No Makin It: Aspirations and Attainment in a Low Income Neighborhood*. Boulder, CO: Westview.

Mehan, H. (1978). Structuring School Structure. *Harvard Educational Review*, 48, 32–64.

Moll. L. C., & S. Diaz (1987). Change as the Goal of Educational Research. *Anthropology and Education Quarterly*, 18(4):300–311.

Oakes, J. (1985). *Keeping Track: How Schools Structure Inequality*. New Haven: Yale University Press.

Ogbu, J. (1992). Understanding Cultural Diversity and Learning. *Educational Researcher* (Nov.), 5–14.

Spindler, G. (ed.) (1982). *Doing the Ethnography of Schooling: Educational Anthropology in Action*. New York: Holt, Rinehart and Winston.

Spindler, G., & L. Spindler (eds.) (1987). *Interpretive Ethnography of Education: At Home and Abroad*. Hillsdale, NJ: Lawrence Erlbaum Associates.

Trueba, H. (1988). Culturally-Based Explanations of Minority Students' Academic Achievement. *Anthropology and Education Quarterly*, 19(3): 270–287.

Willis, P. (1977). *Learning to Labour: How Working Class Kids Get Working Class Jobs*. New York: Columbia University Press.

Rebecca Constantino and Christian Faltis

4

Teaching Against the Grain in Bilingual Education

Resistance in the Classroom Underlife

Many teachers working in bilingual classrooms oppose what is happening generally with bilingual education across the U.S. and within their school settings in particular. Their opposition ranges in practice from boycotting the National Association of Bilingual Education (NABE) for its past corporate sponsorship association with Coors beer company, and its collective silence concerning the governmental promotion of transitional bilingual education, with learning English and its primary goal, to the use of commercial language proficiency tests such as the Language Assessment Scales (McGroarty, 1987) and the IDEA Kit (McCollum 1987) for sorting children by English proficiency levels and assigning them deficit-oriented labels (e.g., limited English proficient, a government adopted label). There is resentment of efforts by school districts to place non-English-speaking students with teachers who are not considered to be good teachers and with teachers who are not proficient in their students' primary language (Sánchez & Walker de Felix, 1986). Others have decided to work within the NABE organization to resist NABE's apparent promotion of the U.S. government's approach to bilingual education. For example, in 1994, María Torres–Guzmán and Alma Flor Ada formed a Critical Pedagogy interest section within NABE to organize bilingual teachers to work against some of the practices and theoretical stances commonly endorsed in NABE workshops and presentations. Likewise, Edelsky

(1991) and Faltis (1993) have argued strongly against the use of BICS and CALP by bilingual teachers and educators to explain why bilingual children fail in academic language-oriented tasks in school. At the local level, bilingual teachers are openly resisting school mandates that focus on basic skills and curriculum packages that present distorted content about life and knowledge in the U.S. in favor of more holistic approaches to language and learning (Fournier, 1993). These teachers "raise their voices against teaching and testing practices that have been 'proven effective' by large-scale educational research and delivered to the doorsteps of their schools in slick packages" (Cochran–Smith, 1991, p. 284).

Resistance in Teaching: Opening the Discussion

In this chapter we present examples of teachers working in bilingual settings who actively resist and find ways to subvert status quo pedagogy and curriculum they believe is counterproductive to providing language minority children an education that not only prepares them to be creative, inquisitive, sensitive, and literate, but also to be critically consciousness of the world around them. We subsume the acts of resistance within the general literature on resistance in school. Our goal is to focus the discussion on resistance particularly within bilingual education, and specifically on teacher-initiated resistance activities. Resistance in school settings has been discussed mainly in terms of a struggle between local and official knowledge (Apple, 1993). Very often, the struggle centers on the whether the students and the teachers have voice (Bakhtin, 1981), the power to counter the dominant cultural values played out in school. Teachers who gain voice do so by drawing from a pedagogical stance that necessarily values and hence encourages social heteroglossia within the classroom setting. Moreover, at many points in their daily lives as teachers, they interrupt and subvert attempts by the school powers to take away either their voice or the voices of their students because these voices collectively and individually threaten the survival of the status quo (Giroux, 1983; Shannon, P., 1995). In most schools where there are children whose native language is other than English, the script handed to teachers values English and Western (male) cultural discourse and practices over non-English, non-Western and non-mainstream values, preferences and practices. This dominant script is invoked differentially across time and place as the need to resocialize perceived deviancies arise (DeVillar, 1994).

The Resistance Zone or Living in the Underlife in Teaching

Those bilingual teachers who oppose the dominant script—or forms of knowledge and ways of participating in the construction of knowledge generally accepted as legitimate for schools—work in what we refer to as the *resistance zone*. Operationally, the resistance zone in the context of bilingual education represents the area between the dominant script and a counterscript—pedagogical activities that interrupt or subvert the dominant script. Gutiérrez, Kreuter, and Larson (1995) define *counterscript* as acts of noncompliance with the larger society's rules for participation within a community of practice—namely, teaching in a bilingual setting. They explain further that space for a counterscript to develop is created when the teacher's local knowledge and that of her students is regularly displaced by holders of and brokers for the dominant script.

We view counterscripting as a primary act of teaching against the grain (Simon, 1992). Moreover, sustained counterscripting within the resistance zone results in the development of an *underlife*, which Goffman (1961, in Gutiérrez, Kreuter & Larson, 1995) defines as the ranges of strategies people use over time to distance themselves from dominant institutions. According to Goffman (1961), there are two primary ways of living the underlife which give character to how resistance is carried out: 1) *living a disruptive underlife* where a goal is to radically change the status quo, and 2) *living a contained underlife* in which the participants seek to subvert the status quo by working within and around the institution. Most bilingual teachers that we talked with seem to adhere to the contained way of living underlife as Goffman depicted it. (See below for information on the teachers we studied). Accordingly, although teachers who resist within the zone and adopt a contained underlife within their school setting are not likely to change the dominant script in a radical manner, they can interrupt and alter the impact of dominant forces on the quality of activities they implement with their students. Giroux (1983) cautions, however, that not all acts of resistance are counterscripts to the dominant script or acts of living in the underlife. For example, leaving school early to avoid attending faculty meetings may be an act of resistance, but not one that opposes the dominant script. Teaching in the resistance zone means that teachers are actively opposing, albeit clandestinely, the schools' attempts to hinder the development of social heteroglossia in learning.

The resistance zone as counterscript spans the entire realm of pedagogy, from teaching activism for social justice and probing how students' lives are connected to and restricted by society to using the students' native language in social interaction that the school expects students to conduct in English (Peterson, 1994). Teaching against the grain as an underlife activity is a sociopolitical and an ethical-moral act of resistance to the status quo in bilingual education in particular, and society and schooling in general (Hudelson & Faltis, 1993).

Politically Neutral: Ain't No Such Thing

Many teachers in bilingual education believe that they should be politically neutral with regard to ideology and pedagogy; that their focus in teaching should be to provide students with comprehensible input (Krashen, 1985), and to make sure that students reach grade level performance on achievement exams. As one teacher who supports the status quo commented to us, "I want my students to read in Spanish and to learn English, and be ready for the next grade. If I can do that, I am happy." This is a dominant script in bilingual education. Our stance is that teacher decisions about what to teach and what not to teach, as well as how to teach are inherently political. Efforts to "get students on grade level" is a political act that supports rather than goes against the grain in education. Why? The answer is simple: *grade level* is a concept that is linked to academic achievement tests which assess a student's ability to reproduce the dominant discourse. Likewise, the decision to conduct literature studies in Spanish is a political act. It becomes an act of resistance, however, when the school authorities forbid Spanish for certain kinds of activities and with children who are deemed to be "fully English proficient." Using school mandated basal readers is a political act in support of the dominant discourse. Teachers who resist them in favor of trade books for promoting oral and written language are teaching against the grain (Fournier, 1993; Moll, 1989; Pease-Alvarez, García, & Espinosa, 1991).

In the following sections, we present some of the ways that bilingual teachers who live in the underlife of bilingual education by teaching against the grain and resisting practices that support social inequality and injustice. These teachers work to help their students gain a critical view of the world in which they and their families live, work, shop, and play. We begin with a narrative which describes some of the condition of Los Angeles area schools and their bilingual program, and then discuss areas of resistance that teachers act upon in their classrooms. In the second section, we draw on a case study conducted by Sheila Shannon of a teacher who fought against the hegemony of English in her bilingual program in Colorado (Shannon, 1995).

Acts of Resistance in the Classroom: The L.A. Underlife

In Los Angles, California, teachers who work in bilingual education may be African American, Latino, Chinese or Anglo; there is no one to one relationship between the teacher's and the students' ethnicity. Moreover, it is not uncommon for English speaking African American teachers to work extensively with bilingual students. Many ethnic minority teachers in Los Angeles carry with them a primary Discourse, or "identity kit" (Gee, 1992) that is discouraged and often disparaged by the school district and the mainstream society the district claims to represent. In Los Angeles, the lion's share of school district administrators expect classroom teachers to exit language minority students from bilingual classrooms and move them quickly (within two to three years) into all–English settings.

Many school districts support bilingual education primarily as means to procure federal money for the district. As one resistance teacher we interviewed stated:

> "[school districts] are not concerned with the needs of the students, we have no money for Spanish materials. We have to grab them [materials] when no one is looking. This is because the district does not encourage the use of Spanish for literacy or even everyday talk. The district personnel still sees literacy as English literacy. There is no room for Spanish. We really don't encourage it [using Spanish] past getting federal funding" (field notes, 11/94).

Efforts to curb the use of Spanish in schools that house bilingual programs occur on multiple levels. Spanish language children's reading and classroom materials are often only available to children in the primary grades. Students in secondary bilingual programs rarely have the opportunity to read literature and other authentic materials in Spanish (Constantino, 1994). Furthermore, when Spanish language literacy materials are available to older students, they tend to focus on drill and practice exercises rather than for pleasure or as learning resources. In the study described below, we found that school districts actually discourage teachers from using Spanish and nonstandard English vernacular in the bilingual classrooms. In one school, we observed teacher supervisors cruise the halls and classrooms to make sure that the daily lesson objectives were written clearly on the board and that the teacher and students were making an effort not to use Spanish and that the teacher was not using nonstandard English. Teachers caught not carrying out school policy are given a written notice of the infraction. Two or more infractions can lead to nonrenewal of the teaching contract.

The four teachers that we studied were all relatively new to the profession of teaching. Two were first year teachers; one was in his third year; and one was in her sixth year. Three of the four teachers we interviewed and observed grew up in the areas where they now teach. They report that they see the same system in operation that was in existence when they were in school, and they believe that it does work with children from the communities it intends to serve. Nonetheless, as members of the community, they see themselves as possessing insight into the needs of the community, and therefore, are hopeful for positive change. Robert, a bilingual teacher, views himself as a kind of resistance fighter against the system: "I just know this system [of schooling] is not working. I was reared in a system that was encouraging and warm—I am merely trying to model that system. It's clear, we don't need to reinvent the wheel. We just need one" (field notes, 11/94).

Robert and the other teachers we interviewed and observed are a minority in their school sites. Most teachers have many years of classroom experience, and as one teacher put it, appear to be "beyond caring. They are either numb or not interested" (field notes, 11/94). One teacher told us that the experienced teachers often mocked and ridiculed the newer bilingual teachers. Robert said that he gained support from teachers who talked openly about teaching against the grain when he took a graduate class for teachers throughout his district. According to Robert, these teachers gave him encouragement and listened to him about the kinds of practices that were taking place at his school. Robert now interacts with them regularly for support and for classroom ideas to counteract the dominant script in teaching at his school.

During the time we interviewed and observed the teachers (4/1994–2/1995), a new school district superintendent came into office. The new superintendent immediately implemented a new set of stiff guidelines for teachers to follow. The guidelines required teachers to write out lesson plans not only week to week and day to day, but also hour by hour. Moreover, unit supervisors were able to "drop in" classrooms at any given time to ensure that teachers had written out on the chalkboard an agenda for the unit plan and objectives to be covered that day. According to John, one of the teachers we interviewed, "this is to appease the district administrator who walks into your classroom. It does not take into consideration the daily reteaching of concepts and comprehension checks that are required for teachers to mediate learning. It does not take students into account." For John, this meant that his involvement in helping students' learn was expected to be subordinated to district objectives.

Supervisors also monitor language use within group activities. That is, according to district policy, when students are working together in groups on a project they are supposed to speak standard English. Student-to-student translation assistance is frowned upon because it is viewed as cheating, and the district discourages the use of group work in general (see Trueba & Delgado–Gaitán, 1985). Teachers who did not follow these policies received written notices of the infractions, which were also placed into their personnel files.

At the secondary level, students are not allowed to enter the classroom after the tardy bell has rung. District policy requires teachers to lock their doors after the tardy bell. Teachers are expected to send students who arrive late to "a holding room" for anywhere from 15 to 30 minutes. "This is valuable learning time; they miss a major portion of the class time" says Deana, a secondary bilingual teacher. John agrees, adding, "they are the students who would most benefit from the first fifteen minutes of the class when we are either reading, discussing or reviewing. They are the students who most will tend to opt out. I want them in class." John and Deana, as well as others in the underlife, resisted this policy by hiding a spare copy of the room key outside the door near the room. That way, if a supervisor comes by, the door is locked. If a student arrives late, she lets herself in. John, in particular was eager to talk with his students about opposing the rules. One of this students commented to us that in this [John's] room "we are learning to play the clean sweep for the big people" (field notes, 10/94). We interpreted this metaphor to mean that at least this student was well aware of how this teacher was creatively subverting the system.

Resistance Action

Within these types of educational setting, teachers are confronted with political decisions on a daily basis. Based upon school visits and one-on-one conversations with four teachers who work in the underlife of Los Angeles schools, we learned that these teachers resist the dominant script for how school is made for them by taking action against the grain of their daily experiences. We will highlight two areas that came up repeatedly in our discussions and observations: Classroom discourse and classroom materials.

Discourse. Many of the teachers who participated in this study are members of ethnic and language minority groups (Latino or African American) who interact with their students in nonstandard forms of English and Spanish. They negotiate meaning and teach in what Gee (1992) refers to as a primary nondominant discourse. At the secondary level, the teachers we talked with expressed a need for standard language in society as a whole. They also stressed the importance of affirming their own and their students' primary discourses, in Bakhtin's terms, multiple voices or social heteroglossia. They told us they consciously reworked classroom discourse to enable multiple varieties of spoken and written language, in both Spanish and English. On one occasion the teachers read and discussed intensively Lisa Delpit's (1992) article on the acquisition of literate discourse, along with the following poem written by an Apache child in Cazden (1988):

> Have you ever hurt about baskets?
> I have, seeing my grandmother weaving
> for a long time
> Have you ever hurt about work?
> I have because my father works too hard and he tells me
> how he works
> Have you ever hurt about cattle?
> I have, because my grandfather has been working on the
> cattle a long time.
> Have you ever hurt about school?
> I have because I learned a lot of words from school.
> And they are not my words.

These two works spurred students to reflect on and talk about how discourse can shape the world around them, and how it can determine who gets what. The Delpit article, in particular, generated a lively discussion on the role of standard English in school and society, and whether learning to use a standard variety of language is enough to change a system that is built on racism and social injustice (as Delpit argues in the piece).

John, a third year bilingual secondary English teacher, made a commitment to his class that he would try to connect what the students read in class with their lives outside of class. Though he follows the district guidelines in terms of what to teach and when to teach it, he goes against the grain of what the district wants because he presents most of the readings, such as *The Iliad*, in nonstandard English. His justification for this action is as follows:

> "For me, they must understand. Many of my students have little contact with standard English and they neither relate to or understand it. That misunderstanding is multiplied when you discuss a work such as *The Iliad*. I have made the choice to teach them in a language they understand and can relate to. It's not that easy: First I put it in their language, we discuss it, and then we move into standard English. That's the easy part. I have to hide this from the district. I am not allowed to instruct my kids like this. I hide my dittos, keep my door shut and immediately switch to standard English when a supervisor comes in (field notes, 2/95).

Robert, a first year teacher, was placed in a "bilingual" classroom and immediately told by the principal not to speak Spanish. The principal also warned him not to use Spanish language materials, since "all kids should be reading in English by the end of the year." He was also told that using Spanish could result in him not being rehired the following year.

Robert, in an act of resistance, has learned to maneuver classroom discourse in order to get around the principal's directives. He developed the "speaking game" in which he speaks Spanish for important parts of the lesson to his students except when a visitor is in the classroom. The students have become quite adept at warning Robert when a supervisor is headed toward the room and they signal each other to revert to English as best they can. While this strategy sends a fragmented message about value of Spanish in school and society, it also teaches students that they too can subvert a system that works against them.

Discourse in the written form is a powerful force in the classroom. In John's district, all students are required to write in standard, mainstream English for all homework and class assignments. Zelda, an African American veteran seventh grade teacher upholds this requirement for apparent district purposes. However, behind the scenes of her classroom is a different scenario. Zelda encourages students to write essays and other assignments in their comfortable voice because, she asserts, "what is critical is that they understand, participate and feel as if they belong in the class and the school society. I want them to contribute" (field notes, 2/95). After students have written in their voices and they discuss their pieces, Zelda then has the students work with partners to rewrite the pieces in a style of English that is acceptable in the district and in general society. Like Lisa Delpit, Zelda believes in the value of helping minority students learn the dominant voice:

> "I think I am encouraging their voices while also giving them the tools for a mainstream voice. It is difficult because their voice is part of who they are and their culture but it is devalued in this society and so they feel devalued. I walk a thin line of encouraging them while also pulling them into mainstream ways of talking and communicating" (field notes, 2/95).

One type of secondary Discourse that is far removed from the repertoires of students in many bilingual programs is that found on standardized tests such as the Scholastic Aptitude Test (SAT). The secondary teachers we talked with encourage and expect bilingual students to go on to college; nonetheless, they realize that the SAT score can easily be the barrier to admissions. As John put it, "I see the SAT as a gatekeeper for these kids and they have to learn to jump that gate 'cause it will never be opened for them" (field notes, 2/95). Accordingly, from January to March, the students in John's high school bilingual class prepare for the SAT tests during the last minute of class three days a week. They practice vocabulary drill and word recognition games with the understanding of what doing well on the games can bring. John says:

> "I see this test as completely removed from their lives and how they talk and communicate. Still, they must pass this test to gain access to more than what is in their community. If we drill them to death with this stuff, they will remember it for the test. They will probably never remember any of the material again. But, hey, if it increases their scores and they get into a junior college or even university, then it was all worth it" (field notes, 2/95).

Classroom Materials

The teachers in this district spend, on average, $1,500 a year on materials for their classroom. Since most of the materials provided by the district entail rote memorization and skill and drill activities in both English and Spanish, teachers who believe in values of literacy and more holistic practices spend a great deal of money on native language books and reading materials.

As with discourse in the classroom, the use of nondistrict materials is secretive and materials are stashed away. Here is how Carolyn, a fourth grade bilingual teacher handles this problem:

> "Since I have district people dropping by my class at any given time and I must be following their guidelines, it can be tricky at times. What I do is put my students in groups and the group in the front of the class is working on district materials while the groups in the back are working on my materials. Then I switch groups so that all students can take part. But when the district personnel person comes in, for all purposes, we are working in district materials. It is hard, and I am tired but what can I do?" (field notes 2/95).

Robert has set up his reading sections of his classroom with a large number of books. With a cursory glance, it is easy to assume that the books are all English. However, Robert has set up the stacks so that the English are out front but behind them are even more Spanish books. Story time is done in both English and Spanish, against school supervisor orders. Students are invited and encouraged to speak whatever language is more comfortable to them. That includes English, Spanish, switching between Spanish and English, and Ebonics (sometimes referred to as Black English). Robert favors having the students write in their primary language. However, Robert displays very little of the students' work and writing on the walls of the classroom, since only English is permitted by the district. Though Robert doesn't like this practice, he feels that it does "keep the district off my back!" (field notes, 11/94). Also on a regular basis, Robert reports that he acknowledges to his students the beauty and strength of their native languages.

"As I encourage students to write and speak in Spanish, it helps them to feel good about themselves. Because students teach me about their language and culture, they feel empowered. I also stay away from stories that are not meaningful to them. We do not read stories about white suburban people; we read stories about their people. I know if my principal knew this he would be offended and I would be unemployed, but they are only kids once" (field notes, 11/95).

The teachers we talked with had to resist the dominant script and discourse on a daily basis, and this wore them down. Robert was fortunate that he found a support group of teachers to discuss strategies and to vent his anger. The other teachers continue to struggle with a system that seems destined to do them and their students in.

Resisting the Hegemony of English in One Bilingual Classroom

The pull toward English in bilingual education has been well documented (Escamilla, 1995; Legarreta, 1977; Milk, 1986; Ramírez & Merino, 1989; Sapiens, 1982; S. Shannon, 1990). Spanish is considered the marked language; English the unmarked one. Teachers in these studies preferred English for large group instruction, for giving instructions, and for explaining important concepts. While the teachers used Spanish for parts of the lesson, and allowed students to use it for small group work, the message was clear that learning English was the goal, and that Spanish was the subordinate language. For example, S. Shannon (1990) reported that errors and unconventional usage were generally tolerated in Spanish; but the teachers were careful to correct students' developing English.

S. Shannon (1995) presents a case study of a fourth-grade bilingual classroom "in which the hegemony of English is recognized, challenged, and resisted (p. 185). The concept of linguistic hegemony means that "whenever more than one language or language variety exists together, their status in relation to one another is often asymmetric. In those cases, one will be perceived as superior, desirable, and necessary, whereas the other will be seen as inferior, undesirable, and extraneous" (S. Shannon, 1995, p. 176). S. Shannon goes on to explain that a powerful consequence of linguistic hegemony is that the speakers of a dominant or dominated language assume the status of the languages. In other words, because speakers of the subordinate language or language variety perceive their language or language variety as inferior, so too do they view themselves as inferior in relation to speakers of the dominant language. Once this occurs, it is likely that speakers of the dominated language will abandon it over time in favor of the higher status language, unless efforts are made to resist hegemony head on (Skutnabb–Kangas, 1994).

Mrs. D's Oppositional Stance

One small, but significant effort to resist the hegemony of English took place in a fourth grade bilingual classroom in Denver, Colorado, taught by Mrs. D.'s, a native speaker of Spanish born in Mexico who came to the United States as a young adult. The bilingual program at the school in which Mrs. D.'s classroom is located represents the status quo in bilingual education: transitional with the goal of moving students into English only classrooms as quickly as possible. Mrs. D. teaches against the grain of this transitional, hegemonic approach to bilingual education. For Mrs. D., a bilingual classroom has to be a place where children can develop to be fully bilingual in Spanish and English. But Mrs. D. knows that English is the prestigious language, so she has to convey to her students that English and Spanish have equal prestige in her class, that everyone in class is a second language learner, and that bilingualism is the goal for all students.

How does Mrs. D. resist the hegemony of English in a transitional bilingual education program? How does she ensure that the children in her classroom use and value Spanish in a school and society that value English first and foremost? First of all, Mrs. D. believes strongly that teachers have to monitor themselves constantly about how they use language when preparing every single activity of the day, and with every interaction with students, co-workers, parents and visitors. Accordingly, the teacher is in control of how language is used, for which purposes, and how it fits the situation. Mrs. D. makes sure that everything that goes home from the school in Spanish is written in an appropriate variety of the highest quality. In the classroom, Mrs. D. distributes Spanish and English more or less equally so that all students are second language users. She also allows students to work and interact among themselves in the language of their choice.

Mrs. D. supports Spanish literacy by disallowing in the classroom any materials in Spanish that are of lesser quality than their English counterparts. She believes that not having the same quality and number of Spanish-language materials available in English sends students a strong message that Spanish is not as good a language as English for learning and enjoying literature. To counter this possibility, Mrs. D. works very had to show all students that Spanish is an important language and to engender in her students an enthusiasm to learn and use Spanish in all sorts of fun and pleasurable activities.

In Mrs. D.'s class, students, parents, and others are expressly forbidden to tell racist jokes or to make racist comments about people of color and white people in either Spanish or English. She understands that racist jokes and comments result from unequal social and economical relationships between dominant and subordinate societies. Racist jokes and comments, she tells her students, are very much a part of the discourse that keeps certain people down at the expense of others.

Mrs. D. also enjoys talking with students in their second language. She uses lots of extralinguistic support to engage in exchanges with students. She expects students to interact in their developing language, and students try out language when they know that the goal is communication, and not humiliation. She is a risktaker with her students, always working hard to ensure that her students use the two languages generously and for a wide range of purposes so that one language does not dominate the other.

The belief that students and their families should be able to use and maintain their primary language because they have a right to do so (Skutnabb–Kangas, 1994) is not shared by all bilingual teachers. Promoting the use and maintenance of Spanish in school while children learn content in English is a counterscript to the dominant perspective in education in general and among many bilingual teachers as well. One reason for this is that for many bilingual teachers using Spanish for teaching is difficult. A stronger reason may be that many teachers are coerced with maintaining the status quo, rather than opposing and exposing it as hegemony.

Conclusion

Every one of the teachers that we highlighted believes that schools are products of human interests, and thus, that they are transformable. As Patrick Shannon (1995) maintains: "If the social world is a human artifact, then it is changeable through the acts of other human beings" (p. 108). Although they live in the underlife of schools, these teachers have decided that they can change the conditions and practices that keep bilingual students down socially, linguistically, and critically. Their struggles will continue, to be sure, as the new movements against bilingual education, from both within and without, surface. This chapter narrated how a number of bilingual teachers teach against the grain and oppose conditions and practices that favor the dominant discourse and the hegemony of English.

There is much to be learned from resistance teachers in bilingual education. One of the more interesting findings from our research is that although all of the teachers opposed the dominant discourse, several of them taught in ways that we felt were traditional. For example, bilingual teachers in high school still had students completing what we considered to be remedial exercises. And in Mrs. D.'s class, there were few instances of critical literacy in which the children read literature that is specifically about channeling resistance and providing alternative ways of understanding activism. P. Shannon (1995), for example, mentions several resistanceoriented children's books written in English, such as *Smoky Nights* (Bunting, 1994) a picture book about the uprising in Los Angeles after the Rodney King verdict and *Trouble at the Mines* (Rappaport, 1987) about a collective demonstration against oppressive working conditions. Kohn (1995) also discusses how children can learn about social injustice using certain books written for children. Faltis (1989) and Hudelson and Riggs (1994/1995) present a discussion of children's books that show how children can be helpers in solving societal problems. What we would like to see in the future then, is more work on how resistance teachers in bilingual education can also become critical literacy teachers as well. We believe strongly that teachers and students alike need access to literature, songs, and films that portray active resistance to the status quo and the dominant discourse of schooling. Moreover, those of us in bilingual education need to learn more about the struggles that bilingual teachers face on a daily basis.

References

Apple, M. (1993). *Official Knowledge: Democratic Education in a Conservative Age*. New York: Routledge.

Bakhtin, M. M. (1981). *The Dialogic Imagination*. Austin, TX: University of Texas Press.

Bunting, E. (1994). *Smoky Nights*. New York: Harcourt Brace.

Cazden, C. (1988). *Classroom Discourse: The Language of Teaching and Learning*. Portsmouth, NH: Heinemann.

Cochran–Smith, M. (1991). Learning to Teach Against the Grain. *Harvard Educational Review*, 61(3):279–310.

Constantino, R. (1994). Knowledge and Uses of the Library Among Immigrant ESL High School Students. Unpublished doctoral dissertation, School of Education, University of Southern California.

Delpit, L. (1992). Acquisition of Literate Discourse: Bowing Before the Master? *Theory in Practice*. 31(4):296–302.

DeVillar, R. A. (1994). The Rhetoric and Practice of Cultural Diversity in U.S. Schools: Socialization, Resocialization, and Quality Schooling. In R. A. DeVillar, C. Faltis, & J. Cummins (eds.), *Cultural Diversity in Schools: From Rhetoric to Practice* (pp. 25–56). Albany, NY: SUNY Press.

Edelsky, C. (1991). *With Literacy and Justice for All: Rethinking the Social in Language and Education*. London: Falmer Press.

Escamilla, K. (1995). The Sociolinguistic Environment of a Bilingual School: A Case Study Introduction. *Bilingual Research Journal*, 18, 21–48.

Faltis, C. (1993). Critical Issues in the Use of Sheltered Content Teaching in High School Bilingual Programs. *Peabody Journal of Education*, 69(1):58–69.

———. (1989). Spanish Language Cooperation–fostering Story Book for Language Minority Children in Bilingual Programs. *Journal of Educational Issues for Language Minority Students*, 5(1):41–50.

Fournier, J. (1993). Seeing with New Eyes: Becoming a Better Teacher of Bilingual Children. *Language Arts*, 70, 177–181.

Freeman, Y., & D. Freeman (1992). *Whole Language for Second Language Learners*. Portsmouth, NH: Heinemann.

Gee, J. (1992). *The Social Mind: Language, Ideology, and Social Practice*. New York: Bergin & Garvey.

Giroux, H. A. (1983). *Theory and Resistance in Education: A Pedagogy for the Opposition*. New York: Bergin & Garvey.

Goffman, E. (1961). *Asylums: Essays on the Social Situation of Mental Patients and Other Inmates*. New York: Anchor Books.

Gutiérrez, K., B. Kreuter, & J. Larson (1995). James Brown vs. Brown vs. the Board of Education: Script, counterscripts and the underlife in the classroom. Unpublished manuscript. Graduate School of Education, University of California, Los Angeles.

Hudelson, S., & P. Rigg (1994/1995). My *Abuela* Can Fly: Children's Books about Old People in English and Spanish. *TESOL Journal*, 4(2):5–10.

Hudelson, S., & C. Faltis (1993). Redefining Basic Teacher Education: Preparing Teachers to Transform Education. In G. Guntermann (ed.), *Developing Language Teachers for a Changing World* (pp. 23–42). Lincolnwood, IL: National Textbook Company.

Kohl, H. (1995). *Should We Burn Babar? Essays on Children's Literature and the Power of Stories*. New York: New York Press.

Legarreta, D. (1977). Language Choice in Bilingual Classrooms. *TESOL Quarterly*, 1(1):9–16.

McCollum, P. (1987). Idea Oral Language Proficiency Test. In J. C. Alderson, K. J. Krahne, & C. W. Stansfield (eds.), *Reviews of English Language Proficiency Tests* (pp. 37–39). Washington, DC: Teachers of English to Speakers of Other Languages.

McGroarty, M. (1987). Language Assessment Scales. In J. C. Alderson, K. J. Krahne, & C. W. Stansfield (eds.), *Reviews of English Language Proficiency Tests* (pp. 51–53). Washington, DC: Teachers of English to Speakers of Other Languages.

Milk, R. (1986). The Issue of Language Separation in Bilingual Methodology. In E. García & B. Flores (eds.), *Language and Literacy Research in Bilingual Education* (pp. 67–86). Tempe, AZ: Arizona State University Press.

Krashen, S. (1985). *The Input Hypothesis: Issues and Implications*. New York: Longman.

Moll, L. (1989). Some Key Issues in Teaching Latino Students. *Language Arts*, 65(5), 465–472.

Pease–Alvarez, L., E. García, & P. Espinosa (1991). Effective Instruction for Language Minority Students: An Early Childhood Case Study. *Early Childhood Research Quarterly*, 6, 347–361.

Peterson, B. (March/April, 1994). Teaching for Social Justice. *Rethinking Schools*, 2–3.

Ramírez, J. D., & B. Merino (1990). Classroom Talk in English Immersion, Early–Exit and Late–Exit Transitional Bilingual Education Programs. In R. Jacobson & C. Faltis (eds.), *Language Distribution Issues in Bilingual Schooling* (pp. 61–103). Clevedon, England: Multilingual Matters Ltd.

Rappaport, D. (1987). *Trouble at the Mines*. New York: Bantam–Skylark.

Sánchez, K., & J. Walker de Felix (1986). Second Language Teachers' Abilities: Some Equity Concerns. *Journal of Educational Equity and Leadership*, 6(4):313–321.

Sapiens, A. (1982). The Use of Spanish and English in a High School Bilingual Civics Class. In J. Amastae & L. Olivares (eds.), *Spanish in the United States: Sociolinguistic Aspects* (pp. 386–412). New York: Cambridge University Press.

Skutnabb–Kangas, T. (1994). Linguistic Human Rights and Minority Education. *TESOL Quarterly*, 28(3):625–628.

Shannon, P. (1995). *Text, Lies, & Videotape*. Portsmouth, NH: Heinemann.

Shannon, S. M. (1990). An Ethnography of a Fourth–Grade Bilingual Classroom: Patterns of English and Spanish. In D. Bixler–Márquez, G. Green, & J. Ornstein–Galicia (Eds.), *Mexican American Spanish in Its Societal and Cultural Contexts* (pp. 35–50). Brownsville, TX: Pan American University.

Simon, R. I. (1992). *Teaching Against the Grain: Texts for a Pedagogy of Possibility*. New York: Bergin & Garvey.

Trueba, H. T., & C. Delgado–Gaitán (1985). Socialization of Mexican Children for Cooperation and Competition: Sharing and Copying. *Journal of Educational Equity and Leadership*, 5(3):190–204.

James F. Shackelford, Penelope L. Shackelford, and Enrique (Henry) T. Trueba

5

Affirmative Action in Engineering Education

A Case Study

Affirmative action has for roughly three decades been an integral part of the policy of American colleges and universities in regard to the recruitment and retention of students. This effort has been a central part of the college or university's mission of teaching and research. Nonetheless, by early 1995, challenges to affirmative action were being reported in the print and broadcasting media at an increasing rate (Roberts, 1995:32–38; Klein, 1995, 36–37). The election of 1994 had provided increased vigor to the voice of long-time opposition to affirmative action policies. Affirmative action had also become intimately associated with discussions of multiculturalism and diversity, two other frequent targets of criticism. Affirmative action may be seen as a remedy to our long social history of sanctioned segregation (West, 1995). The 30-year history of affirmative action is relatively short in comparison to the previous 300 years of mandated racial separation. On the other hand, the challenges to affirmative action require those long involved in the effort to reflect on its nature and its appropriate future (Shackelford and Shackelford, 1995:25–26).

One should begin with a definition of what affirmative action is and what it is not. Affirmative action is a national policy that grew out of the 1964 Civil Rights Act, as amended in 1972. Title VII of the 1964 Civil Rights Act prohibits discrimination based on race, religion, gender, color, and national origin. Affirmative action was introduced by President Lyndon Johnson through Executive Order 11246 in 1965. The Executive Order allowed voluntary programs to take issues such as race and gender into account in trying to overcome past discrimination in employment, education, and contracting. Affirmative action implies a determined effort to ensure that those ethnic groups that are significantly underrepresented in colleges or the workplace are more equitably represented. The definition of affirmative action has been expanded to include disabled and other groups that have historically been underrepresented in certain fields. Properly applied, affirmative action is most definitely not a handout. Instead, it is an opportunity that meets the students or employees halfway. They must respond with their own hard work and enthusiasm to succeed.

It is precisely in the interpretation of affirmative action where the debate lies. If conceived as a quota system, one can argue that it is inherently unfair to any other students deprived from preferential treatment, from the advantages and additional consideration given to persons on the grounds of their race, ethnicity, gender, or other characteristics not related to qualifications. If conceived as an additional mechanism to identify qualified students and to assess the special nature of their qualifications in the larger context of long-term benefits for all students, for the appropriate representation of all ethnic, racial, linguistic, and socioeconomic groups of society, then affirmative action must presuppose the existence of a level of academic excellence (a standard required from all students). The additional consideration given to the richer experience and other qualifications brought by socioculturally diverse students can be constructed as enriching the experience of all students and providing a fair opportunity to students from underrepresented groups. The fundamental assumption in this concept is that society does not create fair and equal conditions for academic success; indeed, the literature (to be discussed below) indicates that society perpetuates the social order precisely through schooling by continuing to give an advantage to those students whose culture, language, social class, economic class, and ethnicity is closer to the mainstream, middle-class university personnel. To the degree that affirmative action is not punitive of previous unjust practices by making today's mainstream students suffer for the sins of their parents, it can be constructed as fair and within the limits of justifiable policies at the university. Indeed, many universities have four years added preferential criteria for admissions beyond tests and scores (as of themselves not completely reliable). Affirmative action can only be understood in the context of societal changes that places a great deal of value on recognizing as part of the civil rights of all Americans the opportunity to achieve an education of comparable quality regardless of race, gender, language, religion, ethnicity, and social class.

The Larger Sociocultural Context for the Debate on Affirmative Action

The United States is going through a most difficult historical period that will test the strength of democratic institutions and values in the years to come. According to recent reports, the estimated U.S. population as of May 1, 1996 was 265,022,000, and its race, ethnicity, and age trends in 1995 show a dramatic contrast. Of the population 65 years of age and over, whites are 85 percent; blacks, 8 percent; Hispanics, 4 percent; Asian and Pacific Islanders, 2 percent. Altogether, blacks, Hispanics, Asian and Pacific Islanders and Native Americans account for 34 percent of the U.S. population under 18 years of age (*Population Today*). Equally shocking are the poverty races for children. From the over 16 million poor children, one-third (5.6 million) live in "working-poor" families (at least one parent working 50 or more weeks a year and making less than $11,821, the poverty standard for 1994). Working-poor families increased 30 percent from 1989 to 1994; most children in these working-poor families are born to women over the age of 25, and half of these children live in two-parent households with one parent working all year. These children (27 percent of them have no health insurance) are often not immunized, do not do well in school, and are more likely to be poor as adults (*ibid.*). Overall, a state-by-state picture of U.S. children is depressive. From 1985–1993, low-birthweight babies increased 6 percent; the rate of violent deaths of youth aged 15 to 19 (by suicide, homicide, or accident) increased 10 percent; violent crime arrests of youths aged ten to 17 rose 66 percent; singleparent families with children increased

18 percent. There are, however, some positive signs. From 1985–1993 the infant mortality rate decreased 21 percent, rate of deaths to children ages one to 14 decreased 12 percent; high school drop-outs ages 16 to 19 decreased 18 percent; idle teens decreased 9 percent; and the rate of child poverty remained the same (*ibid.*).

The above data are only part of the story for the country as a whole. Looking into the distribution of poverty among the various ethnic groups, and the age differences between whites and ethnic or racial minorities gives us a more accurate picture of the challenges ahead. One of the recent reports (*Current Population Reports*, published by the Bureau of the Census, U.S. Department of Commerce, Economics and Statistics Administration, June 1996), examines longitudinal poverty data: the number of people who were poor in a given month during 1992–1993, the chronically poor, median durations of poverty spells, and so on. About 21.6 percent of people who were poor in 1992 were not poor in 1993; children and elderly, however, were less likely to leave poverty; 4.8 percent or 11.9 million people were poor all 24 months of 1992–1993; one-half of all poverty "spells" lasted 4.9 months or longer, but blacks had longer spells (6.2 months) than whites. About 52.7 million people (or 20.8 percent) were poor two months or more in 1993; about the same numbers, 52.9 million, were similarly poor in 1992. The median duration of poverty in the period from 1992 to early 1994, for selected groups shows that those 65-year olds and older had a median 7.2 month duration and female householder families a median 7.1 month duration; blacks had 6.2, and Hispanics 5.2. Poverty trends show that 8.6 percent of Hispanics enter poverty in 1993, in contrast with 2.6 percent white, and 6.7 percent blacks (*Current Population Reports*, June 1996:2–5). Immigrant families and village networks are instrumental in managing the choice of jobs for persons from particular Mexican communities.

The economies and labor markets of rural communities are increasingly layered or segmented in a manner that pushes many of the costs of seasonal farm work onto the most flexible or absorptive people present, recently arrived immigrants. Today's rural poverty is being created via the immigrants of persons with low earnings and little education into an expanding fruit and vegetable agriculture that increasingly exports the commodities produced by immigrant farm workers. Rural poverty affects California cities as local residents, particularly the children of immigrants, seek a livelihood outside agriculture. The transfer of rural poverty to urban poverty highlights the importance of education and training to improve the prospects for California's rural-to-urban migrants in the urban economy. (Martin and Taylor, 1996:2)

The sense that there is no end in sight to the waves of immigrants was pervasive, and created serious reflection on the contradiction between immigration and integration policies, especially considering that children of seasonal farm workers raised in the United States do not choose season farm work. A fundamental question is whether we are allowing unregulated immigration to create rural poverty, and if so, what is likely to happen to the children of these immigrants? If the only option left for growers is to import new farm labor from Mexico, then new immigration will bring new poverty and more segregation. If the United States wants to curtail immigration from Mexico, we must invest in rural Mexico to develop sources of employment for rural Mexican seasonal farm workers so that they can repatriate. Otherwise, the continued arrival of unskilled immigrants transforms the economy into something resembling the "migrants' place of origin" or the "import-Third-World-immigrants-and-get-Third-World-conditions-syndrome." On the one hand, their labor is critical to an expanding labor-intensive agricultural sector. On the other hand, immigration into rural communities is associated with rising poverty, public assistance, and underemployment rates. (Martin and Taylor, 1996:4)

In this volume Suárez–Orozco argues that in this country a general discontent of the American people, based primarily on economic and political crises and the resulting pervasive sense of anxiety about the future, has contributed to a xenophobic and anti-immigrant sentiment. The President campaign of 1996 raised the level of intolerance and immigrant-bashing attitudes when the Republican candidates "blamed illegal aliens for overcrowded public-school classrooms, bankrupt hospitals, crime, high taxes, and even potential voter fraud" (Cornelius, 1996:B4). Naturally, the response by the current administration was equally vigorous in promoting immigration control and in increasing the Immigration and Naturalization Services budget in order to strengthen the surveillance of the southern border. The expression of these sentiments is not unusual in this country. What is unusual, however, is its occurrence during a period of economic recovery as manifested by lower unemployment and rising productivity. According to a number of polls cited by Cornelius (1996), including the General Social Survey conducted by the National Opinion Research Center at the University of Chicago, in the last three years we find a larger portion of the population demanding cuts in immigration and favoring the construction of a Berlin-like wall between Mexico and the United States. Other national surveys by political scientists seem to indicate that the individual's particular economic situation (income, type of employment, job loss, or other circumstances affecting the quality of work) has nothing to do with his or her position on immigration. Cornelius states such findings may reflect the realities of a labor market in which fewer and fewer Americans—particularly white, middle-class voters—ever compete directly with immigrants for jobs or hold jobs whose wages have been depressed by large numbers of immigrants in a given company or industry. But the data also may indicate that noneconomic factors, especially culture and ethnicity, have become more salient in shaping Americans' attitudes toward immigration. Survey respondents who have negative views on Hispanics and Asians as ethnic groups—not just as immigrants—are more likely to prefer a restrictive immigration policy than are other people. (Cornelius, 1996:B4) Other recent research seems to indicate that Anglos who see themselves as "conservative" (particularly as fiscal conservatives) oppose cultural diversity, the use of languages other than English in elementary education or on the ballots, and favor restrictions on immigration. Their main concern, however, seems to be a replication of a society based on European antecedents—one with ethnic purity, a single national identity, and pragmatic and conservative fiscal policies. Unfortunately, the general public seems to view Latinos as more likely to draw welfare benefits, to be less educated, and to contribute less to the general economy of this country. The combination of a desire for cultural and ethnic purity with fiscal conservatism makes it very difficult. In previous decades, notably at the turn of the century, racism, xenophobia, and intolerance were clearly identified and expressed. Scholars today have not been able to produce a clean set of data to inform policymakers. Cornelius cites George Borjas, Michael Fix and Jeffrey Passel to illustrate the classic disagreement between fiscal conservatives who calculate the percentage of immigrants using public assistance at 26.1 percent (George Borjas, a Harvard economist), in contrast with the 5.1 percent used by demographers Michael Fix and Jeffrey Passel of the Urban Institute. The disagreement goes from the unit of analysis (whether they count immigrant households or individuals—documented or undocumented; or whether they include political refugees to the definition of "welfare" (food stamps, noncash assistance programs, and so on). Politicians then are free to inflate figures to advance their political agendas and opinions. In the end, the benefits of immigration are rarely documented because they present themselves in rather intangible ways of long-term development and contributes to the state and federal taxes. How does one measure, for example, the consumption of goods and services, the creation of jobs, the competitiveness of industries (agricultural, textile, and so on) in the international arena? The oversimplified notion, advocated by Borjas, that this country is importing Third-World poverty by bringing in uneducated immigrants has no empirical foundation. According to Cornelius, demographer Dowell Myers of the University of Southern California "has found that Latino immigrants settling in southern California are becoming homeowners at a faster rate than native-born residents" (1996:B5). The point that Cornelius consistently raises is that we have no empirical evidence, no substantive research to back up policies such as those advocated by Proposition 187 denying public education and other services to children of undocumented workers. (For a more in depth discussion on this, see Suárez–Orozco, 1996, AEQ.) In fact, it does not make economic sense initially to save money in the education of these children if we consider the tax revenue losses resulting from reduced lifetime earnings and the additional costs of law enforcement, incarceration, emergency medical assistance, and other social problems related to uneducated youth (Cornelius, *ibid.*).

In the opinion of highly credible social scientists (including Suárez–Orozco and Suárez–Orozco, 1995, 1996, this volume; and Cornelius, 1996; Rumbaut and Cornelius, 1995; Chavez, 1992), the issue of affirmative action does not occur in a vacuum, rather it is part of a national current stimulated by political agendas during a general malaise, a crisis of national identity, desire for ethnic and cultural purity, and struggle over control. Affirmative action, in this context, is seen as one additional social mechanism initiated by "those others," who do not belong in this country, to take over the nation. The "paranoic conspirational theories," the conspicuous crimes against immigrants of color, the intolerance of law enforcement officers, and all the data presented by Suárez–Orozco in this volume, help to understand the subtle and not so subtle strategies of conservatives determined to "regain" control of "their" country by limiting the access of persons of color to positions of power. In this context, Proposition 209 is read by different persons/people and interpreted in entirely different ways. The text alone presents a language that seems acceptable at face value: "The state shall not discriminate against, or grant preferential treatment to, any individual on the basis of race, sex, color, ethnicity, or national origin in the operation of public employment, public education, or public contracting." The end of affirmative action by Proposition 209 was interpreted as a serious and profound threat to the future of the students of color, including black, Latino, and Filipino student associations (supported by gay, lesbian and bisexual student groups). Student demonstrations (the "Weeks of Rage") articulated the short and long-term consequences of this proposition: (1) a drop in the number of Black and Latino students admitted to public colleges, (2) the existence of ethnic studies, clubs, organizations, and overall exclusive presence of non-Anglo students in public colleges, and ultimately (3) an attack on people of color, women, low-income, and other marginalized groups (Schmidt, *Chronicle of Higher Education*, 1996).

The blocking of Proposition 209 by Federal Judge Thelton E. Henderson on the grounds of a strong probability of being unconstitutional angered a number of politicians. In his ruling, the judge suggested that courts, "must look beyond the plain language" of the amendment and determine whether the burden imposed by it "necessarily falls on minorities and women." Judge Henderson said he was issuing the restraining order because Governor Wilson and Attorney General Lundgren appeared to be acting "with considerable dispatch" to carry out the measure, which could cause "irreparable harm" to the rights of the state's minority citizens. Mr. Wilson and Mr. Lundgren had asked state agencies to provide a list of all affirmative action programs that could conflict with the proposition (Schmidt, 1996). The American Civil Liberties Union lawyer Edward Chen felt that Proposition 209 would have the glass ceiling for women and minorities turn into an iron cage (*ibid.*). Public reflection was also heightened by the expediency of other states to replicate California's initiative. Racial tension also resurfaced in corporate America.

As Bob Herbert stated in his *New York Times* article on the Texaco scandal, in the context of the remarks revealed by executive Richard A. Lundwall's tapes, "Who needs affirmative action when discrimination is a thing of the past? . . Racial discrimination is as common as commercials on television" (Bob Herbert, *New York Times*, Nov. 11, 1996, p. A15). In those tapes, Blacks had been called porch moneys, orangutans, uppity so-and-so's black jelly beans and niggers; the executives found it funny the fact that "All the black jelly beans seem to be blued to the bottom of the bag," referring to the lack of upward mobility of black employees.

Obviously racial and ethnic prejudice are not exclusive to business and industry; in fact, they begin in the school setting with the way children are socialized into academic achievement, and they continue through the entire educational processes, especially at the university level. Much of the work in critical theory is devoted to this issue (Freire, 1973, 1993, 1995; Apple, 1989, 1993, 1996; Aronowitz and Giroux, 1991, Gadotti, 1996; Giroux and McLaren, 1996; Leistyna, Woodrum, and Sherblom, 1996). The *Chronicle of Higher Education* has published college enrollment and other educational statistics on the educational gains of Latinos. In 1984 there were 535,000 Latinos enrolled in college, and in 1994 there were 1,046,000 Latinos in college (the actual Latino population more than doubled during this period); in 1994, there were slightly more women than men in college, and more in two-year colleges than in four-year colleges; 968,000 were undergraduates, 64,000 were graduate students and 13,000 were professional school students. The overall educational attainment of Latinos, in 1990, was the lowest in the country, with 30.7 percent of the Latino population having eight or fewer years of education, in contrast with whites (with only 8.9 percent), Asians (12.9 percent), blacks (13.8 percent), and Native Americans (14.0 percent). Of the 64,000 graduate students only 903 Latinos obtained doctorates in 1993–1994. In 1995, Latinos (United States Citizens and permanent residents) obtained 1.8 percent of the nation's doctorates in business and management, 2.2 percent of doctorates in the physical sciences, 2.3 percent in engineering, 3.0 percent in the life sciences, 3.1 percent in professional fields, 3.7 percent in the arts and humanities, 4.2 percent in the social sciences, and 4.3 percent in education. In 1992, of the 526, 222 fulltime faculty members with regular instructional duties, Latinos held 12,076 positions. Latino men had 1.7 percent and Latino women 0.8 percent of the total number.

In the late sixties, there were more than three times as many blacks as Latinos in the school population, and there was one Latino for every 17 white students; 20 years later Latino enrollment is two-thirds of the black student population, and there is one Latino student for every seven whites. The white student population decreased 17 percent, while the Latino student population increased 103 percent in that period (Orfield, cited by Valencia 1991:18–20). This trend has been accentuated for complex historical reasons in the 1990s (Orfield and Eaton, 1996). Paradoxically, the economic and technological future of this country will depend precisely on the educational success of Latinos, blacks, and Asians as, by the middle of the twenty-first century, they will constitute half of the total United States population. Latino children will be the majority in many of our schools. The United States has not prepared for this challenge. Educators need to be trained to communicate with Latinos effectively and to understand the critical role of Latinos in our future. Latinos will continue to view the family and community as the center of religious, economic, and social life. Latinos clearly occupy the most strategic position among immigrants as we approach the twenty-first century; the success of Latinos can easily become the success of the United States' democracy, as well as its economic, technological, and military survival. The world is increasingly complex and less controllable by the United States government and its political institutions. During the twenty-first century, American democratic institutions will struggle for survival in the face of the rising power of other nations.

Affirmative Action Efforts at the University of California, Davis

Giving preference to underrepresented groups in recruitment and retention of university students is a remedy to be used only if there is a showing of past discrimination. An affirmative action program must take, according to law professor Martha West (1995), a very narrow window to be legal. It should not be the basis for forcing unqualified individuals into any institution. In fact, affirmative action typically involves selecting from a pool of candidates who are otherwise qualified. For example in Professor West's academic unit, the School of Law at the University of California Davis (UC-D), 3,000 people apply each year for 160 openings in the first year class. With at least half the pool well qualified, the School Admissions Committee selects from a pool roughly ten times the possible class size. Affirmative action does not appear to have impaired the quality of the resulting law students. The graduates of the School of Law at UC-D typically pass the State of California Bar Exam at a rate of 90 percent on their first try, consistently placing the school among the top performers in the State.

In May 1988, the Regents of the University of California adopted a policy on undergraduate admissions that states that the University's intent is to enroll students who both meet high academic standards and who encompass the broad cultural, racial, geographic, economic, and social diversity of California. This policy is based on the idea that a diverse student body, one that represents all segments of society and therefore differing points of view and experiences, is fundamental to enhancing the quality of education received by all students. Therefore, the University used several criteria including race and gender in determining admissions. It is reasonable to assume that no responsible opponent of affirmative action advocates returning to the blatant discrimination we witnessed in this country during mid–century. Most opponents seem to suggest that, with more than three decades of civil rights legislation firmly established, we can now move to totally race-and-gender-blind policies. It is true that a completely successful affirmative action program will render itself unnecessary at some point in time. Some suggest that this time has come. In late 1994, UC Regent Ward Connerly said this in regard to a renewed debate about Medical School admissions policies (*UC Focus*, 1994). Others argued that we had not yet reached that point and that we are well served as a society to continue policies that will reduce the severe differences between the population of our professions and the community as a whole. For example, the Federal "Glass Ceiling"

Commission reported that after three decades of affirmative action, 95 percent of senior management positions in American industry are held by white males who constitute 43 percent of the total work force (Kilborn, 1995).

On July 20, 1995, the Regents of the University of California voted to adopt two resolutions, SP-1 and SP-2. This historical action was the focus of intense media attention and has remained the subject of close scrutiny and intense debate. SP-1 dealt with admissions and provided that "the University of California shall not use race, religion, sex, color, ethnicity, or national origin as criteria for admission to the University or any program of study." SP-2 dealt with employment and provided that the University "shall not use race, religion, sex, color, ethnicity, or national origin as criteria in its employment and contracting practices." The action of the Regents was followed by a statewide ballot measure, Proposition 209, which used language similar to that used by the Regents. Proposition 209 was passed by a majority vote on November 5, 1996. In its first section, Proposition 209 read, "The state shall not discriminate against, or grant preferential treatment to any individual or group on the basis of race, sex, color, ethnicity, or national origin in the operation of public employment, public education, or public contracting." Although the impact of SP-1, SP-2, and Proposition 209 is substantial, both university and state action excluded any course of action that would jeopardize federal funding. As will be seen below, this shields federally-funded affirmative action programs as long as federal legislation comparable to Proposition 209 does not exist. Similarly, the university and state are still obligated to meet federal affirmative action employment guidelines that stipulate good-faith efforts to meet affirmative action objectives.

On December 23, 1996, Judge Thelton Henderson of the United States District Court for the Northern District of California issued a preliminary injunction against Proposition 209. Judge Henderson concluded that Proposition 209 was probably unconstitutional and would likely be overturned in the appeals process. This action initiated a legal course expected to last for years. In the meantime, the action of the Regents (SP-1 and SP-2) is still in effect, although a more gradual phase-in of new admissions policies is possible.

As a case study of affirmative action policies that work and that have evolved with university and state policies, we shall review a variety of programs within the College of Engineering at (UC–D). These programs are historical ironies when seen within the context of local history (Dreyfuss and Lawrence, 1979). UC-Davis is located in Yolo County which is part of the great Central Valley of California. Yolo—"a place abounding in ruses," according to its early settlers—has a history of discrimination. Its first settlers are held to be immigrants from the migrations across the Bering Strait two to three thousand years before Columbus. The Spanish explorers discovered the Patwin Indians living along the Sacramento River in 1817. The gold rush of the mid-century brought thousands to the nearby Sierra Nevadas. Disappointed gold prospectors saw a value in the fertile land in Yolo, and they enslaved the local Yolo Indians. With time, colonization and epidemics destroyed the Indians. Later the Chinese, who came to build the railroads, were not allowed to live in Yolo county. Chicano farm workers added to Yolo's diverse history. There was a time when these Chicanos had to catch a ride to Sacramento in order to get a haircut.

Another significant local event in the history of affirmative action is the landmark *Bakke* case of 1978, which demonstrated an "ancient and honored form of preference—wealth power and privilege—could still be an obstacle when the son of a mailman and a schoolteacher tried to become a doctor" (Dreyfuss and Lawrence, 1979). Specifically, Allan Bakke successfully sued the Regents of the University of California when he was not admitted to the UC-Davis School of Medicine, although he was more qualified than certain ethnic minority students admitted under a quota system. The significant result of the *Bakke* decision was that quota systems were ruled illegal, but racial or ethnic "targets" could still be used. Until the Regents' passing of SP-1 and SP-2 on July 20, 1995, some consideration was given to race, ethnicity, and gender in admission selections. In the year following that action, policies and procedures regarding admissions and programs dealing with the recruitment and retention of students were modified to comply with these new guidelines, while retaining the underlying goal of increasing the diversity of the student body. A great irony of this entire process was that virtually all the academic management structure, systemwide and at individual campuses, was supportive of the 1988 policies and recommended against passage of SP-1 and SP-2. Nonetheless, all university administrators were obligated to carry out the Regents' orders and did so. It is important to note, however, that even those Regents leading the effort to remove race and gender as factors in admissions expressed strong support for increased efforts in recruitment and retention to bring about a diverse student body. As will be seen in the following specific examples of programs that fall within the broad areas of recruitment and retention, the mission of each program has largely remained the same. Compliance with the wishes of the Regents (SP-1 and SP-2) and the voters (Proposition 209) has occurred generally by removing restrictions in access to the programs.

In reviewing the activities within the College of Engineering at (UC-Davis), we would submit that they illustrate a spectrum of programs that meet the definition of affirmative action in a positive and constructive sense. They also are representative of similar programs in colleges and universities nationwide. (A significant distinction, of course, is the effort to broaden access to these programs within California.) At the outset, one should note that these efforts have been made easier due to the widespread awareness among industrial partners of the college that a more diverse work force, representing more closely the community at large, is an essential goal for our society as a whole.

Engineering Summer Residency Program. The Engineering Summer Residency Program (ESRP) is a one–week residential summer program that introduces populations that have traditionally been underrepresented in engineering. These include African American, Hispanic American, Native American, Filipino, women, low-income, and disabled individuals. Each year the program is open to 60 male and female students who will be juniors or seniors in high school the following academic year. Acceptance into the program is based on math and science courses taken, the GPA in math and science courses, the overall GPA, student essays, and recommendations from teachers. ESRP focuses around three questions: What is engineering? What does an engineer do? How can I know if I might like to be an engineer? Students are led to see that engineering applies math and the natural sciences for the benefit of humanity. Students find that an engineer uses technical knowledge to seek solutions to problems that deal with human needs. If students find they like math and science, like to problem solve, and enjoy working with people, they are encouraged to consider engineering as a possible profession. The cost of the program is funded by various grants from industry, but the only cost to the student is transportation to and from UC-Davis. The primary modification to this program since SP-1 and SP-2 is to avoid the emphasis on "minority" recruitment and emphasize instead that we are seeking students who "might not otherwise be exposed to engineering." Economic disadvantage is more than ever a factor in selecting participants.

Mathematics, Engineering, and Science Achievement. In the late 1960s, a group of concerned educators including Mechanical Engineering Professor Wilbur Somerton initiated a study to determine why so few African Americans, Hispanic Americans and Native Americans enrolled in engineering programs at UC-Berkeley. The result of their study was the basis for a precollege interventionist program that became Mathematics, Engineering, Science Achievement (MESA) (Somerton, Smith, Finnell, and Fuller, 1994). The initial MESA program was offered to 25 students at Oakland Technical High School in 1970 by math teacher Mary Perry Smith. MESA has developed into a statewide program that serves 18,000 students of color from preschool through graduate levels. It is funded by the California Legislature and private industry (Somerton, Smith, Finnell, and Fuller, 1994). "In today's society, an educated community is the best business for all involved," PG&E Executive Vice President James Shiffer has said in explaining why his company supports MESA (MESA News, 1995). MESA's Capitol Center, located in Sacramento, is the largest precollege center in the state, serving 5,000 students. Two unique features of Capitol Center include (1) The Joint sponsorship of the UC-Davis College of Engineering and the CSU-Sacramento School of Engineering and Computer Science and (2) substantial funding support from the Sacramento Metropolitan school districts. In addition significant funding is provided by local industry and various governmental agencies such as the National Science Foundation. Services provided include tutoring, career awareness, summer jobs, college advising, and incentive awards. An important by-product of the interaction with local school districts was the insistence by some that students other than the traditionally underrepresented minorities be served. As a result, a parallel program named Business Education Science Team (BEST) was developed in 1991, well before the actions of the UC Regents. Patterned after MESA, BEST is open to students of all ethnicities. BEST also reaches underrepresented students in non-MESA schools where a large minority population may not be present.

MESA Engineering Program. The MESA Engineering Program (MEP), the university-level component of MESA, celebrated its twentieth anniversary in 1994. Currently, it serves some 5,300 university-level students in 24 universities including the University of California and California State University systems and private institutions. In anticipation of the Regents' action, MESA changed the name of MEP in mid-1995 from the Minority Engineering Program to MESA Engineering Program. Although still focusing on underrepresented students, MEP services are not restricted to that population. MEP supporters see the ongoing need to provide for personal and career development. The state and corporate supporters have determined the following ethnic groups to be underrepresented in the engineering professions: African Americans, Hispanic Americans, Puerto Ricans and Native Americans. Individuals from these groups admissible to the College of Engineering at UC-Davis are an important part of the group receiving MEP services. Extensive services are offered at UC-D through the MEP Center. The MEP staff recruits students from high schools and junior colleges by visiting MESA clubs. In the fall, a special admissions process facilitates the early admission of qualified students. Again the emphasis on "qualified" applicants is to be noted. Incoming freshmen are invited to participate in a four-week or five-day summer program to prepare them for college life and to help them develop the study skills required for the rigorous engineering curriculum. MEP also works with other campus officials to assist students in securing housing, financial aid, and other key services.

A special orientation course is given in the fall quarter to help new students adjust to college life. Assistance is provided in course and career planning as well as opportunities for developing learning skills. Working as a team, the faculty, staff, and corporate representatives offer presentations to the newcomers. Special academic support is given through one-on-one and group tutoring services in key courses such as calculus, physics, chemistry, and in selected engineering courses. Additionally, a "survival skills" seminar is offered to help MEP students avoid academic difficulty. In addition to providing tutoring, the MEP center is a resource and information center that houses carer information, test files, a library of engineering magazines, and industry-donated computers for student use. To provide career development information, MEP sponsors many field trips and presentations by corporate representatives throughout the academic year. These events offer insights into the engineering profession and how to prepare for it. Particular attention is given to helping students develop the skills of self-assessment, resume writing, interviewing and job searching. Assistance is also provided for securing summer jobs in engineering-related work. Incentive grants and awards are offered to students with strong academic records by private industry and the National Action Council for Minorities in Engineering (NACME). UC-Davis has one of the largest groups of NACME scholars in California. MEP also offers periodic incentive awards as funds are available.

Rebecca Arrocha is an example of the kind of outstanding student that MEP in conjunction with MESA has been able to help. Rebecca transferred to UC-Davis from Modesto Community College. A high school dropout, Arrocha was a mother by the time she was 15 years old. Although she had always wanted to attend college, her husband did not encourage her to pursue her education as their family grew to three sons. After a divorce, however, she became convinced that education was the only way to ensure a better life for her children. Although she did have to wait until her sons were older, she took the General Education Development test and passed ten years after dropping out of high school. A combination of financial aid, Aid to Families with Dependent Children (AFDC), and child support allowed her to attend Modesto Community College as a full-time student. Modesto was one of the early community colleges to adopt a MESA program comparable to those developed at the precollege level. An obvious benefit of her MESA involvement was the transfer to the MEP program at UC-D. Her career goal now is to finish her bachelor's degree in Civil Engineering and to pursue a Master's degree in the structural engineering specialty.

California Alliance for Minority Participation. UC-D is an active participant in the California Alliance for Minority Participation (CAMP) that is turn is one of 20 Alliance for Minority Participation (AMP) centers funded nationwide by the National Science Foundation. Due to its federal source of funding, CAMP is able to focus specifically on underrepresented minority groups. The faculty and staff who work together in the CAMP program are dedicated to removing the barriers to minority participation at principal transition points within the science career pipeline. The AMP mission is similar to that of MEP, but is expanded to include science and mathematics students. Also a greater emphasis is placed on research participation and faculty mentoring. A specific goal is to double the number of underrepresented students receiving bachelor's degrees in science, engineering, and mathematics in the University of California system. CAMP provides monetary support to undergraduates in the form of research stipends for work conducted under the direction of a UC-D faculty member. CAMP also provides Workshops for Excellence Programs (WEP) coordinated by UC-D at the Los Rios Community College campuses in Sacramento and other community colleges in northern California. WEP are collaborative learning experiences for underrepresented students in science, engineering, and math. They are modeled after the Professional Development Program (PDP) developed at UC-Berkeley by Dr. Uri Treisman. Enrolled undergraduate students with United States citizenship or permanent residency are eligible for participation in CAMP programs. They are referred by the CAMP coordinator or directly accepted participation in CAMP programs. They are referred by the CAMP coordinator or directly accepted into an established research program. The underrepresented groups that are served by CAMP are African American, Hispanic American, and Native American students.

Mentorships and Opportunities for Research in Engineering. Mentorships and Opportunities for Research in Engineering (MORE) is an undergraduate research program for upper-division students providing funding to work on faculty and graduate student research teams. Over 30 students are served. MORE is a UC-D based program, but, like the statewide MESA programs, it has undergone a name change to reflect increased access to the program. Originally formed in 1987 as Minority Opportunities for Research in

Engineering, MORE had always included access for students outside the traditional MESA targeted groups, vis-à-vis Filipinos and women. College of Engineering funding and corporate sponsors made this possible. Now any student can participate, although recruitment efforts still focus on minorities and women. The primary goal of MORE remains to motivate students to seek graduate degrees. It provides an enhanced understanding of engineering principles by showing students practical applications. MORE helps to demystify graduate study by providing exposure to the research work of graduate students and faculty.

Center for Women in Engineering. Historically, women have been a very small fraction of the engineering profession. Until the early 1970s, women represented less than 1 percent of the graduating class of engineering schools nationwide (Henes, Bland, Darby, and McDonald, 1995). As a result of changes in math instruction at the precollege level (no longer discouraging girls from pursuing math courses), the number of female engineering graduates gradually rose during the 1970s reaching a steady state level of roughly 20 percent during the 1980s. With a slight drop-off nationwide in that percentage in the last few years, various institutions have increased their efforts to reverse this downward trend. At UC-D, the Women in Engineering (WIE) center has been formed to help develop a community for women students and provide support and resources for their pursuit of both undergraduate and graduate degrees. Funding from the National Science Foundation has been especially helpful in this formative stage. One of the goals of WIE is to encourage research on issues of gender in engineering and natural sciences. In this regard, WIE initiated the development, implementation, and evaluation of two faculty workshops in 1992 and 1993 to address the issue of women in engineering (Henes, Bland, Darby, and McDonald, 1995). The workshops were aimed at increasing faculty awareness of and sensitivity to the difficulties that women face. Secondly, the workshops were to encourage faculty members to generate specific ideas that they could use in their own teaching to enhance the learning environment. The third objective of the workshops was to develop a workshop model that could be disseminated to other engineering faculty groups or institutions interested in examining and addressing gender issues in the academic environment. A key message offered to faculty members was that becoming sensitive to issues that women face in the classroom enhances the learning for all students. The dissemination of the workshop results has provided increased awareness of gender equity in the classroom beyond the College of Engineering, as well as beyond the UC-D campus. As SP-1, SP-2, and Proposition 209 have included gender as a factor excluded from admissions and hiring considerations, various campus women's programs have had to reconsider their mission. It appears that the tradition of WIE and similar programs to include men as active participants in various panels and workshops meets the spirit of the new regulations. The activities of WIE have therefore not been significantly affected.

National Consortium for Graduate Degrees for Minorities in Engineering. A significant goal of our overall Affirmative Action Program is to increase the number of minority graduate students. At the graduate level, minority students are even more severely underrepresented. There is widespread agreement that only by increasing the number of graduate students can we, in turn, increase the number of minority faculty who will then serve as role models for undergraduates thereby increasing the undergraduate population further. A significant benefit to this effort is National Consortium for Graduate Degrees for Minorities in Engineering (GEM), composed of over 50 universities and over 60 corporations providing fellowships at member universities for Master's studies. Pursuit of the doctorate degree follows using institutional resources. The target population is the same as for MEP, but within an additional stipulation of United States citizenship. Given the long-range legal debate over Proposition 209 and the substantial amount of non-state corporate funding for GEM, this program is being allowed to continue to run essentially unchanged, with its focus on a narrow group of target minorities.

Summary and Reflections

In a period of substantial reevaluation of affirmative action policies, a useful exercise is to review a comprehensive set of programs associated with a single academic unit, the College of Engineering at the University of California, Davis. Through cooperative interactions, these programs involve students from the first grade through the doctoral programs. Precollege efforts prepare traditionally underrepresented groups for admission to undergraduate college programs in science, engineering, and mathematics. Affirmative action admissions policies ensure that a significant number of those underrepresented students qualified for admission to college programs are included in the admitted class. Once the students are enrolled, college-level programs provide well-established workshop methods for enhancing performance in technical course work. In addition, research mentoring experiences improve the chances for underrepresented students continuing for advance degrees. Ultimately, the completion of the Ph.D. degree is an essential prerequisite for entry into a university teaching position. Underrepresented faculty will provide critically needed role models for the next generation of undergraduate students. The actions of the University of California Regents and the voters of the state in the recent past years have caused many of these programs to be broadened, providing services to some students who were not traditionally underrepresented in the field of engineering. Nonetheless, the central goal of increasing the diversity of the graduating class at both the undergraduate and graduate levels remains the same.

The reaction of certain groups of ethnic students to SP-1 and SP-2 was one of shock and disappointment. Considering the many years of struggle faced by these groups to reach the university level, and the hopes for upward mobility of these students, we can certainly understand their response. The demographic predictions of the 1970s for California had been to conservative. For example, the increased immigration of Latino and Asian populations rapidly shifted both the total number of children in schools and their racial and ethnic balance vis-à-vis the white, non-Latino population. California has faced radical changes before any other state. In 1970 there were only 30 percent ethnic and racial minority students in K–12 public schools. After 140 years of predominant white enrollment, in 1990, 50 percent of the California public school students belong to ethnic and racial subgroups. There is no longer a numerical majority of whites. By the year 2030, white students will constitute about 30 percent of the total enrollment and Latino students will represent the largest group (44 percent of the total enrollment) (Valencia, 1991:17). Other school demographic projections suggest that the white school-age population will decrease for the country at large, while the Latino school-age population will continue to increase. Latino children (aged five to 17) numbered 6 million in 1982 (9 percent of the national youth population); by 2020 they will number 19 million (25 percent of the country's youth population). That is, the Latino school-age population will more than triple in eight years (Valencia, 1991: 18–19).

In the long range, attempts at curtailing the power, the visibility, and the active participation of ethnic minority groups in American democratic institutions, particularly school, will have the very detrimental consequences of destroying the democratic traditions of this country and its inherent strengths. But these efforts are particularly dysfunctional and irrational if we consider the demographic trends and the economic needs of American society during the next century. It would seem that rather than attempting to prevent the participation of minorities in academia, this is the time to make difficult roles in the century that is fast approaching. More than ever, we will need intellectual leaders, teachers, doctors, engineers, professionals in all the fields, technical experts, researchers, and business people with the academic and human abilities to interact with highly diversified populations both at home and abroad. This is the worst time to direct our hostility inward toward our own people as they make their best efforts to belong in American society and become productive through higher education training. The ultimate outcome of antiaffirmative action policies would be to make this country's population less competitive in the business world, in the professions that require high skills and serious interdisciplinary research approaches. It seems that the problem is not one of equity principles, but an ideological one tinted by racism, cultural or ethnic nativism, and simple myopia. We cannot turn the clock back, the reality of American society is that it is already diversified and in search of new frontiers in science and technology that will require a new ideology of tolerance and respect for cultural, gender, racial, and ethnic differences both at home and abroad.

References

American Association of Engineering Societies (1991). *Engineering Manpower Bulletin, No. 109,* May 1991.

Carspecken, P. F. (1996). *Critical Ethnography in Educational Research: A Theoretical and Practical Guide.* New York, NY: Routledge.

Chronicle of Higher Education, Almanac Issue, *Chronicle of Higher Education*, XLIII (1) Sept. 2, 1996, 17–26.

Cornelius, W. (1995). Educating California's Immigrant Children: Introduction and Overview. In R. G. Rumbaut & W. A. Cornelius (eds.) *California's Immigrant Children: Theory, Research, and Implications for Educational Policy* (pp. 1–16). University of California, San Diego. San Diego, CA: Center for U.S.–Mexican Studies.

Dreyfuss, J., & C. Lawrence III (1979). *The Bakke Case: The Politics of Inequality.* New York: Harcourt Brace Jovanovich.

Freire, P. (1973). *Pedagogy of the Oppressed.* New York: Seabury.

———. (1993). *Pedagogia da Esperanca: Um Reencontro Com a Pedagogia do Oprimido.* Sao Paulo, Brazil: Editora Paz e Terra, S. A.

Gamio, M. (1930). *Mexican Immigration to the United States: A Study of Human Migration and Adjustment.* Chicago: University of Chicago Press. (The 1971 Dover Publications, Inc. of New York reproduces exactly the 1930 version.)

Hayes–Bautista, D. E., W. O. Schink, & J. Chapa (1988). *The Burden of Support: Young Latinos in an Aging Society.* Stanford, CA: Stanford University Press.

Henes, R., M. Bland, J. Darby, & K. McDonald (1995). Improving the Academic Environment for Women Engineering Students through Faculty Workshops. *Journal of Engineering Education,* 14 (1):59–69.

Kilbourn, P. (1995). Women and Minorites Still Face 'Glass Ceiling'. *New York Times* (March 16) p. C22.

Klein, J. (1995). The End of Affirmative Action. *Newsweek* (Feb. 13), pp. 36–37.

Martin, P., & E. Taylor (1996). *Immigration and the Changing Face of Rural California: Summary Report of the Conference Held at Asilomar, June 12–14, 1995.* Unpublished manuscript, to be published in *Rural Migration News.*

Menchaca, M., & R. R. Valencia (1990). Anglo-Saxon Ideologies in the 1920s–1930s: Their Impact on the Segregation of Mexican Students in California. *Anthropology and Educaton Quarterly* 21(3): 222–249.

Mesa News (1995). Special Twenty-Fifth Anniversary Supplement, p. 4.

Miranda, L., & J. T. Quioz (1989). *The Decade of the Hispanic: A Sobering Economic Retrospective.* Washington, DC: National Council of La Raza.

Moore, J., D. Vigil, & R. Garcia (1983). Residence and Territoriality in Chicano Gangs. *Social Problems,* 31 (2):183–194.

Orfield, G., & S. E. Eaton (eds.) (1996). *Dismantling Desegregation: The Quiet Reversal of Brown v. Board of Education.* New York, NY: The New Press.

Palerm, J. V. (1994). *Immigrant and Migrant Farm Workers in the Santa Maria Valley, California.* Center for Chicano Studies and Department of Anthropology. University of California, Santa Barbara. Sponsored by the Center for Survey Methods Research, Bureau of the Census, Washington, D. C.

Population Today: News, Numbers and Analysis 24 (8) (Aug. 1996), p. 4–10.

Roberts, S. V. (1995). Affirmative Action on the Edge. *U.S. News and World Report* (Feb. 13), pp. 32–38.

Rodgers, H., Jr. (1996). *Poor Women, Poor Children: American Poverty in the 1990s.* Third edition. New York: M. E. Sharpe.

Rumbait, R. (1995). The New Californians: Comparative Research Findings on the Educational Progress of Immigrant Children, in R. G. Rumbaut and W. A. Cornelius (eds.), *California's Immigrant Children: Theory, Research, and Implication for Educational Policy* (pp. 17–69). University of California, San Diego. San Diego, CA: Center for U.S.–Mexican Studies.

Shackelford, P., & J. Shackelford (1995). Affirmative Action Defended: Case Studies in Engineering Education. *Multicultural Education* 3(1):25–26.

Smith, D. G. (1996). Faculty Diversity When Jobs Are Scarce: Debunking the Myths. *The Chronicle of Higher Education,* (Sept. 6), (B3–B4).

Somerton, W., M. Smith, R. Finnell, & T. Fuller (1994). *La Mesa Way.* San Francisco, CA: Caddo Gap Press.

Spindler, G. (ed.) (1955). *Anthropology and Education.* Stanford, CA: Stanford University Press.

Suárez-Orozco, C., & M. Suárez-Orozco (1995). *Transformations: Immigration, Family, Life and Achievement Motivation Among Latino Adolescents.* Stanford. CA: Stanford University Press.

Department of Bureau of Census. (1996). *Current Population Reports* published by the U.S. Department of Commerce, Economics, and Statistics, and Statistics Administration (June 1996) p. 2–5.

University of California Focus (1994–95). Medical School Admissions Policy Sparks Debate. *UC Focus,* 9(2):1.

Valencia, R. R. (1991). The Plight of Chicano Students: An Overview of Schooling Conditions and Outcomes. In R.R. Valencia (ed.) *Chicano School Failure: An Analysis Through Many Windows* (pp. 3–26). London, England: (Falmer Press).

Vigil, D. (1983). Chicano Gangs: One Response to Mexican Urban Adaptation in the Los Angeles Area. *Urban Anthropology* 12(1):45–75.

———. (1988). Group Process and Street Identity: Adolescent Chicano Gang Members. *Journal for the Society for Psychological Anthropology, ETHOS,* 16(4):421–444.

———. (1989). *Barrio Gangs.* Austin: University of Texas Press.

West, M. S. (1995). An Historical Overview of Affirmative Action. Address at the University of California, Davis. Symposium on Affirmative Action and Civil Rights, March 10.

Beatriz Calvo

6

The Policy of Modernization of Education

A Challenge to Democracy in Mexico

Public education in Mexico is offered by the State and, according to Article 3 of the Political Constitution, it comprises "all kinds and modes of education—including higher education" (Cámara de Diputados, 1993). However, elementary school (from first to sixth grade), and now secondary school (from seventh to ninth grade), are mandated by the State, while the State's duty regarding higher education is reduced to "promote and attend [to it]" (*ibid.*).

Public education dates to the beginning of this century and was an essential achievement of the revolutionary movement of 1910, that was generated by the conditions of injustice and great social inequalities that had been long in the making. Article 3 of the Constitution of 1917 offers education to the great excluded masses by establishing the right and obligation of every Mexican to receive elementary education and the obligation of the State to offer it. Public elementary education—and currently secondary education—has distinguished itself by three attributes that give it its popular character: it is free, mandatory, and nonreligious.

In 1992, Mexico began the latest education reform called the "Modernization of Basic Education," which was expressed in the form of a "new educational federalism." This official policy has given a new structure and meaning to Mexican public education and covers the levels of preschool, elementary, and secondary school, as well as teacher, indigenous, and special education.

Official rhetoric and discourse on this new policy reflect the democratic nature of education. *Democracy* as a value, is considered "... as a way of life based upon the constant economic, social, and cultural improvement of the people" (*ibid.*), that is, upon a collective wellbeing. Therefore, this value must be reflected in those things that impact the standard of living of the majority: employment, larger purchasing power of salaries, public safety, education, public assistance and health, food, housing, services, creation of culture, sports, and recreation.

Democracy, as a value, appears in the official discourse together with others that complement the definition of education. Thus, it also means *social participation,* understanding by this a society interested in social demands, in political processes, and matters such as ecology and human rights.

Solidarity supposes that as Mexicans, we should be especially committed to those who have less, such as marginal urban groups, peasants, and aboriginals of the poorer regions of the country. *Nationalism* means defending and protecting our political and economic independence, and increasing our culture. *Sovereignty* refers to autonomy in making those decisions that regulate the life of the country, of a region, state, or locality. *Equity* implies offering the same to all, but starting out from compensatory strategies, such as specific federal financial mechanisms to support the governments of those states that are lagging behind. By this, it is expected that the social and economic inequalities that exist among the groups throughout the country will even out.

These values allow us finally to speak of *justice*. Public education will be fair, as long as homogenous results are obtained, understanding by this a reduction in the differences in the standard of living of all Mexicans and the achievement of better living conditions for all. Homogeneity is not achieved by enforcing the same measures for all, but by following differential strategies; those who need more should receive more, and each group should receive what it requires. Not all of us need the same things, or in the same quantities. Individuals and groups all have their own requirements, but socially, economically, and culturally different ones. In education, this homogeneity means offering quality education for all, but with a differential approach, meeting the specific needs of the different social groups.

Translating these values to the field of education within a framework of modernization and federalism requires carrying out specific measures, such as allocating more money for education; achieving a true process of federalization and decentralization of basic education, therefore answering the historic problems of centralism, bureaucratism, and tending to regional needs in a specific way; and offering compensatory measures for the neediest of groups.

Regarding the school system, other measures include looking for mechanisms that allow students to remain in elementary school to graduation, reformulating curricula and teaching materials, with a national sense and with strong emphasis on local and regional matters, trying in this way to link directly educational processes with the realities of the students, and allowing education to be meaningful and useful.

A democratic education requires other measures as well, such as creating school councils for social participation at the national, state, municipal, and local school levels to promote the participation in education by parents, teachers, their union, and other sectors of the community interested in regional and local education; establishing new ways of organization, management, and functioning of the schools; bringing teachers up to date so they can be more professional; redefining teachers as social subjects and their professions from a broad and social perspective; raising and standardizing salaries of all teachers in the country, and improving their living conditions.

In this chapter some serious contradictions that exist between the official discourse on Mexican public education and reality will be approached. I will attempt to give specific historic content to the values that appear in the official discourse, especially democracy and justice. To do so, I will use empirical information obtained from a school located on the border region in the north of Mexico—the city of Juárez, Chihuahua, that lies next to El Paso, Texas.

The text is divided in four sections. In the first section, some theoretical and methodological aspects are explained. The second section includes a brief description of the historic context of the current educational situation. The everyday perspective is approached in the third part, including ethnographic information from recorded observations, testimonials by teachers, and life histories. I describe how the public educational policy is implemented in schools such as the one studied, and I try to approach the public and hidden speech of the teachers that has to do with the way they interpret, live, and feel the public policy modernization of education (Scott, 1990). In the final section, I present some reflections on the viability of modernized and federalized Mexican public education as a democratic process oriented toward "achieving better levels of social well-being" and, therefore, "better ways of life for Mexicans" (Cámara de Diputados, 1993).

Some Theoretical and Methodological Aspects

Certainly it is not new to say that there are contradictions or divergencies between what is said and what happens. However, the important thing is to detect the contradictions, point them out, and more importantly *explain them,* which takes us to the plane of concrete facts where these take place. To achieve this, it is necessary to approach to the sphere of study of social relations, from a *historical and everyday perspective* (Calvo, 1992, 1995). Relationships shape values and concepts under specific conditions. These nourish democracy and justice within a specific historical content, that in official rhetoric turn out to be abstract, general, and universal, that is, indifferent to cultural, social, economic, ethnic, and other specifics.

Through qualitative follow-up, the broader investigation, "Modernization of Basic Education: a Perspective from the Northern Border of Mexico," resolved to find out what happens in reality with the launch of an educational policy. This research intends to explain how a national education policy takes historically specific shape at the regional and local levels. For such purpose, during the school term August 1992–June 1993, when the modernization policy was set in motion throughout all the elementary and secondary schools in the country, I carried out an ethnographic project at a federal elementary school located in a peripheral underprivileged zone in the city of Juárez. I wanted to see how a poor school, like many others in the country, was modernized (Calvo, 1994).

The theoretical axis that has guided this research has been the new educational federalism. Its construction as a concept has required working on four levels of analysis: the discursive (official discourse and rhetoric), the normative (new legal and juridical framework of Mexican education), the operative (specific measures that follow "modernization," such as the new plans and curricula, educational content and teaching materials, continuing education for teachers) and the everyday perspective (educational facts at school and the classroom), which constituted the heart of the research. In such a manner, I try to articulate the micro or local processes within socially larger ones (Geertz, 1983; Erickson, 1986), since the discourse, the norm, and the operation are valid for all the country, that is, they relate to processes that have to do with the workings of the educational system at the national level.

I see these four levels of analysis as a process of filtration of official policy, that goes from the top down; that is, that flows through different levels and social spaces. During this flow, not all elements of the policy filter down and those that do, do not flow the same way. The way the official policy filters down depends on the juncture of conditions at every space and at every moment. Therefore, it is important to analyze how those policies, when they are implemented, run into power structures, with relationships between social subjects, with "institutive" forces, until finally arriving at "institutionalized" moments (Lappasade and Lourau, 1974). It is here that the everydayness of the facts gives content to the values, norms, and rules upon which the social subjects act and relate in concrete spaces.

In this work I wanted to know what aspects of the democracy and justice values that are part of the national educational policy and of the new educational federalism have filtered down, why they were able to do it, and how they are manifested in reality, that is, at the local level, where the everyday, the particular, the historical, as well as juncture moments happen.

In order to give concrete, historical content to these values we have to understand them as *concepts* that enclose relationships among social subjects, and that take a specific shape at certain junctures.

Historical Context: The Moment and the Space

The educational modernization came about at a concrete juncture that was delineated by the presidential administration of Carlos

Salinas from 1988 to 1994. Salinas promoted the neo–liberal project and that of modernizing the Mexican State, as a viable reality that would allow for the achievement of a democratic way of life. It was believed that the new economic model would increase productivity, make the economy competitive and, above all, would make Mexico part of the global market. Modernizing the Mexican economy was understood as a democratic process, since it meant entering the social landscape: the increased productivity would create jobs and increase purchasing power.

In education, modernization meant the launch of a new educational federalism. As a first measure, decentralization began in the national educational system. All matters related to education in every state that once had been operated and administered by the federal government would have to be solved by their respective state governments. It was believed that higher efficiency would ensue by rendering services with direct and adequate attention paid to regional and local educational needs.

It was already said that the values of public education acquire content in the field of the everyday, and this necessarily sends us to a specific place. In our case, it is a locality on the northern border of Mexico. The city of Juárez has been an important center of attraction for many diverse groups from all over the country. The economic development of the region during the last three decades, based on the *maquiladora* of twin-plant industry, offered employment for non–skilled workers. This type of industry relies on foreign manufacturing corporations allowed into the country—mainly from the United States—to assemble foreign-made components into both finished and unfinished products of all kinds. These products are shipped back to their country of origin, where they are finished, packaged, and distributed to customers. *Maquiladoras* take advantage of the abundance of labor in countries with high unemployment rates by hiring young men and women for very low wages. (Between 110 and 140 pesos per week, which currently, with the accelerated rate of devaluation of the peso, represents between 15 and 20 U.S. dollars for a 40–hour week).

On the other hand, Juárez' proximity to the United States means that the city is used as a gateway into the "American paradise," where men, women, and children become "illegals" and "undocumented" immigrants, and offer their cheap labor. Therefore, the *maquiladoras* and "going to the other side," are facts that distinguish the local culture of Juárez.

As a consequence, thousands of people, carrying on their backs their customs, traditions, beliefs, and ways of life, leave their place of origin that spans the different states of the Mexican Republic, looking for possibilities of subsistence, and take up new places of residence. Their children enter the schools of the regioń, which have been turned into veritable cultural mosaics given the complexity and heterogeneity of the student population. This reality has given a special hue to the local educational processes.

Macroprocesses and the globalization of the economy, through the twin-plant industry, are made present in this region and in the local education. *Maquiladoras* have been an undeniable source of work for thousands of women—single and married, many of them mothers of students in basic education public schools—and of young people of both sexes, graduates of the basic public education system (secondary level). The participation of these new groups in the regional economic development transforms the ways and routines of life prevalent for generations, and traditional schemes are being broken and family and social roles are being redistributed. Women have become a very important part of the family economy; many single mothers are the heads of their families. On the other hand, public schools at the local level, as the facts show, are carrying out the function of preparing young people to work as *maquiladora* workers, earning low wages.

On another level, phenomena such as the North American Free Trade Agreement (NAFTA) are generating new economic needs in this region. Many of these needs are solved through technological and higher education which prepares and trains skilled labor, new technicians and, although in lesser numbers, high level professionals. However, this education is reserved for certain social groups that make up the economic elite of the population.

School, Students, and Teachers

Studying a school as a social space is studying what happens in it (Geertz, 1989). I was interested in studying one school to find out what elements of the national education values filtered down, how these were interpreted by the different subjects, especially principal and teachers, and what shape they took. Understanding these processes within their space-time context requires explaining them within their institutional space.

Structural processes such as a general crisis, a change in the economy, new governmental policies, a harsher attitude in enforcing them, an increasing population, the fading away of the middle class, and an increase of poverty and extreme want, impact educational institutions. They do so by bringing about the implementation of policies for excessive utilization of existing resources with the consequences this entails, such as low academic achievement, high drop out and failure rates, absenteeism, overcrowding of city classrooms, rural classrooms simultaneously used by two or more groups of students that belong to different grades under the care of one teacher, etc.

However, these conditions are not the only ones that cause educational problems. There are new elements for explanation that recent qualitative investigation discovered. These refer to conditions of performance of the educational system itself and to its deficiencies, and have to do with everyday processes such as: training and continuing education for teachers, working conditions for teachers (institutional, technical pedagogical, administrative, material, labor, union, legal, political), ways and conditions of organization and management of schools (role of the school's principal, teacher organization, and ways for the community to participate in the school), supervision and consulting about the technical and pedagogical work of the teachers, their living standards, the presence of the teacher's union in education, and so on.

Periphery and Isolation

The school under study is located on a peripheral neighborhood of the city, yet it is relatively near its downtown area, and very near the Rio Grande, which serves as the border with the United States. This area, like many other poor neighborhoods in the city of Juárez and other cities in Mexico are affected by serious social and economic problems such as low family income, substandard living conditions, unemployment, alcoholism, delinquency, prostitution, unsanitary conditions, lack of public services, and other factors.

The school was relatively isolated. Aside from suffering from a lack of urban services, it also lacked educational benefits. Little attention was paid to it from its educational authorities (advisers and supervisors) as from their union representatives. In that regard, a teacher said: "Nobody ever wants to come here . . . Many say that this is a school of punishment [since it is at the periphery]. We are told: If you misbehave, we'll send you there . . . "

The school took care of students with severe problems. Their parents, among them many single mothers, worked in jobs that generally paid low wages. They were workers in the *maquiladoras,* in the construction business, in the informal economy, or else, "in whatever they can," as the teachers explained. Others crossed the border daily to work in El Paso, offering their cheap labor. And there were also many unemployed parents.

Functioning

This school, like every school, was directed by the official ordinances and bylaws established by the Department of Public Education (Secretaría de Educación Pública, hence SEP) and valid throughout the country. The adaptation—or the lack thereof—of the national aspect to their local reality was the source of serious problems that were felt daily by the teachers as they worked. Let us see how the school functioned.

Economic and Material Conditions. The lack of economic resources is a situation that distinguishes federal public schools. The federal government does not usually give them a budget; it generally gives them office and janitorial supplies that usually do not last for the year.

This reality has forced schools to look for ways of generating their own resources. These schools have demanded that parents "cooperate" with a family fee that parents give the principal on registration day at the beginning of the school year. These funds are used for teaching materials, sports equipment, cleaning tools, and for school maintenance.

The family fee is a generalized and informally instituted practice at public schools that has now become, through the years, an unwritten law. That is, the fees function as a veritable tuition, since they are not "voluntary," ignoring the fundamental constitutional principle of free public education (Mercado, 1991). The parents who cannot pay the "cooperation" will not be able to register their children. During the 1992–1993 academic year, the school under study charged 30 pesos (approximately U.S. $90) per family, an amount similar to what is charged by schools located at the outskirts of the city. Other schools located nearer downtown, in more affluent areas, which are attended by middle– or lower–middle class students, set fees that go from 60 to 250 pesos (approximately from U.S. $180 to $750), depending on the economic situation of the surrounding area. These numbers are based upon the 1992–1993 rate of exchange. Currently, due to the peso devaluation, these fees can go from U.S. $5 to $90.

For that reason, schools did not function under the same economic conditions. Those schools where parents have more money are generally located in more urban sites near or around the downtown area. Those parents will be able to give more, and, therefore, the school will have a larger budget. In this way the need for teaching materials and equipment are solved. Those schools with poor parents that are often located in peripheral zones of the city can give little and their needs will be proportionally solved.

In part this situation explains why the school functioned under deficient material conditions. Even though its facilities were of good construction materials, the classrooms had lighting problems. Natural light was not always sufficient and there was no money for light bulbs. The school also lacked a ventilator for hot days and some rooms had firewood stoves for the winter.

There was no library; a small room served as principal's office, but also as reception area, an infirmary, a place for the punishment of students, a cafeteria, and a rest area for teachers. It goes without saying that bookshelves, file cabinets, telephones, fax machines, televisions, and computers were but a dream. The furniture of the classrooms was made up of single- and double-writing desks. These were old, damaged, and even broken, and often there were not enough desks for the students.

The school also did not have teaching materials. Teachers and students had only the free official textbooks, two geometry sets for teachers and some maps, all circulated through the nine classrooms. Moreover, chalk had to be rationed by the principal, and teachers requested parents to buy materials, such as paper, scissors, pencils, erasers, and glue for their children, or else the teachers would have to buy these materials themselves.

The material conditions under which the teachers had always worked worsened with the arrival of modernization, and this caused many of the teachers to reject it. The modernization program required specialized material that SEP never provided. Modernization meant two things: either the teachers acquired the required teaching materials out of their own pocket, or else, they went without it, worsening still the deficiencies of the pedagogic work.

Organization of the Teaching Personnel. The school, which offered grades first to sixth, functioned with one principal and a teacher to every class. There were ten teachers in total. With the exception of two teachers who had taken some courses in higher teacher education (equivalent to a bachelor's degree), the rest, including the principal, only had a basic teacher education (equivalent to a high school degree plus one year of undergraduate study).

The teachers had to carry out several activities as part of their daily duties; they had to tend to their groups, which generally had from 35 to 45 students; they played the part of physical education coach, since the school did not have one; and they had to offer special attention to children whom they deemed needed it, since the school also lacked a psychologist and a social worker. Furthermore the teachers spent a great part of their academic time in two other activities that Mexican school culture has made mandatory. First they had to prepare the students for traditional academic contests among schools that belong to the same district; rehearse the routines for the honor guard for the nation's flag in official ceremonies; and prepare the festivities for Children's Day, Mother's Day, and Christmas, that meant time needed to rehearse dances, choral poetry, singing, and gymnastic numbers.

Second they had to do the work entailed by their assigned commission. The organization of teachers in commissions is traditional in Mexican public elementary schools. Usually the commissions are intended to meet the needs of the schools. Thus, if there is no nurse; a teacher had to head the first aid commission; if there is no one hired to keep the order, another teacher would be commissioned as school guard; if a janitor was needed, another teacher, along with her or his group of students, would clean the school grounds and the restrooms; also, every teacher and his or her students would have to clean their classrooms every day before leaving, so it is ready to be used by the afternoon shift. In turn, the afternoon students must do the same. This is an everyday ritual that takes at least 15 minutes.

Because of all this, the time devoted to teaching was greatly reduced.

Bringing Teachers Up to Date: Pedagogic Seminars and Technical Counseling. Continuing education for teachers is one of the most serious problems of Mexican education, given the impact it has at the national level. According to the legislation, it is the responsibility of the SEP to bring elementary school teachers up to date. For that reason, with one week left before going back to school, SEP simultaneously organized in all the states of Mexico, training seminars on the new modernizing programs that would be implemented in that school year. The activities and contents were the same throughout the country.

In five days the teachers were supposed to be "modernized" on the pedagogic principles of education, which basically meant they had to undergo radical changes to their regular methods of scheduling by objectives breaking down in detail the corresponding activities, as had always been done. "The teacher/researcher," the "freedom" and "creativity" of the teachers to choose their own ways of working, the pedagogical techniques of "teaching through play," and "freedom in the classroom," all were meant to make the teacher into a constructivist. This entailed the difficult task of breaking away from old and deep rooted behaviorist schemes acquired from teacher education schools and reinforced during their experience as teachers, and forced them to take on new attitudes and roles. It is obvious that qualitative changes such as the ones charted by modernization, which have to do with processes of formation and not with information only, are not accomplished with such courses.

The new plans and curricula and teaching materials of a national nature constituted the axis of the training. Excluding the regional contents, it formed the fundamental aspects in the proposal of the new educational federalism. It was explained that education would no longer be organized by areas of knowledge (social and natural sciences) as had been done with the former program used since 1971, but by subjects instead (such as history, geography, or ecology) as had been done before the 1971 programs.

It was also said that for the first year of modernization the definitive teaching materials would not be available; these would be ready in 1994. For that reason, work would have to be done using "emergency programs" (given their character of urgent and provisional), that included four sources for teaching material: two new ones made specifically for this year, a manual used in the previous school year, and the free text books from 1971 that dealt with education by areas of knowledge.

According to the explanation of the teacher who offered the training, the teachers should learn to find the objectives in one source and look for the content in others. The content was scattered through different sources. Finally the teacher should locate the corresponding activities for the content in the free textbooks of the 1971 program.

This information did not clarify modernization for the teachers, but confused them even further. The technique, and not so much the content of the programs, the "how" more than the "what" and the "what for," became their main concern and greatest worry, since traditional teaching had always relied on it. Teachers had always been instructed to carry out their work in a directed manner and had always been told how to do it.

Therefore, telling them all of a sudden about "creativity," "freedom," and about their role as "researchers" did not make much sense to them. Their anguish grew when they saw, one week before the beginning of classes, that they did not have clear explanations on the handling of emergency programs or anything on the four sources.

Another way of bringing teachers up to date was by means of technical counseling as a permanent service for teachers during the school year. But in the school of study, the technical-pedagogic problem was compounded by the lack of this service during the whole year. Teachers hoped for the presence of the counselor assigned by the authorities to support them. They felt that the counselor would come to solve as "by magic" their problems, since she kept "the secret" of the technique. "Permanent technical counseling" suffered from two great deficiencies.

On the one hand, the visits from the technical counselor were quite scarce—four or five during the entire year. Moreover, when the counselor finally did come, she only worked part of the morning with first-grade and second-grade teachers who requested it. On the other hand, the counselor's skills were questioned by the teachers, who doubted her capability to manage the modernization programs. She had received special courses for counselors about the emergency programs, in an improvised manner, just like the teachers. Several of them would comment about it:

> She is somebody nobody wanted in the afternoon shift [for political reasons] and then they "relocated" her. She isn't one who really knows what she is doing. . . . When [the educational authorities or union representatives] don't know what to do with someone, they relocate them. Just imagine, one day a teacher asked her for help in I don't know what. She didn't know and told her: 'let me check into it, and I'll tell you later,' and she never came back.

The Principal and Administrative Tasks. The Mexican educational system privileges administrative matters. They take the form of official dispositions coming directly from the high authorities in SEP in Mexico City, and are assumed as mandatory by local authorities, including the school principals. Principals can interpret, assume, and implement the administrative dispositions almost as they see fit. School principals give their own characteristic touch to the school she or he directs, depending on her or his inclinations toward administrative or pedagogical matters.

In the case of local authorities, as well as that of the principal of the school considered in the research, it seemed that they were more interested in the form of the dispositions, made into rituals, that in their substance. The school principal never lead the pedagogic work. He did not have the teachers meet to discuss the new programs for modernization, the educational content or the way they could solve their common problems. The freedom of teachers, a new principle established by educational modernization to encourage their creativity and interest in research, was interpreted by him as not interfering in their classrooms; that is, to remain outside and uninformed of what happened in there; not making collective decisions or supervising the teachers' work.

Paper work and administrative activities took a great deal of the teachers' time during the workday. This was the case with the new registration forms that the teachers had to fill out and submit to SEP. This became quite an event. For several days the school's activity was centered around filling out those forms. Teachers lived for them, neglecting their teaching jobs. There were two "great problems" with the forms: one related to the instructions for filling them out, and the other dealt with information requested about the students.

The "very complicated" instructions for filling the forms out had to be closely followed, according to the principal, or else the computers would not be able to process the information: *z* had to written with the plus sign; *o* had to be written as a vertically slashed zero; all numbers up to nine had to be preceded with a zero; all capital letters had to be used; nothing could be scratched or crossed out; and black ink had to be used. The principal exploited this "difficult and delicate" work to exert pressure, and assert his authority, over the teachers. He did not employ his power in matters of education; his power lay in administrative matters.

> You mustn't make mistakes; if you do, there are no more sheets and these are official; we can't make photocopies. If there's anything wrong, SEP won't take them, and what's worse: all the forms are counted. There are no more. Therefore, nobody can make mistakes.

The second problem had to do with basic information that the forms requested about the students: first names and last names, names of the mother and the father, and birth dates. Some children used the mother's last name, causing confusion: "In those cases they don't have a dad. Then, the child is listed as the mother's sibling."

But the situation took a turn for the worse when the teachers discovered how difficult it was to get the birth dates of all the children. For one thing, the school did not have a school archive, lacking any personal documentation about students as well as about teachers. For another, many children did not have a birth certificate. Getting this data gave rise to a chaos that tortured the teachers and forced them to abandon their duties as teacher for many days.

They turned to many alternatives. For instance, they asked the parents to estimate the information: "Well, I got married in such year and I had the boy two years later. Then, he must have been born . . . "; or else, they calculated it themselves: "It would seem that you are about eight years old." This problem got so bad, that according to a teacher:

> Now the principal wants us to do temporary birth certificates. . . . We have to ask the parents to do a makeshift one: "I, so and so, certify that my son is so and so." Just imagine, I had to make dates up! The other teacher did the same. And so did the others. It's all full of mistakes. What's going to happen when it's all compared to the official certificates?

So, administrative tasks, and the principal's concern about enforcing them harm effective teaching by subordinating it to bureaucratized control routines (Ezpeleta, 1989).

Collegiate Organizations. Two collegiate organizations had to function at the school according to the official modernizing ordinances: a technical council and a social participation school council. The first one, by official regulation of SEP, must be composed of the principal and teachers of each school. The modernization tried to refunctionalize and make this agency into a true collegiate and collective work space. However, in practice it continued working according to tradition: for discussion of administrative issues (distribution of the groups among the teachers, organization of the teaching body into commissions, definition and modification of schedules, student discipline, etc.) and for the preparation of special events: Mother's Day, Children's Day, Christmas and get-togethers. Pedagogic matters were not appropriate to be dealt with; every teacher had to solve them by herself or himself.

At heart there was not interest by the principal or the teachers in making the technical council work according to its goals. The principal expressed that interest in the first meeting of the technical council at the beginning of the school year. All the teachers agreed with him.

> We are going to deal with administrative matters. . . . This is just administrative stuff. We can't deal with everything. . . . We are going to appoint the Technical Council. We are going to define the duties of the teacher on guard. . . . We are also going to check schedules, positions, contests, books and campaigns, general matters. There are just too many things.

Regarding the councils for social participation, which were created by the modernization of education with the purpose of enhancing participation in pedagogic matters from the parents and their associations, teachers and their union, authorities from government and education, as well as the groups of the local community, these were never established. The teachers opposed their creation for several reasons, among these, because it implied working longer hours and they were not willing to do so. Moreover, they saw parent participation on pedagogic matters as an encroachment in matters that did not rightfully concern them, and as supervision for the teachers, things that "there is no way we will ever allow."

This attitude had to do again with a Mexican school tradition. Parents are not expected to intervene in technical-pedagogic matters. Moreover, that is the way it should be according to the regulations for parent associations issued by SEP. This custom is adamantly defended by the teachers. They consider education their exclusive prerogative.

Salary Conditions, the Standard of Living, and Teachers' Disillusionment with Their Profession. In the Mexican teaching system, full time means the time in front of a class. It does not include the time required for preparing classes, carrying out collegiate work, or for professional enhancement. This situation is especially serious in secondary education in which fulltime teachers have to work with ten, eleven, or more classes, each one with approximately 50 students. It means that teachers have to teach, evaluate, and grade at least 500 students at a time.

If we add to this the very low salaries teachers belonging to the public educational system receive, we can easily understand why their working and living conditions have become a deep problem. For many teachers, a fair wage would be the solution of their personal problems, as well as for their educational ones. As long as the current salary does not cover their basic needs, they will have to look for additional jobs, which are detrimental to them personally, as well as interfering with their teaching assignments. Not only in the City of Juárez, but everywhere in Mexico, teachers hold two, three, or even four jobs, or work fulltime teaching, or look for work outside of teaching.

At the school, seven of the eight male teachers, including the principal, had to perform other work outside school hours: by working a second job in the afternoon shift in another school (elementary or secondary); by selling cigarettes or lottery tickets; by working temporarily as farm laborers in the United States; and even by promoting cockfights. The two female teachers had one job each. During the afternoon they would tend to their homes and look after their family.

Work situation and salaries were topics often discussed by the teachers:

> As long as teachers don't have a worthy salary. . . . One of the great problems is having to hold two jobs. A teacher works then ten hours. What time do they have to prepare for their classes? They return tired. They only want to take a shower, have dinner, and go to bed.
>
> Teachers earn an average of 900 pesos (approximately 300 U.S. dollars in 1993). Some of them are paying for their own home. They take away from them 30 per cent. They end with . . . nothing. That's why we . . . no longer dedicate ourselves 100 per cent to teaching nor professional enhancement. To come here, all teachers have to spend for gasoline or two *rutas* [a type of collective transportation]. That comes out of our salary.

In the face of the simultaneous presence of several factors (low wages, having several jobs, attention to large classes made up by children with so many problems, the lack of true training and professional improvement, the lack of adequate and sufficient material and technical-pedagogic conditions, as well as technical support from educational authorities), the teachers showed an understandable decrease in interest for teaching. A testimonial can give us a good idea of their position toward teaching:

> At this school . . . there are so many children that they can't and don't learn. Moreover, teachers don't adapt to each child's learning pace. . . . The children learn what they can from 8:00 until 12:30 and that's it. If they learned, fine, if they didn't, too bad. And another thing, teachers just have to run to another job.

This situation is not unique. Teacher salary policy has to do with the national educational system budget. It was during the eighties that teacher salaries began a process of deep devaluation, and when the dissident movement inside the teachers' union was at its peak, it became quite popular so say "they make believe they pay us, we'll make believe we work,' which, as we can see, is still heard and practiced."

From the Everyday to Official Discourse

What Was Learned During the School Year

What did students learn during that first year of modernization? In sum, we can say that teachers, even those who in the beginning of the year had tried to carry out the modernization programs, after having improvised a few months, were defeated by obstacles beyond their control. For that reason, little by little they went back to their usual teaching methods. A teacher said: "If you visit every classroom, you will see that all back to the old program. They are still using the free textbooks [from 1971]. We are ignoring the objectives of modernization."

During that year, two things were emphasized by teachers: national over regional content, and elemental skills over other knowledge. The combination of both gave as a result an education that emphasized teaching writing, reading, and basic mathematics (addition, subtraction, multiplication, and division), virtually excluding the acquisition and development of other skills, as well as acquiring other knowledge, especially that having to do with regional content.

But this situation, which apparently contradicts official, government rhetoric, is not really contradictory. According to the National Agreement for Modernization of Basic Education, signed in May 1992 by the Secretary of SEP, the 31 governors of the states and the general secretary of the teachers' union, established what seems enough for the children to learn in public basic schools.

In a paragraph, this document presents the discrimination of educational content in skills and knowledge, and ranks them according to their importance:

> The *FOUNDATION* of basic education are *READING, WRITING,* and *MATHEMATICS, SKILLS* that are to be grasped at an *ELEMENTAL* level but *FIRMLY.* . . . *SECONDLY,* every child must acquire a *SUFFICIENT KNOWLEDGE* of the *NATURAL AND SOCIAL* dimension on the environment where they will live, as well as about themselves. . . . (Secretaría de Educación Pública, 1992).

Not only was this thinking present in the official rhetoric, but in practice, this criteria became operative for discrimination and ranking. The official forms for grading the students instructed the teachers that in order to promote the students from one grade to the next they should have a minimum passing grade of 6.0 on a scale from 1.0 to 10.0 in Spanish and mathematics (that constituted the national content), regardless of the grades obtained on their other subjects (social and natural sciences that had to do with local and regional content).

So it seemed that children really were not expected to learn very much. It seemed enough for them to graduate from school and be able to read, write, add, subtract, multiply and divide. In practice, the emergency programs asked for little; therefore, the teacher could work little and yet comply with the requirements; as a result, students learned little.

Through the year it was common to hear teachers say: "I do what I can as I can." And in fact, they did what they could as they could. This phrase, far from being taken as an excuse of the teachers, is quite suggestive. Analyzing closely its meaning allows us to approach the way teachers, as subjects, constructed their teaching practice.

In spite of the fact that what happens every day at schools and more specifically inside the classrooms, has little to do with the official rhetoric of educational policy, and despite the series of adverse conditions that beset teaching, *teachers are always subject, and as such, they relate to knowledge, to their students, to other teachers, to their principals and supervisors, to the parents, and more importantly, they keep teaching, continually defining themselves as teachers, they keep on constructing their own educational practices every day and, therefore, their students keep on learning.*

Reality and Values

What concrete meaning did democracy and the other values that accompany it take on in specific situations as part of the educational modernization? Has the new education complied with its function to achieve collective wellbeing, especially of underprivileged groups, in this case the school beneficiaries (students, teachers, parents)? The specific everyday conditions in which educational work was carried out take education away from these values. The marginal, isolated situation of this school as that of many others does not allow us to speak of equality, solidarity, justice, that is, of democracy.

The lack of federal economic resources is a serious problem that troubles public schools in general, but in poor schools this situation is even worse. The material resources given in kind are very little. Besides the problem goes hand in hand with another. The "obligatory" cooperation from parents to the school are in proportion with their economic possibilities. And, since these are meager, so is the quality obtained. Therefore the needs are unsatisfactorily solved.

Marginal schools suffer from another deficiency—a lack of capable teachers. The farther away a school is, the less attractive it becomes for teachers, since that remoteness has implications of lack of resources, difficulty for getting there, socioeconomic problems of its community of students, non-cooperative parents, etc. It is common that less prepared teachers, or recent graduates from teacher schools with no experience, are assigned to these schools. The teachers must "earn" the privilege of working at "better" schools: nearer, with more resources, and with fewer problem students. Instead of having better prepared teachers serving needy schools, just the opposite is true.

Social participation is not brought about with laws or by decree, especially in schools such as this one where there is little commitment to education, and where there are long standing traditions among Mexican teachers, such as the feeling that education is their exclusive "property." But, on the other hand, to demand that parents, overwhelmed with family and money troubles, participate on these boards makes little sense. Their time is devoted to working to be able to survive. Their presence and participation in educational processes is, therefore, no much.

If we speak of solidarity, we find little at marginal schools. They do not have the support, attention, and interest from educational authorities. Therefore they function under autonomous processes that do not promote self-management processes or political maturity from the subjects for making decisions that direct and benefit education in their community, but rather that suggest loneliness and subjection to local dynamics that do not allow them to work together with the system as a whole. Teachers at these schools can only share their solitude (Galván, 1991).

About gratuitousness, it has turned out to be a myth. Public basic education not only exacts fees from its less fortunate beneficiaries—students and parents living in underprivileged communities—but also from teachers. Parents, besides paying for registration expenses and for acquisition of teaching and support materials, must also give money and their labor to improve their children's schools. Teachers feel forced to acquire, out of their own pocket, teaching and support materials. That is, in one way or the other, public basic education is not free. Then, if this is so, how do we comply with the constitutional mandate of obligatoriness when parents have to, and sometimes can not, pay for the education of their children, and the State has no economic capacity to comply with this obligation?

Also, equity, which implies equality of opportunity for all Mexicans to enter and remain in the educational system, as well as to receive a quality education, and justice, which implies giving more to those who need it more and giving what each social group needs, by differential strategies with the goal of achieving homogeneous results, are uncertain values.

Not all Mexican children enter the educational system, and those who can, do not do it under conditions of equality. Situations outside the school, such as extreme social, economic, and family problems that the students have to live with every day are reflected in poor performance. Internal processes, generated through inadequate and insufficient material, technical and operative conditions, also prevent us from speaking of equality in education. The same education is not offered in the school of this study as that offered at other public schools that are less isolated and neglected. Neither is it the same as that offered at other more marginal and forgotten schools, such as many rural and indigenous ones.

The value of justice takes on a certain empirical shape. What is differential seems to be misunderstood as what is *different.* Thus, our education if differentiated in that it offers a firstrate education, as well as a secondrate one, and even a thirdrate one, depending on who the beneficiaries are. Let us remember again that urban area schools have better circumstances: a direct relationship with authorities, supervisors, and technical counselors; enough teaching and support materials; students who come from the middle class; better economic resources; more affirmative participation from the parents; teachers with higher levels of education; and so forth. And schools away from the city function under circumstances of greater isolation. Remoteness and isolation go hand in hand with poverty. Poor schools are the ones that require more and better attention. But the opposite happens; the schools that have fewer economic resources and function under a deficiency of material and didactic conditions, the ones forgotten by the educational authorities, and the ones that have the least prepared teachers are the ones that get the least amount of attention.

Let us return to the city of Juárez and see the meaning that basic education, and consequently, the value of justice acquire at a regional level. First, basic education is subordinated to productivity. Productivity has become an important value determined by the neo–liberal model and by a market economy, more than by social needs, and it takes on a concrete shape in this region with the presence of *maquiladoras*. It has meant an important source of employment that requires nonskilled personnel. Therefore this industry is interested in young graduates from public secondary schools (equivalent to seventh, eighth, and ninth grades), since the job requires only that the applicant be 15 years old and have a secondary school diploma.

Second, intimately related to the previous topic, productivity and *maquiladoras* are related to the hierarchy of knowledge as determined at basic education schools. The National Agreement for Modernizing Basic Education defines as a priority the skills related to reading, writing, and basic mathematics. *Maquiladora* workers do not need more. The twin-plant industry is concerned only that the job applicant can read, write, and do basic math operations. Industry's main interest is not on what their workers know about the social and natural sciences.

Third, the acquisition of skills and knowledge has to do with living conditions. Graduating from a secondary public school opens a possibility for young people who do not have the resources and conditions to continue studying due to their social and economic situation, of entering the job market occupying subordinate positions. This, more than being a way to improve their standard of living, means a way for them to survive.

At this moment of deep and almost permanent crisis plaguing all Mexicans in all aspects of life, the constitutional values of education seem to get farther away from reality. Popular education in Mexico has been a synonym with public education, and it will continue to be so for as long as the historical conditions allow it.

Changed lifestyles for many families which used to keep a certain standard of living has forced them to look for alternatives that, even though they prevent them from living in the same way, at least allow them to substitute some things for others. It is the same for education. The economic crisis is giving rise to the trend of students who before could afford A private education and that now in some way will continue to study, but at public institutions. Therefore those whose only possibility of study was at a public institution, will no longer be able to do so. As a consequence, the differences between opportunities of education of the most privileged groups and those with less money, will broaden ever more, leading to a loss of the democratizing principles that sustain public education. We could run the risk of continuing to have public schools in name only; in practice they would be just like private ones. Where would obligatoriness, equity, equality, justice, and democracy stand in public education?

A Light at the End of the Tunnel

The current landscape that characterizes Mexican public education evidently does not seem flattering. However, getting to know the realities from a historic-everyday perspective yields some benefits.

One of them refers to the advancement toward theory construction and the search for new explanations for educational facts that surpass and overcome the traditional ones. It means discovering new data and carrying out new readings of the realities. In this same sense, the historic–everyday perspective takes us to the field where day-to-day educational processes and social relations are constructed. Education is in continuous movement, transformation, and construction by subjects that participate in it every day.

Therefore, we cannot speak of a future for education that is predetermined or predictable. It is an open future, subject to the shape given it by social relationships at specific moments. For that reason, it is an encouraging future. Subjects concerned with education acquire a great responsibility with this way of conceptualizing education, since we understand it as a collective alternative for construction of original and necessary paradigms based on new epistemological supports. That means that we now must turn our attention and look in a different direction, that is, from the bottom up, and from the inside out. In other words, our commitment must be to privilege the local and everyday accounts and the "attempt to position the popular sectors as social actors at the centre of educational processes," in order to search for new conditions for transforming "political-pedagogical consciousness; promoting resolution of immediate problems in daily life, and distilling organisation of the popular sectors around cultural preservations and participatory democracy, comprehended in its most profound ramifications" (Austin, 1995).

One way, among many, of channeling this commitment is looking for spaces for participation. I would like to mention an experience: the workshops where the teachers carry out the hard and sometimes burdensome work of collective reflection. In these spaces, each teacher retrieves her or his own daily experience from what happens in their schools and classrooms. Based on this, teachers rescue themselves as social subjects and become protagonists in their own history. It means breaking with traditional paradigms with regard to the historic role that education, the teacher, and the teaching-learning process play. The teachers' experiences then are no longer unexamined, mechanical, and disjointed tasks, and become collective construction. "Making the invisible visible" out of what happens in the arena of everyday life, we will be able to understand the implicit assumptions to be found in teaching. These new elements of interpreting educational facts will push aside rituals that are performed many times without awareness. They will make education and teaching into actions that will strive toward transforming local educational realities and spaces, that is, into their schools and classrooms. With great effort, teachers will begin to transform their own teaching practice. The changes that can be foreseen in this pedagogic alternative, are not "national," they are woven, they are constructed at concrete places. These are qualitative transformations in which every situation finds its own solution.

References

Austin, Robert (1995). "Second Thoughts on the Third Phase of Popular Education: Towards a New Popular Pedagogy." Unpublished manuscript. Brisbane, Australia.

Calvo, Beatriz (1992). "Etnografía de la Educación" en *Nueva Antropología, Revista de Ciencias Sociales, XII* (42):9–26. México.

———. (1994). "Modernización de la Educación Básica en la Frontera Norte de México: Una Experiencia ethnográfica en una Escuela Federal Urbana." *La etnografía en Educación: Panorama, Prácticas y Problemas* (pp. 329–370). Centro de Investigaciones y Servicios Educativos de la Universidad Autónoma de México.

———. (in press). "Ethnografía de la Educacion: Una Perspectiva Histórico-Cotidiana." In Mario A. Rivera and Luis Fernández y Zavala (eds.) *Evaluación Programática y Educacional en el Sector Público: Enfoques y Perspectivas. Washington, D.C.: Organization of American States, Government Printing Office.*

Cámara de Diputados, Congreso de los Estados Unidos Mexicanos (1993). *Constitución Política de los Estados Unidos Mexicanos*. Mexico, D.F.: Congreso de la Union.

Erickson, Frederick (1986). "Qualitative Methods in Research on Teaching," Merling Wittrock, (ed.), *Handbook of Research on Teaching*. Third Edition (pp. 119–161). New York: MacMillan Publishing Co.

Ezpeleta, Justa (1989). *Escuelas y Maestros: Condiciones del Trabajo Docente en Argentina.* Santiago, Chile: UNESCO.

Galvan, Luz Elena (1991). *Soledad Compartida: Una Historia de Maestros.* Publication #28. Mexico, D.F.: Ediciones de la Casa Chata.

Geertz, Clifford (1983). "From Natives Point of View: On the Nature of Anthropologial Understanding." In Morris Freilich (ed.) *The Pleasures of Anthropology* (pp.). New York:

———. (1989). *El Antropólogy Como Autor.* Madrid, España: Paidós Studio.

Lapassade, George, & René Lourau (1974). *Clavez de la Sociología.* Barcelona, España: Laia Publishing Co.

Mercado, Ruth (1994). *La Educación Primaria Gratuita: Una Lucha Popular Cotidiana.* Mexico, D.F.: Departamento de Investigaciones Educativas del Centro de investigación y Estudios Avanzados del Institute Politécnico Nacional.

Secretaría de Educación Pública (1992). *Acuerdo Nacional para la 1992 Modernización de la Educación Basica.* Mexico, D.F.: Secretaría de Educación de la República Mexicana.

———. (1993). *La Ley General de Educación.* Mexico, D.F.: Secretaría de Educación de la República Mexicana.

Scott, James (90). *Domination and the Art of Resistance: Hidden Transcriptions.* New Haven, CT: Yales University Press.

Robert DeVillar

7

Indigenous Images and Identity in Pluricultural Mexico

Media as Official Apologist and Catalyst for Democratic Action

The Notion of *National Cultural Unity:* Its Rhetoric, Practice & Consequences

The sociocultural development of many minority culture groups in the Americas is framed within an extraofficial context of subordination to the dominant national societies, despite that any or all of these national contexts may be officially self-described as democratic (cf Yinger, 1994:167, *passim.*). In his work *México Profundo, Una Civilización Negada* (loosely translated here as *Deepest Mexico, A Civilization Denied*), for example, Bonfil (1990:11) states:

> The coincidence of power and civilization at one extreme, and subjugation and civilization at the other, is not by serendipity, rather the inevitable result of a colonial history that to now has not been eradicated from the heart of Mexican society.

The official rhetoric in these dominant culture contexts expresses that minority groups are seen as integral parts of the nation's democratic enterprise, or in the process of continually integrating themselves toward this end. There is a question as to how substantive change in their actual status—whether social, political or economic—can occur when dominant institutional practices belie institutional rhetoric. Stavenhagen (1994:78), for example, makes clear that although Mexico's National Indigenous Institute (INI) is "the principal vehicle of the government to integrate Indians into the national society," its ability to effectively address the indigenous circumstance is compromised since in "modern Mexico, the concept of national culture was founded upon the idea that indigenous cultures do not exist" other than as a reference to its past (p. 78).

The following discussion addresses principles that sustain or constrict the schism in Mexico between the official rhetoric which seemingly advocates democratic inclusion of indigenous groups and official practices that actually move significantly toward it. Making an issue of the degree to which a particular national (minority) group has a right to conserve and develop that set of elements which comprises its cultural identity is itself a significant power peculiar to the dominant cultural group. At the same time, the very need to address the question through minority group voices, resources and actions—and those of minority group rights advocates—attests to the perceived expendability of the minority cultural paradigm by the dominant culture.

The drama of minority group cultural existence—the right to identity in a self-designated democratic nation—is particularly evident in the print and images conveyed through the mass media, a form of expression which is increasingly accessible to indigenous groups. In this presentation, the recent indigenous rights events in Chiapas, Mexico will serve as an example of the official and minority voices, resources, and practices that characterize modern armed conflict settings in Mexico, to illustrate how this interplay sustains or constricts the schism between official democratic rhetoric and actual democratic practice. In a subsequent text (DeVillar & Franco, this volume), a second example will compare and contrast how two indigenous groups attempting to achieve the same end through different means each utilize media: the Zapatista insurgency in Chiapas—an example of armed conflict—and the Ñähñu, or Otomí, cultural community in the Mezquital Valley in the state of Hidalgo, Mexico. This latter example addresses the use of indigenous voices, resources and actions to produce native language videos of contextual relevance for purposes of internal community dialogue and cultural action to preserve and develop their identity within the larger cultural settings in which they inevitably interact.

Mexican Media: Apologist vs. Change Agent Orientations

The rhetoric-practice schism in Mexico, and the mechanisms by which it is kept in place, have been graphically represented and enjoyed widespread distribution since the Mexican Revolution (1910–1921). The popular, eerie engravings of José Guadalupe Posada (1852–1913) and the majestically emotive murals—didactic, anti-capitalist, pro-indigenous, worker-centered—of Rivera (1886–1957), Orozco (1883–1949), and Siqueiros (1896–1974) provide a common note which still resonates within that which is graphically Mexican. These artists through their works captured especially well the tragedy which persists in Mexico and which bemused writers of their era (for example, Samuel Ramos [1897–1959], *Profile of Man and Culture in Mexico;* José Vasconcelos' [1881–1959] notion of *the cosmic race*), those immediately following their era (e.g., Octavio Paz [1914–], *The Labyrinth of Solitude*), and the present (e.g., Roger Bartra, *The Cage of Sadness: Identity and Metamorphosis of the Mexican*): the conflictive development of the Western self through the ambivalent denial of the indigenous identity. Bartra's (1987:127–128) succinct interpretation embodies the yet-to-be-resolved cultural conundrum haunting Mexico:

> The Revolution is an impressive spectacle for the intelligentsia: by some strange manner those who seemed destined to live with their heads bowed rebelled and were transformed. At the bottom of the wells of the Mexican soul there is more than mere sadness: there is also an unsuspected potential for violence. It is possible—many think—to take advantage of that energy to create the new man, so as to place the Mexican in the current of world history. To do so requires finding the true personality of the Mexican, discovering his authentic spirit. This is the obsession of Antonio Caso and, above all, of José

> Vasconcelos. The muralist school and the so-called novel of the Mexican Revolution contribute to the search for the true *I* of the Mexican, submerged in the sad otherness of the strange beings exiled from their native Eden . . . It should not surprise anyone that the submissive peasant rise like a *Zapatista* revolutionary and that "progress" transforms him into a new man: the proletariat, hero of the modern age.

The question remains active in popular debate as to whether the soul of this indigenous cultural group—which, however much stifled, continues to palpitate after 500 years—should be eternally stilled and forever fossilized as a revered museum piece in the memory of the Mexican mind, or allowed to develop unfettered to unleash the creative power of the existentially complete Mexican; or, as Mexican writer Enrique Krauze (1994:9) points out, at least to not continue to make a total mockery of Mexican democracy.

> Mexico is the land of anti-democracy . . . a system that perverts democracy through electoral fraud, corruption and patronage. In Mexico there is no republican, representative, democratic federal regime . . . as our constitution proclaims. Rather, we have a kind of six-year paternalistic monarchy dressed up as a republic.

The international intelligentsia and informed media specialists are well aware of Mexico's brand of democracy, its structural mechanisms, and its likely consequences:

> Unlike most of Latin America, Mexico is not a recognisable democracy with alternating governments. A strong, centralized bureaucracy has ruled the country since the revolution, with the Institutional Revolutionary Party (PRI) as its electoral vehicle. Elections have been marked by fraud and other biases in the PRI's favor . . . Now it has become a liability. At the top, it stifles independence of thought and impededs accountability. At the bottom, state and municipal governments cannot hope to respond to the inequalities (which NAFTA will exacerbate) between a prosperous north and a poor south . . . Above all . . . the PRI has ceased to be an effective transmis-

> sion belt for the tensions and conflicts of an increasingly complex and diversified society. (The clash in Mexico, *The Economist,* Jan. 22, 1994:15)

The North American Free Trade Agreement (NAFTA), a trade agreement among the nations of Mexico, Canada and the United States, which formally began on January 1, 1994, was ostensibly then-President Salinas's shining path along which Mexico was to transport itself to modernity, upon the wheels of his platform of neoliberalism. Early projections in reputable media were less sanguine:

> Even before Chiapas, skeptics feared that Mexico was condemning itself to having to sprint in a competitive world when much of its economy was still learning to walk unaided. NAFTA, momentous as it is for Mexico, is merely a trade agreement which in itself can guarantee neither growth nor prosperity and which involves none of the social and regional funds that the European Union offers its poorer members. (The Revolution Continues, *The Economist,* Jan. 22, 1994:19)

That same January 1st, the Zapatista National Liberation Front (EZLN)—an indigenous insurgent army seemingly led by Subcomandante Marcos—occupied six towns in Chiapas, including Altamirano, Ocosingo, Las Margaritas, and San Cristóbal de las Casas, at which the EZLN declared war on the Mexican government, proclaimed NAFTA a "death sentence" for the Indians of Mexico, and announced the EZLN's ten-point manifesto: "work, land, shelter, nutrition, health, education, liberty, democracy, justice and peace" (Zapata's Revenge, *Time,* Jan. 17, 1994:33). Their Declaration from the Lacandon Jungle read, in part:

> We are the product of 500 years of struggle: first against slavery, in the war of independence against Spain, then to escape being absorbed by North American expansion . . . we have nothing to lose, absolutely nothing, no decent roof over our heads, no land, no work, poor health, no food, no education, no right to freely and democratically choose our leaders, no independence from foreign interests, and no justice for ourselves or our children. But we say it is enough! We are

> the descendants of those who truly built this nation. We are the millions of dispossessed, and we call upon all of our brethren to join our crusade, the only option to avoid dying of starvation! (Simpson & Rapone, Why did Chiapas revolt?, *Commonwealth,* June 3, 1994:16)

In today's Mexico—understandably rent by armed civil strife, by political assassinations, corruption and intrigue, by economic convulsions—media serves as the stage upon which the struggle for an inclusive, if not synthetic, Mexican identity plays itself out before a mass, captivated audience. Although the official culture dominates the national media (cf. Riva Palacio, 1992), the stone of the minority voice can momentarily still its goliath-like threat of inevitable advance and censure. Cockburn and Murray (1994:20[3]) provide a recent example of media repression momentarily gone awry in the early stages of the Chiapas uprising:

> Most Mexican get their news from TV, particularly the Televisa Network, owned by Emilio Azcárraga, one of the five richest men in Latin America, which captures ninety per cent of the viewing public . . . Azcárraga is a major supporter of the government . . . Televisa's news programmes presented grotesque misrepresentations of the [Chiapas up] rising. The [insurgents] responded by disinviting the TV giant from the peace negotiations, and judiously selecting friendly newspapers and other TV channels for its communiqués. Meanwhile, angry crowds in Mexico besieged Televisa's headquarters. (Cockburn & Murray, A Fistful of Promises, *New Statesman & Society,* 1994:20[3])

These voices of Mexico—now indigenous, now official; the one unpredictable, captivating, yet rare; the other, a bee's drone whose mutant sting is its incessancy and omnipresence—are captured by contemporary Mexican and international media in contexts of intra- and intergroup struggle. These are contemporary voices assailing, as Paz (The Media Spectacle Comes to Mexico, *New Perspectives Quarterly,* 1994:59[2]) states, old, yet unresolved, issues:

> The [Chiapas] rebels are not proposing to change the world . . . Their demands, many of them justified, are directed toward

> mending traditional abuses and injustices against indigenous communities and asking for the establishment of an authentic democracy. This last point is an aspiration as old as the Revolution of 1910.

These are voices that are relentlessly driven to the pursuit of cultural identity despite exclusion. These are voices which combat the repressive operating principles alluded to earlier that thwart movement toward democratic inclusion.

The Voice of Repression

Rhetoric toward indigenous groups carries with it institutional actions of high visibility and geographic extension but of minor significance in terms of serving as mechanisms of democratic, inclusionary change, whether economic, political or social. At the beginning of his six-year term (1988–1994), for example, President Carlos Salinas de Gortari established the National Program of Solidarity (Pronasol) to coordinate collaborative works throughout Mexico between communities in need—including indigenous ones—and the national government, that is, the Institutional Revolutionary Party, or PRI. The PRI has been, as is all too well known, in continuous power since 1929. Over the past few years and particularly the past three, however, it has witnessed widespread challenge to its hegemony—in the provinces by voting blocs and armed movements, and nationally, through its self-destructive internal conflict. During the Salinas de Gortari presidency, however, Solidarity's supposed integrative and democratic accomplishments were touted biweekly in the *Solidarity Gazette* (*Gaceta de Solidaridad*), the party's propagandistic organ for the program. *As indigenous groups in Mexico tend to be marginalized physically as well as socioculturally, the dominant rhetoric proclaims the governmental obligation to help them in their integrative development. This rhetoric implies that the inability of the indigenous group to integrate reflects cultural elements that are, on the one hand, in conflict with development or modernity and, on the other, related to an embedded indigenous cultural deficit.*

The August 15, 1994 issue of the *Gazette* illustrates these principles in the words of a PRI functionary:

> *The Otomí–Tepehua region, in the State of Hidalgo, is one of the zones having the greatest marginalization in the country . . . [I]ts respective communities suffer from all of the backwardness that poverty carries with it: dispersion, serious deficiencies in basic services, insecurity, injustice, illiteracy, health problems, and lack of communication, among others . . .* [W]e have spurred participation on the part of the communities, but also democracy . . . This is very important taking into account that the Otomí–Tepehua region, due to its very backwardness, has for years suffered from the presence of a host of diverse chieftains . . . In order not to contribute to the reproduction of that problem, what we are now doing is trying to avoid rule by chieftains (page 30, original emphasis).

Attending more to the program's actual intent than to its rhetoric, Teódulo Guzmán's report (1993:7) exposes the acknowledged embedded impotence of Pronasol's impact:

> Currently, the National Solidarity Program (Pronasol) is presented as a glorious entity, even with its own patron saint celebration to Solidarity. However, even government officials have criticized it for not being tied to a macroeconomic policy that has a clear intent to redistribute income, congruently assign fiscal resources and restructure the productive base of the most backward regions.

These institutional actions are evident even at the broadest level of national policy. In 1992, for example, through a constitutional amendment, Mexico for the first time recognized the legal right of indigenous communities, their people, customs and forms of organization (Stavenhagen, 1994). A similar program to Solidarity of Salinas' was the National Farm Support Program (*PROCAMPO*). Although having quickly retro-mutated into a traditionally predictable PRI "vote–buying mechanism," under analytic scrutiny it was not considered sufficient even in its original form to compensate the maize growers for the losses incurred by having to compete with international price levels introduced through NAFTA (Summa & Harris, Chiapas storm, *dollars and sense,* January/February, 1995). This coercive "buying favors" approach, however, is not predictably as successful as in the recent past. In Morelia, Chiapas, for example, government officials offered the townspeople an expensive corn grinding mill and "generous" agricultural credits in exchange for PRI votes. The townspeople rejected the offer and voted unanimously for the popularly-oriented ("left-of-center") Democratic Revolutionary Party (PRD), a result that Summa and Harris (1995) attribute to the positive democratizing influence of the Zapatista insurgency.

Official rhetoric, moreover, fails to recognize either the role of the dominant group in the current subordination of any minority group or that structural subordination presently is institutionalized within its own geopolitical borders. On the contrary, official rhetoric tautologically asserts that whatever inferior state in which a minority group finds itself is due to features found within the same minority group. Mexico's indigenous groups in prehispanic and recent times have participated in a communal land practice which ensures that whatever modest amount of land members hold, it will remain in their possession. Since the Mexican Revolution (1910–1921), this right has been assured—and fought for in courts and in the fields—through Article 27 of the Mexican Constitution, a right which then-President Salinas repealed in 1992 to accommodate the demands of national and foreign investors who desired those lands (*Multinational Monitor,* 1995; Summa & Harris, 1995).

An editorial in *The Economist* (January 22, 1994) critiqued this action specifically in terms of Chiapas:

> Mr Salinas's land-tenure reforms, which have allowed communal farmers to buy or sell their own plots . . . do little for the Chiapas Indians, whose land has been stolen from them by rapacious incomers, often under the complaisant eye of corrupt state officials and judges.

There is widespread consensus among Mexico's intellectuals and reporters in the international media that the conditions in Chiapas are among the worst in Mexico and that state politicians and commercial interests there continue to exacerbate the schism. The words of Paco Ignacio Taibo II (1994:406[5]), a Spanish-born

Mexican writer of national and international acclaim, reflect perspectives found generally in media descriptions regarding the subordinate status, economic misery, and powerlessness of the Chiapan indigenous groups, and peasants in general:

> Fifteen thousand indigenous people have died of hunger and easily curable diseases in Chiapas in the past few years. Without crop rotation, the fields are not very productive. The price of coffee has dropped, so the landowners have seized more land for cattle; they create conflicts between the communities and assassinate community leaders. Although the land cannot feed any more people, the population has been growing by 6 percent annually with the arrival of indigenous refugees from Guatemala and the internal migration of Indians whose land has been taken by the owners of the large haciendas. All this in a region where there is no electricity, 70 percent of the population is illiterate, most houses have no sewage systems or hookups for potable water and the average monthly income of a family is less than $130.

Especially poignant are the consistent accounts enumerating the hardships, punishments and death toll of indigenous and peasant community leaders in their struggle for democratically sanctioned cultural and socioeconomic self-sufficiency and determination against the super-wealthy landowners of insatiable material appetite:

> By 1990, 15,000 indigenous people were in prison on charges related to land conflicts, and in the last 10 years over 30 peasant leaders have been assassinated (Simpson & Rapone, *Commonwealth,* 1994:16[4]).
>
> Since mid-summer, at least 2,000 Indian peasants who are [Party of the Democratic Revolution, or P.R.D.] sympathizers fled their homes to seek refuge in distant villages because of harassment by bands of armed PRI followers, who burned houses and made threats, with guns and machetes, according to refugees, human rights monitors and opposition party officials. (Preston, *New York Times International,* Oct. 16, 1995) Chiapas is an actively racist state; its cattle ranchers enlisted moonlighting policemen, soldiers, and ranch hands

> to terrorize—and, fairly often, to murder—the Indian peasants who . . . were daring to organize themselves (Guillermoprieto, *The New Yorker,* March 13, 1995:43).

Hernández (The new Mayan war, *NACLA Report on the Americas,* March–April, 1994:6) reports on the public voice given to racism and related acts of violence by the *élite* in Chiapas even in the early 1970s:

> In the Ocosingo Lions Club, as recently as 1971, there hung a sign that was the ranchers' motto: "In the Law of the Jungle it is willed/that Indians and blackbirds must be killed." Threats, jailings and killings of peasants—sometimes at the hands of the ranchers' private armies, other times the result of the army or a judge acting on the ranchers' behalf—fill the pages of Chiapas' tabloid press. Several international human rights organizations, among them Amnesty International and Americas Watch have documented these attacks.

These overtly racist behaviors were occurring at the same historical moment, report Simpson & Rapone (1994), when Bishop Samuel Ruiz began his efforts to organize the indigenous community in this part of Chiapas to give voice to their grievances through the Indigenous Congress.

Pathetic as the Chiapas situation is—compassionately so in the case of the indigenous and peasant community; contemptuously so in the case of the private and government sectors—other states, such as Oaxaca and Guerrero, are infested with similar, and even worst, politically-instigated blight gnawing persistently, rabidly at their cultural and socioeconomic circumstance. Michael Serrill, in *Time* magazine (Jan. 17, 1994), paraphrased Peter Hakim—president of Inter–American Dialogue, "a think tank and forum for exchange among leaders in the hemisphere—[as saying that] the gap between haves and have-nots is wide, and inequity and discrimination are rife." Hakim is quoted in the article (p. 33) with respect to the implications of such anti-democratic official actions: "With those kinds of abuses—alienation, disaffection, isolation, exploitation . . . the prospect of some kind of uprising is always there."

This principle of minority culture deficit operating in tandem with the principle of the majority culture turning a blind eye to its own blatant and violent contribution to sustained subordination also may operate, and indeed be reproduced, in the one-way (i.e., from minority culture to majority culture) integrationist strategies of minority leaders (cf Said, 1993; Munslow, 1992). In reviewing more than a hundred Mexican and international press accounts dating from January, 1994 to late 1995, however, there was not a significant presence, much less a pattern, of indigenous voices in conflict with the uprising in Chiapas. Whether *integration,* perceived as a sociocultural force leading minority groups into the majority context, is more appropriate than *marginality,* perceived as a preferred state undergirded by concommitant expectations of cultural self-determination, is not the fundamental issue. The main problem is that either scenario reflects a rhetorical platform structured and perpetuated by dominant groups who actually have sufficient power to continue their self-development while persistently limiting the cultural development possibilities of marginalized groups (cf Yinger, 1994:234–238). One particularly effective form of limiting cultural development is through differential acculturation.

Differential Acculturation: Selective and Restrictive

The phenomenon of acculturation, as applied here, occurs in those instances where a group labeled by the dominant culture as being outside of, or foreign to, it, nevertheless finds itself in physical or social contact with the dominant group. Differentiated status carries embedded within it the notion of equity and its internal elements: access, participation and benefit (DeVillar & Faltis, 1991, 1994). The differentiated group's developmental possibilities are positively related to their type and degree of equity status within the dominant culture. Their quantity and quality of contact with relevant social, political and economic institutions (including formal education) of the dominant culture are directly related to the ultimate benefit they will derive as a group from that experience. Thus, the degree to which a particular group acculturates is bound significantly to the type of integrative channels made available to the differentiated group by the dominant group. If the group is perceived as significantly similar to the dominant group in physical appearance, value system, religion, historical or potential status parity, then the type of acculturation process to which they are exposed will lead the outside/foreign group in relatively short order to a status significantly similar to the first class citizenship accorded nativeborn dominant culture members. If, on the other hand, the group is perceived as significantly different from the dominant group along these same parameters, then the acculturation process to which they are subjected will work to maintain their outside or foreign status regardless of the amount of native–born generations produced by the outside or foreign group within the dominant group geopolitical context (see DeVillar, 1994a, 1994b for initial elaboration upon this and the following points).

Clearly, under the above conditions, the simple fact of having been born within a particular national context designated as democratic does not guarantee *socialization,* applied here as the process of integrative guidance to the culture and its institutions reserved for newborns considered natives to the dominant culture. *Successful transmission, interaction and internalization of the socialization process results in enculturation, that is, the state of the general consensus that one has become a full-fledged member of the native context. Successful socialization also implies that those who have internalized the culture's guiding principles will be, at once, its inheritors (cultural preservation through transgenerational social conformity) and architects (cultural regeneration through cumulative transgenerational development*). In this manner, the culture sustains the fundamental principles associated with its survival formula and pretends to refine itself indefinitely.

Conversely, minority group members who are native to the national context are generally perceived by the dominant culture as foreign and in need, not of socialization, but of acculturation. Thus, indigenous minority groups find themselves in a peculiar type of cultural existence characterized by the imposition of severe restrictions on their cultural development within their native geographic, and nominally national, context. Factors which superseded mere birthright include skin color together with other physical features, native/ancestral language, cultural ancestry, ancestral geographic origin, and religion, among others.

Acculturation, moreover, is comprised of two major classes: restrictive and selective (DeVillar, 1994a, 1994b). *Restrictive acculturation,* a segregative phenomenon, is applied to those *groups* whose features are considered significantly different from the dominant group. There are two types of *selective acculturation,* but integrative in nature: *Type I* applies to those *groups* whose set of composite features is considered significantly similar to those of the dominant group; *Type II,* to *individuals* from any restrictive group who, by exception, gain entry and success—however fleeting—within the dominant culture.

Such forms of acculturation, and the relegation of minority groups to the restricted, inevitably means that the restricted group loses the strength of its own voice—that is, its unique form of interacting within, perceived control of, and understanding of its cultural context, both historically and in the present. In its place is a *subdued voice,* that of a culture denied, permitted only that which has been sanctioned by the dominant culture to remain or that has been effectively hidden from it. In any case, what remains will be slight, and without the necessary force to significantly influence on a sustained basis the democratic enterprise within the majority culture, much less forge its own significant alternative cultural trajectory—not even as a minority culture.

Culture and freedom are interdependent; to the extent that minority cultures survive in subjugated circumstances, however subtle, they are bound significantly by the norms and values of external dominant cultural forces and, at best, in a continual process of reaction, albeit to seek freedom and equality through peaceful or armed, overt or covert, means. In short, *minority groups of restricted status are characterized by their dependency, albeit involuntary, and reaction in the vise of the cultural dynamics forged by the dominant group within and external to the minority context.* Subjugation does not of course equate to minority group cultural paralysis. The following discussion elaborates upon the interactive nature of the dominant-subordinate relationship.

Dominant–Subordinate Intergroup Dynamics

Subordinate marginality does not imply complacency (Yinger, 1994:169), since the minority group will continue to greater or lesser degrees its search, and to fight—as in the recent case of Chiapas—for those forms which will assure its authentic cultural survival and voice. Nevertheless, the limitations imposed by the politics of the majority context are of sufficient strength to preclude the expression and development of the more potent features of the minority culture. At a snail's pace and with little possibility of eventual success, the minority groups will continue their incessant march toward cultural resolution, particularly to regain or attain control and development of their own economic and socialization elements—including their native language.

Even within this rather bleak scenario, as a predictable form of consolation-cum-condescension, *the dominant culture will permit the least threatening but visually strong cultural characteristics of the minority group to exist, such as traditional garb, music, dance, typical foods, and festivities, among others, associated with holidays from the ancestral cultural context. Additionally, the dominant culture will adjust its official rhetoric, widening its rhetorical parameters to extol the value that minority culture contributions have made to the general national context.*

Through these means, the dominant culture maintains the myth of unity, freedom and democracy, as it reaps economic benefit from consumerizing the typical and folkloric, and keeps cultural stereotypes vitally intact (cf Stavenhagen, 1994:79). Within this model of purposeful subordinate marginality, the dominant culture neither seeks, nor, even less, values, the social or professional integration of minority groups, although on an exceptional basis individual members (Type II) from the restricted group are able to cross over into selective acculturation membership (Type I).

Cecilia Rodríguez, the U.S. Coordinator of the National Commission for Democracy in Mexico (NCD), makes reference to this dominant group practice of duplicity in describing Mexico's official government dealings with the *Zapatistas*:

> People have to realize the dual face of the Mexican government. [It first sent] the head of the Justice Department of dialogue with the EZLN. In that way, they gave sort of a *de facto* legitimacy to the EZLN. However . . . [by later] labeling the [Z]*apatistas* as terrorists and criminals, the government has essentially shown the other side of their face, the real

side; their intent was never to deal with the EZLN in good faith (The Zapatista struggle: An interview with Cecilia Rodríguez, *Multinational Monitor,* April, 1995:17).

The ebb and flow of minority group discourse and action with the official sector is perpetual and the goal predictable: Continued insistence on minority group transformation from its historical circumstance of second class citizenship to equal first class citizenship status. *Equality, in turn, carries with it the expectation that the group will participate completely in the rights and responsibilities of the nation, influence and contribute to its direction and development, and fully enjoy the benefits associated with first class citizenship.*

At the same time, a concommitant minority group expectation is that its particular collective identity will not be significantly sacrificed, even though the group is well aware of the need to negotiate its own vision in light of the complex reality within which it interacts with the dominant culture (cf Parenti, 1988: 308–317). In fact, negotiation between groups so distinct—the one extremely powerful, the other without adequate material or institutional resources—is difficult, and so, while the discourse process may eventually or at times lead to semblances of change, transformative social change itself—in this case, democracy at the pluricultural level—remains abstract and distant, perhaps at the moment increasingly distant, although the struggle is constant.

Too, the dominant culture is allied with other cultural groups of similar ilk in other settings. Mexico, for example, has had an especially contentious historical relationship with the United States since the U.S.–Mexico War of 1848 in which Mexico lost territory to the U.S. including Arizona, California, Colorado, New Mexico, and Texas. Mexico has an equally contentious economic relationship with the U.S. since the Porfirio Díaz regime (1877–1880; 1884–1911), in which foreigners were encouraged to invest heavily in Mexico. Nevertheless, official government and business ties between the two nations have continued to develop, the latest being the NAFTA agreement, which has brought some 50 billion U.S. dollars to Mexico. These binational ties between partners—however unequal—cut from the same materialist cloth can carry with them similar attitudes, perspectives, and judgments toward the role of minority groups and the exercise of democracy. An analysis circulated on Capitol Hill by Riordan Roett, an expert on Mexico employed by Chase Bank, relative to the steps that the PRI should take to thwart the zapatista movement, was summarized and quoted in part by *Time* (Feb. 20, 1995:9):

> The Mexican government, still reeling from the peso crisis, must "eliminate" the opposition in the rebellious southern state of Chiapas . . . and should "consider carefully whether or not to allow opposition victories [even] if fairly won at the ballot box." And indeed, President Ernesto Zedillo's soldiers rolled into Chiapas last Thursday to crack down on the rebels and arrest their leaders as criminals.

Said (1993: xix) alludes to the historical precedent for such reactions—prevalent since Western Europe came in contact-*cum*-conquest with Africa, Austral-Asia and the Americas, and criticized by Joseph Conrad in *Nostromo* (1904)—and predicts their continuation by United States institutions with international interests and a lamentably *au courant-yet-passé* attitude of imperialistic destiny:

> . . . The United States government is still unable to perceive, as it tries to implement its wishes all over the globe . . . At least Conrad had the courage to see that no such schemes ever succeed—because they trap the planners in more illusions of omnipotence and misleading self-satisfaction . . . and because by their very nature they falsify the evidence.

In short, the dialectic tends to reflect a struggle—at times circular, dormant, festering, silent or physically active, but rarely permanently resolved on the side of equity—between the dominant and subordinate classes, each in a sensitive but not predictable relationship with the middle calss, itself increasingly weakened in economic and political strength (Bardhan, 1993). Reavis (Chiapas is Mexico, *The Progressive,* May, 1994:28ff) refers to the diminution of purchasing power across Mexico since 1982:

> Across Mexico, the purchasing power of urban families has declined by about 60 per cent since the oil crunch of 1982 put neoliberalism into the presidential seat. Maquiladora [inter-

> nationally owned and operated assembly plants in the northern states of Mexico] workers who labor in American-owned plants are as poor as the rest: base wages run $4 to $5 a day, and top scales halt at $100 a week. In comparative terms, Mexican factory pay is lower than that in Hong Kong, Singapore, even Haiti. Neoliberalism's push to keep wages stagnant and food subsidies low brought about most of the decline.

The struggle itself relates to *the practice of the construct democracy in contrast to what this construct encompasses in its ideal semantic sense.* The notion of democracy is strongly held within subordinated groups; it represents concretely what rights they are entitled to as denizens and allows them to envision the ways and means by which they can influence development, stability, and prosperity. At the same time, *the notion of democracy is strongly supported in the rhetoric, although not in the practices, of the official government*—witness, for example, the Mexican Constitution, particularly with respect to land distribution rights for all Mexicans, although the clear intent was the landless tillers, mainly comprising mestizo peasants and indigenous groups (Article 27).

Salinas, the epitome of the Mexican neoliberalist political figure, international darling of the Bush administration and U.S. mainstream media, repealed Article 27 in 1992, enabling the private sector to purchase previously unsellable lands:

> President Salinas introduced a shift in Mexican agriculture that only a Western stooge, World Bank economist, or Cortes would have dared to try. In 1992, he steered through amendments to the Mexican constitution that repealed the promise of land and, for the first time, also permitted the sale and encumbrance of ejido [common] plots. That is why Subcomandante Marcos, in his hyperbolic way, accuses Salinas of plotting indigenous suicide. The disappearance of *ejidos* would wipe out the roots of Mexican culture (Reavis, *ibid*).

It is little wonder that the topic of equally distributed justice plays a prominent and enduring role in this uneven and persistent negotiation process.

Although the prospects for resolution, or even for significant movement toward particular agreements, are not encouraging between the Chiapan indigenous groups and the official government, the enterprise of insurgency may well continue undaunted. Rodríguez (*Multinational Monitor,* 1995:18) explains the willingness of the insurgents to struggle tirelessly in terms of world views:

> You have this clash. Even if we didn't have the Chase Manhattan Bank report that calls for the *Zapatistas'* elimination, even if we didn't have the statements of financial leaders in Mexico that call for the elimination of the *Zapatistas,* that's the reality. They must eliminate the *Zapatistas* because those two world views completely clash, and the survival of one means the elimination of the other.

Rodríguez presents a decidedly pessimistic scenario; one that implies that monoculturalism is the natural human response in this case rather than a negotiated bi-, multi-, or syncretistic-cultural reality. Certainly, evidence sustaining a democratic imperative is as strong as that which sustains its hegemonic counterpart; the difference being that the former remains a vision to be achieved through struggle, while the latter is a reality maintained through coercion.

Thus, alternative scenarios of coexistence—if not conviviality—between cultures in permanent contact and persistent conflict within Mexico are important to understand and offer a gauge of democratic possibilities or their lack. It is to the notion of culture and intercultural coexistence in pluricultural settings, and the characteristics of dominant–subordinate interactions within them, that we now turn.

Domination's on the Notion of *Culture* and Related Terms

The construct *culture* in pluricultural contexts, self-designated by a dominant group as democratic, does not lend itself to simple or precise definition, either in reference to a single group within the larger national context or to the unified amalgam of groups that are perceived as culturally distinct. *Culture, as applied here, is understood to be the codified yet dynamic survival formula of a particular group, that demands constant interaction and negotiation with its immediate context to preserve and improve the group's circumstance across time and space* (see DeVillar, 1994). The phenomenon and results of cultures in contact within the same geographic context impose developmental restrictions upon this particular notion of the term *culture*. The most historically obvious and widespread example of cultural developmental restriction is one culture being dominated by another.

A cultural group ultimately becomes dominant over other cultural groups through subduing them—in the denotative sense given in *Merriam Webster's Collegiate Dictionary,* tenth edition, 1993:1171: "to conquer and bring into subjection." In the modern era, that is from the period of Western global expansion which dates particularly from 1492, cultural contact was followed by an act of violent domination, engaged in by Spain and Portugal, at the beginning, and, by 1800, to an even greater degree, by France and England, although many other European countries were involved to a lesser degree.

The general attitude and thrust toward the task of dominating the lands they invaded—which expanded from 55 percent of the earth's surface being held by Western powers in 1800 to 85 percent by 1914—is, I think, illustrated particularly well by Said (1993:8) in his depiction of U.S. expansionism:

> There were claims for North American territory to be made and fought over . . . ; there were native peoples to be dominated, variously exterminated, variously dislodged; and then, as the republic increased in age and hemispheric power, there were distant lands to be designated vital to American interests, to be intervened in and fought over . . . Curiously, though, so influential has been the discourse insisting on American specialness, altruism, and opportunity that "imperialism" as a word or ideology has turned up only rarely and recently in accounts of United States culture, politics, history.

Subsequent actions of the dominant group will, not surprisingly, influence the degree to which the subordinate group is included, excluded, restricted, or exploited within the geographic context in which it attempts to interact in accordance with its particular survival formula (cf Horowitz, 1994; Stephens, 1993). The dominant group, then, is practicing culture in the operational sense of the term as described above; the subordinate groups are not. Rather, subordinate groups practice involuntary cultural repression ("to prevent the natural or normal expression, activity, or development of . . . ," *MWCD,* 1993:993) through suppression by the dominant group, whether blatant or disguised—("*sup•press . . . 5 a:* to restrain from a usual course of action : ARREST . . . *b :* to inhibit the growth or development of : STUNT," *MWCD,* 1993:1185).

The subordinate group of restrictive acculturation status neither has control over the significant implementation of its particular principles of survival nor the probability of integrating itself at the whole group level within the dominant group's context to significantly influence the democratic process—of which it is supposedly a part—or, much less, its outcomes. The process of negotiation—that is, involvement in those acts of communicative exchange which produce shared meaning as a result of equitable participation and consensus—theoretically serves to direct, influence and sustain the democratic process. In fact, however, in national contexts designated as democratic within the Americas, the degree of negotiation between these two hyper-differentiated groups toward equitable, pluricultural democratization has been slight and of minor consequence, in spite of the persistence with which minority groups have maintained their engagement in the dialogue process. An institution as important and universally accessible to dominant group members as a school, for example, can become in restricted minority group contexts a routinely ignored request until a crisis occurs, as in the case of the Chiapas insurgency: "We've been asking for a school for five years. But we've never gotten anything from the government until now" (McDonald, A Cry from the People, *Maclean's,* 1994:42).

The aforementioned type of democratic nations, therefore, is more readily characterized by the dominant presence of a particular cultural group. This group controls the nation's social and economic institutions and its politics. It also controls the access which different groups have to these same institutions and political contexts, their participation within them, and the benefits derived through them. *Differential benefits, moreover, tend to be a function of the degree, type and quality of each group's relative access and participation: The less the access or participation, the less benefit derived.*

The fact that the dominant group's control is not absolute is interesting in that it leads to a corollary statement: Its predominant control over time and space is sufficient to deny restrictive minority groups significant opportunities and benefits, and maintain their dependent marginality within the national context (cf Diamond and Platter, 1994; Munslow, 1992—particularly Chapter 6; Parenti, 1988). Said (1993:109) points to the "quotidian processes" that solidify domination and subordination; the patient, steady toxic flow of one-way communication that signals the superiority of the dominant, the inferiority of the subdued (his work of course generally relates to direct European imperialism/colonialism and how culture and its intellectual products collaborated with expansionism; I extend his meaning here to include the *imperialist model* inherited and currently practiced by the European-oriented Mexican *élite* in political and economic power against indigenous groups and the nonindigenous poor in Mexico):

> . . . an ideological vision implemented and sustained not only by direct domination and physical force but much more effectively over a long time by *persuasive means,* the quotidian processes of hegemony . . . [Studies of the] underpinnings of such hegemony . . . show the daily imposition of power in the dynamics of everyday life, the back-and-forth interactions among natives, the white man, and the institutions of authority. But the important factor in these micro-physics of imperialism is that in passing from "communication to command" and back again, a unified discourse . . . develops that is based on a distinction between the Westerner and the native so integral and adaptable as to make change almost impossible.

Constructions related to the term *culture,* such as *intercultural* and *intracultural,* also lose some of their descriptive force, especially when interwoven with other constructions such as *nation* and *democracy.* According to the official rhetoric of American countries, for example, minority groups all belong to the national majority culture, whether called Mexican, American (U.S.), or other; moreover, all presumably have the same rights within the majority culture. Any exception to this perspective is justified historically—as in the case of the native reservations in the United States which supposedly conserve the identity of the indigenous nations and express the will of these same indigenous peoples. Enrique Krauze, writing in *The New Republic* (Jan. 31, 1994:9), illustrates this perspective in his allusion to "biological and cultural mixing"—that is, European, or "white" with indigenous—having been key to Mexico's positive economic and group development, while indigenous groups suffer relative to those two attributes due to their original genetic and cultural composition:

> The north of Mexico is an area of progressive, individualistic businessmen and farmers. The center, home of the Aztecs and the main stage of the Spanish Conquest, is stable, having passed successfully through a period of biological and cultural mixing—*mestizaje*. Both areas are now oriented toward the political and economic values of the West . . . Chiapas, by contrast, is economically backward and ethnically divided . . . There was no *mestizaje* here.

This type of mythic regional perspective is common historically and globally among intellectuals and biased investigators: the supposed industriousness and polish of northern Italy versus the slothfulness and crudeness of southern Italy is one example; the supposed "contamination" of American Spanish versus the perceived correctness of Peninsular Spanish is another—there is no shortage, unfortunately, of examples. On the contrary, ever increasing numbers of examples of these lamentably ignorant stereotypes continue to exist and because they are promoted, even encouraged, through the official media and state–sanctioned intellectuals, they persist as does the need to refute them. The state of Nuevo Leon in northern Mexico, for example, does not provide sewer lines to 40 percent of its population (Reavis, 1994); 16 percent—13.5 million people—in Mexico are classified as living in "extreme poverty" and almost twice that number—23.6 million people—are classified as "poor" (*The Economist,* The Revolution Continues, Jan. 22, 1994). Krauze's mythic regional perspective is also refuted by large scale organized reactions

(20,000 in the account below; 150,000 demonstrators in a later similar incident referenced by Taibo [1994]) in Mexico City—mere days after the *Zapatista* insurgents momentarily seized a handful of towns in Chiapas on January 1st—to protest the "government brutality" in Chiapas toward the insurgents and townspeople:

> Waving placards reading "All of Mexico is Chiapas" and "Mexico First World—Ha, Ha, Ha!," the demonstrators shook the government by adding mainstream weight to the guerrillas' battle cry. Together, they have shattered the myth of a slick, modernized Mexico—an image cultivated by the government with the help of the U.S. public relations giant Burson–Marsteller, which collected some $7.7 million in fees and expenses to promote Mexico's cause in NAFTA talks since 1990 (McDonald, A Cry from the People, *Maclean's,* January 24, 1994:42–44).

The fact of marginalization, then, is attributed to factors associated with the very same marginalized group's survival formula—in a word, its culture. The lamentable fact that this latter attribution has become significantly incorporated into the collective self-image of minority groups did not occur by accident, rather through persistent institutional experiences in school, everyday contact with mainstream society, and the hierarchical reality of the workplace (cf Memmi, 1968; Noël, 1994; Yinger, 1994). In reference to Mexico, Bonfil (1990:13) labels this phenomenon *desindianización,* or de-Indianization, that is: "the loss of the original collective identity as a result of the process of colonial domination."

The alternate identity that the indigenous groups are to assume, in Bonfil's term, promotes the *Fictitious Mexico* (*México imaginario*), which propels "the Western civilization project" (*ibid.*). This project envisions Mexico as a monocultural European entity, relegating its indigenous cultural roots and expression to the historical, preferably pre-Colombian.

Within the above scenario, conflicts between minority groups and the majority group in theory would not be *intercultural* in type as all groups ostensibly belong to the same national culture. Nevertheless, *from a practical standpoint, the discrepancies between the dominant group and minority groups are deemed officially of sufficient strength to warrant particular institutional effort toward their remediation, supposedly to bring minority groups into closer proximity with the perceived everyday practices of the nation at large* (*i.e., Type I acculturaltion*), *but in fact the group is to remain in constant process of remediation* (DeVillar, 1994). The *Solidarity* program during the Salinas presidency in Mexico is, as we have seen, one example of this dominant group strategy. Other examples include schooling in the official language (or, put another way, forcing the minority group children to learn subject matter in a language other than their own and in which they are not sufficiently proficient to receive instruction), preschool remediation, personal and family hygiene instruction, nutrition classes, and adult literacy. All the above are dominant group-imposed indicators reinforcing and applying the judgement that the minority culture contains elements of its own demise and must be remediated to achieve the expected standard level of behavior to participate in, and benefit from, the dominant culture, which is of course construed as the nation.

Hence, from the logic of the dominant group's official perspective, these practices are *intracultural* in nature as they supposedly attempt to integrate minority groups into the majority cultural context through *remedial* activities. As intracultural phenomena, minority group practices are seen as *deviant* from the mainstream norm and in consequent need of repair; thus, there is little to no room for *negotiation* with the minority group as to the form remediation will take since it is not perceived as a legitimately functioning cultural entity.

Nevertheless, these same minority groups have their own languages, sociocultural histories and contexts, as well as ways of interacting among themselves within their particular context and those of others. These elements serve to maintain and nurture the development of the particular group, even within its marginalized circumstance. What is damaging within this sociopolitical context of marginality relates to the lack of development based on the minority group's own vision, since development is characterized more by restrictive and reactive properties in relationship to the constraining elements emanating from the dominant culture.

Also, in their role as a subordinate group, members learn the language and customs of the dominant group, but usually not in their standard forms—a predictable consequence of (quasi-) fossilized marginal status. Hernández Hernández (1977, cited in Ros Romero, 1981:253), for example, summarized the Mexican government's attempts in the area of bilingual-bicultural education from 1964 to 1977 in the following manner:

> Theoretically, at present there exists bilingual and bicultural education for indigenous communities. However, we observe within objective reality that young natives who have completed their elementary schooling have a deficient control of Spanish; but even more serious is that they are ashamed to speak in their native language, a situation that leads to psychological trauma that [in turn] limits their confident self-development within the national society.

The description by Bonfil Batalla (1990:184–185) of Mexico's current government–supported education indicates that the situation remains the same:

> [T]he instruction given at school ignores the culture of the majority of Mexicans and attempts to replace it rather than develop it . . . It is schooling that negates what exists and provokes in the student a schizophrenic dissociation between his concrete life and the time he spends in the classroom. And to this there is an explicit extension . . . due to an even deeper conviction: what you know has no value, what you think makes no sense; only those of us who participate in the imaginary Mexico know what you need to learn in order to replace what you are with something else.

Thus, in practical terms, the official politics of Mexico reflect a practice of restrictive acculturation which minimizes and attempts to discard what exists within the minority culture *through remediation,* to replace it with new cultural elements from the dominant culture. Historically, neither completion of the remediation process nor the ardent pursuit of the so-called new elements, even when acquired, has been judged sufficient by dominant culture standards to enable the minority group to move from restricted status to equal status within the majority culture.

This model of the politics of subordination results in a dysfunctional experience for the minority group given that: (a) the minority group is not permitted to develop in accordance with its native cultural formula; (b) the expression of native cultural forms which could be adapted or modified to fit the new sociopolitical context is not permitted by the group in power, even within the minority group's segregated context; and (c) the ideal posited in the majority group's rhetoric—that is, *the forsaking of the minority group's cultural way of being and the corresponding acquisition of the majority group's way of being—is not permitted at the minority group level rather only by exception, as an individual phenomenon.* This prevailing political model characterized, on the one hand, by the imposition of practices which initiate and maintain minority group subordination, and on the other, by an entrenched institutionalized rhetoric of equality which denies subordination, obviously lacks vital democratic elements, yet is extremely difficult to eradicate.

In summary, these operational terms associated with the description of cultural phenomena are neither stable across contexts, absolute in their precision, nor free from significant bias. The relative political dominance of the one group over the context in which it and all other groups interact, coupled with its corresponding power to indiscriminately impose its own culturotropic stimuli (whether through armed control or, to use the term coined by the French some decades ago to describe insidious control through global marketing, *cocacolonization*), produce culturocentric definitions and applications of these terms. Thus, a term's meaning depends on what cultural group controls the tropes that influence the particular cultural reality in which multiple cultures interact ("the language of objectivity" of the dominant group described by Lise Noël [1994] in her work *Intolerance, A General Survey*).

It is important to reiterate that the minority group response to this phenomenon and circumstance is not complacency but struggle. The historical manifestation of the pro-democratic struggle by subordinated groups within supposed democracies for the right to forge and integrate their respective group identities can involve instances of armed violence or nonviolent processes, even within the same historical moment. In a following text (DeVillar & Franco, this volume), two such examples of minority group responses are presented, within the same year (1994) and geopolitical context (Mexico, a country self-designated as democratic).

The first example offers a brief description relative to the role of semantics and of symbolic interpretations produced by official and insurgent voices in contexts of armed conflict, conveyed and sometimes filtered by the national and international media. The second example is a description of three video-based narratives created by members of an indigenous minority group (Ñähñu, also referred to in a more generic sense as Otomí) relative to literacy, economic self-sufficiency, and immigration. The video enactments are grounded in the Ñähñu cultural context and circumstance, born of cultural conflict and restriction, and reflect their community-voiced options in pursuit of cultural self-determination. Community-based video production in the indigenous native language at first blush strongly contrasts with the armed conflict response in Chiapas, yet it is in keeping with the spirit of the challenge posed by Chiapan insurgents at the Democratic National Convention (CND), August 8, 1994. The answer lay in the peaceful, civil resolution of their issues—as in a democracy:

> In the CND you had many arguments between seasoned and new people who are tired of rhetoric, and who are attempting to find genuine solutions and methods for getting the message out, for getting people organized, for getting a democracy movement in place. That's what they called upon civil society to do. They said armed struggle is not the solution. It cannot be the only form of struggle. We call upon you, civil society, to organize yourselves and to figure out a way to change this situation and to have a peaceful transition to democracy. (Interview with Cecilia Rodríguez, *Multinational Monitor,* April, 1995:17.)

Chiapas and Mexican Identity: Before, at Present, and Beyond

The examples provided by Chiapas continues to reinforce that today, as for the past five centuries, indigenous cultures in general live as foreigners in their native lands, with few prospects of currently directing the course of their own destiny as a group or significantly participating in helping to determine national development efforts. This marginal, powerless status becomes more rigid as their native voice and image become increasingly weak, increasingly faded, and their very existential development more tenuous.

Alvin M. Josephy, Jr., in his *The Indian Heritage of America* (1968, revised 1991), succinctly describes the general condition of indigenous communities since their contact with Europeans:

> From Alaska to the Southern Cone of South America, wherever Native Americans continue to exist, after five centuries of dispossession, physical and cultural genocide, repression, and paternalism, they are by and large among the economically poorest of all the peoples in their respective countries (377).

This sentiment is currently echoed even in everyday popular magazines, regardless of their political orientation. Victor Manual Juárez, for example, writes in the Mexican conservative magazine, *EPOCA* (1993:22) that:

> The cold, but eloquent, figures give an idea of this situation that persists after more than five hundred years, originating due to the [Spanish] Conquest, aggravated by colonization and perpetuated by the marginality and the ransacking to which they have been subjected . . . In them, in the Indians, there lies the disquieting contradiction that, of all the Mexicans, they are culturally the richest [yet] in an inadmissible state of poverty.

When left unchecked, this general state of subordination ultimately goes beyond the borders of restrictive acculturation and inevitably touches those of cultural extermination.

DeVillar & Franco (this volume) describe a collaborative effort to present and represent through a series of ethnographic videotapes the voice and image of an indigenous community characterized by subordinate marginality. The objective was to give voice and image to the community's own themes, contexts and conditions in video form. These video representations, once assessed for level of authenticity by the community participants, will be shown to the wider Ñähñu community to incite reflective dialogue and cultural action among themselves. While the Ñähñu context may be distinguished from that of Chiapas due to its lack of being an armed movement, it approximates the Chiapas context in its economic, social, cultural, linguistic and educational marginality from the dominant Mexican contexts.

It is worthwhile to ask how this vicious cycle of cultural subordination can be peacefully broken. The forms that successful change could take are understandably multifold, a logical reflection of the many different factors that have contributed to the type and degree of cultural restriction of the indigenous groups by the dominant culture in the first place. What we offer in the forthcoming text is the experience of a research-based practical intervention, still in progress, which by way of a video project has meant to capture two culturally related phenomena: (1) particular problems of subordination of a specific indigenous Mexican group and (2) the way the group developed its own image and voice in order to dialogue more deeply and consciously about its cultural circumstance and alternatives.

Additionally, we seek to illustrate the cultural strength extant in the minority group that enables it to project and move toward its particular vision of cultural development through peaceful means. Finally, we wish to document a cultural vision of identity that carries with it a capacity for negotiation sufficient to influence the making and taking of decisions relative to the group's own course of cultural action. A course that sustains and refines the indigenous group's identity and, through the group's meaningful participation in the wider, plural society, reinforces the collective democratic enterprise.

References

Bardhan, P. (1993). Comments on J. D. Stephens, "Capitalist Development and Democracy." In D. Copp, J. Hampton, & J. E. Roemer, eds., *The Idea of Democracy.* New York: Cambridge University Press, 447–449.

Bartra, R. (1987). *La Jaula de la Melancolía, Identidad y Metamorfosis del Mexicano.* Mexico, D.F.: Editorial Grijalbo.

Bonfil Batalla, G. (1990). *México Profundo, Una Civilización Negada.* México, D.F.: Grijalbo.

Cockburn, A., & K. Murray (1994). A Fistful of Promises. *New Statesman & Society,* (March 18) 7(294):20–23.

DeVillar, R. A. (1994a). The Rhetoric and Practice of Cultural Diversity in U.S. Schools: Socialization, Resocialization, and Quality Schooling. In R. A. DeVillar, C. J. Faltis, & J. P. Cummins (eds.), *Cultural Diversity in Schools, From Rhetoric to Practice.* Albany, NY: State University of New York Press, 25–56.

———. (1994b). Racismo y Educación en Estados Unidos. *La Jornada Semanal,* 280(23 de octubre) 18–23.

DeVillar, R. A., & C. J. Faltis (1991). *Computers and Cultural Diversity, Restructuring for School Success.* Albany, NY: State University of New York Press.

———. (1994). Reconciling Cultural Diversity and Quality Schooling: Paradigmatic Elements of a Socioacademic Framework. In R. A. DeVillar, C. J. Faltis, & J. P. Cummins (eds.), *Cultural Diversity in Schools, From Rhetoric to Practice.* Albany, NY: State University of New York Press, 1–22.

DeVillar, R. A., C. J. Faltis, & J. P. Cummins (eds.) (1994). *Cultural Diversity in Schools. From Rhetoric to Practice.* Albany, NY: State University of New York Press.

Diamond, L., & M. F. Plattner (eds.) (1994). *Nationalism, Ethnic Conflict, and Democracy.* Baltimore, MD: The Johns Hopkins University Press.

Economist, The. The Clash in Mexico, January 22, 1994:15.

———. The Revolution Continues, January 22, 1994:19.

Gaceta de Solidaridad, Sí a Los Liderazgos, Pero con Vocación de Servicio, v(105) (15 de Agosto): 30–31.

Guillermoprieto, A. (1995). The Unmasking. *The New Yorker* (March 13): 40–47.

Guzmán, T. (1993). La Educación Neoliberal. Retos y Perspectivas. *Renglones.* Revista del Instituto Tecnológico y de Estudios Superiores de Occidente. 8(24) (Diciembre 1992–Marzo 1993), 3–14.

Hernández, L. (1994). The New Mayan War, *NACLA Report on the Americas* (March–April) 27(5): 6–10.

Horowitz, D. L. (1994). Democracy in Divided Societies. In L. Diamond & M. F. Plattner, eds. (1994). *Nationalism, Ethnic Conflict, and Democracy.* Baltimore, MD: The Johns Hopkins University Press, 35–55.

Huerta, A. (1994). Seeds of a Revolt. *Commonwealth,* Jan. 28, 1994, 121(2):5.

Josephy, A. M., Jr. (1991). *The Indian Heritage of America.* Boston, MA: Houghton Mifflin (originally published in 1968).

Juárez, V. M. (1993). El Indio Mexicano: La Cultura de la Supervivencia. *EPOCA, Semanario de México,* 97 (12 de abril), 18–22.

Krauze, E. (1994). Zapped: The Roots of the Chiapas Revolt. *The New Republic,* 210(5), Jan. 31, 1994:9–10.

McDonald, M. (1994). A Cry from the People: The Chiapas Revolt Shatters Mexico's Slick New Image, *Maclean's,* Jan. 24, 1994, 107(4):42–44.

Memmi, A. (1968). *Dominated Man.* Boston, MA: Beacon Press.

Merriam–Webster's Collegiate Dictionary. Tenth edition. Springfield, MA: Merriam–Webster, 1993.

Multinational Monitor (1995). The Zapatista Struggle, An Interview with Cecilia Rodríguez, April, 1995:16–19.

Munslow, A. (1992). *Discourse and Culture, The Creation of America, 1870–1920* London: Routledge.

Noël, L. (1994). *Intolerance, A General Survey.* Montreal, Canada: McGill–Queen's University Press (a translation of *L'intolerance: Une problématique générale* published by Boréal, 1989).

Parenti, M. (1988). *Democracy for the Few.* Fifth edition. New York: St. Martin's Press.

Paz, O. (1961). *The Labyrinth of Solitude.* New York: Grove Press (originally published in 1950).

———. (1994). The Media Spectacle Comes to Mexico. *New Perspectives Quarterly,* 1194:59–61.

Ramos, S. (1967). *Profile of Man and Culture in Mexico.* Austin: The University of Texas Press (originally published in 1934).

Preston, J. (1995). Rebels' Impact Felt in Mexican Vote, *The New York Times International,* Monday, October 16, 1995:A8.

Reavis, D. J. (1994). Chiapas is Mexico, *The Progressive,* May, 1994, 58(5): 28–32.

Riva Palacio, R. (1992). La Prensa Mexicana, ¿Controlada? *Revista Mexicana de Comunicación,* No. 5 (Septiembre–Octubre, 1992):7–14.

Ros Romero, Ma. del Consuelo (1981). *Bilingüismo y Educación, Un Estudio en Michoacán.* México, D. F.: Instituto Nacional Indigenista.

Said, E. W. (1993). *Culture and Imperialism.* New York: Vintage Books.

Serrill, M. S. (1994). Zapata's Revenge. *Time,* January 17, 1994:32–34.

Simpson, C. R. & A. Rapone (1994). Why Did Chiapas Revolt?, *Commonwealth,* June 3, 1994, 121(11):16–19.

Stavenhagen, R. (1994). The Indian Resurgence in Mexico, New thinking about old issues. *Cultural Survival,* 18(2, 3):77–80.

Stephens, J. D. (1993). Capitalist Development and Democracy, Empirical Research on the Social Origins of Democracy. In David Copp, Jean Hampton, & John E. Roemer, eds., *The Idea of Democracy.* New York: Cambridge University Press, 409–446.

Summa, J. & S. Harris (1995). Chiapas Storm. *Dollars and Sense,* Jan./Feb., 1995:30–33.

Taibo, P. I., II (1994). ¡Zapatista! The Phoenix Rises. *The Nation,* March 28, 1995, 258(12):406–410.

Time, Banker to Mexico: "Go Get 'em," Feb. 20, 1995, 145(7):9.

Yinger, J. M. (1994). *Ethnicity, Source of Strength? Source of Conflict?* Albany, NY: State University of New York Press.

Robert DeVillar and Victor Franco

8

The Role of Media in Armed and Peaceful Struggles for Identity

Indigenous Self-Expression in Mexico

Mexico is a nation characterized by a longstanding and deeply entrenched inequality based fundamentally, rather than explicitly, on the notion of race. While it is not sustainable scientifically (Barkan, 1992; DeVillar, 1994a; Montagu, 1964), the notion of race continues to enjoy an operational vitality in nations across the globe to maintain and explain differential status among racially classified groups (DeVillar, 1994b). In Western countries, or within those mimicking the Western model, the colorbound hierarchy of racial classification ascends to white and descends to black. In Spanish- and Portuguese-America, where significant racial blending has occurred, the extremes of the human color spectrum are more accurately characterized as tones which range from "fair" to "really dark" (cf Mörner, 1967, who refers to the term *pigmentocracy;* see Stuart Chase's 1931 work, *Mexico,* which by 1945 had been reprinted 19 times, for a highly subjective, but well-reported field account).

In Mexico, this self-perpetuating, racially based scenario, which now spans more than 500 years, still finds the remaining 56 indigenous groups—at present numbering between 8 and 13 million people—co-existing in a subordinate and economically depressed state *vis-á-vis* their two intranational counterparts. On the one hand, there is a huge but relatively powerless group of American Indian-European heritage (the *mestizo,* a racially based designation of little intellectual but enormous social, economic and cultural consequence); on the other, a small, *élite* group who socially, economically and politically control the country, and whose numbers are comprised of those who are of European heritage or, being of European-American Indian heritage, ultimately claim their heritage as European.

The *mestizo* group, whether popular or *élite,* has been described by Bonfil (1987:42) as comprising the "contingent of deindianized Indians;" Bonfil is referring to the fact that while the racially based distinction between *mestizo* and *indígena* in all too many cases may not be readily apparent, the former's denial of their past heritage and transformative ignorance of their present indigenous heritage combine to mark and sustain that distinction. Other Mexican intellectuals throughout this century—Gamio (1930, 1931, 1960), Ramos (1934), Paz (1950), Bartra (1987), to name but a few who have contributed significantly to this discourse of Mexican identity—have tended to agree that "being Mexican" is an unresolved existential dilemma at the individual, group and national level.

Over the past five years, the pattern of co-existence has shifted from an uneasy stability based on the fear of, and coercion by, the combined forces of the official and private sectors to one collective action for reform. This collective response, although not uniform or unified across Mexico, is founded upon social unrest, economic need, and political desperation—factors that signal that the public tolerance threshold for dysfunctional government practices has been exceeded.

Social disquietude has been especially visible in the provinces, where indignant groups of Mexican citizens in numerous states have rejected the official party's (the Institutional Revolutionary Party, or PRI—in continuous power since 1927) gubernatorial choices, and the rigged elections upon which they were voted in to office. The advent of "second time around" elections began in 1991, when the states of Guanajuato and San Luís Potosí challenged the PRI's tallies and established interim governments (Sánchez Susarrey, 1993); protests continued in the 1992–94 election periods, and included the states of michoacán, San Luís Potosí (again), Tamaulipas, Yucatán and Zacatecas (see, respectively, Beltrán, Castellanos, & Galarza, 1992; Galarza, 1993; Beltrán, 1992; García Colín & Villarreal, 1993; and, Correa, 1992).

Social action took a second form during this period: a decidedly, if short-lived, militaristic turn on January 1, 1994—the official launch date of the North American Free Trade Agreement (NAFTA), a trinational agreement involving Mexico, the United States, and Canada. The indigenous Zapatista Army of National Liberation (EZLN) gained control of various towns within the state of Chiapas in the name of democracy and indigenous rights (see DeVillar, this volume). While the armed conflict between the insurgents and the Mexican military lasted only four days, its aftermath lingers, morphlike, in the global media, whether in text, video, television, radio or electronic forms. Media coverage has generated discourse, controversy, and doubt with respect to Mexico's overall stability, especially in the wake of NAFTA and the dire economic straits of the country that forced the Mexican government to request scores of billions of dollars in loans from the U.S. and other countries. The Chiapas conflict serves as a metaphor for the ills plaguing the whole of Mexico, nattily expressed by the Mexican university professor, Jorge Castañeda (quoted in Reavis, 1994:28[5]) as: "The problem with Chiapas is Mexico."

A third form of social action is visible within this same period and national context: indigenous groups who continue to peacefully develop their own alternatives to (a) regain their denied cultural status and the institutions which support it, (b) strengthen the range and influence of their proper cultural voice, and (c) forge their sustained, progressive economic development. These alternatives embrace immigrating to other parts of Mexico and, without documentation, at times without spouse or children, to what we "Americans" (narrow sense of the descriptor) call the United States, but what to millions of Mexicans, immigrants and nonimmigrants alike, is known in popular Spanish parlance as "the other side," or "the North."

How media is used within official and popular contexts merits attention (see DeVillar, this volume). Today's *commercial* media enables, for example, instantaneous access to conflicts of power, whether racially, ethnically, religiously, politically, or otherwise motivated, through its ubiquitous high-technology infrastructure. *Public* media in the United States—it has no authentic counterpart in Mexico—under heavy pressure of late by political and private agencies to mimic the official news posture and mores of the consumer *infotainment* model, also has instantaneous access, although not the distribution of the audience available to commercial media. Nevertheless, the tools and channels of distribution of media, however, can generate two-way communicative production, a relatively new phenomenon. The *Zapatista* insurgents, for example, have proved not to be mute beings in a goldfish bowl where the eyes and ears of the world are upon them, or where their surrogate voice, likely to be filtered and distorted, is solely spoken and heard through field- or handsomely paid studio-reporters of commercial media. On the contrary, their rebel voice has been produced through their own leaders and supporters, who have utilized fax, telephone, the information highway, video and bound printed matter, as well as newspaper print and radio, to communicate with, and gain support from, the outside world.

Concomitantly within this same national context, media production is being used in indigenous contexts where the struggle for cultural and economic self-determination is localized, peacefully confronted, and not readily perceived or considered newsworthy. For example, the aim of one particular intracultural indigenous communication project, which we address in detail in this chapter, is to locally produce a series of videos to serve as a discourse catalyst to identify and discuss problems and solutions relative to their cultural circumstance. While commercial (i.e., widespread) dissemination of these indigenously produced videos is yet viable (nor particularly desired), there is recent evidence that international and regional organizations are working toward improving dissemination beyond the community setting. The Festival of Films in Languages of Limited Diffusion, for example, will hold its third annual festival (July 1996) in the Basque Country. It is supported by the European Union and local Basque government institutions, and founded by cinematic-related professionals, translators and associations of linguistic normalization to:

> [Create] an International Review which would serve as the data base and vehicle for information and debate on films in languages of limited diffusion, and the strengthening, together with the Festival, of a Film and Video Market for films of limited diffusion (Nolley, ERaM-list, April 3, 1996).

This chapter describes how media is utilized by these two indigenous groups in their common culturo-democratic quest. We offer a brief overview and analysis of the January–August, 1994 insurgent experience in Chiapas gathered from commercially available, *Zapatista*-authorized, video and print documents and follow it with a summary of a video-based project which we undertook with the participation of Ñähñu community members in the state of hidalgo (The term Ñähñu is a self-designation by this particular indigenous community group; a more well known designation, although not internal to this particular community, which refers to this and kindred groups in other part of Mexico, is *Otomí*). The *Zapatista* group is characterized by armed conflict or the perceived threat of it; the Ñähñu, by marginal, but peaceful actions, one of which—undocumented immigration to the U.S.—is viewed as illegal according to U.S. laws. As the April 1, 1996 videotaped beating of two Mexican nationals by two Riverside (California) police officers has clearly shown, undocumented immigrants remain subject to severe and brutal consequences which violate human rights guaranteed by the U.S. Constitution, international accords, and official police protocol (Silverman, *Voice of America,* April 3, 1996).

Both indigenous groups are struggling for rights: the right to their self–identity and cultural self-determination; the right to meaningfully participate in the democratic venture to negotiate their type and level of integrated status within the larger Mexican community and thereby have a say in the nation's overall development; and the right to use their own voices and images to express and develop themselves in the process of claiming these rights. Both groups employ media to express their cultural plight and to garner support for their endeavors. Nevertheless, the focus of each is distinct. The drama of the *Zapatista* insurgency is played out before a theatre that houses a world audience; the most recent and globally publicized example being the visit to Chiapas by the successful and controversial U.S. screenwriter-director Oliver Stone, photographed on horseback and accomplished by one of his screenwriters, to meet with *subcomandante* Marcos (*Newsweek,* April 8, 1996). Nevertheless, the drama, however worthy, is an armed reactive phenomenon, triggered by desperation (see DeVillar, this volume). The Ñähñu case differs in that it is an internal, nonviolent response to their particular cultural dilemma—complex in its alternatives, limited perforce in its linguistic extension, and resonating solely and unpredictably within its regional borders.

Thus, the scale of media diffusion between the two indigenous groups, in reality and in potential, is vastly different. In keeping with the descriptions cited above, the Zapatista phenomenon might be designated a Scale I magnitude; the Ñähñu, a Scale II magnitude. It is to these two cultural voices that we now turn to gain an appreciation for the contexts within which they reside, the problems they face, the aspirations they hold, and the words and images they choose to communicate their quest for a self-determined cultural survival and selfidentity that will enable group success within, and beyond, Mexico.

The Rhetoric of Conflict

The current indigenous armed uprising in the state of Chiapas reflects the subordinate relationship of the 56 indigenous groups to the Mexican nation–state. Mexico's official indigenous policy, that is, those practices which are fomented and supported by the State's National Indigenous Institute (*Instituto Nacional Indigenista,* or INI), have not led to securing the autonomous rights of Mexico's indigenous groups. To the contrary, the INI policies can be characterized as reflecting the sustained, repressive antagonism by the nation's dominant group toward formal acknowledgment of indigenous groups' movements to change their persistent, widespread marginalized cultural status and circumstance (see DeVillar, this volume).

Cultural conflict and, more broadly, societal change in Mexico have been at the center of national and global media attention since early 1994. Chiapas offers a particularly poignant example of dominant cultural rhetoric in the face of minority culture discourse. Chiapas serves as the stage upon which the present day drama of complex cultural conflict is passionately and intricately revealed. The conflict itself is thorny and knotted, involving age-old disputes and unanswered questions, specific to Chiapas and common to all Mexico. How should majority and minority groups interrelate and what should be their relative power *vis-á-vis* the other? To what degree, if any, and when, if ever, should official goals override popular needs? How are democracies justified and sustained in the face of oligarchical, anti-democratic practices? To what extent should the Western societal adoptive model—expansionist, materialist, individualist—hold sway over indigenous and peasant group self-determination?

The discourse generated by these questions takes place, on the one hand, against the backdrop of a small, humbly attired, though dignified and widely popular, indigenous army in their natural sylvan environs. Its counterpart setting is official Mexico, where sanitized settings peopled with well-heeled bureaucrats, military officers and captains of industry, mirror comparable institutional contexts and mainstream leaders in Western and other Western-mimicking countries.

The dialogic exchange between these two groups is key in terms of content and style. Faced with the recent demands for democracy, lands, and self-determination by the indigenously comprised insurgent group, State representatives repeatedly have expressed doubt relative to the legitimacy of EZLN demands, alleging, for example, that the rebels were delinquents controlled by "professionals of violence." The traditional image of Indians—noble yet subservient, out-of-place and backward, and therefore unwilling or unable to organize themselves, whether through peaceful or armed means, to take control of their own destiny—continues to play well within official Mexico. In Chiapas, the indigenous negative stereotype persists in large part due to economic interests of the regional and national power groups, who actively and violently resist challenges to their central power by the indigenous community (cf DeVillar, this volume; Kleist, 1995).

The insurgent army's masked leader, *subcomandante* Marcos, rejects this demeaning perception and the socio-political status quo in favor of practicing democracy along the lines outlined in the Mexican Constitution. His passionate, unpredictable expression—elegant and stately at times; at others, humorous and earthy—justifies, locally and across the globe, the EZLN demands.

Dialogue between the State and populist armed movements in Mexico is of course a recent phenomenon, one that is heavily mediated by the presence of immediate and global two-way media communications, even in the isolated, rural and infrastructurally sparse setting of Chiapas. The massacre at Tlatelolco in 1968–a government subsidized housing project for mid-level bureaucrats and their families in Mexico City—occurred immediately prior to the Olympics held there. When government soldiers gunned down peacefully assembled students and other citizens, there were no instantaneous communication options comparable to that associated with the Chiapas insurgency to influence global democratic discourse and worldwide sanctions against the Mexican government. Mexican media was then even less of a viable outlet, given their near absolute state of control (see DeVillar, this volume).

Access to immediate and universal media has enable the insurgents' collective voice to preempt the official State celebratory voice at the national and global level and to plead their democratic case before a world audience. Media coverage in various forms, including fax and video, together with reports in highly diverse and prestigious newspapers, magazines, and professional journals, have combined to keep the Chiapas conflict, and the related general plight of today's Mexico, in the forefront of international discourse.

Official Mexico indeed feels the twisting pinch of international pressure and continues to scramble to recover the international trust, now misplaced, in its future. This trust reached its peak in the six-year (1986–1994) presidency of Carlos Salinas de Gortari, who is now self-exiled from Mexico and whose jerry-built neoliberal platform caved in under the weight of its own corruption, internal party squabbling, and negative global media exposure.

In sum, two groups, one a majority, the other a minority, are attempting to communicate as much with the outside world as with each other, perhaps more. In the following section, we describe the insurgent voice and that of the official government, extracting examples from local, national and global media to illustrate ways in which each uses rhetoric and practice to reinforce concepts of cultural and national identity, to justify their immediate actions, and to gain support for their respective development perspective.

The Voice and Practices of the *Zapatistas*

A review of the video documentary, *Journal to the Heart of the Jungle, A Zapatista Journal, January–August, 1994,* and its accompanying glossy booklet of the same title, both authorized by the

Zapatistas, illustrates the sociopolitical elements associated with the insurgents' discourse. The *Zapatista* voice, largely represented by that of the insurgent leader Marcos (his title of *subcomandante* is here loosely translated as *second-in-command*), justifies the uprising in the name of democracy, liberty, the Mexican Republic, Mexico itself, the Mexican flag, and the collective body that supports the uprising, a "mainly indigenous" phenomenon. This same voice, expressed in the above-mentioned video documentary, denies any association with classical forms of socialism or communism and emphasizes its democratic roots:

> There does not exist in the movement of ideology perfectly defined in the classical sense of Marxism/Leninist, of socialism/communism, of Castroism. What does exist is a common thread which runs through all of Mexico's major national problems, and that for any and all sectors always coincides with the lack of liberty, the lack of democracy.

The *Zapatista* voice recounts the 15,000 fatalities per year in Chiapas due to hunger, lack of adequate medical services, and extreme poverty, while their proclamations unabashedly favor democracy, education, patriotism, and respect and obedience to the will of the citizenry. The *Zapatista* movement is further self-characterized as being "in search of the homeland," which, they reason, has left its populace poor, in misery, and worse off than ever.

Their collective voice literally asks why their country has left them destitute and why it was necessary for them to rise up in armed struggle in order to be heard. The rebel group holds their National Democratic Convention on the seventy-fifth anniversary (1919–1994) of the assassination by the "triumphant government" of Emiliano Zapata—the Mexican revolutionary leader whose slogan of "land and liberty" has continued to be associated with the voice of the common people, particularly in the provinces. Held under conditions of strictest security in August, 1994, the need for comprehensive change is characterized as long overdue, and the collective voice concludes to its widespread audience that today they "also cannot depend upon the government." Here, deep within the Chiapas jungle, the insurgents celebrate their "conquered fright" and, upon parading their military troops in public, Marcos explains the meaning to the decorative items on the *Zapatista* rifles. In doing so, Marcos reinforces the solidarity between the *Zapatista* movement and the Mexican populace, the latter symbolically represented by the public citizens who attended the convention (quote from video documentary referred to above):

> At the tip of the *Zapatista* rifles you will see a white ribbon, which symbolizes the calling that inspired [our] movement. It symbolizes that these are not weapons with which to confront our civil society. It symbolizes, as everything else here, a paradox: weapons that aspire to their own uselessness.

The *Zapatistas* express regret over the promotion of the government's position by the national communications media, which claims that the struggle is not an indigenous one, rather that the indigenous are being manipulated and coerced by the *Zapatistas.* The insurgents also express their dissatisfaction toward those in the media who cry "poor Indians, they don't understand politics," since this implies that others are controlling the indigenous insurgents and that their actual circumstance does not warrant armed response as an internally motivated option. The analysis by Riva Palacio (1992:7–14) of the Mexican press lends credibility to the *Zapatista* criticisms:

> Mexico has practically institutionalized the practice of compromising the media through indirect bribery, enlisting reporters on the government's payroll . . . [Moreover, the] government [and] its politicians . . . pay the newspapers to publish their propaganda . . . under the guise of newsworthy information . . . The Mexican government exercises almost total control over that which it desires published.

The Voice and Practices of the Mexican Government

The official voices heard—in addition to those already indicated in the preceding paragraph and elsewhere (DeVillar, this volume)—represent a range of reactions that is not difficult to interpret. At first the Mexican government responded to the Chiapas situation with enormous force: troops toting rifles, machine guns, and explosives; armored, artillery-bedecked tanks; bomb-carrying fighter planes. The words of General Miguel A. Godínez reflect the time-worn official interpretation of these types of events: The insurgents are "victimizing the general public;" they belong to a "group of individuals trained in matters of violence, well-trained, and armed;" they are a "small group" that form part of "other militants," and whose numbers are enlarged by their "supporters." However, after the national and global reaction to the government's heavy-handed tactics, the then-President of Mexico, Carlos Salinas de Gortari, proclaimed the suspension of "all firing initiatives in Chiapas," and assigned Manuel Camacho, the ex-Mayor of Mexico City, as Peace Commissioner. Camacho's rhetoric supported the notions of negotiation and democracy:

> I think that the road to peace in Chiapas will be in new responses for the State, not only for the [Zapatista Army] but for all society . . . in a new treatment of the indigenous communities throughout the country . . . in a commitment to democracy in Mexico.

Nevertheless, as pointed out earlier, the Zapatistas thought of Camacho as a mere mouthpiece of the government, echoing words produced through official sources.

Meanwhile, the Mexican people, especially those from the poorer socioeconomic sector, allowed themselves to be seen and heard in City Hall squares throughout Mexico, even in its capital, in favor of "self-determination for the Indian communities." Jorge G. Castañeda, professor at the National Autonomous University of Mexico, writing in the July 1995 issue of *The Atlantic Monthly,* analyzed Mexican class conflict from the perspective of three nations: the élite and upper middle class, predominantly *criollo,* or European in origin, and being few; the poor, which is comprised predominantly of the *mestizo,* that ethnic, cultural and racial combination of European and Indian; and "the utterly destitute minority of what in colonial times was called the Republic of Indians—the indigenous peoples of Chiapas, Oaxaca, Tabasco, Michoacán, Guerrero, Puebla, Chihuahua, and Sonora, all known today as *el*

México profundo: the deep Mexico" (p. 72). Castañeda adds that these divisions, and the inequity and segregation associated with them, explain in part the violence that persists in Mexico throughout its history, particularly as the ruling class remains, even now, too far removed from indigenous groups, students, and others, to understand or predict internal uprisings.

Chiapas and the Future

At present, the voices of both the government and the insurgents are uncomfortably mute with respect to the Chiapas conflict, their mutual postures indicating a stalemate (Reitzammer, November, 1995). Containment does not favor the insurgents, as their resources and numbers are comparatively sparse; at the same time, global voices and governments have relaxed their pressure on the Mexican government once it made overtures to negotiate with the Zapatistas. Insurgent-produced and -inspired global media exposure has definitely increased exposure, if not understanding, of democratic struggles, and, at the same time, has made the interpretation of events more complex, less naively facile. Yet, resolution is not readily at hand, and it is not possible to predict how the *Zapatista* conflict, now more than two years old, ultimately will be resolved, or what role media will play, or whose voice will be conveyed, listened to, or prevail.

The role and effect of media in this context are likewise difficult to predict. The conveying and receiving of messages, however timely or graphic, do not necessarily lead to conflict resolution of a democratic nature, or even to a sustained interest level on the part of the media audience. On the contrary, self-designated democratic societies can justify heterogeneous co-existence in a state of uneasy peace, one that includes the phenomenon of periodic localized violent conflict. The world audience to whom the *Zapatistas* speak is itself complex, an amalgam of televideo voyeurs and information hunters and gatherers, whose sustenance depends upon receiving the message and integrating it immediately into their respective social circles, not taking sustained action upon it. Information is not praxis, merely an element necessary to it.

The Videographic Development of a Cultural Voice and Image

This section describes the rationale and methodological process of a research project in which cultural and language features of an indigenous community in Mexico were combined with ethnographic video production to enable the community's own voice and image to express itself through the production of three video recordings. The purpose in producing the set of videos was twofold: (a) to disseminate each one among the wider Ñähñu community in the state of Hidalgo, Mexico to generate internal dialogue of a critical nature relative to the community's current cultural circumstance, and (b) to identify and discuss the viability of proposed alternatives for individual and social development within the scope of their cultural context. As outbound migration and external cultural encroachment are realities that affect the community's circumstance, they were included thematically in the videos to generate discussions of intracultural alternatives in relationship to intercultural contact at the national and international level.

A key point relating to the indigenous cultural phenomenon of restrictive marginalization *vis-á-vis* the larger Mexican society concerns the lack of clarity regarding the identification and use of ingroup processes to demarginalize themselves and regain control of their cultural self-determination. This collective ambiguity extends itself into areas with respect to how the indigenous community strengthens traditional cultural elements, forges its self-selected complementary cultural alternatives, or establishes viable negotiation paths with other cultures—including the dominant culture—toward democratic coexistence and conviviality. The project's intent, therefore, was to find and document evidence of current group processes relating to marginalization and demarginalization within a particular indigenous community in Mexico, the Ñähñu.

Through collaborative engagement with the community, our goal was to articulate and record themes identified as salient by members of the community relative to their cultural survival, using their native voice and everyday images within authentic social and economic (i.e., field) contexts. As a result of these collaborative efforts, three ethnographic videos were produced with two future goals in mind: (1) to promote reflexive dialogue within the immediate and extended indigenous community; and (2) to document and analyze the nature of the dialogue relative to its elements of *cultural self-determination* with respect to the community's present context, and *acculturation* (see DeVillar, this volume) with respect to its extended contexts and contact with majority cultures, both in Mexico and the United States of America.

Each video—in addition to representing a specific theme identified previously by particular members of the Ñähñu community for its cultural value—reflects the collective process of these same members, jointly with the other project team members, toward producing a finished ethnographic video product. The other members of the project team (two linguists, two screenwriters, an educational/cultural studies researcher, a professional videographer, and two audio specialists) were not from this particular indigenous cultural community, but were, with the sole exception of the first author, from Mexico. The following segments of the chapter will describe the nature and extent of this multicultural, multilingual, and multidisciplinary collaboration, especially as it pertains to the process of conceiving and completing the project.

By reflecting upon this investigative experience, we seek to illustrate the cultural strength extant in the minority group that allows it to project a self-defined vision of cultural development. A cultural vision that carries with it a capacity for negotiation sufficient to influence the making and taking of decisions relative to the group's own course of cultural action and the extent to which the minority group participates in the wider, plural society. Thus, the following is an attempt to show by way of contextualized images and authentic voices the form in which a minority group can recoup the power to express its cultural circumstance and vision. The experience to which we refer is based on the production of videos as practical action—as praxis: the giving of communicative form to a group's own cultural image, including the values and themes considered fundamental to reflect its actual cultural circumstance.

Video as Ethnography

The initial concern with respect to our goal of capturing an authentic indigenous communicative form on video revolved around how to achieve it. Our approach was to enlist members of the indigenous community in all facets of video production, from these conceptualization to assessment of the finished products. Typically, the media (TV, video, radio, press) have excluded the indigenous-produced voice and image when portraying aspects of the indigenous cultural circumstance (Reeves, 1993). In contrast, this project used video, a communicative medium from the dominant culture, in order that the indigenous group itself produce its own cultural reflection.

Methodologically, the project is based upon the tradition of ethnographic documentary, which has its origin, according to Loizos (1993), in 1960 with *Chronique d'un été* in which cineasts Jean Rouch (an anthropologist) and Edgar Morin (a sociologist) not only used characters who were not professional actors but at the end of the project asked them to reflect and discuss upon the "cinematic authenticity" of the product. Also, we think that our project adheres to the set of criteria delineated by Jay Ruby (1975) and Karl Heider 91976)—cited by Loizos—in that it (a) related to an important aspect of an entire culture, (b) is based on a theory of culture, (c) explicitly shares its methods of research and videorecording, (d) presents its discourse in anthropological language, and, adding Heider's criterion, (e) has filmed actual people interacting in a faithful manner around real events in actual contexts.

This project also respects, in our opinion, the personal criteria outlined by Loizos (1993:9) and an additional criterion he cites by Nichols (1991) relative to attitudinal *elements* associated with achieving *realism* in an ethnographic documentary: (a) the desire to achieve faithful representation of the social world and how each group lives within it; (b) keeping oneself open to include the totality of human experiences, without excluding those which are troubling or do not comfortably fit, or those that break the appearance of continuity; (c) filming that which is concrete without communicating metaphorically that life is an illusion, or a repetitive cycle, or having but smoke for substance; (d) avoiding the presentation of fictional genres, such as romance or comedy, or dramatic encounters such as the struggle between the forces of good and evil; (e) utilizing an editing style that permits breaking away from the absolute continuity found in commercial movies as these are designed visually and orally beforehand; and, the criterion offered by Nichols, (f) attempting to produce the situation in a manner that reflects how a "typical observer" might have experienced the same situation.

Analytic Overview of the Present Ñähñu Cultural Context

In the scenario of conflict between self-determination and restrictive acculturation, the struggle for cultural development by the Ñähñus transpires within the context of marginality, discrimination and powerlessness. Maintenance of cultural values are centered, not illogically, on those social and economic activities that are least remunerated, such as work in seasonal agricultural production, elaboration of handicrafts, and raising of livestock. These types of activities tend to be strongly linked to community life, and, by extension, to the survival of a particular collective way of being that is constantly threatened by multitudinous elements from the dominant Mexican culture, and even from within. The policies of cultural revitalization struggle to find development models that avoid cultural constriction, paralysis or extinction. Strategies that attempt to recapture or regain cultural expressions that are native and valued, however, are far from invigorating the total group. The objective indicators, from a decreasing number of native speakers to the disappearance of communities that identify with the native culture, attest to the enormity of the native development task faced by advocates who value maintaining the viability of the Ñähñu culture.

In contrast to the struggle for cultural survival, there are cultural expressions linked to marginality, to group devaluation from outside forces, and to the lack of social prestige attributed to the indigenous culture, that result in stereotypes tying "being Indian" to poverty, ignorance and misery. Another misguided form, while not exactly the converse to the above stereotype, couches itself in romanticizing Indianness, ennobling all that is indigenous at the expense of objective or critical awareness of a group's needs and possibilities. The state of marginalization, likewise, is in many instances seen as emanating logically from the Ñähñu cultural context. Thus, the way to escape from marginalization is to escape from the minority culture that produces it. Within the Ñähñu ethnic experience, therefore, there appear to be few elements that point toward effectively surmounting marginalization, or even critically discussing its nature and consequences. The need for a sociocultural catalyst is obvious, and the present project, through its video productions and the process it used in their making and projected distribution, is an attempt to address that need.

Project Description

The project's central idea resided in proposing an applied approach to express those conditions of cultural socialization and reproduction that would enable the Ñähñu group to become conscious of its particular situation, and collectively articulate the possible directions, and perhaps visions, relative to its future. The production of a set of videos seemed appropriate to address this central idea as the video medium allowed recording and distributing of the group's voice and image throughout much of the community.

Under the academic institutional auspices of CIESAS (Center for Research and Higher Education in Social Anthropology) and with the economic support of CONACYT (National Council for Science and Technology), the project was in a position to invite the Academy of the Ñähñu Culture (ACÑ), comprised of indigenous professionals in education, to participate in the project. These Academy members, bilingual in Hñähñu and Spanish, are looked upon locally as cultural leaders, and together with other, nonindigenous, professionals in the areas of anthropology, linguistics and communications, formed the project team. Thus, in March, 1993, the project *The use of television-video for linguistic revaluation in minority groups* began; its objective being to determine if the medium with its broad communicative range and prestige would enhance the group's appreciation of its own culture and serve to invigorate it. The medium, as well as the message it conveyed, suggested the possibility of enhancing the minority group members' critical awareness of the developmental and debilitating elements of their cultural circumstance.

The use of video was deemed viable based on the years of linguistic and anthropological research experience in the region by some of the project team members, most notably the second author.

The team was of the impression that this experience had produced a general cultural knowledge of the Ñähñu group and familiarity with specific sociocultural aspects which could be effectively expressed and supported through a video documentary. This knowledge and experiential base helped to categorize and prioritize the multiple ideas which resulted from the implementation of the pre-project, where we sought to identify the salient themes to be expressed in the video-documentary set. Ideas included improving the economic situation of the group, learning new skills, gaining greater knowledge of the Ñähñu language and culture, assessing their migratory practices, and disseminating the group's most significant cultural practices. We saw the project not only in terms of its academic research, but fundamentally as an intervention, a concrete action and dynamic experience which the members of the Ñähñu community would construct and participate in.

The central question which resulted from the expectations cited above was: Is video a significant medium to help structure and express the issues associated with the Ñähñu context, and additionally serve as an effective elicitation and distribution medium that would enable the Ñähñu community to discuss these issues? To address this question, we had to attend to various elements, including a dialogue among the participants and the elaboration of methodological resources that would ensure the authentic expression of the community members as they discussed their values and visions relative to their cultural group. Video technology would facilitate making visible the group's cultural context and making audible the members' verbal expression with the context, internally to the members themselves and to others outside the community. Strictly speaking, the essence of the project was not about making videos *per se,* rather that the medium was seen as sufficiently flexible to achieve the objective of obtaining an authentic representation of a culture by capturing and projecting a particular minority group's own voice and image.

Methodological Concerns

The most salient methodological concern was to systematically ensure the active, free and spontaneous participation of community members. Toward this end, the design encouraged participants to construct their cultural image and apply their cultural voice; it also spurred the expression of elements within the culture that restricted or constricted the group's preferred cultural development route. Broadly speaking, the methodology was divided into two stages: the first stage comprised the project's beginning through the production of the three videos; the second stage was to disseminate the videos for viewing by the participants themselves, the members of their community, and the various other communities in the region for their assessment. The first stage, then, entailed video production; the second, diffusion and evaluation.

Currently (early 1996), the project has completed its first stage and initiated the second stage, specifically by showing the completed videos to the Academy of Ñähñu Culture team members for their assessment. Below, we summarize the principal methodological steps that guided our work during the video production stage, namely: the formation and preparation of the work team; preparation for working within the communities; initial proposal of cultural themes; pilot testing of the proposed themes; selection of themes and their narrative sequence; script proposals; videorecording; and coding and editing the material. The evaluative comments of the ACÑ team members are also summarized and presented.

Formation and Background of the Work Team

The research team consisted of two different groups: the academic researchers from CIESAS and the group of researchers and professors from the ACÑ, who were themselves indigenous, university educated, and native Hñähñu speakers. Team development, moreover, was based on the notion of shared expertise; consequently, members form these two institutions reflected anthropologists, linguists and bilingual educators, the latter being mainly ethnolinguists by professional training. The ACÑ is comprised of a group highly specialized in education and the Hñähñu language who dedicate themselves to the promotion of bilingual education in the elementary schools within the Mezquital Valley region. Among their principal duties is the design and production of books in the native language for use as texts across elementary grade levels. This group of indigenous professionals could well be regarded at the vanguard of regional cultural leadership.

Due to the democratic orientation to the project's mission, the Academy's role rapidly transformed from being an interested party to one of strong advocacy, which in hindsight was indispensable to the project's completion. The Academy, aside from contributing support and participating directly in all facets of planning and production, acquired self-sustaining alternative means, including computer and video equipment, to continue the development of educational materials.

From the beginning of the project and throughout its duration, a methodological task agreed upon by the team involved seeking out the voice of the community and fomenting the construction of images that would be culturally representative. Rather than an *a priori* methodology imposed *in toto* from the beginning of the project, a spate of methodological resources were constantly examined and selected by the team in accordance with, and throughout, the project's phases. The resulting methodology, designed dynamically by this multidisciplinary team, helped ensure that the vision projected by the Ñähñu community members from within its already complex context of conflict was neither diluted nor inaccurately represented.

Community Relations and Participation in the Project

All team members understood that it was crucial for the project to base its work on the participation of the native speakers. Given the composition and *modus operandi* of the team, this crucial element was successfully achieved through networks or linkages formed among the team members with various inhabitants of the 15 communities in the municipalities of Ixmiquilpan and El Cardonal, in the Mezquital Valley. Communities which participated in the project were: Bondo, Decá, Orizabita, Boxuadá, B'oye, Remedios, Nith, San nicolás, Sauz, Pozuelos, El Olivo, El Durazno, Ixmiquilpan, Cardonal and Santuario. Men, women and children participated in the project's diverse aspects, demonstrating ample cooperation by community members in the decisions taken during the course of the project.

It was essential that our methodology achieve the participation and representation of the communities in order to capture the expression of their quotidian cultural reality. The primary criterion used to select the communities was the prior relationship established by team members with them. Thus, it fell largely to the Academy members to propose and invite the communities and individuals having the inclination to support the project's activities.

The goal of gathering proposals from the communities relative to the themes that each video might reflect meant that we would return to each community to discuss the proposed themes with them. The communities responded enthusiastically to this proposal. This feedback mechanism enabled the communities to express significant elements reflecting cultural tendencies, particularly those associated with cultural and linguistic valuation and devaluation. With this information, we began to examine the effects of domination by the majority group, as well as those valued cultural elements that reflected adherence to a group vision that moved toward reconfiguring its dominant-subordinate relationship through cultural development and self-determination.

Initial Criteria for Selecting Cultural Themes

Once the initial opinions from the communities were gathered, the research team began to discuss the topics and storylines relative to each prospective video. The production presuppositions had already been identified and agreed to by the team: to respect the spontaneous expression of the speakers, to invite participants to primarily use the native language—Hñähñu, and to represent the positive and negative attitudes relating to cultural reproduction and development.

The themes themselves sprang from various sites and occasions. To cite one initial experience, we were permitted to videorecord a meeting of the Common Lands and Communal Assembly (Asamblea Ejidal y Comunal) of a small village of some 1,200 inhabitants. The discussion on the part of the Assembly, at which about 150 heads of family participated, produced a long list of cultural topics of interest to those present and served as the initial momentum to move the project from its planning stage to its application. Topics relative to socioeconomic and cultural issues—of group survival—were immediately raised, such as the lack of water for irrigation purposes, lack of sources of employment, economic shortages, low selling prices for regionally produced goods, the herding of small livestock (goats, sheep and pigs), plant cultivation, and traditional foods as forms of nourishment.

Each proposed topic touched upon different needs and accentuated one cultural form or another, but fell within the general pattern of developing a cultural and visual image based upon their actual life experiences. Regardless of the degree to which they elaborated upon their opinions, community participants projected their cultural vision of the group, confronting the cultural and intercultural conflict existing in their current context or expressing a perspective with respect to it. Our task subsequently consisted of proposing adequate structures within which to develop the storylines. Following this method allowed us to return to the communities with the proposed storylines in order to further develop and enrich them.

Ultimately, we selected the following three themes: *Writing in the native language and schooling, The cultural and economic life of shepherds,* and *The family and migration.*Each of the themes represents a field of issues comprised of aspects that relate to the self-sustainment or debilitation of the Ñähñu culture. Below, we summarize a few of the salient aspects associated with the thematic contexts selected.

Theme 1: The Ñähñu Alphabet and Writing

This literacy topic originally revolved around the function of writing in minority societies where typically the indigenous language in written form is not present, or is restricted to particular sectors of the group. In this type of situation, the actual use of writing in the native language is associated with formal schooling. Moreover, as we had observed from the outset, the minority society, at the same time that it placed a high value on writing in the dominant society's language (Spanish), held strong prejudices and negative stereotypes toward the value of writing in its native language (Hñähñu). The slight social efficacy of native writing, the weight of its stereotypic association with indigenous marginality, and the support given learning to write in the Spanish language, all conspired against its development. The gravity of the situation is increased significantly when we consider that these same pressures are also brought to bear on oral language expression in Hñähñu. Nevertheless, we looked upon the above as common characteristics associated with linguistic and cultural subordination framing the context in which the project unfolded.

Basing our judgment criteria upon the above experience and perspectives, the development of the central thematic treatment selected was the social importance accorded literacy in the native language by its own speakers. The topic, then, would have to reflect those cultural spaces where the native written language is socially used and relate it to the cultural space of perceived greatest importance, that is, bilingual education at the elementary school level.

Theme 2: The Life of Shepherds (Production of Small Livestock)

The topic of traditional tending of flocks (shepherding) represents a central economic activity in the regional economy. In most of the Valley, the production of small livestock (goats, sheep, pigs) is an additional means of subsistence, which becomes a necessity, for example, where irrigation does not reach, such as the middle and high areas of the Valley. In the mountainous parts, shepherding is an everyday activity, almost exclusively conducted by women, who frequently spend their entire day tending to their herds in the mountains. Moreover, it is a practice that represents one of the important cultural activities of those considered to be among the poorest community members.

In the majority of cases the flocks of goats and sheep are not meant to be sold, rather they are a form of nonmonetary economic reserve that supports the needs of the extended family. Animals are only sold in case of emergencies, such as illness or a festive commitment. The animals represent a means to meet social obligations, since, whenever required, one or two can be taken and barbecued. Thus, this topic was seen as representing a self-sustaining economic activity of the region, linked to two points: (a) the image of economic marginality in which the group lives, and (b) a cultural image in which strongly held indigenous cultural values persevere in the form of shepherding.

At the same time, this traditional aspect of the Ñähñu economy is related to perspectives of *modernization of the production of caprine and ovine livestock*. Many indigenous field workers, for example, enter into livestock development projects with the hope of converting their herd into a source of monetary income. In many communities, therefore, small organizations of producers exist that seek to increase their earnings. This implies a transition in the manner in which herds are produced and also confronts outside ways of doing business. It is necessary to point out that investing in these methods of improving production through access to higher yielding technologies, does not mean that this outcome in fact occurs. Many small producers instead of improving their lot actually increase their losses.

In light of the above, the team decided to propose the idea of expressing the relationship between the traditional shepherds with those producers who desired to modernize. By introducing this particular relationship, we could also express the uncertainties of economic development and reflect one of the economic activities most closely associated with the Ñähñu culture. The basic story revolved around various shepherdesses—as women are the principal managers of shepherding—through representations of their everyday life in the mountains and at home. Also, we combined the above with content about various livestock production techniques, both traditional and modern, and highlighted at the end of the story the festive banquet in which the barbecued goat represents a deeply rooted cultural form.

Theme 3: Family Life and Migration

One of the most salient factors in the life of the inhabitants of the Mezquital Valley is migrating in search of employment opportunities. The migratory tendencies for some decades now have been toward the urban centers, such as Mexico City, Pachuca (the capital of Hidalgo), diverse agricultural regions in Mexico itself, and over the past two decades in a strong fashion, the U.S. The migratory phenomenon, together with the sociocultural shifts and patterns which result from it, have significant repercussions in the lives of the indigenous inhabitants of the Valley and in the communities from which the migrants originate. One of the principal repercussions is reflected in the family lives of indigenous field workers. The conditions of marginality and the low production yields in the semiarid zones, exert pressure on the inhabitants to leave their families and communities on a seasonal or permanent basis. The problems associated with migration, then, are effectively, though harshly, reflected in the separation of one or more members from their families.

The context of family and migration is a key factor in the reproduction of family groups attached to the Ñähñu culture. The nuclear family, as a principal reproducer of cultural agents, experiences the repercussions of migration, including family disintegration, the leaving behind of their community and cultural roots by some individuals, and the rejection of local cultural life. Moreover, with the ebb and flow of the immigrants, the families and communities come face to face with diverse, interrelated changes in sociocultural attitudes, including disdain for things indigenous, rejection of the vernacular language, permanent departure from the community, and abandonment of spouse and children. There are changes, of course, that reflect values introduced by the migrant population which are appreciated in particular contexts. These influences can be seen, for example, in the form of improvements in the indigenous living standards, in alimentary nourishment, in housing, in learned skills and productive trades, and in religion, among others.

Given this complex dynamic, it is clear that the culture sees migration as a form of economic development that brings with it the risk of abandoning particular forms of indigenous culture. Taking the above into account, we proposed the topic of migration in which we would strive to identify and interrelate three distinct individual experiences representative of the migration phenomenon: migration of a single individual, migration of a husband and wife who leave their children behind, and the experience of an individual who decides to remain with his family rather than migrate.

Piloting and Assessing Spontaneous "Enactments"

Before developing each of the stories, we first had to conduct some tests—impromptu rehearsals, so to speak—in order to observe the form in which: (a) speakers would express themselves relative to a particular theme, (b) principal ideas would be articulated, (c) values would be accorded to particular cultural patterns, and (d) prejudices and stereotypes would be associated with each theme. Thus, the improvisations provided elements that would enable the team to assess the content, characters, sequence, conflicts, dialogues, and values associated with each of the three narratives.

The extemporaneous enactments were produced by requesting some of the community members to represent the role of a character within the narrative structure. With but a few brief indications with respect to the roles to be represented, the protagonists invented their dialogues and interacted extemporaneously with each other, to create a quasiauthentic cultural experience. The interpretation of the topic, with its conflicts and alternatives, by the participant-enactors, then, was to reflect their actual perspective toward the situation. Through this process, we were able to identify qualities associated with the cultural voice and vision of each participant. The extent to which these voices and visions reflect a regionally-specific wider community indigenous perspective will be determined at a future assessment stage.

Self-assessment by the Enactors

Once the scenes had been recorded, the enactors were immediately invited to preview on a monitor their performance and critique their enactment and the dialogue created. In this manner, those persons who had participated confronted their own acting and dialogue and those of others. At this juncture, they could simply agree with what they saw and heard, or they could set themselves apart from the scene, critiquing it and providing alternatives. Recording on videotape did seem to influence the creative process of the participants, increasing their interest and motivation to provide more authenticity to the characters they were representing. The participants' comments, for example, alluded to the need to speak correctly, the manner in which one should dress, the image that one was projecting to others, the types of ideas that were expressed, the crucial points of a discussion, and the faithfulness with which a character was developed.

Production: Organization, Settings and Videorecording

With respect to camera operation, we counted upon the presence of experienced and trained personnel to visually capture the desired video form. The role of the camera operator was centered principally around capturing the scenes as they developed extemporaneously, trying, as it were, to capture the dynamics of improvisation associated with the actors' movements and dialogues. This implied that before the shoot, the camera operator had only a general idea of what would happen, and that it was left up to the operator's expertise how best to frame and obtain the shots most appropriate to the action within this natural setting.

The participants in the recording—aside from the basic work team—were those members from the various indigenous communities who had previously participated in the pilot takes, and who because of this experience had a certain level of confidence and ability in spontaneously acting out the storylines. In most instances, the community participants were acting out roles that they actually had in real life. For example, the role of teachers was done by teachers; the shepherdesses in the video were shepherdesses in everyday life; the migrants were individuals with actual experience in migration, etc. The work team not only selected those who would act in the videos, but also selected the locations, they types of setting, the appropriate dress and objects utilized, in constant search of authenticity. The pilot takes had demonstrated to us that our goal was in fact achievable, particularly the fact that the actors had shown such ease in portraying their roles and creatively developing their lines.

Although the basic work team understood the complete storyline of each video, the participants were constructing their respective stories in logical sequence and within the immediate demands of their role. In this sense, they did not rehearse or memorize anything prior to their enactments. Nevertheless, on each occasion the participants were apprised of the context of the situation within their setting, the characteristics associated with their role, and the type of dialogue sought. Other than the introduction of these elements, the participants' integration was very similar to their pilot test experiences. The fact of having dialogues already prepared served only to guide the participants, as the intent was not that they memorize lines since such a mechanism would negatively influence their creativity and spontaneity. Moreover, having the participants engage in free dialogue enabled them to express the knowledge gleaned from their own direct and indirect experiences within similar settings.

The greatest difficulty we faced was development of the dialogues. We found that attempting to have the participants prepare their lines was counterproductive, yielding stilted language and behaviors. Hence, the development of each videorecording moment was left up to the spontaneity expressed by participants relative to the idea sought. Scenes were recorded in continuous segments, such that dialogues lasted up to 15 minutes without interruption. On numerous occasions, scenes were comprised of six or eight speakers. In sum, the video creation of the situation could only function insofar as it could demonstrate what was known about, discussed within, or done in a comparable real life situation by the participants. To this degree, their charge was to be the interpreters of their own social reality.

Editing. Having completed the videorecording phase, we proceeded to review, code and select the material considered to be the most representative and best in terms of video quality. To accomplish this, the team met several times and came up with a preliminary edited version. At this juncture, the first macrostage of the project was concluded: the production of three videos whose contents sprang from the very speakers of the culture being videotaped and expressed their own cultural values.

Preliminary Results and Future Project-related Activities

To gauge the authenticity and relevancy of the three videos, we decided to compile and analyze the judgments of three distinct groups within the same Ñähñu cultural community. The first group was to be comprised by the teachers within the Ñähñu Cultural Academy (ACÑ), who were directly involved in the conceptualization and production of the ethnographic videos; the second group, by those persons who had production or character roles in each video; and the third group, by member of the Ñähñu community within the Mezquital Valley who had not participated in the project and who would be invited to view the videos subsequent to the first two groups' critiques and consequent final editing. We report here upon the outcomes of the first stage of assessment, which involved the teachers within the ACÑ, who, as project team members, participated in the design and elaboration of the videos, served as community and production coordinators, and participated as actors in the videos. The Academy members' comments relate only to their single viewing of the videos; thus, we qualify this assessment as initial, as their critiques may vary with more frequent viewing.

Previous to visiting the Academy site, the authors structured the questions and format of the assessment meeting. One of the fundamental questions refers to the attainment of the main goal: (1) To what extent did the videos reflect the projected expression of an authentic image and voice representing the cultural life and vision of the Ñähñu group? Other salient general questions that we formulated to guide our evaluation included: (2) To what degree did the selected themes represent cultural alternatives in the face of the reality of subordination within which the indigenous group lives?; (3) to what extent was linguistic revaluation enabled through the video themes; (4) what actions could be generated from the presence of linguistic revaluation?; and (5) what, if any, would be the perceived educational effect of the videos in the Ñähñu community? There were other questions of related interest: (6) What did each like most/least about each video?; (7) was the length of each video appropriate?; (8) what was lacking in each video?; (9) was the language correct?; (10) was the acting authentic or false?; (11) was the story authentic or false?; and (12) in what ways would one change the video?

The videos were shown at the Academy site on January 20, 1995 to seven of the ten Academy team members. Due to the open-door policy of the Academy, a retired bilingual teacher who happened to drop by also was present throughout the review of the videos. The first author introduced the nature of the meeting and the types of questions to consider as each member viewed the videos; he also expressed that he and his colleague (videotaping the session) were there to listen to their comments and underscored the immense value of their anticipated input to the final editing of the videos. For purposes of this assessment, each video was run only once and without interruption. The videos were shown in the sequence that they were produced—respectively, literacy, immigration and shepherding—and comments were given after each video was viewed.

ACÑ Teachers' Initial Assessment

Generally, the set of videos was considered to have great potential for creating cultural discourse and promoting native language literacy within the Ñähñu community. The Academy members expressed their desire to now show the videos to the community at a formal function where local and federal functionaries, together with university officials, would be invited. They also voiced their desire to continue making documentary videos to further elaborate upon critical aspects of their cultural life, particularly with respect to immigration. More specific evaluative comments by the Academy members fell into the following categories:

1. Language. Academy members expressed that the videos would enable them to show the value of speaking and writing in the native language (Ñähñu) and of bilingualism. Moreover, they value multilingualism, and see a concrete need for their community, particularly the children, to become literate in Ñähñu, Spanish, and English. English is particularly prized as it is associated with attaining a higher standard of living. They felt that language instruction should be a responsibility of the schools and parents. Further, as the community members must go to the U.S. with an employment skill and English, the schools should teach specific skills and English to the children to prepare them for this eventuality. Code-switching—that is, the alternate use of two languages within a string of utterances (intersentential) or the same utterance (intrasentential)—was considered to detract from comprehension and to be a shame (*una pena*).

2. Editing. The use of cinematic conventions such as cutting, dissolves, wipes, fades, panning, sound, music, rate of motion, flash forwards and flash backs, montage and others (see huss and Silverstein, 1968; Spottiswoode, 1950) make up a film grammar. These conventions enable film makers to present a story within the confines of the two dimensionality of the medium and the length generally accorded to it as entertainment value (90–120 minutes). Through these conventions, audiences comprehend and evaluate a film; moreover, audience recognition, for example, of a film's genre, say as a comedy or drama, of its time span as one day or hundreds of years, or of its use of one or more of the above techniques to accelerate or constrain (even to the point of fixity) time, is facilitated. As movies (and their offspring, television and videos) in Western cultures have enjoyed immense success since the first quarter of the twentieth century, audiences generally have become functionally literate in decoding these cinematic conventions. We found that the use of particular film conventions did not translate to the Academy audience.

2a. Literacy Theme. In the literacy video, for example, we used an *intercut* (in this case, a story inserted in between a previously introduced sequence) to introduce a dream sequence precipitated by the illiterate grandfather having fallen asleep while thumbing through the text he had borrowed from the ACÑ to show his grandson. The dream sequence was signalled by having the grandfather remove his hat and glasses, and rest his head and arms on the desk at which he was sitting. The next show shows him sitting at a desk in a classroom with other adults and children—including his grandson—forming part of a literacy lesson. He is asked to come to the chalkboard by the teacher where he demonstrates his ability to read and write in Hñähñu (note the spelling variation to designate the language). The next cut shows the grandfather with his grandson at the reading room in which he had fallen asleep; the grandfather had internalized an appreciation for learning to read and write in the native language and was sharing that value with his grandson.

These two interrelated sequences, threaded together by way of the intercut, did not convey their intended message. The dream sequence was interpreted literally, that is, as if it actually had transpired in actual life rather than a dream. Consequently, the members suggested that a particular scene previously shot but excluded from the final version be reinserted and that *the sequence of shots be corrected*. The scene referred to showed a teacher, outside the context of the school and school day, tracing letters in Hñähñu in the dirt with a stick to capture the interest of the children who were present. The Academy teachers thought that this shot when reinserted would give the audience an indication that the grandfather had been learning to read and write as it was thought to match with the shot of the grandfather writing at the chalkboard.

2b. Immigration Theme. The immigration video also consisted of the use of *flash back* and *visual simile* to tell the story of three types of prospective Ñähñu immigrants. It used the technique of *visual simile* to separate the individual telling of the stories yet link them together contextually. Specifically, as each immigrant's individual story was told, a truck was showing going down the mountainside to signal two messages: the first, that the particular story just viewed was over and that another one was being introduced; secondly, that the repetition of this technique would convey that each of these stories was linked to a greater whole—the story of their community's involvement with immigration and the feelings of illusions and loss that relate to it. The flash back technique was used to place the prospective immigrants together at the setting which they attended where the *coyote,* the Ñähñu community member who would lead them from the village across the border to the U.S., described to them the nature and risks of the immigration experience. Neither technique worked well for the Academy members. In the case of the flash back, they felt that the shots were out of sequence and should be placed in the correct sequence; in the case of the visual simile, the truck was considered to be a superfluous insertion, and the fact that in one cut it was proceeding down the mountain in one direction and in another cut it was moving in another direction only compounded the lack of visual-cognitive cohesion.

The fact that these editing techniques did not translate into the visual-cognitive schema of the Academy members helped us—both as authors and as project leaders—to understand two interrelated points relative to our media project. First, that in community-based projects, the community members (in this case, particular members of the Academy) must be involved in all stages of the project, including the editing phase. Distance, in this case a formidable barrier, must not be a determining factor in excluding team members from full project participation and contribution. Second, media conventions that may be understood (or overlooked) by community members in one type of media (say, television programs reflecting the dominant Mexican society and transmitted by its networks into their homes) are not necessarily perceived as adequate to convey stories and messages that are locally produced and meant for local viewing, reflection and dialogue. In a sense, the grammar of film/video is subordinate to the language of culture; and editing, which strings together the shot sequences that result in the syntax and ultimately the semantics of the produced film or video, reflects the language of its intended speech-community audience. We were, so to speak, code-switching inappropriately in our editing process and obscuring the stories and their respective messages.

3. Veracity. There were various types of comments that touch upon the perceived authenticity of the videos, particularly elicited by the immigration video. All in all, the videos were considered authentic representations, from the perception of the dress that people wore to the story lines, enactments and dialogues. More interesting was the interpretation given by particular audience members upon viewing each video. The most dramatic response was on the part of the retired teacher upon viewing the immigration video. Waiting until each Academy member had voiced his opinion, the retired *maestro* asked permission to speak and in the course of doing so could not contain his tears or sadness. He stated that he had seen such cases as those that we presented and that the community needed to see such sadness so that they would be award of what immigrants were leaving behind. Who would care for their children?, he asked. The *maestro* also wanted the video to show the hardship of immigration, citing the lack of money, food and justice that parallel the immigrant experience, asking us if this "sadness" could be presented through video.

Interestingly, the Academy members view immigration as *positive,* and that the hardships endured are minimal and lead to an improved standard of living. They agreed with the *maestro* that the immigrant video should be extended to include the actual process of immigration (i.e., going to and crossing the border, and even returning) but *to motivate immigration* by showing how immigration takes place, the risks that are taking, the treatment and discrimination the immigrants are subjected to, and where they are employed (examples given included tobacco fields, agriculture, construction, restaurants, and gardening). Thus, the value of immigration is employment and the higher standard of living that employment allows. This higher standard of living is particularly symbolized by the houses that the immigrants can afford once they return to their community.

Immigration was viewed by the Academy members as an opportunity to contribute needed employment skills to the United States and, in turn, to learn English and earn a respectable wage. The standards that the immigrant was expected to conform to included having an employable skill and a working knowledge of English, both acquired prior to the act of immigration, preferably through schooling. It appeared to us that in the cosmological vision of the Academy members, travel to and from the "other side" (such as the United States) was a necessary and natural experience, in which harmony was reachable by both parties (the United States and Ñähñu community members) meeting each other's needs. (In Spanish, *cosmovisión,* is defined in the *pequeño Larousse ilustrado* 1992 as "the way one sees the world and the form in which one considers it.") The question of legality of entry or the consequences of apprehension by U.S. authorities were never broached.

4. Summary Comments by Members. The videos would, in the words of the director of the Academy, "help us think about our destiny." In the case of the Shepherd and Immigration videos, the suggestion was made to produce related videos to delve more fully into their culturfal phenomena (e.g., country veterinary and economic practices in pastoral contexts and the immigration points covered previously). The next steps suggested were to make the recommended modifications to the videos, set the date to show the videos to the community at an event and venue to be attended also by local, federal and university officials. The suggestion was that this event take place soon. Lastly, the director stated his desire that the university in the United States at which the first author teaches enter into an agreement with the ACÑ for future collaborations.

Next Steps

The next stage of the evaluation process will take place once the suggested revisions are completed. This step will enable us to observe the reaction by distinct nuclei within the Ñähñu community upon viewing the scenes within each video and reactions to the total video and set of videos. We will also assess the degree to which the themes are well received and identified with by the community. Finally, the evaluation will assess the nature of the cultural communication among the group members upon viewing the videos in relation to the image that they have of themselves and the horizon toward which they wish to direct themselves as individuals and as a cultural group. We also plan to have the video dialogues translated into Spanish and English and have the videos subtitled in each language for wider diffusion and dialogue by audiences in national and international settings.

References

Barkan, E. (1992). *The Retreat of Scientific Racism.* Cambridge: Cambridge University Press.

Bartra, R. (1987). *La Jaula de la Melancolía, Identidad y Metamorfosis del Mexicano.* Mexico, D.F.: Editorial Grijalbo.

Beltrán del Río, P. (1992). En Tamaulipas el PRI Enfrenta, Debilitado, el Reto de la Coalición PAN–PRD. *Proceso.* (Sept. 7, 1992):26–29.

Beltrán del Río, P., F. Castellanos, & G. Galarza (1992). "Que se Queden en sus Plantones": Dice Villaseñor; 'Nos Quedamos Hasta que se Vaya," Dicen los Perredistas. *Proceso.* 829 (Sept. 21, 1992):20–23.

Bonfil Batalla, G. (1990). *México Profundo, Una Civilización Negada.* México, D.F.: Grijalbo (Originally published in 1987).

Catañeda, J. C. (1995). Ferocious differences. *The Atlantic Monthly,* 276(1), July, 68–76.

Chase, S. (1945). *Mexico.* New York: The Macmillan Company (originally published in 1931).

Correa, G. (1992). Perredistas y Panistas Toman Alcaldías entre Cargos de Fraude; Romo, Gobernador. *Proceso.* 826 (August 31, 1992):31–32.

DeVillar, R. A. (1994a). The Rhetoric and Practice of Cultural Diversity in U.S. Schools: Socialization, Resocialization, and Quality Schooling. In DeVillar, R. A., C. J. Faltis, & J. P. Cummins (eds.), *Cultural Diversity in Schools, From Rhetoric to Practice.* Albany, NY: State University of New York Press, 25–56.

———. (1994b). Racismo y Educación en Estados Unidos. *La Jornada Semanal,* 280 (23 de octubre de 1994):18–23.

Galarza, G. (1993). Sorprendieron a Todos las Elecciones de San Luis. *Proceso.* 860 (April 26, 1993):26–29.

Gamio, M. (1971a). *The Life Story of the Mexican Immigrant.* New York: Dover (orig. pub. in 1931).

———. (1971b). *Mexican Immigration to the United States.* New York: Dover (orig. pub. in 1930).

———. (1960). *Forjando Patria.* Mexico, D.F.: Porrúa.

García Colín, M. & R. Villarreal (1993). Dulce María se Arrepiente, El PAN se Ensoberbece y Yucatán Ríe. *Epoca.* 100 (May 3, 1993):28–31.

Huss, R. and N. Silverstein (1968). *The Film Experience, Elements of Motion Picture Art.* New York: Dell Publishing.

Kliest, T. (1995). Chiapas: Roots of a Rebellion. *Santa Clara Magazine* (Summer):16–21.

Loizos, P. (1993). *Innovation in Ethnographic Film, From Innocence to Self-Consciousness.* Chicago: University of Chicago.

Montagu, A., (ed) (1972). *The Concept of Race.* New York: Collier Books (orig. pub. copyrighted 1964).

Mörner, M. (1967). *Race Mixture in the History of Latin America.* Boston: Little, Brown and Company.

Nolley, K. (1996). Festival of Films in Languages of Limited Diffusion (EREMUAK '96), e-mail correspondence via EraM-list, April 3, 1996.

Payan Velver, C., E. Ibarra, & H. Vera (1994). *Viaje al Centro de la Selva, Memorial Zapatista.* Mexico: Argos (Proceedings and video).

Paz, O. (1961). *The Labyrinth of Solitude.* New York: Grove Press (orig. pub. in 1950).

———. (1994). The Media Spectacle Comes to Mexico. *New Perspectives Quarterly,* 1194:59–61.

Pequeño Larousse Ilustrado. 16th ed. (1992). Mexico, D.F.: Ediciones Larousse.

Ramos, S. (1967). *Profile of Man and Culture in Mexico.* Austin: The University of Texas Press (orig. pub. in 1934).

Reavis, D. J. (1994). Chiapas Is Mexico, *The Progressive* (May, 1994) 58(5): 28–32.

Reeves, G. (1993). *Communications in the Third World.* London: Routledge.

Reitzammer, L. (1995). The Consulta Nacional. *Z Magazine* (Nov. 1995): 6–8.

Riva Palacio, R. (1992). La Prensa Mexicana, Controlada? *Revista Mexicana de Comunicación* 5 (Septiembre–Octubre, 1992):7–14.

Sánchez Susarrey, J. (1993). La Lección de San Luis Potosí. *Epoca* (May 3, 1993):20–21.

Sigesmund, B. J., & L. A. Locke (1996). "What's Up, Oliver?," in Newsmakers, *Newsweek* (April 8, 1996):83.

Silverman, A. (1996). Immigrant Beating, *Voice of America* (correspondent report on Netscape) (April 3, 1996).

Spottiswoode, R. (1950). *A Grammar of the Film.* Berkeley and Los Angeles: University of California Press (this version, 7th printing, 1969; originally written in 1933–34).

Lotty Eldering

9

Mixed Messages

Moroccan Children in the Netherlands Living in Two Worlds

Identity formation is a process of interaction between a child and the socio-cultural environment in which it grows up. The environment shows the child its place and role in society and the values and norms it is expected to internalize. The child reacts to these socializing forces by conforming to the standards or by changing and sometimes even rejecting them. Identity formation can be studied from a socio-anthropological or a psychological point of view. In the first case the study focuses on the socializing environment and in the second on the developing child. In this contribution a socio-anthropological approach is used. The socializing environment of ethnic minority children will be described from a cultural-ecological perspective (Eldering, 1995), using a cultural-ecological model based on Bronfenbrenner's ecological model and Harkness and Super's framework of the developmental niche.

The process of identity formation is more complicated for ethnic minority children than for children from majority groups, because of the mixed messages ethnic minority children receive from their environment. This is particularly the case with children of first generation immigrants. The messages these children get from their ethnic environment may even be contradictory to those form society at large.

In the following sections the cultural-ecological model will be presented and applied to Moroccan parents and children in the

Netherlands. First the socialization context of Moroccan children growing up in two-parent families surrounded by a Moroccan network and community will be sketched, then the backgrounds and environment of Moroccan children living in female-headed households will be depicted. These cases are illustrated with examples from my research on Moroccan immigrants (Van den Berg-Eldering, 1978, 1986; Eldering & Vedder, 1993; Eldering & Borm, 1996).

The Cultural-Ecological Model

In reaction to traditional approaches of developmental psychology Bronfenbrenner (1977) has developed a broader research approach viewing human development as the progressive accommodation, throughout the life span, between the growing human organism and its changing environments. This approach is based on the paradigm that the ecological environment in which a child grows up has a strong influence on its development and behavior. The *ecological environment* is conceived as a topologically nested arrangement of structures, from microsystem, mesosystem, exosystem to macrosystem (Figure 9.1).

Microsystems are the most important environments of the developing child. A *microsystem* is a pattern of roles, interpersonal relations and activities experienced over time by the child in a given setting with particular physical and material characteristics (Bronfenbrenner & Crouter, 1983, p. 380). Family, daycare centers, school and work are examples of microsystems. As a child grows up, it participates in a growing number of microsystems, the whole of which is called *mesosystem.* Microsystems directly influence the child by face to face contacts, whereas the exosystem's effects on children are mainly indirect. The *exosystem* refers to formal and informal social structures that influence the immediate settings of children. Parents' social network, the neighborhood in which the family lives and parents' world of work are relevant elements of the exosystem. The *macrosystem* differs from the preceding systems in that it refers not to a specific context but to cultural prototypes, originating from religion or world view, that influence structures at macrolevel, such as the law system, the educational system or the

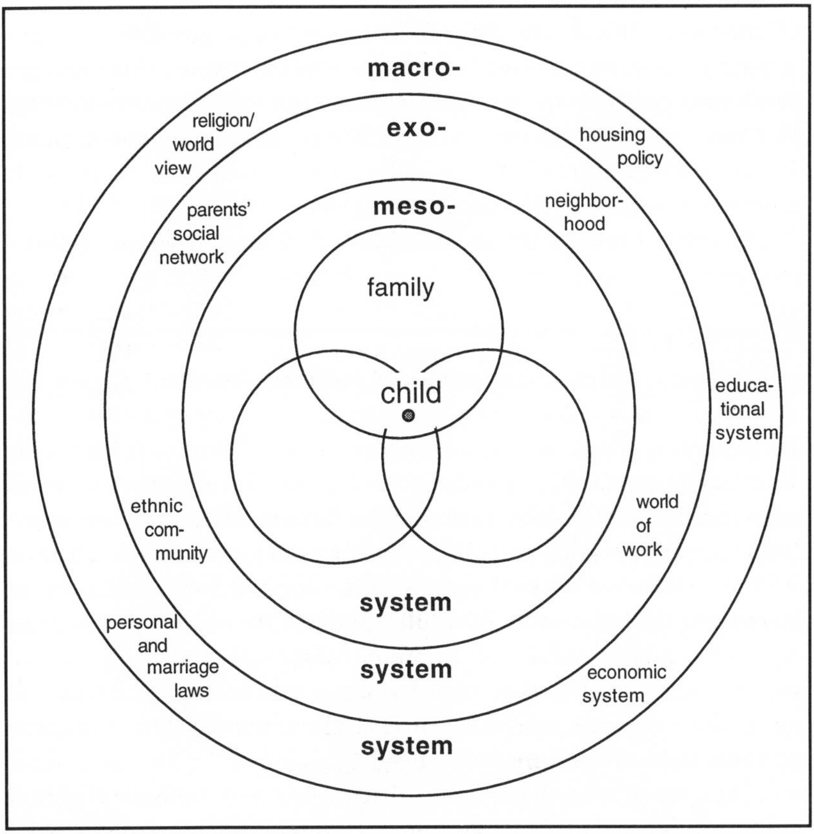

Figure 9.1 Socio-ecological environment of the child

economic system. A macrosystem is the 'cultural blueprint' of society. Culture permeates society from macrolevel to microlevel.

Bronfenbrenner's socio-ecological model offers a useful approach for studying the social environment of the ethnic minority children from micro- to macrolevel. Although there is no universally accepted definition, *ethnic minorities* are mostly characterized as groups having a subordinate position in society and a culture different from that of the mainstream society (Eldering, 1996). A theoretical model to study the development and education of ethnic minority children should therefore take into account the social and cultural factors in their daily life. The socio-ecological model acknowledges the vital role of the parents' social world (exosystem) in the daily life of children. The subordinate position of ethnic minority parents in society and their social network after emigration, influence the way they raise their children (Eldering, 1995; McLoyd, 1990; Ogbu, 1987, 1992). Moreover, this model can elucidate the determining influence of the host society as well as the country of origin at the macrolevel.

Bronfenbrenner's model enables the social aspects of the environment of a child's daily life to be mapped, but it pays scarcely any attention to its cultural dimension. To study the latter dimension I use the model of the developmental niche, an anthropological-psychological framework developed by Harkness and Super. The *developmental niche* consists of three interrelated subsystems: the physical and social settings in which a child lives, the culturally determined customs of childcare and rearing, and the belief systems of the caretakers (parental ethnotheories) (Harkness & Super, 1993; Super & Harkness, 1986). The physical and social settings of children include elements such as the size and composition of the household, the activities of adults and children, and physical aspects of the house and environment. Observation of the children's settings leads to the second subsystem: culturally regulated customs and practices of childcare and childrearing. These customs and practices are so commonly used by members of the community and integrated into the larger culture that they do not need individual rationalizing. Both systems are rooted in the parents' belief systems regarding children and the development of children. Parental belief systems, or parental ethnotheories, play a vital role in structuring the customs and practices of childcare and childrearing and the settings in which children live (Figure 9.2).

Parental belief systems are specialized cultural models, derived from more general cultural models in society. For example, in Western societies where independence is highly valued, autonomy is a key value in childrearing. In contrast, ethnic minority parents originating from societies with a more collectivistic orientation, such as Morocco or Turkey, more often emphasize relational values in their childrearing practices. Parents in these societies attach high priority to obedience, respect for parents and older family members, group loyalty and solidarity (Eldering & Vedder, 1993; Kağttçtbaşt, 1989, Pels, 1991). Another key value in childrearing, which will be discussed later, concerns family honor. Parents in

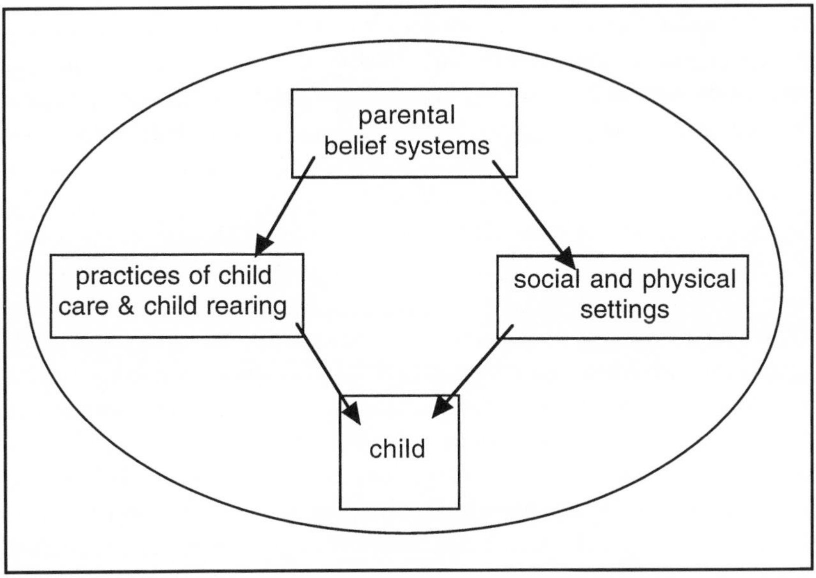

Figure 9.2 Framework of the developmental niche

non-Western countries appear to attach more value to the moral development of children than to their cognitive development. To them, the concept of intelligence more often means social intelligence than cognitive intelligence (Harkness & Super, 1993).

The developmental niche is on the one hand seen as a well-balanced system of subsystems, but on the other it is assumed that the subsystems can be influenced and changed from the outside. Although subsystems initially resist change, they will change in the long run under the influence of the exosystem and the macrosystem.

The model of the developmental niche has mostly been used to compare child rearing across cultures, but until recently it has not been used in research on children growing up in multicultural settings. This framework, however, is particularly suitable to study the cultural dimension in the daily life of ethnic minority children. It enables the cultural belief systems of ethnic minority parents to be described in addition to their practices of childcare and childrearing and the setting in which their children grow up.

The framework of the developmental niche can also be applied to other microsystems, such as schools. Schools can be viewed as geographically located microsystems, in which teachers' ethnotheories about children's development and learning regulate classroom settings and teaching practices. By describing the developmental niche of ethnic minority children at home and at school, discrepancies between both niches can be identified and analyzed.

The integration of Bronfenbrenner's socio-ecological model and Harkness and Super's framework of the developmental niche into a cultural-ecological model makes it possible to study the social and cultural environment of ethnic minority children. With the help of this model, discrepancies and risk factors in the daily life of these children may be identified and analyzed (Eldering, 1995).

Moroccan Children Growing Up in Two Worlds

Moroccans (165,000) are the third biggest ethnic minority group in the Netherlands, after the Surinamese (258,000) and the Turks (203,000) (CBS, 1995). Ethnic minorities comprise six to eight percent of the total population in the Netherlands (15 million).

Morocco experienced a short period of colonization by the French from 1912 until 1956. The divide-and-rule policy of the French magnified the differences between the Arabs and Berbers. The rural regions, mostly inhabited by Berbers, remained underdeveloped because of insufficient sources of subsistence and poor schooling. At the end of the previous century an exodus began from these regions to urban areas in Morocco and, after independence in 1956, also to Europe: France, Belgium and the Netherlands. About 40 years ago, the first Moroccan men arrived as "guest workers" in the Netherlands. More than half the Moroccans currently living in the Netherlands are Berbers originating from the Rif mountains in Northeast Morocco.

Böhning (1972) distinguishes three stages in the labor migration process from Mediterranean countries to Northwest Europe:

- the arrival of (predominantly male) workers
- the family reunion process
- the formation of ethnic networks and communities ("ethnic colonies").

Most immigrant groups from Mediterranean countries in the Netherlands have completed the three stages. I'll illustrate this with examples from my study of Moroccan families in the Netherlands (Van der Berg-Eldering, 1978). The sample consisted of 45 Moroccan families settling in a small Dutch town with an expanding industry. Initially, I helped these families to settle (buying furniture, filling out forms for loans, accompanying women to the family doctor, introducing children to schools, and so on.); later I received a grant from the Ministry of Welfare to study the family reunion and accommodation process of these families in greater depth. In order to be able to talk with women as well as men without an interpreter, I learned the Moroccan-Arabic dialect, the language Moroccans speak in daily life. I visited many of these families in Morocco before and after they emigrated. This gave me the opportunity to compare their situations in their home country and in the Netherlands. After my research I kept in touch with a number of these families and have followed their lives over a period of about twenty years.

In the following sections I will outline the formation of ethnic networks and communities, the social position of the Moroccans in the Netherlands and their home country, and the developmental niche in which their children grow up.

Moroccan Networks and Communities

The Moroccan families in my sample originated from three geographically and culturally distinct areas: the Rif mountains, the regions surrounding Tanger and Tetouan, and the big cities (Casablanca, Fez, Marrakech, Kenitra). The Moroccans from the Rif mountains perdominantly speak a Berber language, are mostly illiterate and they seclude their women and girls after puberty. The immigrants from the regions surrounding Tanger and Tetouan speak the Moroccan-Arabic dialect and their literacy rate is higher than that of the Rif people. Many of their families in Morocco grow and sell the soft drug hashish (*kif*). The immigrants from the big cities are, on average, better educated and they read and write Standard Arabic. Most of the men worked in factories or service industries before they emigrated.

Regional differences proved to be a relevant identity marker and criterion for network formation in the Netherlands. Within the Moroccan community these people primarily felt themselves to be a *Riffi,* a *Tetouani,* or a *Bedaui, Fessi, Marrakchi or Kenitri,* yet to the Dutch people they presented themselves as Moroccans. They primarily trusted people from the same region and they held prejudices against people from other regions. The prejudices often concerned religion (being good Muslims or not) and behavior of women and girls (behaving according to the standards of modesty or not). The Rif families had the strongest preference for their own group. Men from the Rif, for instance, did not ask women from other regions to help when their wives gave childbirth, and their name-giving parties were mostly attended by related families and other people from their home region.

Over time the networks of the Moroccan families have grown as a result of chain-migration, births and marriages. When I started my research, none of the families had relatives living in the same Dutch town. Three years later, many families, particularly the Rif people, had attracted other related families to settle in the same town. A family from Tetouan was joined by nearly all the man's brothers and their families. Now, twenty years later, all the families which had small children at the time of my research have married children and grandchildren. Most parents arranged marriages for their children with Moroccan partners, preferably from the same family or region. Although basically consisting of relatives and people form the same region, most networks included some Moroccan friends and colleagues from elsewhere. Moreover, most families had contacts with one or more Dutch families living in the same neighborhood or from the workplace. These relations were predominantly instrumental in character, and were not intended for sharing emotions.

Ethnic networks and communities have various functions: reconstructing cultural life, providing mutual aid and solidarity, and exercising social control. Many families from rural areas in Morocco had lived in villages, surrounded by their extended family. During their first period as "guest workers," the men invested in housing and land in Morocco in order to maintain the extended family network. In the Netherlands, the families initially lived in nuclear families without related families nearby. Many postponed the celebration of life cycle rituals, such as name-giving and circumcision ceremonies and marriages until their holidays in Morocco. As their stay lengthened, their network of relatives developed and their opportunities for ritual slaughter increased, so more rituals were celebrated in the Netherlands. The kinds of rituals, however, have changed in the course of time. Whereas in the first period after the reunion of the family in the Netherlands many children were born and name-giving and circumcision ceremonies had to be organized, now, 20 years later, there are many marriage parties and celebrations for older people who have made the pilgrimage to Mecca (*hadjdj*).

> In the first years of the family reunion process the name-giving ceremonies were usually held in one house. The women sat in a bedroom upstairs, so that they could not be seen by men, whereas the men sat downstairs in the living room. Women prepared the meal in the kitchen and boys served the men first and girls served the women later, often after midnight.
>
> Recently, my husband and I were invited to celebrate the marriage of a daughter of one of the Moroccan families in my sample. She is the third daughter in a family with nine children. Her elder brothers and sisters are already married. Their in-laws were also invited to the wedding. The bride's father has four brothers who live nearby with their families. They and their children and in-laws also attended the party. The party was held in three houses: one for the older men, one for the younger men and one for the women. This division over several houses was caused not only by the number of guests, but also by the differences in age categories and interests of the men. Older men are more interested in serious topics, while younger men want to dance and joke, which is not allowed in front of their fathers and uncles. My husband who was invited to join the older men had to listen to a tape of Qur'an recitations the whole night and I joined the girls and women, who joked, gossiped and danced Arabic dances.

Islam is a religion with a great influence on daily life. The Muslims are forbidden to drink wine and liquor (many Moroccans drink beer) and they do not eat pork. Muslim children are expected to respect these dietary rules at school too.

Besides life cycle rituals, the Moroccans have several yearly religious celebrations, such as the *Ramadan,* the month of fasting which ends with the *'Id al Fitr,* and the *'Id al Kbir,* the celebration of the sacrifice of Isaac, the son of Abraham. The Moroccan network and community play an important role in the reconstruction of cultural and religious life and the confirmation of its underlying values.

Giving mutual aid and showing solidarity is a second important function of the social network. Women help each other in illness and pregnancy and they prepare meals for rituals. Men loan each other money, help their compatriots with buying and selling cars, translating letters, filling out forms and interpreting in contacts with Dutch people.

A third function, which will be dealt with more in detail later, is the exercise of social control. The existence of a tight ethnic network and community on the one hand enables Moroccan families to reconstruct their cultural and religious life and protects them against alienation, but on the other it impedes them from deviating from the accepted cultural and religious standards by controlling the behavior of its members. In principle, the social control concerns all the behavior that can be observed in public, such as the compliance with religious standards, the behavior of Moroccan children and, particularly, the modesty of married women and adolescent girls. The many mosques that have been established in the Netherlands over the past 20 years are not only centers for religious worship, but also places where people—mainly men—gather to discuss the state of affairs in the community. Recently many mosques also seem to have become involved in drug dealing and money laundering (Müller, 1996).

Social Position in the Netherlands and Morocco

First-generation immigrants usually participate in two macro-systems, that of the country of origin and that of the country in which they live. In this section I'll point out that the Moroccans occupy different social positions in both countries.

1. Social Position in the Netherlands. First-generation Moroccans on average occupy a low social position in the Netherlands; indeed, they are the most disadvantaged ethnic minority group in our country. Moroccans, particularly the women and those originating from rural areas, have a high illiteracy rate. Although most men had work at the time their women and children joined them in the Netherlands, more than half the Moroccan families currently live on welfare or receive benefits from the Sickness Benefits Act (CBS, 1995). The prospects for their children in the Dutch opportunity structure are even worse. Many Moroccan children, particularly boys, leave school without a diploma. A relatively high percentage of Moroccan boys currently come into contact with the police and as much as one-quarter of the youngsters in Penitential Youth Establishments are of Moroccan origin (Boendermaker, 1995; Junger, 1990). Unemployed Moroccan boys with low educational qualifications are easily tempted to become involved in drug dealing.

Some 60 percent of Moroccans in the Netherlands live in cities of more than 100,000 inhabitants, compared with only 22 percent of the total Dutch population (Roelandt *et al.,* 1991). Although the housing conditions of ethnic minorities have improved over the past ten years, many Moroccans still live in overcrowded apartments in ethnically mixed neighborhoods. Only four percent are houseowners (CBS, 1995).

2. Social Positions in Morocco. The Moroccan emigrants are accorded a higher social status and more prestige back in Morocco. Many Moroccans in the Netherlands still invest in housing, land and other commodities in Morocco, even after their wives and children have joined them in the Netherlands. Initially the houses were bought to live in during the holidays and after retirement (Van den Berg-Eldering, 1978). Another reason for these investments was to have a house and some capital in case of the emigrants were forced to leave the Netherlands in times of economic recession and growing racism. As one Moroccan said: "If a father does not have enough food for his children, he'll first send his guests away."

About 95 percent of the Moroccans in the Netherlands still have Moroccan nationality. They equate giving up their nationality with giving up being Muslim. Recently the Dutch parliament decided that foreigners such as Moroccans and Turks could be granted Dutch nationality, but still retain their original nationality. Since then, many Moroccans have requested Dutch nationality. Having Moroccan nationality, Moroccans are governed by Moroccan Family Law (*Moudawwana*). The *Moudawwana* is characterized by inequality of men and women. Under Moroccan Family Law men are entitled to have several wives (polygyny) and to repudiate their wives. Women have much less opportunity to get a divorce under this law. Moroccan women living in the Netherlands, therefore, file for a divorce in a Dutch court. But, as will be shown later in this contribution, a divorce acquired in a Dutch court, is not accepted in Morocco. As explicitly noted in the marriage contract, girls are expected to remain virgin until their first marriage and they are forbidden to marry a non-Muslim (Van den Berg-Eldering, 1986). Moroccans living in the Netherlands usually contract their marriages in the Moroccan consulates in this country or in their country of origin.

The Developmental Niche of Moroccan Children

Having described the socializing context at exo- and macrosystem level, I will now discuss the developmental niche in which Moroccan children in the Netherlands grow up.

1. Changing Settings. The setting in which children grow up changed drastically in families who emigrated to the Netherlands. Apart from being housed in a one-family house or apartment in an ethnically mixed neighborhood, the most remarkable changes were the absence of members of the extended family and the daily presence of the husband and father. When they migrated as "guest workers," most men had left their wife and children under the control of their family. Many such women were forbidden to leave the home during the absence of their husbands. I met several women in Morocco, mostly young women, who were not even allowed to show their face at the door. Their father-in-law or brother-in-law did the shopping and represented the family outside. Most men visited their family only once a year for one or two months. Although the women became more dependent on their in-laws for contacts outside, they acquired more autonomy within the household, particularly when they and their children moved to their own house. (As pointed out in the previous section, many men invested in housing during the first period of migration.)

Over time, however, the social control function of the extended family decreased, for various reasons, and in many families problems with the children arose, particularly with the sons. Because of their seclusion and limited authority in public, the women were unable to control the behavior of their sons outside. This was one of the main motives for the migration of the family to the Netherlands. Remarkably, the women stimulated this family reunion process, because they wanted their husbands to resume the responsibility for the household and the raising, or rather the disciplining, of the children, even if this meant emigrating to a foreign country (Van den Berg-Eldering, 1978).

In the Netherlands, mother and children had to accommodate to the daily presence of the father and vice versa. The role pattern and responsibilities of the family members had changed in his absence: the mother had acquired more autonomy in the management of the household and the raising of the children, one of the older sons had often assumed the role of the father. Mother and children usually had a warm and close relationship, the father's role had attenuated to that of a visitor. The accommodation process did not proceed without difficulties, and had mixed success. In some families the man did not succeed in resuming his position as head of the household and disciplining father. He never regained control over his growing sons, who marginalized and became delinquent (Werdmölder, 1990). In some other families the mother and the older sons continued to manage and control the household and the father had to accept to subordinate position in the household; he represented the family only formally in public (Buijs, 1993).

Most men in my research resumed their responsibility as head of the household and the women had to accept a subordinate position once more. They had no knowledge of Dutch society and language and were dependent on their husbands for a residence permit. Moroccan men from rural backgrounds, particularly the men from the Rif, were very strict with their women and secluded them after migration. The women were not allowed to work outside the home, to go out shopping or to follow Dutch courses. The men accompanied their wives to the family doctor and other medical services. They not only feared the social control of their compatriots, but were also afraid that their women would be attracted to the greater freedom of women in Dutch society. Most women in my research accepted the rules their husbands set for them and acquired more autonomy when their children were older. Moroccan women originating from urban areas were more often allowed to work outside the home. The women with a stable marriage invested in family projects, such as housing, education or marriage of the children; other women invested their savings in golden jewelry as an insurance against repudiation (Van den Berg-Eldering, 1978).

When the families came to the Netherlands, all the men were working. Indeed, to have work was a condition for being granted a permit for family reunion. Now, about 20 years later, many men are no longer working. The families live on welfare or receive benefits under the Sickness Benefits Act.

Although the children were mainly socialized in the Netherlands, many families in my sample succeeded in visiting Morocco every two or three years. During these visits marriages were celebrated, circumcision ceremonies held and celebrations for pilgrims to Mecca organized. The families displayed a conspicuous consumption pattern, which raised their status and prestige within their community. Their investments in housing and religious and life cycle celebrations were financed partly by their savings, partly by income from drug dealing. The children experienced and enjoyed the higher prestige of their family during their stay in Morocco. Over the years, however, they began to feel more Dutch. Many children asked their parents to return to the Netherlands after a few weeks, because they missed their friends. Their proficiency in Moroccan-Arabic and Berber decreased and because of this they tended to play with Moroccan children also living in the Netherlands.

2. Beliefs and Practices. It will be clear that the first years after the family reunion in the Netherlands proved to be a confusing period. The family had to find a new role pattern and at the same time to cope with influences from Dutch society. Moroccan parents have an ambivalent attitude toward Dutch society. On the one hand they attach much value to a modern education for their children, but they also want to preserve their cultural and religious values and to prevent their children adopting certain Dutch values, such as autonomy, independence and Western style relations between men and women.

The Moroccan families in my research initially expected that graduating from Dutch high schools would give their children a better position in Dutch society. The parents were unwilling to request the municipality to organize mother tongue lessons for their children, because they wanted them to concentrate on learning Dutch. Only after they became aware that their children did not succeed under the permissive teaching style of the Dutch school system and began to play truant, did the parents ask for more authoritarian teachers and mother-tongue lessons (Van den Berg-Eldering, 1978). About 70 percent of the Moroccan students in primary schools in the Netherlands currently follow mother tongue lessons during school hours (CEB, 1994). Moroccan parents see the home and the school as settings with separate responsibilities. The school is responsible for the cognitive development of the children, whereas the parents' responsibility primarily lies with the children's religious and moral development. Moroccan parents want these domains to stay separate, a wish that is proving to be elusive (Eldering, 1996; Rex, 1991).

Moroccan parents have become afraid that their sons will marginalize, become delinquent and addicted to drugs. This fear is well-founded, give the high percentage of delinquent Moroccan boys. In order to protect their children against permissive Dutch society and to preserve their cultural and religious traditions, many Moroccan parents arrange marriages for their children at a relatively young age. The percentage of mixed marriages of Moroccans in the Netherlands is still very low.

> A Moroccan father asked me once to interpret during a visit to a Dutch couple, the parents of his son's girlfriend. Two older brothers fetched me from the station on the appointed day and in the car told me what the problems were. The Moroccan family was afraid that the son, not too stable a figure, would become a drug addict by being affiliated with this Dutch girl and her friends. During the visit I tried to translate as literally as possible, without asking questions.

After having introduced themselves, the Dutch parents politely pointed out that they had no objections against Moroccans, but that they thought that their respective cultures were too different to make a relationship or marriage work. The Moroccan father—the Moroccan mother was also present, but she did not speak Dutch—used another and (as proved later) very effective strategy. He painted a very negative pictue of his son by saying that his son was like the wind, blowing from another direction every day, and was so unstable that he would never succeed in providing for his family and that he though that their daughter was too good for him. Finally, he requested the Dutch couple to persuade their daughter to allow her friend visit Morocco with his family. The relationship ended shortly after this visit, as might be expected. A brother of the Moroccan boy helped him to find a job and his parents arranged a marriage for him with a Moroccan girl. They expected that he would behave as a responsible man after his marriage.

First-generation Moroccans attach much value to the honor of the family as determined by the modest behavior of the women and the girls after puberty. Moroccan children are raised with gender-specific rules in the family. A predominant rule is that a girl remains a virgin until she marries. Her virginal status is even described in the marriage contract of a girl's first marriage (Van den Berg-Eldering, 19860. Although Moroccans value education for their children, many parents, particularly those from rural backgrounds, do not want their girls to continue schooling after puberty. They are afraid that their daughters will meet boys and eventually become pregnant. Loss of virginity and pregnancy of an unmarried girl brings great shame to the family and leads to a severe loss of family honor within the community. A pregnant girl is threatened with death, exclusion from the family, or a marriage with a poor man in Morocco. Moroccan parents particularly fear that Dutch teachers and social workers will help their daughters gain greater autonomy and freedom. Confining adolescent girls to the home, however, does not always prevent them from becoming pregnant.

Fatima is the second daughter of a Moroccan family from Tanger. At the time the family emigrated to the Netherlands

> she and her older sister were twelve and fourteen years old. When I proposed that the father send the girls to school, he reacted by saying: "What will they do there? Make coffee and tea for the teachers?" The municipality imposed no sanctions on absenteeism from school at that time, so the girls stayed at home. Several years later, the father asked me to accompany him to the specialist who was treating his daughter who was in hospital. When I heard that she was in the gynecology ward, I asked the father to allow me to see the specialist first on my own. It turned out that the girl had been pregnant and had had a spontaneous abortion. A cousin from Morocco, who stayed with the family in the Netherlands, had seduced the girls and promised to marry her next year in Morocco. She implored us not to say anything about the pregnancy to her parents. When I returned I told the father that his daughter had had an ovarian cyst. He reacted by saying that the family doctor had told him that his daughter had been pregnant. When confronted with two contradictory versions of his daughter's illness he immediately chose the specialist's version because "a specialist has more knowledge than a family doctor" and asked me to tell this version to any Moroccans who enquired about his daughter. The girl's mother entreated me not to tell her husband's brothers and their families anything about the affair. A few years later the parents arranged a marriage for this girl with the son of a neighbor of the mother's brother in Morocco. After the marriage had been celebrated the girl's mother told me that she had informed the groom that Fatima was no longer a virgin due to an operation in hospital. He nevertheless accepted her because he needed a residence permit for the Netherlands.

This case shows that loss of virginity is a very serious threat to the honor of the family, particularly when it becomes public. Both cases show that maintaining the family honor in public is the responsibility of the whole family. Elder brothers and sisters control the behavior of the younger ones outside, and vice versa.

So far I have pictured the socializing context of first generation Moroccan children living in relatively stable families embedded in a Moroccan network and community. That the accommodation process of the family does not always proceed so smoothly will be demonstrated in the next section.

Moroccan Children Growing Up with Divorced Mothers

A few years ago the Center for Intercultural Pedagogics was requested to study the conditions of single (divorced) Moroccan mothers and childen. Social workers had indicated that these women were having problems in rearing their children. For this study we interviewed 15 Moroccan mothers from different backgrounds (Eldering & Borm, 1996). Despite differences in age, regional and ethnic origins, and educational level, the history and daily life situation of the single mothers were strikingly similar. I'll give a shortened version of the story of Wafia.

> Wafia is a 30-year-old divorced Moroccan woman. She was raised in Morocco, first by a childless aunt in the country, where she lived like a princess, and then, when she was eight years old and had to go to school, by her parents (which was a rude shock for her). At the age of 17, her parents arranged a marriage for her with a man, Driss, who worked as "guest worker" in the Netherlands. After the marriage he left her in his parents' home, where she had a hard life. After a few years of marriage, Wafia persuaded Driss to take her to the Netherlands. Here her life became even more miserable. In a short time she bore three children, a son Rachid and two daughters. Driss secluded his wife and forbade her to have contact with other people. When he returned from his work, he raised the children and set them against their mother. After a couple of years Driss took his wife and children to Morocco and left them with his family after taking away their passports and his wife's residence permit. A policeman in Morocco who sympathized with Wafia summoned Driss to return to Morocco. Driss promised to better his life and to take the family back to the Netherlands. Back here the situation worsened. Driss was very angry that Wafia had made

> the family problems public and he maltreated her and the children. Finally, after eight years of marriage Wafia ran away with her children to a battered women's refuge. To prevent Driss abducting the children, Wafia and her children were sent to a refuge in another part of the country. She filed for a divorce in a Dutch court. Now, seven years later, Wafia still has many problems with the education of Rachid, her eldest son. Rachid has been in residential care for many years, but the situation has not improved. Wafia suspects that Rachid has been sexually abused by his father. Recently the father requested the Dutch court to give him the right to visit his children. This action has again caused great unrest in the family.

Most divorced Moroccan women were given in marriage by their family at a young age. On the date the marriage was celebrated, their husbands were usually working in the Netherlands. The women usually joined their husbands in the Netherlands after a couple of years. Emigration meant a stressful change in daily life settings for the women. They had to leave their parents and other family members in Morocco and had to adjust to a husband they scarcely knew and to life in an unfamiliar society. The men generally failed to help them adjust. Typically, the husband simply forbade his wife to participate in Dutch society and insisted she remained secluded at home, even if she had not lived in seclusion in Morocco. Many women were maltreated by their husbands. Problems also often arose between fathers and children. The fathers neglected or maltreated their children. Finally, after a marriage of, on average, twelve years, the women fled with their children to a battered women's refuge and decided to get a divorce. They sought help from Dutch social workers and lawyers. By making their family problems public and seeking a divorce in a Dutch court, they injured the reputation of their husband and his family and their prestige in the Moroccan community decreased. Divorced women are viewed negatively in Moroccan society. They are blamed for the marriage problems and are seen as threatening for other marriages (Naamane-Guessous, 1988).

The divorced mothers deliberately chose to settle in the Netherlands and to integrate. They applied for Dutch nationality, requested to be housed in a neighborhood without Moroccans, entered Dutch education, and tried to find a job. Clearly, the social and cultural environment of these Moroccan mothers and children changed drastically after the divorce. Before their divorce, the women were part of a Moroccan community, although they had few contacts outside the family. After their divorce, they tried to participate actively in Dutch society and avoided the Moroccan community.

Will this participation lead to a quick acculturation of mother and children? Although this question can only be answered after a longitudinal study, here I want to discuss the link between the women's avoidance of the Moroccan community and the transmission of religious values. A striking phenomenon in the daily life situation of the single Moroccan mothers was their limited informal network and their heavy dependence on formal social work and health institutions. Their informal network consisted mainly of women. Because they had low prestige in the Moroccan community and they feared harassment from their former husband and his family, the women avoided contact with other Moroccans, except Moroccan women in similar circumstances. Most women had one or more Dutch female friends. On the other hand, they depended heavily on professional workers from health and social organizations, because they had many health and financial problems.

Islam is a religion which influences the daily life of the believers in various ways. Some religious rules can be practiced without the presence of other believers, such as praying, fasting or not eating pork or drinking alcohol. But on the other hand Islam is a religion to be practiced with the community of believers. By celebrating the yearly holy days and the rites of passage of the life cycle, the community reconfirms its religious beliefs and values and transmits them to the next generation, as I pointed out in the previous section. Some Moroccan women in our sample had turned away from Islam. Others tried to continue to practice the religious food prescripts and to fast during Ramadan. Most mothers, however, reported that they did not celebrate religious holidays, since they were no longer part of the Moroccan community. Moreover, about half of the women had been unable to visit their family in Morocco for many years, because they feared they would be imprisoned upon arrival in Morocco. Many women were in the curious position that they were viewed as divorced women under Dutch law and as married women under Moroccan Family Law. A point, which also needs to be studied further, is that some children rejected Moroccan culture and Islam because of the negative experiences with their father and his family, and the Moroccan community.

Conclusion

In this contribution the socializing environment of two categories of Moroccan children in the Netherlands has been sketched from a cultural-ecological perspective. The socialization of Moroccan children living in two-parent families appears to proceed differently from that of Moroccan children growing up with a divorced mother. The parents in two-parent families try to transmit their cultural and religious traditions to their children and in this process they are supported and controlled by their Moroccan network and community in the Netherlands and Morocco. The children are expected to internalize gender-specific values and codes and to comply with Islamic rules. At school these children are socialized with values and norms different from those in their home setting and community. They enjoy their family's high status and prestige during their holidays in Morocco, but at the same time they are confronted with the low position and prestige Moroccans have in Dutch society. In short, these children are socialized in various settings in the Netherlands and Morocco, which sends them mixed messages about their role and identity.

In contrast, the children of the divorced mothers are raised in settings with more Dutch than Moroccan influences. The mothers have deliberately opted for integration in Dutch society and they avoid contacts with the Moroccan community. The female-headed families have limited informal networks and visit their family in Morocco infrequently. Moreover, as divorced women they have a low status in Morocco. Consequently, their children have less opportunity to learn and practice Moroccan cultural and religious rules. Because of the negative experiences before and after their mother's divorce, these children develop at best an ambivalent attitude toward the Moroccan culture and community. Will these children and their mothers become pioneers in the acculturation and integration process, or will they become marginalized in both cultures and societies? Viewed from the increasing frequency of Moroccan women requesting help from battered women refuges, these issues need to be studied more thoroughly.

Although the two cases I have sketched are based on small samples of informants, the comparison of Moroccan children growing up in different settings, makes it clear that to get more insight into the socialization and acculturation process of immigrant children requires more comparative research. Comparative research in various settings in the country of immigration, as in our case Moroccan children growing-up in two-parent families versus children raised by divorced Moroccan women, will enable the changes in the developmental niche within one generation to be identified. The questions I have raised in presenting these cases need to be studied in a longitudinal study. Research which compares across generations and includes samples in different countries enables the changes over the generations and the differences between the emigrants and those who stayed behind to be identified (cf. Suárez-Orozco, 1995). Comparative research makes clear that one cannot speak of *the* socialization and identity formation process of immigrants or ethnic minorities.

References

Berg-Eldering, Lotty van den (1978). *Marokkaanse Gezinnen in Nederland.* Alphen aan den Rijn: Samsom.

Berg-Eldering, L. van den (1986). Marokkaans Familierecht in Nederland. In L. van den Berg-Eldering (ed.) *Van Gastarbeider tot Immigrant, Marokkanen en Turken in Nederland 1965–1985* (p. 78–109). Alphen aan den Rijn: Samsom.

Boendermaker L. (1995). *Jongeren in Justitiële Behandelinrichtingen.* Den Haag: WODC.

Böhning, W. R. (1972). *The Migration of Workers in the United Kingdom and the European Community.* Oxford: Oxford University Press.

Bronfenbrenner, U. (1977). Toward an Experimental Ecology of Human Development. *American Psychologist,* July, 513–531.

Bronfenbrenner U., & A. C. Crouter (1983). The Evolution of Environmental Models in Developmental Research. In P. H. Mussen (ed.) *Hand-*

book of Child Development Vol. 1. History, Theories, and Methods (pp. 357–414). New York: Wiley.

Buijs, F. (1993). Leven in een nieuw land: Marokkaanse jongemannen in Nederland. Utrecht/Leiden: Uitgeverij Jan van Arkel/Rijksuniversiteit Leiden, COMT.

CBS (1995). *Allochtonen in Nederland 1995.* Voorburg/Heerlen: CBS.

CEB (Commissie Evaluatie Basisonderwijs) (1994). *Onderwijs gericht op een multiculturele samenleving.* Den Haag: SDU.

Eldering, L. (1995). Child Rearing in Bicultural Settings: a Culture–Ecological Approach. *Psychology and Developing Societies, a Journal,* 7(2) Sage, 133–153.

———. (1996). Multiculturalism and Multicultural Education in an International Perspective. *Anthropology and Education Quarterly,* 27(3): 315–330.

Eldering, L., & J. A. Borm (1996). *Alleenstaande Marokkaanse moeders.* Utrecht: Jan van Arkel.

Eldering, L., & P. Vedder (1993). Culture Sensitive Home Intervention: The Dutch HIPPY Experiment. In L. Eldering & P. Leseman (eds.) *Early Intervention and Culture: Preparation for Literacy. The Interface Between Theory and Practice* (pp. 231–252). Paris: UNESCO.

Harkness, S., & Ch. M. Super (1993). The Developmental Niche: Implications for Children's Literacy Development. In L. Eldering & P. Leseman (eds.) *Early Intervention and Culture: Preparation for Literacy. The Interface Between Theory and Practice* (pp. 115–132). Paris: UNESCO.

Junger, M. (1990). *Delinquency and Ethnicity.* Deventer/Boston: Kluwer Law and Tanalion Publishers.

Kağttçbaşt, C. (1989). Child Rearing in Turkey: Implications for Immigration and Intervention. In L. Eldering & J. Kloprogge (eds.), *Different Cultures Same School: Ethnic Minority Children in Europe* (pp. 137–152). Amsterdam: Swets & Zeitlinger.

McLoyd, Vonnie C. (1990). The Impact of Economic Hardship on Black Families and Children: Psychological Distress, Parenting and Socio–emotional Development. *Child Development,* 61(2):311–346.

Müller, Henk (1996). Dope in de Djellaba. *De volkskrant, 13 Januari.*

Naamane-Guessous, S. (1988). *Au-delá de toute pudeur. La sexualité féminine au Maroc.* Casablanca: Eddif.

Ogbu, J. U. (1987). Variability in Minority School Performance: A Problem in Search of an Explanation. E. Jacob & C. Jordan (eds.) Explaining the School Performance of Minority Students. *Anthropology and Education Quarterly,* 18(4):312–334.

———. (1992). Understanding Cultural Diversity and Learning. *Educational Researcher,* 21(8):5–14.

Pels, T. (1991). Developmental Expectations of Moroccan and Dutch Parents. In N. Bleichrodt & P. J. D. Drenth (eds.), *Contemporary Issues in Cross–Cultural Psychology* (pp. 64–71). Amsterdam/Lisse: Swets & Zeitlinger.

Rex, J. (1991). The Political Sociology of a Multi–Cultural Society. *European Journal of Intercultural Studies,* 2(1):7–19.

Roelandt, Th., J. H. M. Roijen, & J. Veenman (1991). *Minderheden in Nederland. Statistisch Vademecum 1991.* 's-Gravenhage: SDU Uitgeverij/CBS Publikaties.

Suárez-Orozco, Carola, & Marcelo (1995). *Transformations.* Migration, Family Life, and Achievement Motivation among Latino Adolescents. Stanford, California: Stanford University Press.

Super, Ch. M., & S. Harkness (1986). The Developmental Niche: A Conceptualization at the Interface of Child and Culture. *International Journal of Behavioral Development,* 9, 545–569.

Werdmölder H. (1990). *Een generatie op drift.* De geschiedenis van een Marokkaanse randgroep. Arnhem: Gouda Quint bv.

Marcelo M. Suárez-Orozco

10

State Terrors

Immigrants and Refugees in the Post-National Space

The purpose of this essay is to insert the current delirium over immigration in the context of a cultural *malaise* afflicting nearly all postindustrial democracies. Although I shall concentrate on the recent American experience, the story—both about immigration and about cultural *malaise*—is a larger one: playing with Tolstoy's famous diagnosis, when it comes to immigration all of the families of the postindustrial world are unhappy in the same way.[1]

In both sides of Atlantic the debate over immigration is now routinely linked to economic concerns, fears about crime, and anxieties about preserving local cultural identities in light of new, little understood transnational forces (Espenshade and Hempstead, 1996; Suárez–Orozco, 1996). Yet no one to date has placed the immigration delirium—including the intensified violence against immigrants—in the context of an unprecedented crisis of meaning which has generated an array of dystopic cultural responses.

In the United States today there is a widespread sense that the sense has failed to solve an array of pressing domestic problems—such as poverty, inequality, and youth crime—and is now increasingly irrelevant in the context of powerful transnational economic and social formations. There is anger over the irreverence of a political class that is seen as arrogant, corrupt, and "out of touch." There are unprecedented anxieties engulfing the American middle class over economic decline, job insecurity, and the "disappearance" of good jobs to the developing world. There is anger over a judicial system that is seen as "broken." And there is a feeling of fatalism about schools that cannot teach, maintain discipline, or prepare our students to compete (with overseas students) in an increasingly globalized arena.

The distinguished political theorist Michael Sandel summarizes the nature of our current "discontent,"

> Two concerns lie at the heart of democracy's discontent. One is the fear that, individually and collectively, we are losing control of the forces that govern our lives. The other is the sense that, from family to neighborhood to nation, the moral fabric of the community is unraveling around us. These two fears—for the loss of selfgovernment and the erosion of community—together define the anxiety of the age. It is an anxiety that the prevailing political agenda has failed to answer or even address (Sandel, 1996: 1).

Furthermore this crisis of trust has engendered a vacuum of legitimacy that now is overflowing with unsettling paranoid conspirational theories, detached cynicism, and a culture of resentment. The debate over immigration is one of the most visible threads in the tapestry of our discontent.

In this essay I approach immigration as drama. Viewed through psychocultural lenses, immigration talk—in the media, in the Internet, in the neighborhoods, in the political pulpit—emerges as a stage articulating some of the more unstable, contradictory, and paradoxical formations of our age. In the first part of this essay, I paint in broad strokes some of the most visible landmarks of our dystopic landscape. Then I craft argument about how a sense of "dislocation"—a defining feature of our increasingly global world—relates to extremely unsettling anxieties about economy, society, and culture. Lastly, I explore how "immigration talk" offers a powerful symbolic order—including a reworking of the idea of "culture"—to articulate anxieties and to focus rage.

Mourning

Immigration talk intensified after the Cold War—and exploded over the public space in the 1990s. The end of the Cold War freed immense amounts of energy: military, political, economic, and psychological. The collapse of the Soviets facilitated new political alliances, new transnational economic projects, and new forms of interdependence. Beyond the Soviet factor, new technologies—particularly information technologies—new means of mass communication, and new ease of mass transportation generated unprecedented forms of international enmeshment.

Old national boundaries—the kinds of boundaries that defined the Cold War—were redrawn, seemly overnight. Places that had been kept apart now would come together—such as the two Germanies. Places that had been kept together now would come apart—such as the former Yugoslavia. Seemingly everywhere "supra-national" projects cropped up opening up new socioeconomic, political, and symbolic spaces. It appeared that a new "global culture" would overwhelm anachronistic national boundaries. A new space of what I will call "post-nationality" decidedly reconfigured the international landscape.[2]

Paradoxically, these globalizing impulses also generated a new mood of inwardness. "Going home" we did not like what we saw. Nearly all of the structures of the nation-state came under scrutiny. By the 1990s social and economic anxieties began to corrode the famed optimism of the American middle classes. After decades of a seemingly unshakable faith that tomorrow will be better than yesterday a new depressive anxiety set in. Millions of workers found out they were "disposable." (Since 1979 more than 43 million jobs have been lost in the United States [Uchitelle and Kleinfield, 1996: 1]). And economists highlighted that many who managed to keep their jobs had in fact been "losing ground." Indeed, "[for the median American worker] there has been no increase in real take-home pay since the first inauguration of Richard Nixon" (Krugman, 1994: 2).[3]

Surveys suggested that many Americans felt that their children would be worse off than they were. A new scary word entered the American vocabulary: "downsizing." Paradoxically, accelerated changes in the global socioeconomic landscape, including new patterns of capital flows, the liberalization of "Third World" economies, and "First World" policies to recruit temporary workers to do the impossible jobs that workers in the "developed" world won't do, ignited unprecedented levels of immigration. By the mid–1990s there were over 100 million immigrants—and an estimated 30 million refugees—worldwide.[4]

The economic downturn, the symbolic death of the state—or, at best, the massive corrosion of trust in the structures of the state to ameliorate enduring problems—and the dawn of a global era in production, communication, and culture constitute a series of major losses. On the work front alone the loses were fantastic. "On the Battlefields of Business, Millions of Casualties" announced an oversized *New York Times* front-page story (March 3, 1996, p. 1). The story went on to tell us that in 1996 ATT will "cut" 40,000 jobs, Delta Airlines will cut 15,000 jobs, Boeing will cut 15,000 jobs and Sears will "kill" 50,000 jobs.

The effects of these loses include, we are told be psychologists interviewed for the *New York Times* piece, patterns akin to "survival guilt" (among those who manage to keep their jobs) and patterns akin to "posttraumatic stress disorder" among those who are "downsized." Other reported symptoms included a deep sense of alienation and withdrawal from community organizations.[5] According to Harvard political theorist Robert D. Putman bowling patterns became a good index of the new social *malaise*. Putman showed that a time when more people than ever were bowling, bowling leagues were decreasing because large numbers of people went "bowling alone" (Putman, 1995).

Yet there was little or no inscribing of these upheavals in the public space—no ritual mourning signifying and elaborating these enormous upheavals and loses. Rather there was a general sense of disorientation and dystopia characterized by feelings that the world was changing in incomprehensible ways. Surveys suggested that was a widespread sense of loss of security and loss of control (Uchitelle and Kleinfield, 1996).

Dayton, Ohio, near the very (symbolic) center of the nation, we are told in another front-page *New York Times* story entitled "A Hometown Feels Less Like Home,"

> is deep in mid-passage between two economic eras: the old era of making things and job security, and the new one of

> service and technology, takeovers, layoffs, and job insecurity. And the entire cloth of society, which most people in Dayton once wore so comfortable, feels as if it is out of style and could just wear out.
>
> Everything, seemingly is in upheaval: not just the jobs and lives of tens of thousands of people, but also the big corporations, the banks, the schools, the religious and cultural institutions, the old relationships of politics and power, and, especially, people's expectations of security, stability and shared civic life. . . .
>
> They know that thousands of jobs—middle management, government, blue-collar—have disappeared, and more could go at any time. The anxiety is everywhere. From the mostly white East Side to the mostly black West Side; over coffee in the new $300,000 homes of suburban Centerville, in the classrooms at John Patterson High School downtown: the conversation inevitably returns to the loss of jobs, the decline of the middle class, the rise of the global economy, the end of the American dream (Rimer, 1996: 16).

Responsible politicians largely stayed away from the new *malaise* (Sandel 1996). When President Clinton noted that the American people seemed to be in a "funk," the media—and his opponents—immediately went on the attack. Sensing that the topic was too big, too painful, and simply impossible to address in soundbites—the President dropped it. Though sensing that the next election will be won by the candidate who is better able to contain the anxieties of the voters, the President on several occasions did refer to his understanding the "hurt" in the population—specifically (some said strategically) referring to the "angry white males."

Dis-Locations

The new global impulses undermined the old boundaries that served to contain not only political and economic projects but also to structure local identities and cultural psychologies. The upheaval brought about by these unprecedented global changes have affected the political and economic realm as well as the symbolic and psychocultural order. A particularly subversive aspect of the global upheaval has been the tearing of a feeling of "home"—the sense of rootedness, the feeling of continuity and familiarity with one's social space.

A variety of factors suggest themselves as related to a new sense of dis-location: the globalization of production and communication, the ease of mass transportation, and the cognate fact that for many workers—white and blue collar alike—survival in the era of "disposable workers" means manic relocations following or anticipating "downsizing."

The average length of home ownership in Los Angeles county is less than five years. In some school districts, the annual student turnover is nearly 90 percent! (K. Gutierrez, 1996). A teacher told a *New York Times* reporter writing a series of articles on downsizing:

> "Many of these kids I see are on their fifth or sixth move because the company keeps saying "We are not making enough money; we need to downsize more.' . . . 'It used to be military families. Now it's modern life. It really hurts the child's ability to develop those long-term commitments. It's devastating to the sense community'" (Rimer, 1996: 17).

Another informant simply commented, "We are the new homeless" (*ibid.*), after moving from Indianapolis to Wichita, to Dayton, to South Carolina, and back to Dayton in just four years. She added, "I am not building anything here. I attend church. I haven't joined. When they pass around the attendance card on Sundays, I want to write down 'I'm moving.'" (Rimer, 1996: 7).

For upper status workers the concept of "home" comes to mean something new for very different reasons. Rifkin claims that "the new elite of symbolic analysts have little or no attachment to place. Where they work is of far less importance than the global network they work in. In this sense they represent a new cosmopolitan force, a high-tech nomadic tribe who have more in common with each other than with the citizens of whatever country they happen to do business in" (Rifkin, 1995: 1).[6]

The anxieties generated by immigration today cannot be divorced from the worldwide reshaping of the socio-economic and symbolic space. Immigrants and refugees, I contend, have become terribly unsettling not simply because of the economic or political consequences of immigration, important as they are (see Suárez–Orozco and Suárez–Orozco 1995). What has been neglected is that immigrants and refugees are problematic because they have become an uncanny mirror of our own dislocation. Immigrants are subversive—and talk around immigration is so charged and out of control—because they come to embody the very terrifying sense of homelessness which characterizes the age of rapid change and globalization.[7]

Theater

Immigration comes to play a critical role in the symbolic space of the late twentieth century. My point is that today, in nearly all advanced postindustrial democracies, immigration has become a kind of theater engaging our collective anxieties. Immigration and anti-immigration talk captures our uneasiness about lost jobs, lost homes, lost communities, lost faith in the nation. As the old mythologies—of, *inter alia,* "nation," "community," and "home"—collapse, we find ourselves struggling to create a new language to imagine new "postnational" communities. And if the causes of the global transformation in economy and culture are hopelessly overdetermined, immigration offers a powerful metaphorical map to chart the complexes of our era.

Several "acts" can be dissected in the most recent version of the immigration drama. Rather than delve in the various gradations of the anxious talk around immigration, here I concentrate on two oppositional "ideal types." I choose to examine two opposite poles—poles that in obvious ways need and contain each other—because I think they best reflect the radicalization of affect around immigration in recent years. I will call these poles the "pro-immigration and the anti-immigration scripts."

Pro-immigration scripts are mythmaking. They are about (re)creating a sacred language to inscribe the eternal ideals and values that constitute our cultural soul. In these scripts, the new arrivals are cast in terms that are simply irresistible to many audiences. Enter, stage left: humble, hard working folk, killing themselves to become proud and loyal Americans.[8] Looking at this immigration mirror, we find an idealized—if somewhat mournful—picture of our most cherished ideals and values. Immigrants are our alter superego. Celebrating immigration is a kind of pseudo-xenophilia: we loved them for reminding us of what we once were. In the words of Massachusetts Governor and Mrs. Weld,[9]

> We find that to an amazing degree, they [immigrants] share the most traditional of American values: a disciplined work ethic, strong family ties, religious values, an inclination towards entrepreneurship, respect for education, personal independence, appreciation of democracy and a determination that—whatever it takes, whatever sacrifices may be called for, whatever deprivations must be endured—their children will have a better life.
>
> They share with other Americans a conviction that they and their children are smart enough, tough enough and brave enough to answer questions, solve problems, avert disasters and ultimately not only flourish and thrive themselves, but help bring prosperity and honor to their new country.
>
> And they are right. Immigrants are not helpless victims relying on our charity and good will—far from it! They are survivors. It takes courage, creativity, determination and commitment to abandon cherished possessions and people, leave the known for the unknown, cross unfamiliar territory and set up a new life in a new land. It is a tribute to the indomitable human spirit that so many people continue to do this so well.
>
> To those who say that the time has come to extinguish Lady Liberty's lamp and to slam shut the golden door, we say nonsense. Did you ever notice how, in the Olympic games, the Norwegians look like Norwegians, the Chinese look like Chinese, the Ethiopians look like Ethiopians, the Spaniards look like Spaniards and the Americans look like everybody else?
>
> There is a reason for this: Americans are everybody. American is still a young country, somewhat brash perhaps, occasionally prone to stumble and recover, and then stumble and recover again. But the United States posses a vigor and a record of accomplishment that has prompted many an Old

> World aristocrat to drop his monocle and say, 'Wow!' (Weld and Weld, 1996: 29).

For conservative Republicans Abraham, Bennett, Kemp and Wallop immigration is a defining feature of the Reaganesque "shining city" that is (was?) America:

> Immigration policy both reflects and projects our character and level of decency. In his farewell address to the nation, President Ronald Reagan said: 'I've spoken of the shining city all of my political life, but I don't know if I ever quite communicated what I saw when I said it. But in my mind it was a tall, proud city built on rocks stronger than oceans, windswept, God blessed, and teeming with people of all kinds living in harmony and peace, a city with free ports and hummed with commerce and creativity. And if there had to be city walls, the walls had doors and the doors were open to everyone with the will and heart to get here. That is how I saw it and see it still.'
>
> We choose the shining city over fortress America (1996: 39).

In such narratives immigrants play a strategic role: they enact a reassuring scrip which recycles the ur myth of the American project. According to the founding myth of the nation, the exceptionalism that makes America unique is that the United States took in millions of humble foreigners and made them into successful and loyal Americans. Immigrant "courage, creativity, determination" embodies the energy of a "young," somewhat "brash," "tall" and "proud" America. Immigration is the antidote to cultural *malaise*. As the late Barbara Jordan, the former Chairman of the Commission on Immigration Reform, put it, immigrants "remind ourselves . . . what makes us America" (Jordan, 1995: 15).

In the pro-immigrant scripts immigrants are seductive because they reaffirm, and narcissistically mirror, a soothing symbolic order.[10] In an age of cynicism, immigration injects a Panglossian shot of optimism: it is simply irrefutable proof that ours indeed is "best of all possible worlds" (Voltaire, 1961: 16). We are the greatest and the immigrant's desire marvelously mirrors our greatness. After all no other country in the world can claim what we can claim: The United States takes every year more immigrants than all other nations combined. Immigration talk, in this act, is feel good therapy.

Pro-immigration talk has its phantom or double in various rapidly metastasizing anti-immigration scripts. In its most primitive forms the anti-immigration scripts return the pro-immigration talk in an upside-down imagery that conveys a frightening message. In this mirror, humble foreigners become "illegal aliens" abusing social services and successful immigrants become sneaky competitors "stealing our jobs."[11] If the pro-immigration script is laced with cultural narcissism, anti-immigration scripts are typically poisoned with lethal dosages of paranoid ideation—saturated with culturally elaborated envy and jealousy fantasies.[12]

In many of these scripts, immigration articulates powerful anxieties about "losing control" or "losing boundaries." This engenders a near-psychotic panic that we are "inundated, swamped, submerged, engulfed, awash" by immigration (Christenfeld, 1996: 22).[13]

In a world *sans* borders, immigration quickly becomes invasion, and invasion leads to war (see Chavez 1995). In the words of Patrick Buchanan, "When you have one, two, three million people walking across your border every year, breaking your laws, you have an invasion." Ruth Coffey, the head of Stop Immigration Now (SIN!) says, "I have no intention of being the object of 'conquest,' peaceful or otherwise, by Latinos, Asians, blacks, Arabs or any other group of individuals who have claimed my country" (quoted in Christenfeld, 1996: 22).

By the early 1990s the anti-immigration scripts focused on and amplified a panic that the U.S. southern border had "fallen." There were loud cries to further militarize the U.S.–Mexico border to stop the estimated 200,000 to 400,000 people entering the U.S. without proper documentation each year.[14] The Border Patrol of the Immigration and Naturalization Service (INS), working in collaboration with the armed forces, attempted to contain public anxiety over ongoing waves of undocumented immigration by initiating various programs to "seal" sectors of the U.S.–Mexico border. On July 27, 1993 President Bill Clinton presented a new plan to crackdown on undocumented immigration (see Stern, 1993a). Arguing that "our borders leak like a sieve," President Clinton proposed bringing the number of Border Patrol agents to near 6,000. Another priority in the Clinton plan was to curb "political asylum abuses."[15]

Immigration came to be seen through the prism of illegality. One survey reported that "nearly 70 percent of respondents in our data believe that most new immigrants are in the country illegally" (Espenshade and Hempstead, 1996: 553). Powerful homeopathic connections between "illegal," "criminal," and "alien" saturated media coverage of immigration. These charged free associations fed public anxieties that not only are the new immigrants "illegals," but they were here with the purpose of committing crimes and abusing the welfare system. Another poll found that 59 percent of those surveyed agreed with the statement that "immigrants add to the crime problem" (Nelan, 1993: 11).

In mid-1993, the scripts were saturated with reference to the participation of undocumented immigrants and asylum seekers from the Middle East in the Manhattan Twin Towers terrorist bombing. There was also the case of the Pakistani refugee, Mir Aimal Kansi, charged in the killings of two C.I.A. employees just outside the Agency's headquarters. The anxious questions then asked referred directly to the loopholes in asylum laws and procedures: Just how did these terrorists get into the country? How is it possible that they could get work permits and could purchase weapons? How could they operate so freely? And how many other terrorists and criminals are slipping through?

The participation of "illegal aliens" in these terrorist acts injected a decidedly paranoid dose of nervousness into the public debate. To many, these dark men speaking with impossibly thick accents, seemed to capture everything that had gone wrong with immigration policies. The New York Twin Towers came to embody America's collective fears about the new immigrants much as Ellis Island represents what is now a safer and domesticated immigrant past.[16]

In the days following the arrests of the followers of Sheik Omar Abdel-Rahman, charged in the New York World Trade Center bombing, news cameras flocked to major airports to report, somewhat sensationally, on how "just about anyone" can get through immigration officials by simply claiming political asylum. Because of lack of space at the detention facilities, it was reported that asylum seekers are routinely released, pending a future INS hearing (Conover 1993: 58).[17]

In the more archaic versions of this charged talk, the crime problem is something which outside "aliens" bring into our world:

> [The] new criminals are undocumented aliens from Mexico, some of whom live here but many of whom sleep in their native land and cross daily into the United States to commit their crimes. At the end of their workday, they go back into Mexico with a few dollars to show for their efforts (quoted in Chavez, 1992: 16).

There is an everydayness implied in such talk: sleep, get up, cross the border, commit crimes, go back to Mexico. Simply, all aliens crossing the border are criminals.

Indeed, much of the anti-immigration talk came to deploy Hobbesquian images of chaotic disorder and lack of control in which growing waves of criminal aliens and terrorists, threaten to destroy our way of life. In the words of a former director of the INS in San Diego,

> One only need go down to this border just a short distance south of us to see how wildly out of control it is. And when we speak of out of control, we're not just talking about a few folks wanting to come in to get a job, we're talking about a torrent of people flooding here, bringing all kinds of criminal elements and terrorists and all the rest with them (Wolf, 1988: 2).

"Torrents" of "criminals" and "terrorists" "flooding" the country: The language of a country under siege. As someone else said, "Every night I can see the campfires those [immigrant] men make. I know what they are doing out there. I know they are just waiting for the right time to rob us, or worse. I just want you to know that every night I go to bed with a pistol under my pillow to protect myself from them" (quoted in Chavez, 1992: 18). The terror of those men in the dark waiting for the right moment to cross the line to strike has led to renewed cries to further militarize the Border region. In February 1994, Attorney General Janet Reno outlined a plan to add another 1,010 frontline agents to "hold the line" at the southern border.

There is a feeling that parts of California are under siege by gangs of criminal aliens terrorizing citizens, and even children:

> Nowhere in San Diego do you find the huge gangs of illegal aliens that line our streets, shake down our schoolchildren, spread diseases like malaria, and roam our neighborhoods looking for work or homes to rob. We are under siege in North County, and we have been deserted by those whose job it is to protect us from this flood of illegal aliens (quoted in Chavez, 1992: 17).

The terror of loss of control is intertwined with powerful images of waves of criminal aliens terrorizing innocent citizens, including children, robbing as they spread contamination and pollution (malaria)![18]

It is undoubtedly true that some immigrants do commit crimes. Indeed, a case can be made that given the marginalization, lack of opportunity, levels of symbolic violence, and racist disparagement the new immigrants of color face today, their participation in crime and "alternative economies" should be more acute than the data suggest.[19]

Identity: 'Where am I? What's Happened Here?'

I relate the fear of "loosing control" to a very threatening sense that "our" world—"home," "community," "nation"—is changing in incomprehensible ways. In Flushing, New York, a town that in 10 years saw the increase—via immigration—of the Asian-American population from 9% of the total population in 1980 to 22 percent in 1990, the metamorphosis is "proving painful, even traumatic, for many elderly white voters, who reared their children in Flushing and once regarded it as theirs. . . . 'Everything is changing' . . . 'It is very discombobulating, very upsetting. We all recognize that change is part of life, but it doesn't sit well.' The oldtimers' feelings of displacement often center on the Asian market places, where shelves are lined with jars of unfamiliar condiments and vegetable bins are filled with fare they see as exotic" (Dugger, 1996: 38).

Julia Harrison a Flushing councilwoman—and many of her elderly constituents—say "they come to feel increasingly out of place in their own neighborhood as growing numbers of Asian-Americans have settled there, speaking languages the oldtimers don't understand and selling foods they have never tested. She said in an interview that the sudden transforming arrival of Asian-Americans businesses—which city planners and immigration experts say revitalized a declining Flushing in the 1980s—was an 'invasion, not assimilation.' The new immigrants she argued, are 'more like colonizers than immigrants. They sure as hell had a lot of money and they sure as hell knew how to buy property and jack up rents of retail shops and drive people out" (*ibid.*).

Barbara Coe, a leader of the anti-immigration Proposition 187 in California—the initiative that would deny access to a host of publicly funded programs to undocumented immigrants (even school for children [see Suárez–Orozco, 1996]), became involved in the anti-immigration cause after a visit to an Orange County social service agency when she,

> became frightened by the changes immigration had brought into her community. 'I walked into this monstrous room full of people, babies, little children all over the place, and I realized nobody was speaking English,' . . . 'I was overwhelmed with this feeling: Where am I? What's happened here? [Barbara] Coe was trying to help an elderly friend secure some public health benefits but was turned down. 'When the counselor told me that lost of those people waiting were illegal aliens and they were getting benefits instead of citizens like my friend, I walked out of there so outraged I decided I had to do something' (Suro, 1994: 1).

In these scripts, immigrants embody the "uncanny" (Freud, 1955 [orig. 1919]). They are the actors in a nightmare that transforms our social space into something "monstrous." Anti-immigrant sentiment—including the jealous rage that illegals are "getting benefits instead of citizens like my friend"—is intertwined with a unsettling sense of panic in witnessing the metamorphosis of "home" into a world dominated by sinister aliens.[20]

The horror of being lost in this menacing world activates primitive defenses saturated with projections and splitting. Psycholgically the world of unreadable signs becomes peopled with powerful, malevolent criminals, operating, controlling, and manipulating the space of the uncanny. I concur with Julia Kristeva when she writes, "the strange [Freud's uncanny] appears as a defense put up by a distraught self: it protects itself . . . [by] the image of a malevolent double into which it expels the share of destruction it cannot contain" (Kristeva, 1991: 183–184). There is a price to this defensive psychology. The "malevolent double," constructed to contain that which we cannot psychically integrate, activates powerful persecutorial fantasies.21

Much of the current anti-immigration script is laced with paranoid rage. In these scripts immigrants have been singled out to contain unbearable inner tensions and to focus rage.22 Melanie klein (Klein and Riviere, 1964) postulated that infants and others deal with anxiety, frustration, and aggression principally via "projection" and "splitting." Projection is a universal psychic mechanism attributing to others characteristics belonging to the self (De Vos and Suárez–Orozco, 1990). Klein argued that infants "split" their earliest representations and relations into "good" (gratifying) and "bad" (frustrating) objects. Klein claimed that in the so-called "paranoid-schizoid position," the infant is unable to integrate the gratifying and frustrating aspects of certain "objects," such as the mother's breast. Hence, the infant "splits" the object into two alternating images, "the good object" and the "bad object." Klein postulated that it is only later, during the so-called "depressive position," that infants are unable to integrate the frustrating and gratifying aspects of an object into a single representation: sometimes the breast is frustrating and sometimes it is gratifying.

Projective mechanisms become dominant in certain paranoid personalities. Furthermore, in times of crisis and distress paranoid projections are often reactivated (Storr, 1991). Talk of immigration today is decidedly saturated with "projective" and "splitting" imagery. Immigrants, I have suggested, are represented as either dangerously "bad" or unrealistically "good." Today's aliens are criminals and parasites drawn to manipulate and abuse us. Yesterday's immigrants were proud peasants who eagerly gave up their old-world ways and, pulling themselves up by their bootstraps, became proud Americans.

The End of Culture

Psychological theorists of varied perspectives including Freud (1930), Dollard (Dollard *et al.,* 1939), Kohut (1972), Fromm (1973), and Mitchell (1993) have argued that frustration, injury, endangerment, and upheaval offer a powerful context to aggression. Immigrant and anti-immigrant scripts may well serve to articulate anxiety a discharge frustrations over the global remaking of economy and society. Whereas the underlying frustrations are overdetermined anti-immigration sentiment concentrates much anger and frustration into a single focus.

Heuristic models are only relevant when they can elucidate God in the details. Why, we must ask, *is this terror and hatred of immigrants and refugees emerging as worldwide epidemic now*? Beyond psychocultural insight we are in urgent need of a theory of new social formations. I have suggested that some facts present themselves as important to new theoretical understandings. The demarcations of the world principally structured around the bounded nation state have hbeen swiftly unsettled—internally by a crisis of trust and a corrosion of authority and externally by new transnational dynamics. The new formations are engendering unprecedented opportunities but also stunning contradictions, paradoxes, and anxieties.

We are entering the era of post-nationalist, supra-nation building. New technologies, new idioms of communication, new patterns of capital flows, and a new ease of mass travel is erasing many of the boundaries that delineated much of the 20th century. In this post-Wall moment—when a space of global semiotics, economy, and culture is bringing the world together in previously unimagined forms—in there is a furious momentum to rebuild new borders.

The new borders are constructed around the meaning making systems that structure identity and give us a sense of rootedness and continuity with our social space—what cultural anthropologists in the American tradition call "culture."

But the late 20th century is witnessing the reworking of the idea of culture as the idiom of unity and belonging in ways that are far from the traditional anthropological approach to culture. In these new "folk models of culture," culture emerges as fixed and immutable—a last line of defense in a disorienting world. At a time when nothing else can be kept steady, there is a desperate drive to maintain and defend the basic markers that give meaning and structure identity. Fascist anti-immigrant sentiment, whether in France, Belgium, or California captures the tools of anthropology to construct landscapes of Otherness around the incommensurability of cultural forms and the totalization of human differences. The new concept of culture, strategically deployed in anti-immigrant scripts, is at once premodern (culture is fixed, eternal, immutable; race, language and culture are single construct) and postmodern (cultures are incommenurable, demarcating radical Otherness).

Stunningly the grammar of this argument is identical—whether it is deployed in anti-immigrant scripts in the Flanders, Paris, or California. In all of these places we are told the new immigrants are different from previous ways of immigrants because "they will not adapt." In the primitive but direct words of Samuel Francis, until recently a columnist for the *Washington Times*, "immigration from countries and cultures that are incompatible with and indigestable to the Euro-American culural core of the United States should be prohibited" (quoted in Herbert, 1996: 29). Indeed, the new immigrants are most subversive when portrayed as "not wanting to give up their cultures and languages." There is a panic that they will impose their grotesque semiotics on all us. If the post-Boasian observers of the American immigration experience spoke of malleable immigrants melting into the mysterious American alloy, today we are in decidedly beyond the melting pot.

Notes

1. I am not interested here in exploring the formal features and determinants of immigration—"push-pull," "core-periphery," "global capitalism" (see Suárez–Orozco, 1996). This area of scholarship tends to be somewhat

stale often saturated with mechanistic and reductionistic models—which, I must note, served at various strategic moments in the most recent wave of collective hysteria over immigration as a screen of rationality in what is mostly an irrational debate.

2. This new space, I hypothesize, arises with the 1) collapse of boundaries—*inter alia,* national, economic, and political—2) the crisis of authority and the symbolic "end" of the State, and the 3) dawn of phantom "transnational" formations. Immigrant workers, refugees, and "illegals" are seen as key players in the making of this highly charged and dangerous space. Rather than speak of "transnationalism," a term which seems to be used to explore new ways of coming together over national boundaries, I use the term "post-nationality" in a slightly different sense. In this paper, I am concerned the vacuum that is created when social spaces are subverted, reconfigured, and reconstituted. I am interested in the gaps, fissures, and paradoxes that are engendered in the reconfiguration of old boundaries, and in the place immigrants, refugees, and other 'Others' come to play in the making of such spaces. Discourses of "multiculturalism," "difference," and "the culture of diversity" fertilize the space of post-nationality. Entering such symbolic systems probably encourages immigrants to be hesitant to form identities around "assimilationist" models. Immigrants may identify and mimic the kinds of (instrumental) competencies they may see as required to successfully operate in a global economy. On the other hand, entering a "dystopic" ethos, new immigrants seem even more hesitant than previous generations of immigrants to identify with the expressive aspects of the new culture. Forced to leave one nation and yet hesitant to identify wholly with the cultures of their new homes, immigrants create new identities between and betwixt old national systems (see Levitt, 1996).

It is important to highlight the delicious contradictions that saturate what I shall call the space of post-nationality. For example, in the current ethos of anti-immigrant sentiment, the need for foreign workers seems to remain constant (Lydia Chavez, 1994). Since passage of Proposition 187, a number of leading California politicians, including Pete Wilson and Attorney General Don Lungren have been calling for a *new* guest worker program to bring temporary workers to California.

Some immigration experts have argued that such "guest worker" programs are a short–term fix that produces longterm problems. Doris Meissner, the current Immigration and Naturalization Commissioner, has noted that "the notion that a country can add workers to its labor force and not residents to its population is fundamentally flawed" (1992: 66). Furthermore, some studies suggest that because in certain sectors of the economy employers *prefer* to hire the relatives and friends of immigrant workers they trust (see Waldinger, 1994), guest worker programs tend to generate new cycles of undocumented migration.

But the regime's predilection for the "guest worker system" also works to hide the system's phantom. Today's official "guest workers," promoted by Governor Wilson and others as the antidote to "labor shortages" (a dubious claim that cannot be considered here), become tomorrow's "ghost workers." Today there are 2 to 4 million "illegal immigrants" living in the United States. In 1986, Pete Wilson then a Senator, and others from the California Congressional delegation, "held up passage of the Immigration Reform and Control Act until a provision was added to allow several hundred thousand immigrants into the country temporarily so that they could help harvest crops. Under the provision that eventually resulted, more than one million came to stay" (Brinkley, 1994: 1). In other words, the largest wave of illegal immigration into California resulted from the efforts California politicians on behalf of big business.

Who are these "ghost workers"? They are an army of invisible people—picking the harvest in California, babysitting the children of upwardly mobile couples in New York (remember Zoë Baird?), taking care of the elderly in Texas. They live, in the apt words of Leo Chavez, "shadowed lives" (Chavez, 1992). They are the hidden hands doing the jobs that no body wants to do—and doing them at substandard wages. These "ghost workers" are indispensable to an obscene, underground, economy that reaps fabulous benefits from human exploitation. Wayne Cornelius, Director of the Center for U.S.–Mexican Studies at the University of California at San Diego, on this point: "Every sector of the economy here [San Diego] is heavily dependent on immigrants. They all draw heavily on this labor pool, and most of it is illegal. It underwrites an affluent life style. But the anti-immigration line is very popular because of all the anger. People really want to have it both ways" (quoted in Sterngold, 1996: 8).

The ghost workers must at once "be there" (to do the impossible jobs) but not be there (be voiceless and transparent). When it became public knowledge that Pete Wilson and his wife had hired an "illegal alien" as a maid, his response was that he did not "remember her" and that he had "never seen her." Likewise, when California billionaire Huffington was running for the U.S. Senate—of course, on an angry anti-immigration platform—and was found to have an "illegal nanny problem," he too, said he never seen her and did not remember her—although the woman had reportedly taken care of his children for a substantial period of time. These responses make perfect symbolic sense precisely because by definition "ghost workers" must be seen as invisible.

This presence/absence is a defining feature of what I call the "space of post-nationality." This is a space where the State, like the "ghost workers" themselves, is at once hyperabsent and hyperpresent. The State's absence generates a powerful vacuum of legitimacy. For example, it is a Bourdiesque "best-kept secret"—the kinds of secrets that "everyone in the community must keep in order to ensure the complicity of all in collective forms of bad faith" (Scheper–Hughes, 1994: 139)—that there is an industry generating the illegal documents that ghost workers use—not so much to protect themselves but, *voilà,* to protect employers that hire them from prosecution for "knowingly hiring an illegal alien."

It is also well known that powerful California politicians (including Pete Wilson) are *against* the Immigration and Naturalization Service making raids on big businesses known to hire illegal immigrants because such raids "disrupt business." In the words of Demetrios Papademetriou, a senior immigration scholar at the Carnegie Endowment for Peace, "Enforcement has always been the stepchild of the immigration service. Businesses complain about the disruptions" (quoted in Sterngold, 1995: 16).

In fact, California Governor Pete Wilson has "twice vetoed bills that would have held big manufacturers responsible for monitoring their subcontractors' compliance with labor and immigration laws. Proponents of such laws say they would make it more difficult to exploit illegal aliens" (*ibid.*).

What the Governor and others want is "business as usual." In the space of postnationality "business as usual" means working conditions that approximate slavery. In September of 1995 the New York times reported on a series of sweatshops in Southern California where "scores of illegal Thai immigrants were being kept as virtual slaves" (*ibid.*) Likewise, in the agricultural fields business as usual has traditionally meant inadequate or no sanitary facilities and doing impossibly demanding physical labor in the heat—often handling dangerous pesticides—at substandard wages (Trueba, 1996). It took a long time—and the saintly struggles of Cesar Chavez—to address the basic human needs of agricultural workers in California. Before Chavez farm workers were ghosts—"there" to pick the crops but not "there" as human beings—in need of water, bathrooms, not to mention basic dignity.

The early guest worker program was named, making robust symbolic sense, the "*bracero* program." *Bracero* comes from the Spanish word *brazos* meaning "arms:" the arms needed to do the work. But instead of "arms," whole human beings came to do these jobs. The tension here is between two meanings systems: a system that constructs these workers as invisible ghosts or disembodied "arms" and a system that insists on their humanity. The discursive movement from guest workers as "arms" to guest workers as human beings, with needs, with families, with children in need of basic services such schooling—in short workers *qua* humanity—is what is most subversive to the regime.

I must also highlight that in the last few years there has been an unprecedented militarization of the southern border of the United States (see for example Fainaru, 1996; Pear, 1996; Dillion, 1996). In that sense the State is hyperpresent. Violence against immigrant workers is more or less routine (see Suárez–Orozco and Suárez–Orozco, 1995: 35–43). They face violence from the Border Patrol and other policing agencies on both sides of the international border (see American Friends Service Committee, 1992; America's Watch, 1990).

The recent widely reported beatings of two suspected undocumented immigrants by Riverside County police officers after a high-speed chase down a Southern California highway is only novel in that it violated the principle that ghost workers should never be seen.

The responses to the beatings highlight just how fundamental this symbolic principle is: the police beatings generated widespread applause from large sectors of the Southern California population who hysterically called radio and television call in shows announcing that the "illegals got just what they deserve" (see R. Gutierrez, 1996).

3. It is not surprising then that a 1996 survey by The New York Times suggested that 72% of respondents had been "affected by a layoff" (*The New York Times,* 1996: 26).

4. Although the majority of immigrants and refugees remained within the confines of the "developing" world, the "developed" world—including the United States, Germany and France, experienced near record numbers of new arrivals—including substantial numbers of undocumented immigrants and asylum seekers. In the 1990s the United States was accepting, on average, nearly 1 million new legal immigrants. Additionally, there were estimates that 2 to 4 million "illegal immigrants" resided in the United States.

5. PTAs, Rotary clubs, Kiwanis clubs, and town meetings all report lower attendance patters (Uchitelle and Kleinfield, 1996: 26).

6. As if to further unsettle the sense of "home"in public space, new census projections suggest the United States in now in the midst of a major demographic transformation, a change that will have profound implications for the future of American democracy and cultural pluralism. By the year 2050, the United States population will be roughly 50 percent ethnic and racial minorities—of Hispanic, African-American, and Asian origin.

7. How do we ground ourselves in a world that changes at dizzying speed? And how do we look for landmarks in such a world? What new

understandings are to be created to navigate a world where formerly incommeasurable semiotic and epistemic boundaries are instantaneously transversed—and may be even erased—courtesy of the internet, CNN, and MTV?

8. There are data to suggest that immigrants are literally "killing themselves" in record numbers to come to the United States. Immigrant deaths at the southern border have been rising (see Rodriguez, 1996).

9. It is worth noting that Governor Weld's "double" in the immigration issue is his counterpart in California—Pete Wilson. Governor Wilson briefly fantasized during the 1996 Republic primary that he could surf the California anti-immigration wave all the way to the White House. Gov. Weld was Gov. Wilson's main backer in the East Coast. In terms of immigration talk Gov. Wilson was Gov. Weld's alter id.

10. It is critical to emphasize that the pro-immigration script has very carefully defined roles for the new immigrants. The script demands, for narcissistic reasons, that immigrants become just like us. True differences must be erased. In this act, cultural diversity is only celebrated in superficial "folkloristic" forms. The terms of the bargain are clear: immigrants must "give up" meaningful cultural and linguistic differences and become proud and loyal Americans. When immigrants resist this script, massive amounts of anxiety are unleashed—"the disuniting of America!" "The Balkanization of California!" "The tearing of the American fabric!"

11. In a 1996 New York Times Survey, nearly 50 percent of all respondents came to see immigrants as "taking jobs from citizens" and 74% of them felt that immigration "should be decreased" (*New York Times,* 1996: 23). The anxiety around immigration was so out of control that at a time of deep budget cuts, the Immigration and Naturalization Service received a significant increase in its budget. On January 6, 1996 "President Clinton signed legislation increasing the budget for the immigration service to 2.6 billion, from the 2.1 billion provided in 1995. Most of the money is for border enforcement and detention of illegal aliens" (Pear, 1996: 8). In 1995 House Republicans were calling for proposals to limit the publicly funded services legal immigrants could receive. A few months earlier (on November 8th, 1994), California voters overwhelmingly approved Proposition 187. The Proposition, currently under litigation in federal and state courts, aims to bar illegal immigrants from a host of publicly funded services, including non-emergency medical services and public schooling for undocumented children. The focus has decidedly shifted away form discourses

strategically celebrating the immigrant experience for the narcissistic gratification of the citizenry to a nervous building of new walls.

12. As George Foster has brilliantly argued, in a ethos of "limited good" where somebody's gain (immigrant) is framed as occurring at somebody else's loss (citizens), destructive envy becomes a dominant interpersonal concern (see Foster, 1972). Framing immigration as a zero–sum issue ("their gain is our loss") can only fuel righteous anger.

13. Since we do not seem to control much else—be it the economy, crime, or our children—there is a sense that at least we *must* control our borders, which alas, are also said to be out of control. If immigration is about "control" in the "out of control era," it is worth exploring the delicious contradiction that just as national boundaries are increasingly beside the point, new boundaries are furiously being erected. Much of the immigration debate is about making of new boundaries.

14. A side effect of the Bush administration's "war on drugs"—a "war" widely believed to have failed miserably (see García Márquez, 1994)—is that the U.S.–Mexico border is now highly militarized. Consider the following quotation from an American Friends Service Committee (AFSC) report entitled *Sealing our Borders: The Human Toll,*

> [During the first half of the Bush administration] INS attainment and development of sophisticated new equipment continued. The low-light-level television system was expanded to additional, unspecified border sectors . . . Further, the INS was in the process of obtaining new landmobile infrared imaging equipment and additional airborne forward looking infrared radar (FLIR) equipment . . . The INS also requested additional $8.6 million for fiscal 1991 for infrared nightscopes, portable ground sensors, and additional low level television equipment, to enable the Border Patrol to increase its number of apprehensions of undocumented immigrants, though the equipment was also said to detect drug smugglers. Finally, the INS obtained five new A-Star 350-B helicopters capable of carrying seven people each, which were to be used for various special operations . . . Each of these new helicopters is equipped with a 'Nite Sun' search light and forward looking infrared radar (FLIR), that has heat sensing capabilities and is especially useful in night detention and surveillance activities (AFSC, 1992: 9).

15. In February 1994, the INS disclosed plans to begin charging a $130 fee on applicants seeking political asylum. The U.S. would be the

only nation in the world to charge an asylum application fee (see *The New York Times,* 1994b). INS officials argued that in 1993 there were 150,386 formal requests for asylum and only 150 asylum officers to process the claims. According to one observer "The system in the past year and a half just collapsed under its own weight" (quote din Weiner, 1994: 2). Human rights and refugee rights advocates noted that the new fee would simply further undermine the right to asylum when facing a well-founded fear of persecution. Others noted that a universal right is now for sale (see *The New York Times,* 1994b).

16. After the Twin Towers there was a widespread feeling, palpable in media coverage, that the noble idea of granting refuge had been overwhelmed by opportunists, criminals, and terrorists gaining easy access into the country and abusing its diminishing resources (see McDowell, 1993). According to one report, "the wholesale abuse of asylum law must be stopped. Immigrants with no legitimate claim to resettlement in the United States routinely request political asylum knowing that they will likely be released pending INS [Immigration and Naturalization Service] interviews a year or so hence. Many disappear and are never apprehended" (Caldwell, 1993: 4).

17. In many reports, the implied message was that once released, the asylum seekers *de facto* gain more or less permanent entry into the United States. Such reports did little to clarify the disturbing dilemmas all major post industrial democracies face when they attempt to control their borders as they deal with the rights of asylum seekers under international agreements.

Contrary to these sensational reports, researchers in the field of refugee and asylum law are increasingly disturbed by new formal and informal policies developed in the U.S. and Europe to contain what is perceived as a "flood" of asylum requests. Many countries concerned with the volume of asylum requests are putting into place policies which may violate the spirit and the letter of international agreements on refugee and asylum rights.

18. It turns out that the psychologically charged fear of pollution (malaria) was based on an isolated report in which a migrant worker evidently contaminated another *migrant worker* with malaria in their migrant camp (Wolf, 1988: 17). For a study of the history of fear of immigrant "contamination" and disease see Kraut (1994).

19. There is evidence, however, to suspect that recent treatment of the involvement of immigrants in crime is exaggerated by those opposing

immigration (for a particularly outrageous statement on immigration and crime see Brimelow, 1995). For example, Simon concluded that, though there are few reliable studies on this topic, "The rate of all crime has been less among immigrants than among natives" (1989: 304). In the words of Eisenstadt and Thorup, "incidence of such [immigrant] crime has been exaggerated or misrepresented by those opposed to immigration" (1994: 52).

Daniel Wolf conducted a systematic study of undocumented immigration and crime in Southern California. Wolf concluded that in San Diego county, an area heavily populated by undocumented immigrants (Chavez, 1992), on average some 12 percent of those arrested not convicted for felonies are "undocumented aliens" (Wolf, 1988). A more recent estimate indicates that "about 10 percent of the 4,892 inmates in San Diego's jails are illegal immigrants" (Sterngold, 1996: 8).

This is a significant figure. But there are three important caveats. First, undocumented aliens in general tend to be arrested (again, not convicted) at rates higher than the general population (Wolf, 1988). Second, there is reason to suspect that a significant number of the crimes reported as "undocumented alien crimes" are not committed by immigrant *workers* but by professional "border bandits," and international drug runners which are nevertheless counted as "undocumented aliens" when apprehended in the U.S. side of the international border. Third, immigrant workers tend to be the *victims* of much of the crimes committed by professional border bandits.

Wolf writes,

> There exists substantial unanimity among police that, as a group, migrant workers do not appear to be responsible for much serious crime. Most migrant workers are honest and hardworking; and most of the crimes committed by this group are 'public order misdemeanors,' such as urinating in public, and nonviolent 'survival crimes,' such as thefts of bedding, food, and cash (Wolf, 1988: 23).

If it is in fact the case that migrant workers are not responsible for much serious crime, where does such fear of immigrant crime come from? In an atmosphere of neo-nativism the criminal acts of some highly visible migrants and asylum seekers, such as those involved in the Twin Towers bombings, tend to make all migrants "suspect." In addition, there may be two other important sources.

According to the "kernel-of-truth" hypothesis all irrational fears are deformed elaborations based on some kernel of truth (see Allport, 1979).

According to Daniel Wolf much of the concern over "immigrant crime" in Southern California probably grows out of the work of international drug runners and "border bandits," also called the "rob and return bunch." These are professional robbers who are not migrants workers but who operate on both sides of the international border. According to this view, public opinion is unable or unwilling to differentiate between migrant workers and "border bandits." And since both are foreigners, the sins of one (the bandits) are passed on to the others (the migrant workers).

As much else in the experiences of most migrants, there is an Orwellian twist in incriminating migrant workers for the acts of "border bandits." Wolf found that migrant workers are much more likely than non-migrant U.S. citizens to be the victims of border bandit crime:

> The 'border bandits' who commit robbery, rape, and murder, perpetrate almost all their crimes in the dark of night *against* undocumented migrants crossing the border. (Some bandits 'work' the migrant camps further north.) *The undocumented alien worker, preyed upon by these violent criminals, is far more liley to be a victim of serious crime than a perpetrator of it* (Wolf, 1988: 23, emphasis added).

Hence, far from being responsible for much serious crime, migrant workers are more likely to be the victims of serious crime.

20. The sense of disorientation in facing an incomprehensible semiotic order drives the nearly obsessive preoccupation with immigrant languages, signs, and customs. Hence the increasingly unnegotiable demand—even in pro-immigration circles—that immigrants abandon their native tongues and erase any "signs" of difference from the public space.

21. Powerful jealousy and envy fantasies are critical ingredients in the organization of these persecutorial fantasies. In the anti-immigration talk of today "aliens" appear as either parasites who are not "making it" and are taking away our limited and shrinking resources— "stealing jobs," stealing social services, taking your child's place in schools—eliciting jealousy; or, conversely, are imagined as powerful and sinister aliens controlling vast resources and eliciting envy. Consider the ferocity of the language presented to California voters in a recent anti-immigration initiative: "Proposition 187 will be the first giant stride in ultimately ending the ILLEGAL ALIEN invasion. It has been estimated that ILLEGAL ALIENS are costing taxpayers in excess of 5 billion dollars a year. While our own citizens and legal residents go wanting, those who choose to enter our country ILLEGALLY get royal treatment at the expense of the "California taxpayer" (Proposition 187; Argument in Favor of Proposition 187: 54; emphasis in the original). It is far from settled that undocumented immigrants cost the taxpayers of California "in excess of 5 billion dollars a year" (see

Passel, 1994; Simon, 1995). But invoking the parasitic immigrant is of strategic importance to gather up fury in the next announcement, "while our own . . . go wanting . . . [they] get royal treatment." Constructing the debate as a simple—and simplistic—they win we lose proposition becomes a building block in the construction of hatred and angry lashing out.

22. Wolf (1988) argues that undocumented immigrant workers are recipients of obscene amounts of violence. They are the targets of the great majority of crimes committed by "border bandits" as they make the journey North. And what are their experiences once they settle in the new land? Leo Chavez reports, "undocumented immigrants are the victims of random crimes committed by individuals with an irrational hatred or fear of them. For example, in November 1988 two teenagers in the community of Escondido, motivated by their dislike for Mexicans, used an AK-47 assault rifle to gun down two Mexican workers walking along a field of avocado trees" (1992: 60).

Are these the random acts of disturbed and rageful teenagers or is violence against immigrant workers more systematic? In the words of Senator Art Torres, Chairman of the California Legislature Joint Committee on Refugee Resettlement, International Migration, and Cooperative Development:

> 1979, gang shoots, injures migrant workers in a camp; 1980, in Escondido, reports of assaults on migrant workers by law enforcement and gangs; 1981, Del Mar, Mexican man beaten to death; 1982, Escondido, migrant worker beaten severely by gang in a truck; 1983, Oceanside, Pablo Martínez Toledo and Raul Mejía García shot and killed by three white youths; 16-year-old migrant worker shot and wounded in park; 1984, Fallbrook, California, six U.S. Marines conduct, quote, "beaner raids," unquote, armed attacks on Mexican migrant workers in their caves; 1985, Fallbrook, California, sniper shoots and wounds 17-year-old migrant in back, paralyzing him from the waist down; 1986, November, Encenitas, California, three 17-year-old white youths arrested in sniper shootings of migrant workers; San Ysidro, November of 1986, seven undocumented people shot by unidentified assailants on the freeway; 1987, north San Diego County, unidentified bodies of migrant workers—victims of violence—begin to appear throughout the county; 1988, Del Mar, California, killing of two migrant workers by two self–proclaimed white supremacists—victims: Hilario Salgado Castañeda and Matilde de La Sancha; October, 1989, Poway California, gangs of white teens attack and shoot 14 migrant workers with guns and paint bullets; Encenitas, October of '89, California, two border patrol agents shoot

> at, detain, and beat migrant worker; 1990 in Carlsbad, two store owners beat, handcuff, and kidnap migrant; 12-year-old Emilio Jimenez shot and killed by unidentified assailants; Carlsbad, California, robberies continue on migrant workers; Chula Vista, California, 1990 Border Patrol Agent shoots into a van filled with Salvadorians [sic], wounding two; Vista, California, 1990, Sergio Mendez, farm worker, shot in the back by paint pellet fired in drive by shooting (California Legislature, 1990: 24).

It might be argued that Mr. Torres, who after all is a State Senator, might be motivated to inflate the crime against immigrants issue (Latinos, after all, are a powerful voting block) to promote his own political ambitions. Let us turn to a review of the problem of violence against immigrants by more independent observers. According to a report by the human rights monitoring organization, Americas Watch,

> U.S. Border Patrol agents have committed many serious abuses against Mexican nationals . . . In 1989, the American Friends Service Committee's U.S./Mexico Border program documented the cases of five Mexicans who were killed and seven others who were wounded by Border Patrol agents in five separate shooting incidents in the Tijuana area. Some of the incidents involved only border control agents. Others involved the Border Crime Prevention Unit, a joint venture of the Border Patrol and the San Diego police. One of those killed was 14-year-old Luis Eduardo Hernández who was run over and killed by a Border Patrol vehicle on August 20, 1989. The following week 15-year-old Pedro García Sánchez was shot in the back and wounded while trying to run back into Mexico. In December, officers of the Border Crime Prevention Unit shot and wounded another minor, Manuel Martín Flores . . . Flores is now paralyzed from the waist down. On May 25, 1990, a U.S. Border Patrol agent fired three bullets from his service revolver . . . a 16-year-old Mexican boy was hit in the neck and seriously injured, and a woman was hit in the arm by the gun fire. According to Roberto Martínez of the American Friends Service Committee in San Diego, 'No Border Patrol agent has been persecuted for any unjustified killing of an alien in the past five years.' . . .

In addition to violent acts of this type by the Border Patrol and police officials, citizens along the border have waged a campaign of intimidation against Mexican and other aliens trying to cross the border without authorization. Organized under the slogan "Light Up the Border," citizens in the San Diego area hold monthly rallies during which they drive their cars to the U.S. border and turn their headlights onto Mexicans and other aliens waiting to cross. Participants in the campaign blame undocumented immigrants for a variety of social ills, including the influx of drugs into their community.

A more serious menace is posed by gangs of white supremacist youths in the San Diego area who dress in combat fatigues, carry knives, bows and arrows, and high powered rifles, and have been responsible for assaults and killings of Mexican immigrants (Americas Watch, 1990: 86–87).

In a followup report entitled *United States Frontier Injustice: Human Rights Abuses Along the U.S. Border with Mexico* (1993), Americas Watch concludes, "After a followup investigation conducted nearly a year after issuing its first report condemning human rights violations along the U.S. border with Mexico, Americas Watch concludes that serious abuses by U.S. immigration law enforcement agents continue and that current mechanisms intended to curtail abuses and discipline officers are woefully inadequate" (1993: 1).

The report states that even "after heightened scrutiny from legislators, human rights groups, community activists, and the press concerning the conduct of their agents . . . the agencies (INS, Border Patrol and Customs) have failed to introduce measures needed to curtail agent misconduct or to hold abusive agents accountable" (Americas Watch, 1993: 1–2). The reports established that "beatings and other forms of mistreatment are still common during the arrest and detention of undocumented immigrants, U.S. Citizens and legal residents (of Latino origin). While less frequent that beatings and mistreatment, unjustified shooting and sexual assaults also occur" (*ibid.*).

Likewise, the American Friends Service Committee (AFSC) report entitled, *Sealing our Borders: The Human Toll,* concludes that:

> significant and serious abuses continue to occur in the enforcement of immigration law along the U.S.–Mexico border . . . [including] psychological and verbal abuse (use of racial or ethnic insults, rude or abusive language, threats or coercion, and prolonged or aggressive interrogation techniques); physical abuse (shootings, beatings, sexual assault, injury by vehicles and high-speed chases), at least seven of which resulted in death; illegal or inappropriate searchers (including questioning based solely on ethnic appearance, entry without warrant or consent, overzealous execution of search warrants, strip searching without proper motive, and illegal law-enforcement raids); violation of due process (failure to advise persons of their legal rights or eligibility for statutory benefit, denial of access to counsel, and fabrication of evidence); illegal or inappropriate seizures of persons (unlawful temporary detention, false arrest, and illegal deportations); seizure or destruction of property; violations of the rights of Native Americans to cross the border freely (AFSC, 1992: 3).

And a three-part *Los Angeles Times* report entitled "Turmoil at the Border" concludes, "the [Border] Patrol's record includes persistent reports of abusive behavior by agents, improper shootings and crimes including drug smuggling, sexual assault and theft" (Rotella and McDonnell 1993: 1). According to a Human Rights Watch-Americas report released on April 1995, "Border Patrol agents routinely abuse [including beatings, shootings, rapes and deaths] people seeking to enter the United States from Mexico—legally and illegally—and they enjoy virtual impunity under a system that provides little oversight" (*Boston Globe,* 1995: 3). As long as INS officers feel under siege, and in the current ethos of immigrant fear and hatred—and as long as there is impunity and lack of accountability in law enforcement at the border—human rights violations of immigrants by U.S. agents and others will likely continue.

According to my perspective, there is an unmistakably paranoid quality to the fear and hatred of immigrants. Nowhere is this "projective" quality more evident than in imputing criminal motivations to undocumented immigrants. Undocumented immigrants are, some have suggested, among the most vulnerable of all workers (Chavez, 1992; Walsh, 1993; Lewis, 1979).

They are the likely targets by "border bandits" and corrupt and brutal Mexican officials working the frontier (Golden, 1992). If they are able to cross the border without documents and are apprehended, they may be the targets of abuse by U.S. officers. According to Americas Watch, Border Patrol supervisors "encourage the punitive beatings of suspects who run away from agents. The agents termed the practice, 'Thump 'em if they run'" (Americas Watch, 1993). And "the remarks of one Border Patrol supervisor to his agents—remarks made in front of a visiting *Los Angeles Times* reporter—are illustrative: 'Catch as many tonks as you guys can. Safely. An alien is not worth busting a leg.' ('Tonk' is the word used to refer to an undocumented immigrant and refers to the sound of an agent's flashlight striking an immigrant's head") (1993: 11).

On April 1, 1996 a widely aired video recording showed two deputies from Riverside County, CA, repeatedly clubbing two suspected illegal immigrants, a man and a woman, after a high speed chase down a Southern California Highway. Rather than generating any useful public debate over violence against immigrants, the incident became yet another barometer of anti-immigrant sentiment in the atmosphere. Audiences in several national radio and television shows suggested the illegal immigrants "got what they deserved." One caller to the Larry King Show was particularly outraged—not by the brutal beatings—but by the fact that the immigrants are filing lawsuits against the county of Riverside for ten million dollars. A caller to a radio show captured the message saturating the air waves:

"What do these people expect? They are coming here breaking our laws, stealing our jobs, and demanding social services. They got what they deserved!"

If they are able to squeeze pass the INS, National Guard—now serving at the U.S. Border—and the police, immigrants may be attacked by organized bands of anti-immigrant nativists "hunting Mexicans" in the U.S. side of the international border (Americas Watch 1990: 87). Once they make it beyond the border zone and find work, they are arguably the most exploited of all workers. Before "employer sanctions" were in place (the law making it illegal for employers to hire undocumented workers), there were many reports of undocumented migrants working for weeks to find out on pay day that their bosses refused to pay them and instead turned them to INS for deportation (Conover, 1987).

A lawsuit filed in September 1993 at the Sonoma County Superior Court illustrates a pattern of what often happens to make immigrants once they make it North,

> When Adam Zuñiga came to the United States at age 14, he didn't enroll in school. He went to work. A rancher hired him as a stable boy, Zuñiga said, and housed him in a [discarded horse] trailer, with no heat and no running water, charging him $200 a month rent . . . Zuñiga, now 24, charged that he regularly worked 9–12 hour days, sometimes seven days a week, for James Stembridge and Sandra Harper, co-owners of James Stembridge Stables. Zuñiga said he spent most of his teenage years in service to Stembridge and Harper for a promised salary of $125 a week, which he claims, he often did not receive . . . Immigration rights lawyers say Zuñiga's case is important because of what it says about the treatment of newcomers who do jobs U.S. citizens won't take, and the treatment of immigrant children . . . [His lawyer] hopes his story will encourage tough prosecution of employers who ignore the minimum wage and overtime laws as they expolit immigrant workers. [The lawyer hopes] the case will bring public understanding that 'there's a whole hidden economy in this state that depends upon the exploitation of immigrant laborers . . . our neighborhoods and businesses are full of immigrants being treated like slaves or animals, or worse" (Marinucci, 1993: 1).

The reality that immigrant workers are routinely exploited and sometimes "treated like slaves or animals" is reversed in the public fantasy that immigrants come to "exploit" us. (They come to parasitically feed off our wealth, go on welfare, are here to engage in criminal activities, and so forth). This mechanism of defense reinforces the initial exploitative treatment: we should not feel guilty for exploiting human beings because they are exploiting us (stealing, taking our resources, using our services, and the like).

Under certain circumstances of human exploitation and racist disparagement, and particularly when a dominant group feels threatened, there is a tendency to use those who are in a subordinate position (and those who "look and are least like us"), as receptacles to contain unacceptable anxieties and to focus rage.

In addition to often being exploited, we must note that different ethnic groups elicit different conscious and unconscious fantasies from the dominant culture. Disparaged groups are those with whom emphatic linkage is most difficult to achieve—those who look, sound, indeed "are," most unlike members of the dominant group.

In the post–utopian moment, the more pathetic, helpless, and exploited the new arrivals seem—rickety Haitians arriving in rickety boats or undocumented migrants devastated by the Los Angeles earthquake, for example—the greater is the repulsion and emphatic flight. It is as if we are afraid that the drowning are—through the principle of "contagion"—going to drown us all. The fear of being engulfed by their misery can only reflect our own terrifying anxieties in a time of serious cultural dystopia—rampant crime, economic stagnation, demographic changes, and natural disasters.

In the current climate of frustration over the economy, the budget crisis, the health care crisis, the crime epidemic among the youth, stunning demographic changes (Latinos today make over 25 percent of the California population), natural disasters (in California alone since 1990 various floods, urban wild fires, and earthquakes brought much destruction—adding to over 50 billion dollars in loses), those are least like the dominant population—the new immigrants—have been singled out as the cause of much "badness."

These developments are not unlike what is happening in Europe. Consider the words of Daniel Cohn–Benedit, Frankfurt's Director of Multicultural Affairs,

> Over the last several years, we have witnessed the emergence of a new xenophobia in Europe. This ostensible fear of foreigners is as much a product about anxiety about change in society as it is an actual fear of foreigners themselves. Western societies are passing through a difficult stage in the process of modernization. Many people simply cannot handle all the changes. Family relations are changing, jobs are being lost, and people find their social status shifting. Many people developed a vison of personal consumption that is very difficult to realize in today's economic environment. All these uncertainties about individual identity have produced a new assertiveness about national identity. People again feel a need to belong to a secure and well defined group.

> The presence of new immigrants accentuates those fears. To live with foreigners is always something new and uncertain—a challenge (Cohn–Bendit, 1992: 62).

And Stanley Hoffmann writes of the French *malaise,*

> French discontent seemed particularly strong during 1993 . . . The new disillusionment results from a series of blows to French pride and hopes, and from the sense that virtually all of the possible political formulas for dealing with the 'twenty years crisis' that began in 1973 have been tried in vain . . .
>
> Unemployment has been the worst of the shock inflicted on French self-esteem . . . With more than three million people officially out of work—12 percent of the active population—the situation is unprecedented since World War II . . .
>
> Indeed, during much of 1992 and 1993, what was most striking about French political life was its regression into a kind of shrill, defensive, and protectionist nationalism which recalled previous episodes of French chauvinism in French history (Hoffmann, 1994: 10–11).

Hoffmann concludes that things in France are not as bad as the French think they are. He uses the astonishing argument that today there is no "war of French against French" (1994: 13) in assigning blame for the "20 years crisis." But surely, someone must be blamed:

> It is not only the cheap goods produced by overpopulated poor countries that threaten France, it is also their miserable masses attracted by Europe's wealth. As the Gaullist interior minister keeps insisting, the door must be closed to them as well . . . [But] Large numbers of these foreign invaders are already within the wall; hence the government has shown a new vigor in defending the traditional model of an integrated French nation, and in fostering the already widespread view that multiculturalism á l'américaine would balkanize and dismantle the Republic (Hoffmann, 1994: 13).

In the United States, like in Europe, anti-immigrant fever has reached such dangerous proportions that almost any frustration leads to violence against immigrants.

References

Abraham, Spencer, William Bennett, Jack Kemp and Malcolm Wallop (1996). A Manifesto for Immigration. *The Wall Street Journal* (Feb. 29).

Allport, Gordon (1979). *The Nature of Prejudice.* Twenty–fifth Anniversary ed. Reading, MA: Addison Wesley.

American Friends Service Committee (1992). *Sealing Our Borders: The Human Toll.* Third report of the Immigration Law Enforcement Monitoring Project (ILEMP). A Project of the Mexico–U.S. Border Program. Philadelphia: American Friends Service Committee.

Americas Watch (1990). *Human Rights in Mexico: A Policy of Impunity.* New York: Americas Watch.

———. (1993). *United States Frontier Injustice: Human Rights Abuses Along the U.S. Border with Mexico.* New York: Americas Watch.

Brimelow, Peter (1995). *Alien Nation: Common Sense About America's Immigration Disaster.* New York: Random House.

Caldwell, Robert (1993). To Save Sensible Immigration, Curb Current Abuses. *San Diego Union–Tribune* (July 25).

California Legislature (1990). *Joint Interim Hearing on International Migration and Border Violence.* San Ysidro, Calif. (June 22).

Chavez, Leo R. (1992). *Shadowed Lives: Undocumented Immigrants in American Society.* Fort Worth, Texas: Harcourt Brace College Publishers.

Chavez, Lydia (1994). "More Mexicans, More Profits." *New York Times* (December 9).

Christenfeld, Timothy (1996). Wretched Refuse Is Just the Start. *New York Times* (March 10).

Cohn-Bendit, D. (1992). Immigration in Europe. *World Link* (Geneva) March/April: 604–64.

Conover, Ted (1987). *Coyotes: A Journey Through the Secret World of America's Illegal Aliens.* New York: Vintage Books.

———. (1993). The United States of Asylum. *New York Times Magazine,* Sept. 19: pp. 56–78.

De Vos, G. A., & M. Suárez–Orozco (1990). *Status Inequality: The Self in Culture.* Newbury Park, Calif.: Sage.

Dillion, Sam (1996). Border Patrol vs. 'Illegals': Now the Desert War. *New York Times* (March 26).

Dollard, J., L. W. Doob, N. E. Miller, O. H. Mower, & R. R. Sears (1939). *Frustration and Aggression,* New Haven, CN: Yale University Press.

Dugger, Celia (1996). Queens Old–Times Uneasy As Asian Influence Grows. *New York Times* (March 31).

Eisenstadt, T. A., & C. L. Thorup (1994). *Caring Capacity vs. Carrying Capacity: Community Responses to Mexican Immigration in San Diego's North County.* La Jolla, CA: Center for U.S.–Mexican Relations, University of California, San Diego.

Espenshade, Thomas, & Katherine Hempstead (1996). Contemporary American Attitudes Toward U.S. Immigration. *International Migration Review* 30(2):535–570.

Fainaru, Steve (1996). Border Crackdown Adds to Perils. Boston Globe. April 6.

Foster, George (1972). The Anatomy of Envy: A Study in Symbolic Behavior. *Current Anthropology* 13(2):165–202.

Freud, Sigmund (1930). Civilization and Its Discontents. Translated and edited by James Strachey. New York: W. W. Norton.

———. (1955) [orig. 1919]. The 'Uncanny.' *The Standard Edition of the Complete Psychological Works of Sigmund Freud, Volume XVII.* Translated by James Strachey. London: The Hogarth Press.

Fromm, Erich (1973). *The Anatomy of Human Destructiveness.* New York: Henry Holt.

García Márquez, Gabriel (1994). The Useless War. *New York Times Book Review* (February 27).

Golden, Tim (1992). Mexico is Now Acting to Protect Border Migrants from Robbery and Abuse. *NewYork Times* (June 28).

Gutierrez, Kris (1996). Immigration and Language: Contemporary Themes. Paper presented at the Harvard Graduate School of Education. Feb. 6.

Gutierrez, Ramon (1996). The Politics of Scapegoating. *Boston Globe* (April 14).

Herbert, Bob (1996). The Company They Keep. *New York Times* (March 16).

Hoffmann, S. (1994). France: Keeping the Demons at Bay. *New York Review of Books* 16(5):10–16.

Jordan, Barbara (1995). The Americanization Ideal. *New York Times* (Sept. 11).

Klein, Melanie, and Joan Riviere (1964). *Love, Hate, and Reparation.* New York: Norton.

Kohut, Heinz (1972). Thoughts on Narcissism and Narcissistic Rage. *Psychoanalytic Study of the Child* 27(1):360–400.

Kraut, Alan M. (1994). *Silent Travelers: Germs, Genes, and the 'Immigrant Menace.'* New York: Basic Books.

Kristeva, Julia (1991). *Strangers to Ourselves.* New York: Columbia University Press.

Krugman, Paul (1996). *The Age of Dimished Expectations.* Cambridge, Mass: MIT Press.

Levitt, Peggy (1996). "Immigration and Transnationalism." Paper presented to the Harvard Graduate School of Education, May 12.

Lewis, Sasha (1979). *Slave Trade Today: American Exploitation of Illegal Aliens.* Boston: Beacon Press.

Marinucci, Carla (1993). Treated Like an Animal for Years: Immigrant Laborer Charges Abuse Against Employer. *San Francisco Examiner,* September 26.

McDowell, Edwin (1993). Airport Securities Facing Terrorism's New Threat. *New York Times,* July 11.

Meissner, Doris (1992). Managing Migrations. *Foreign Policy* 86(4):66–83.

Mitchell, Stephen (1993). Aggression and the Endangered Self. *Psychoanalytic Quarterly* 62(2): 351–82.

Nelan, B. (1993). Not Quite So Welcome Anymore. *Time,* September 21, pp. 10–12.

Noble, Kenneth (1996). Sympathies Sharply Divided On Beating of 2 Immigrants. *New York Times,* May 6.

Passel, Jeffrey (1994). *Immigrants and Taxes: A Reappraisal of Huddle's 'The Cost of Immigrants.'* Washington, DC: The Urban Institute.

Pear, Robert (1996). U.S. Strengthening Patrols Along the Mexican Border. *New York Times,* January 13.

Putman, Robert D. (1995). *Bowling Alone.* Cambridge, MA: Center for International Affairs: Harvard University.

Rifkin, Jeremy (1995). *The End of Work.* New York: G. P. Putman's Sons.

Rimer, Sara (1996). A Hometown Feels Less Like Home. *New York Times,* March 6.

Rodriguez, Nestor (1996). *Deaths at the Border.* Houston: Center for Immigration Research.

Rotella, Sebastian, & Patrick McDonnell (1993). The Troubled Border Patrol. *Los Angeles Times,* April 22.

Sandel, Michael (1996). *Democracy's Discontent.* Cambridge, Mass: Harvard University Press.

Scheper–Hughes, Nancy (1994). The Violence of Everyday Life: In Search of a Critical and Politically Engaged Psychological Anthropology. In M. M. Suárez–Orozco & G. and L. Spindler, eds., *The Making of Psychological Anthropology II.* Fort Worth, TX: Harcourt Brace.

Simon, Julian (1989). *The Economic Consequences of Immigration.* Oxford: Basil Blackwell.

———. (1995). *Immigration: The Demographic and Economic Facts.* Washington, DC: The Cato Institute.

Stern, Marcus (1993). Clinton Plan for Leaky Borders. *San Diego Union–Tribune,* July 28.

Sterngold, James (1995). Agency Missteps Put Illegal Aliens at Mercy of Sweatshops. *New York Times,* March 23.

———. (1996). For Immigrants, Political Power Can Lead to Harsh Scrutiny. *New York Times,* Nov. 3.

Storr, Anthrony (1991). *Human Destructiveness.* New York: Ballantine Books.

Suárez–Orozco, Carola & Marcelo M. Suárez–Orozco (1995). *Transformations: Immigration, Family Life, and Achievement Motivation among Latino Adolescents.* Stanford, CA: Stanford University Press.

———. (1996a). "Unwelcome Mats." *Harvard Magazine,* 98(6):32–35.
Suro, Robert (1994). California's SOS on Immigration. *The Washington Post,* Sept. 29.
Trueba, Henry T. (1996). "Latinos in the United States: The Emerging Majority in Our Schools and Society." Unpublished manuscript. Harvard Graduate School of Education.
Uchitelle, Louis, & N. R. Kleinfield (1996). On the Battlefields of Business, Millions of Casualties. *New York Times,* March 3.
Voltaire (1961). *Candide.* New York: Ballantine.
Waldinger, Roger (1994). Black/Immigrant Competition Reassessed: New Evidence from Los Angeles. Unpublished manuscript, Department of Sociology, University of California, Los Angeles.
Weld, Susan Roosevelt, & William F. Weld (1996). We Should Always Lift Our Lamp to the World. *Boston Globe,* Jan. 11.
Wolf, Daniel H. (1988). *Undocumented Aliens and Crime: The Case of San Diego County.* La Jolla, CA: Center for U.S.–Mexican Studies, University of California, San Diego.

Elvira S. Lima and Marcelo G. Lima

11

Identity, Cultural Diversity, and Education

Notes Toward a Pedagogy of the Excluded

Culture and education is a theme of relevance in a world that becomes increasingly multicultural both by actual immigration movements and by socialization (at a certain degree-level) of cultural modes through technology.

A major aspect of this situation is the impact it has on the cultural development and learning processes of individuals. From each individual's perspective there is a complexity of factors that intervene in the development of one's personality. Education is one that we will focus on in this chapter.

The approach to culture is that of seeing it as constituted by mediation systems in the development of self identity, which in turn produces specific lived experience in the learning processes at school. That means that we necessarily need to rethink pedagogy in the light of historical processes and culture becomes an inherent element of knowledge construction and not merely a pedagogical tool to improve learning in the case of differentiate groups within society (the usually referred to as minorities).

To discuss the education of differentiate groups they need to be situated in the process of historical formation. Therefore in the first part of this chapter this is the perspective in which the Latino and Latina experience is discussed, bridging it in the second part of the chapter to the basic principles of the pedagogy of the excluded. This pedagogy, though rooted in pedagogical theory developed in

Brazil, is discussed here in its epistemological basis and implications which go beyond the Brazilian historical experience of education. To develop a pedagogy of the excluded means to build possibilities of knowledge appropriation and knowledge construction for everyone, a fact that in itself implies multiplicity.

How can we face education in the framework sketched above? This is the core of the case of Latino and Latina groups in the United States discussed here. The Latino and Latina schooling experience in the United States is thus discussed from a twofold approach: that of historical formation of Latinidad as part of cultural North America and that of pedagogical action for human development.

Cultural Diversity as Fact and Experience

Cultural diversity is a fact in the world we live in and it has been a fact throughout the past history of humanity and, closer to us in time, in the process of development and expansion of the modern nation-states and the modern capitalist economy. A process which has systematically revised the geographical patterns of mankind, destroyed traditional frontiers and regional divisions and has brought together as free or forced collaborators, as equal or unequal partners, or as competitors, peoples from the four corners of the planet. The development of modern capitalism has brought to a new and accelerated stage the historical process of contacts and exchanges between diverse civilizations and cultures, and has contributed to the gradual unification of the many under an increasingly interdependent world market. However, the *fact* of cultural diversity is not accompanied by the *consciousness* of diversity, that is, the understanding of the historical formation and the *role* of diversity in culture. We are faced with the paradoxical result that cultural beings may and in fact many times do have difficulty in dealing with the multiplicity of cultures. And that the cultural dimension of human experience apparently does not by itself prepare the individual to understand (and to value) cultural diversity.

In a nutshell.. ☆

Diversity and Culture: Identity as Mediation

Diversity is constitutive of culture as such in the most basic and general sense that culture implies the negation and supersession of the naturally given. It implies a *doubling* of the agent of the cultural process, at the same time object and subject, producer and product of the workings of culture. In this sense we can say that the cultural self is a mediated self and as a mediated being brings within itself the mark of the negative, of its own constitutive *otherness*. Identity is mediation: the Self can only be conceived *in relation to* the Other.

Diversity is both the result and the condition of the historical development of culture. In fact, culture develops as (formal) system in the medium of time. The identity of a culture, of any culture, is a *result* and a *relation,* as it is the constitution of the self in culture. For the individual, culture is the milieu of his or her development, that is, it provides the forms and it constitutes the medium of experience of the lived self. The identity of the self is immediately the experienced identity with and of the forms of the culture.

The Meaning of Identity

Identity can be understood as the symbolic, significant structuring of social relations which define the appurtenance to group, granting access to collective symbolic codes and assigning participation in the web of relations of a given community, it is "filiation" at collective level. At the same time identity is the internal structuring of sociability that confers visibility and legibility to oneself as member of a group. Identity is "cultural filiation."

The sense of identity mediates the subject's self-understanding at the intrasubjective and intersubjective levels, bridging the gap between the two levels in the process of cultural self-understanding that locates the individual and his-her primary and secondary groups (family, a professional group, class, linguistic group, ethnic, national) in the larger social historic context. In this sense, identity may also be understood as a kind of underdeveloped form of "historical consciousness" at the level of the lived experience, a form of consciousness devoid of the reflective moment of a truly historical consciousness. While able to recognize identity as somehow time bound and historically constituted (that is, the transmission of identity from the past or tradition), this "unreflected" consciousness is unable to distance itself from its own experience in order to constitute it as objet of inquiry, as object of historical *knowledge*.

Identity is in this sense a form of primary identification transferred or translated from the intrasubjective into the intersubjective and intergroup levels. The relational and dynamic nature of identity as historical construct, as the ever provisory mapping of vanishing and transformed or recreated differences, accompanies the sense of identity as its "unthinkable" other.

The Question of Identity

The concept of identity itself, it has been pointed out repeatedly from different quarters, is not without difficulties. Many of these are certainly related to the intersection of domains and of specific perspectives at the point in which we tend to locate the question of identity: between the individual and the collective, between representation and experience, between the intra-psychic and the suprapsychic, between the psychological and the cultural, and with all the consequent ambiguities of language and the difficulties of communication between and among disciplines.

The difficulties with the conceptualization of identity are also due to the fact that the notion of identity at times appears to express or translate "immediately" what belongs to the domain of common experience, to everyday forms of thought and language, the realm of false evidences, that is, of ideology as such. However, what "identity" designates for us today, in one way or another, more or less obscurely, conceptually or intuitively, regards directly the reality of multiculturalism as fact and as problem in the world today.

Multiculturalism as Fact and as Problem

Immigration has become a structural element in world economy in the present. The continuous flow of people in search of jobs and opportunity today follows what in the past was the more or less exclusive flow of materials and goods between continents or the localized or conjunctural displacement of populations. The new mobility of work is part of the deep transformations in the productive sphere by the new process of globalization, the effects of which are distributed all over. Compared to past historical experiences of working force displacements as diverse as, for instance, the African Diaspora, the great European and Asiatic migrations of the nineteenth and early twentieth centuries it is evident that not only the pace of the process has presently changed but that, in a world made closer by the means of communication, human groups are not any longer isolated in space or in time and the new displacements put in direct contact with each other entire communities with their different ways of life and believes. With the change of pace, what constituted before historically a long, at times painful and in many ways "invisible" or "unconscious," process of assimilation of these communities also changes. Multiculturalism is the conscious reflection of a new situation: the demand for the recognition of cultural difference which is also the recognition of the "irreducible" other, individual and community. Multiculturalism unveils the historically and culturally heterogenous in the core of the present process of "globalization" and constitutes itself therefore into a practical and theoretical *problem.*

The Politics of Identity

In a world more and more objectively unified by the demands of capital, the politics of cultural difference and cultural resistance and affirmation may on one hand indicate an objective limit of domination, a limit to the molding of human groups into pieces of the economic machine of universal reproduction of capital. The politics of difference as a strategy of resistance would represent the conscious reflection, that is, the reflection in consciousness, and the affirmation of the heterogeneous reality (social, historical, cultural) of human collectivities (ethnic and cultural minority groups, working class and other subordinated social groups) objectively subordinate to but never fully integrated into the cultural, social and economic patterns of capitalist relations. In this sense, it would point to structural and historical limits of capitalist integration. As the critical analysis of capitalism developed since the nineteenth century has shown, the contradiction between growing socialization of production and increased inequality, economic *and* political, is the core of the capitalist socioeconomic process and represents the heart of the "historical enigma" of capitalism's future.

On the other hand, the fact of the universalization of the capitalist relations, as the dominant if not exclusive relations, in any case as the hegemonic social-economic relations in the present may also indicate that an active miscognition of the structural basis or ground of the new historical developments is in effect in the stress on the cultural sphere and on cultural difference as the privileged or exclusive locus of social criticism and social transformation. Here the function of ideology may be again to mystify real processes into ideal ones and generate imaginary solutions to real contradictions. The criticism of ideological representations does not mean a dismissal of the cultural question, which indeed becomes central to the new historical context, but it intends to indicate the limits of the cultural construction and deconstruction of the political. Indeed the articulation of culture and politics marks the configuration of important oppositional strategies in the present and is central to the project of emancipation of social forces in the context of multicultural social formations. However the stress on culture and identity when used to evade the analysis of structural processes, taking the representation of reality for reality itself, may serve also to legitimize the separations and contradictions it intends to overcome.

Certainly, the experience of difference is the ground for the recognition of identity (self-identity and other-identity), the recognition of the limits of one's world, the limits of the effectiveness of our "original" or "originary" mode of insertion and action in social reality and of the symbolic apparatus and communicative capital we constructed and accumulated. It is also the moment to negotiate new ways of communicating, acting, and symbolizing that will effectively reach the other outside, and recreate the other inside, the transformed self.

Identity may then be understood as the possible site for the reflection and appropriation of historical knowledge and fundamentally for the critical appropriation (and recreation) of the tools for individual and collective development given in cultural experience.

The Social Burden of Identity

Both in the discourse of specialists of various fields and in public debates much of the recent discussion on identity in the United States has focused on minorities. The problematization of identity, that is, the viewing of identity as relatively urgent question or problem to be solved by those whose identity is considered to have been in one way or the other damaged in the historical process of nation building, most of the time assumes implicitly the position that the issue of identity is exclusively a minority issue. Without denying, and on the contrary affirming, the negative individual consequences of constant and systematic practices of (social, racial, ethnic) discrimination, we want to assign the "burden of the proof," which in this case it is the "burden of identity," to the other side, that is to the "self-satisfied" majority.

The social burden of identity, that is, of the identity ascribed or assigned by the cultural and historical other, accompanies the development of the cultural self-consciousness of minority groups in the United States. The process that has brought in the past (and continues to do so, with different means in a transformed historical context) the dominant white majority in contact with the "non-white" peoples was historically a process organized and commanded by the white majority.

Of course it is necessary to qualify this last observation: the white world of the colonizer in North America was itself structurally a fractured social universe of old and new class distinctions and formations. It is true that it in some aspects it was comparatively less structured than its European matrix. It was at the same time an ideologically and practically unified social universe, that is, a universe of social classes unified in the common, practical task of conquest of the land from its native inhabitants (who constituted, in one way or the other, the common enemy), and in the process of creation of the colonial order.

A class society is a society in which the monopolization of effective economic and political power by one class accompanies the distribution of the tasks of material conservation and expansion of the social totality among the various (differently) subordinated classes. If the uneven distribution of the material rewards of the colonial enterprise separated, for instance, the relatively poor white farmer from the rich landowner, both nonetheless benefitted from the expropriation of the natives and, in different levels, from the exploitation of labor and of slave labor. The landless white laborer could at times be caught by the workings of the economic and social colonial processes and end up in servitude (if he did not start already as a temporary serf to pay his trip from England). But the harshest conditions of white servitude never attained in early America the intensity and the cruelty of slavery, which in time were reserved to a special category of foreigners: the Africans.

From the point of view of the subjugated natives or of the imported African slaves the colonization of America repeated initially the pattern of European colonization in other parts of the world with similar results. From a relatively common point of departure, however, the national development of the United States would create a specific and lasting structure of racial domination. The historical process of definition of the national particularity implied not only the imposition of a dominant or unique language, cultural patterns and ways of life but also a racial cleavage in which "whiteness" as such played the role of a crucial defining element of "Americanity." The early democratic ideals that defined the political ethos of the emerging nation could therefore without much internal conflict coexist with discriminatory and segregationist practices in a kind of exclusionary democracy, a social regime of the "more equal" with the boundaries of equality defined also and specially by the "natural" markers of race.

It is possible to say that to the common pattern of European expansionism and colonization, that is, racist ideologies and practices implementing and complementing domination and the merciless exploitation of conquered and transplanted populations, the American national experience added, in a specific development, the enlightened ideology of the bourgeois revolution: the idea of universal rights and its corollary the idea of equality of opportunities. The potential and the actual conflicts between the diverse ideological principles of racism and of the universality of rights would not impede the prevalence in effect of a *de facto* compromise between the discourse of rights and the practice of racism and discrimination. As essential elements of the historical definition of the American *polis* the notions of equality of rights and opportunities were in fact implemented as exclusive accomplishments and privilege of the "originary" American nationals: the white Anglo population.

That the American "other," that is the other Americans (the incorporated minorities) could be defined (and defined in an exclusive way) as "other than American" is the proper historical achievement of the ideology and practice of racial domination in American society. It represents the denial by the majority of the very diversity that has structured and implemented, through inequality and domination, exploitation and oppression, the path of historical development of the United States. From the historical beginnings of the American nation the question of "cultural encounters" was already present. The United States either imported (by violent or other means) or conquered the nonwhite and incorporated diverse racial, cultural and ethnic groups into the national life as subordinated minorities. The common element in the historical experience of Native Americans, African Americans, Latinos among other ethnic and racial groups, is the white majority dominant role and its ideological response to the "practical multiculturalism," that is, the multiracial and multiethnic composition of the population of the United States from colony to independent state and to world power prominence. Against a background of effective dominance and control, the relations between races and ethnic groups imply that in effect it is the persistence of white dominance (a dominance that cannot be countered by cultural means exclusively) which dictates the forms of apprehension and actualization of racial conflict and of racial (and cultural, ethnic) identities (to a great extent defined in conflict). And this is the heart of the problem for the minorities which have to affirm their "otherness," their particularity, their difference from the white world in the face of systematic denial of value, and demand their place in the American universe as constitutive (and not only peripheral, secondary or disposable elements) of the American reality. Their efforts imply none other than a redefinition of America whose consequences go beyond symbolic affirmation to attain the core of power structures and the structures of racial and class privilege.

The structural racial (and cultural, ethnic) conflict also implies for the white dominant group the daily confront, whether conscious or unconscious, with the negative mirror of self-identity presented to the majority by the American "others" both in the sense of the experience of the fractured self (which as such has to be by all means exorcized and therefore negated by the majority) and in the sense of the recognition (which is always at the same time the active miscognition) of the violence at the core of the social order.

The tragedy of American racism, from the point of view of class relations, is that it has served to create a "homogeneous" white majority out of the conflicting and contradictory relations between the social classes, a relationship in which the nonwhite element has played the unwilling part of a third, demonstrating in practice to the subordinated whites what could or would be like without privilege of race in a social order based on universal exploitation, and playing their part also in fueling economic development as one of the vital links (role of slave labor and immigrant labor) in the process of capitalist accumulation.

The social basis of identity in the case of the white majority has been provided historically by the effective experience of race privilege, by the objective advantages generated by institutionalized, structured inequalities of race (coupled with inequalities of class). A specific combination of class division and race division is in fact what defines the American social formation, in which the assumed fluidity of class frontiers contrasts with the strong divisions of race, and class conflicts are "subsumed," and hidden, under the more visible oppositions of race. And it is around this central complex of identity and experience of dominance that racial policies, or policies directed to the questions of ethnic minorities (whether in favor or against those minorities), revolve and are instituted: whether, to counterbalance social tensions and to respond to minorities' demands, policies of integration or dedicated to enlarge opportunity for minority members are proposed and enacted, or whether the threat, real or imaginary, to the status quo generates policies against "unfair advantages" and "privileges" supposedly accorded to minority members (in a curious inversion of the actual realities of the minority social and economic position). We could perhaps indicate that both at the individual and at the social level identity is in effect, in a specific and central sense, the "crisis of identity" itself, that is, it emerges as conscious object in critical contexts when the representation of self no longer fits the reality of a transformed subject or a subject in a process of transformation (individual or collective). Transformation which may be brought about by critical experiences, for instance the experience of oppression no longer masked by common ideological images. At this point identity is experienced as a personal (and collective) riddle, as a social burden in the sense that the identity ascribed by the social and cultural other must be denied and transcended.

Education and Cultural Discrimination

What are the implications of social, ethnic, racial discrimination and cultural discrimination, in the schooling process? That every child can learn in circumstances that promote the construction of meaning is something that has already been demonstrated by international research and educational experiences around the globe. The learning process however can be complicated or disturbed by many factors and specially by the experience of discrimination which generates the need to confront again and again the question "Am I able to learn? Am I capable or not?"

For example, the work developed in Paris by the Centre de Recherche de l'Education Specialisee et l'Adaptation Scolaire (CRESAS, 1978, 1981) in the '70's and '80's has shown that the feeling of failure can be installed in the child at a very early stage of his or her schooling experience. The experience of nonrecognition by the school of the child's cultural behavior, including his or her cultural tools and cultural experience, and, beyond that, the experience of one's cultural heritage being considered as a negative factor, a factor that will act against learning and cognitive development, will accompany the student during his or her schooling process (Lima, 1988).

critical

Failure to learn is thus constructed, in more or less subtle way, in and by the learning context of the school. Students have little power to change the situation and they are forced to conform to the school structure and demands. However, this "adaptation" is a process that interferes with their learning activities: great part of the time in the classroom they are not dealing with subject matters, instead they are dealing with the situation of being in a context that excludes them and discriminate against them as learners. Time that should be allocated to studying, working with concepts and developing thinking skills is in fact time used to try to situate oneself and to understand oneself as a capable learner. The fact of exclusion acts as an element of rupture in the individual's relationship to knowledge. To try to understand (and to locate oneself in) a milieu that is adverse is not a simple matter for anyone, adult or child. It is in fact an enormously difficult and emotionally demanding task.

The experience of discrimination disturbs the individual's involvement with the process of constructing knowledge in the school. Rightly considered, the issue of the education of minorities (and other excluded social groups) has to include the notion that learning depends also on sociological conditions. In this sense it is important to observe that minority status or even social marginality as *such* is not a determinant of individual intelligence and ability to learn and therefore, *considered by themselves,* do not automatically produce educational failure. In the schooling process it is the experience of discrimination, an experience that is part and process of the minority condition and of marginality, that will disturb the individual's process of cognitive (and emotional) development.

To revert the social process of exclusion in school is the way to produce changes in the internal representation of oneself as cultural being, which means to view cultural diversity in the perspective of the dynamic reality of cultural-historic contexts in continuous process of redefinition and recreation.

The Latino Experience

Roughly speaking the formation of a Latino sector of the population of the United States can be divided into stages that correspond, *grosso modo,* to the historical phases of early Mexican, and later Puerto Rican and other Latin Americans incorporation by wars and conquest or by immigration. In the case of Mexicans and Puerto Ricans we have national groups incorporated inside the American formation by territorial conquest, by the political and economic control of the territory of the defeated neighbor state (Mexico) and of the Spanish colony (Puerto Rico). By history, language and culture these populations were distinct national groups (including Puerto Rico whose process toward political independence and nationhood was disturbed and interrupted by American intervention) and in many levels (language, culture) they considered an important core of their national or "transnational" distinctions in the very process of adaptation to American social, political and economic life. To these two main groups were later added the successive waves of immigrants from Latin America and the Caribbean, including again the Mexicans, the peoples from the various Central American nations, Cuba, and South American countries.

The process by which these diverse nationalities, ethnic and cultural groups have been amalgamated into the general category of "Hispanics" is a relatively recent one and has been described in a recent work (Oboler, 1995). The term started to be used in official racial-ethnic classifications by the U.S. government in the late 1960s and early 1970s as a response, on the level of symbolic discourse, to the demands and political struggles of the Mexican Americans on one side, and the Puerto Ricans on the other, during the 1960s. It can be understood as an effort of deflating and controlling the course of Mexican American and Puerto Rican protest and fight for cultural affirmation and social and political empowerment: whatever its publicly declared and consciously intended purposes, the State "recognition" of the role of the "Hispanics" in general in American life had the paradoxical result of creating a new invisibility for the *specific* demands of the *concrete* and *diverse* Mexican and Puerto Rican communities in the United States with their specific histories, questions and problems. As it developed, this process of homogenization included the old and the newly arrived groups of the Spanish-speaking population: Mexicans, Salvadoreans, nicaraguans, Colombians, and others, all of them undistinguished and undistinguishable in their common linguistic, cultural and, at times, racial features as seen through the eyes of the majority. In a sense, the way in which the Spanish-speaking populations have been represented in public discourse in the United States is itself the index of a deeply felt difficulty with the realities and the challenges of a multicultural experience inscribed in past and present history. It discloses the contrast between the ideological discourse of equality, participation, inclusion and mutual tolerance and the practical realities of effective powerlessness, subordination and exclusion.

The masking of history effective in the use of generalized ethnic-racial labels contributes to produce an unidimensional view of society and constructs the experience of a time without dimensions, where the specific histories of social groups become not the possible (although difficult) object of conscious reflection and apprehension but the repressed, unconscious element of collective identities, the object of experience (and representation) as myth.

Identity and Development

The children of immigrants (as minority and bicultural children) accumulate the demands of the process of growth and development with those of the process of symbolic transformation from one culture to the other. The singularity of their situation constitutes a challenge to traditional views of development centered on the isolated, "universal" or generic individual without history, that is, without a past other than the past stages of his/her biological and functional growth, and it is also the occasion to investigate and understand the role of culture in cognitive and emotional development: the imbrications of subjectivity, class, culture, of lived experience, representation, and structural constraints, of self and non-self, self and other, self as other, which constitute the context and substance of the question of identity.

The analysis of Claude Mesmin (1993) of the role of schooling in the developmental procedss of culturally diverse children in France reveals that school failure and developmental problems are produced by the cleavage of the cultural universe of the child. When the symbolic split and communicative fractures between the culture of origin and the new cultural environment are ignored by teachers and school officials, the child is condemned to solve by him/herself the cultural puzzle, to negotiate the often contradictory demands of his or her cultural group and of the school, to bridge and translate with the few instruments available the gap between the self in formation in the universe of the family and the social self required and produced in and by the schooling process. The internalization of the symbolic split as the cleavage of the self is most of the times the result of the conflicts between the cultural worlds of the child's experience. As Mesmin observed, the responsiveness of the school to the cultural needs of children is the key element here: a Bambara, or Soninke, or Malinke child, can indeed learn in a French school, provided the child and his or her culture is recognized. By contrast a child without a cultural identity, that is, whose identity is in question, is denied or is ignored, separated of his or her cultural environment and unadapted to or rejected by the out world culture is a child whose emotional and cognitive development is impaired: suspended as it were between the often contradictory demands of contrasting and diverse cultural environments and at times incompatible cultural systems, the "unidentified" and therefore unnamed and denamed child experiences the situation as a concealment of self that undermine his or her ability to communicate and hence to see and produce himself or herself as subject in the educational and social process of schooling, with consequences for the child's social, cognitive and emotional development. Human development, the development of the emotional and cognitive capacities of the individual, is not simply the automatic correlate of biological growth and individual maturation but fundamentally a concrete social process requiring, among other things, the symbolic tools for interaction which are given in and by culture.

The experience of a plurality of cultures is not in itself the difficulty for the minority child. The difficulty lies in the intolerance for the multicultural elements of the child's experience manifested by the dominant culture in school. When the dominant ideological discourse tolerates diversity as a cultural value while the effective cultural practices, in society and in the school, promote the exclusion of ethnic and cultural groups, the effect for the minority individual is one of great confusion with negative consequences for his or her development.

Education and the Latino Children

Latino and Latina children in the United States, whether recent immigrants, first or second generation, encounter a social context of development that is North American. A social context that includes, whether acknowledged or not by the dominant white majority, the historical experience of diverse minorities groups including the Latinos and Latinas themselves, in short: a multicultural environment.

In our work of research and intervention with Latino and Latina groups living in the area of Chicago we have witnessed that the introduction of cultural tools closer to the Latino and Latina cultural patterns, cultural tools that may be considered secondary or that are neglected by the dominant culture in the school context, such as the uses of symbols and signs characteristics of the aesthetic experience and of artistic practices (painting, music, poetry) will open the possibility of creating meaning and allow children and adults to place themselves in a new relation to the diverse elements in the cultural context of American society and specially to the elements originated in or related to the many Latino and Latina cultures and which are part of the historic development of America.

This has important implications for schooling. The first is that an opening to cultural diversity in school does not mean the reproduction of a Latino and Latina environment as such, not only because of the sociological and psychological impossibility of such a task, but because the Latino and Latina experience in the United States is necessarily that of biculturalism. Perhaps even more than the difficulties of dealing with another culture, the American school has difficulty in dealing with the emotional and cognitive particularity of people who grow up through the mediation of more than one culture and one language. The symbolic systems developed by bicultural/bilingual individuals (or by multicultural/multilingual individuals) are necessarily diverse from those who grow up with just one. Since language is a tool for thinking, to be fluent in more than one language also means that the individual may have different approaches to a new situation or a new problem to solve because his or her symbolic tools have been developed in more than one particular way.

Question for teachers: Look around your classroom – at your walls, desks, curriculum materials: are you promoting a "white" American environment, a "neutral" one; or one which promotes / welcomes cult. diversity?

Latino and Latina children, as children of any other ethnic group, develop their higher psychological functions with the cultural tools offered by their culture. To have access to two cultural systems does not make the Latino or Latina child better or worse than anyone else. It nonetheless means that the child will be faced with more decision making situations, because, being in possession of two diverse ways of perceiving reality, acting and conveying meaning, the child will have to make options more frequently. What the school does not acknowledge is diversity as the general rule rather than the exception.

Latino and Latina cultural diversity can be apprehended in the particular expressive systems, uses the language, patterns of human interaction and temporality. The control of Latino and Latina students behavior in the school passes by more or less subtle issues such as impeding the use of cultural expressive systems and imposing a temporality that not only restricts the usual way Latinos and Latinas organize their actions, but in doing so also prevents them of developing learning.

Can we think of a different educational experience for Latino and Latina children? Yes, if we begin to consider the education of minorities from other perspectives. For instance, in the case of Latino and Latina students the length of time for learning should include elements of social interaction and oral narrative that are culturally specific and are commonly present in the students interactions including the interactions during schooling activities. Rigid structures do not allow Latino and Latina children to present or develop many of the activities, including the culture-based activities, that are necessary for the acquisition of formal knowledge. And since classroom situations are very complex situations and the understanding of the processes and interactions that happen in the micro-level of the classroom are not the least evident, the burden to sort out the situation is left for the student, who is then considered incapable of learning.

Our experience with Latino and Latina groups in and out of school in Chicago reveals that the feeling of failure does exist and affects the attitude that children, adolescent and adults have toward schooling and formal learning. However, in situations in which the norms of the institution are modified or new elements introduced in the social and cultural milieu, the performance can change radically.

Through the experience of the Mural Painting Workshop (Lima and Lima, 1995), which is part of the work we have been developing, it is possible to observe that a totally different situation emerges when the nature of the proposed activity is not the common school structured or school oriented activity, even when it is organized and realized inside the school.

The activity of creating meaning through a production of symbolic contents that need to be visually organized and presented, the solution of a practical problem, reveals clearly the existence of a series of behaviors, abilities and skills of the children which had not surfaced yet in the common schooling activities. For example, in a situation of creating a mural painting children act using voluntary attention and perceptually oriented action, things that they were considered unable to do in the classroom. If those children are able to solve aesthetic problems that are complex in nature and depend on the development of higher psychological functions, they should not have trouble to apply the same resources in different educational situations. These facts raise epistemological issues and the consequent need to review the pedagogical theory supporting the actions inside school.

A Pedagogy of the Excluded

At closing of the twentieth century the challenge confronting the human community is to master the present structural crisis and transform the predatory nature of a process of development based on waste of resources and above all on the waste of human resources. Concentration of power and wealth goes hand in hand with a process of global exclusion and destitution for the majority of the peoples of the planet, oppressed by poverty, that is, by the violence of the social–economic order and social relations, and controlled by the violence of armies and police forces, by wars and other forms of intergroups and intragroup conflicts.

Education, as the area in which the social order fashions its subjects, but at the same time the place of symbolic conflict and of the struggles for individual and collective development, will face the challenge presented by the masses of the earth, the excluded of today and tomorrow, demanding the recognition of their humanity and struggling for a place in a renewed and humanized social order.

Reflecting on the experience of the Brazilian struggles for popular education in the present century as part of the struggles for real democratic participation, sociologist Florestan Fernandes once observed that developments in the theory and practice of education in Brazil in recent times, more and more are directed toward the construction of what he called "the pedagogy of the excluded" (Fernandes, 1989). After the pedagogy of the oppressed the challenge today is to develop a pedagogy that will not only promote the cognitive conquest of schooling for the popular classes—the working class, the underclass, minorities—but that will foster the cultural development of the so called underrepresented groups as tool for empowerment: the development of the cognitive, emotional and imaginative resources for social change. Based on that experience and on our own experience of work with urban communities, disadvantaged groups, working class, minority groups and indigenous groups in Brazil and in the United States we can start to formulate some of the characteristics as well as the main objectives of the pedagogy of the excluded.

Delineated from the particular experience of Brazilian education, the pedagogy of the excluded anticipated by Florestan Fernandes, while focusing mainly on issues of class relations in a so called Third World society, may benefit all the social groups that struggle globally for participation today. The aim of the pedagogy of the excluded is to provide the tools of knowledge for the integration of the underrepresented majority (in fact today a truly unrepresented, "invisible" majority), an integration that is in reality part of the project of creating a new social order.

In its theoretical dimension a pedagogy of the excluded aims at the critical understanding of the structural-historical production of exclusion in the present time, and the role of education for empowerment and participation as a challenge to the new strategies of global exclusion and the new ideological obscurantism. At stake in the present situation is mankind's capability of imaging and constructing the future as the overcoming of its present day structural conflicts and limitations. The aim of the pedagogy of the excluded is the practical and theoretical understanding of education as a process of historically based individual and collective development.

The pedagogy of the excluded is one that in its *practical* dimension redefines the norms that usually control the behavior of teachers and students within the school, specially in what concerns the use of time and appropriation of spaces. It is a pedagogy that allows teachers and students to make decisions about the use of time in school in order to let the nature of the activity proposed determine the time that one is going to spend on it rather than schedules defined by bureaucratic criteria (Lima, 1994). Also, it redefines the usual appropriation of spaces in school and the definition of "learning spaces" usually confined to classrooms and labs. Can community spaces, work place and commercial spaces, be considered and used as continuities of classrooms and the knowledge available in those places be articulated to the construction of formal knowledge in school settings? This is an issue to be explored in its epistemological significance.

This pedagogy implies the redefinition of the role of the teaching adults. Teachers have the primary role of working with form and content. This means that they will devote time to develop strategies of studying, that is, to teach the actions necessary for the construction of formal knowledge. Teachers will work with different symbolic systems and conduct the children in the process of creating meanings. They will focus on relations between facts and develop an interdisciplinary framework for fostering critical thinking and emphasize reflective thinking through accounts and narratives of the actions undertaken in the classroom.

The pedagogy of the excluded is the pedagogy that considers as an essential part of teaching the co-construction of knowledge with the students in the classroom by promoting the transparency of the interactional process between adults and children, and among adults themselves, by making culture and social class issues central themes for debates in the classroom. It will bring the cultural experiences of both children and students as subject matter. That means to reflect about cultural diversity as a given normal fact rather than approach it as an undeniable yet uncomfortable reality.

An important aspect of the pedagogy for the excluded is that it may include acting upon the *milieu* of the educating self, that is, through diverse forms of action it makes possible for the student to interact with sources of information available and to participate in diverse forms of human activity that are constituent of this *milieu.* The milieu exists in effective and potential elements to be learned and/or appropriated by the individual. Not everything that is part of the social cultural *milieu* is [equally] available as mediators for development and learning (Lima, 1995).

It is the role of schooling to enlarge the availability of the resources, information, tools and knowledge to students. Equity involves also acknowledgment of the mediators that are outside school and that are not available to working class and minorities. In fact it recognizes that the schooling process is not dissociated from a broader context, the *milieu,* and that therefore the actions taken inside school have an impact in the individual cultural development that goes beyond the limits of school itself.

The biological-social nature of human development needs to be considered as guiding factors on planning, executing and evaluating educational actions. Otherwise, we risk investing financial and human resources to produce failure. Consequently, in order to develop a pedagogy that will promote inclusion it is necessary to revise the role that universities and colleges have on preparing teachers. It becomes clear that school reforms and curriculum proposals in basic education need to be accompanied by school and curriculum reform in higher education.

Fernandes (1989, 1990) observed that educational changes in Brazilian schooling and more advanced reforms have been made effective by the transformation of teachers' professional profile in the last two decades and by their commitment to the empowerment of the population received at public schools.

That education may not be treated anymore as an exclusive matter of only the school as an institution separated from the social, cultural and political context in which it is inserted is a fact that people worldwide are increasingly aware of. In addition, with technological development the *milieu* in which human beings develop is transformed continuously by the incoming cultural elements, artifacts and ideas, and the consequent new or transformed forms of activity that they promote. Therefore, the mediation for the development of higher psychological functions, essentially related to formal learning, cannot be faced as immutable.

As a factor both in the struggles for equity in modern societies and in the maintenance of the status quo, the role of education in society depends on the uses of education defined by culture and socioeconomic systems. Education therefore cannot be considered as the solution for structural social and economic inequalities alone. At the same time, educational actions that may be a factor of changes in the socioeconomical situation of the dispossessed in society are those that do not reduce the educating self to ethnic and cultural stereotypes.

Education and the Dimension of the Future

As Florestan Fernandes observed, the process of education is rooted on the dimension of the future. The present crisis of the civilization constructed by capitalism, the crisis of its delayed transformation and supersession by a new historical stage of social evolution, necessarily produces a crisis of education itself (Fernandes, 1990). When the imagination of the future is impoverished and blocked by the social (dis)order, the process of education suffers a "crisis of identity." In a contradictory process, the over-instrumentalization of education, whose role as a mere branch in the institutional apparatus of ideological reproduction is reinforced, contributes at the same time to enfeeble its capacity to reconstruct social cohesion at the symbolic level.

Dialectically, the present crisis confers to education a renewed role in the future shaping of a more rational and just social order. A new form of civilization capable of facing the challenges of historical development at the global scale will require the contributions of a new, a different kind of education: an education oriented toward "the abolition of the process of dehumanization of man by man."

References

CRESAS (1978). *Le handicap socio–cultural en question,* Paris: ESF.
———. (1981). *L'échec scolaire n'est pas une fatalité.* Paris: ESF.

Fernandes, Florestan (1989). *O desafio educacional.* São Paulo: Cortez Editora.

———. (1990). *A transição prolongada. O período pós-constitucional.* São Paulo: Cortez Editora.

Lima, Elvira Souza (1988). A escolarização do processo de construção de conhecimento, in *Toda criança é capaz de aprender.* Idéias. São Paulo: Fundação para o Desenvolvimento da Educação.

———. (1994). Tiempo y temporalidad en la escuela, in *La etnografia en la educación. Panorama, practicas y problemas,* Rueda, M., Delgado, G., and Jacobo, Z. (Ed). Mexico: Universidad Nacional Autonoma de Mexico/UNM.

———. (1995). Culture revisited: Vygotsky's ideas in Brazil, in Vygotsky's Cultural–Historical Theory of Human Development, Souza Lima, E., and Emihovich, C. (ed). Theme issue, *Anthropology and Education Quarterly,* 26:4.

Lima, E., and Guimarães Lima, Marcelo (1995). Le développement culturel des enfants par l'experience esthétique. Un projet de peinture murale á Chicago, in *Langages et cultures des enfants de la rue.* Paris: Editions Karthala.

Mesmin, Claude (1993). *Les enfants des migrants á l'école. Reussite, échec.* Grenoble: La Pensée sauvage.

Oborlan, Suzanne (1995). *Ethnic Labels, Latino Lives, Identity and the Politics of (Re) Presentation in the United States.* Minneapolis: University of Minnesota Press.

Donaldo Macedo and Lilia I. Bartolomé

12

Dancing with Bigotry

The Poisoning of Racial and Ethnic Identities

As we approach the end of the century, one of the most pressing challenges facing educators in the United States is the issue of "cultural war," which constitutes, in our view, a code word that engenders our society's licentiousness for racism. Central to this cultural war is the creation of an ideologically coded language that serves, at least, two fundamental functions: on the one hand, it veils the raw racism that characterizes our society and, on the other hand, it insidiously perpetuates the fracturing and the devaluing of ethnic and racial identities. We want to argue in this chapter that although the present cultural war is characterized by a form of racism at the level of language, it is important to differentiate between language as racism and the experience of racism. Even though the former is no less insidious, it hides the institutional racism which bears on the lived-experience of those who are victimized by institutionalized racism.

Language as racism constitutes what Bordier refers to as "the hegemony of symbolic violence."[1] As educators, we need to fully understand the interrelationship between the symbolic violence produced through language and the essence of experienced racism. While the two are not mutually exclusive, "language always constructs and mediates the multiple experiences of identity by both historicizing it and revealing its partiality and incompleteness, its

Portions of this chapter will be published in the *Harvard Educational Review*.

limits are realized in the material nature of experience as it marks the body through the specificity of place, space, and history."[2] This is very much in line with John Fiske's notion that "[t]here is a material experience of homelessness that is of a different order from the cultural meanings of homelessness . . . but the boundary between the two cannot be drawn sharply. Material conditions are inescapably saturated with culture and, equally, cultural conditions are inescapably experienced as material."[3]

By deconstructing the cultural conditions that provide 20 million Limbaugh's ditto heads, we can begin to understand those ideological factors that enable seemingly educated individuals to blindly embrace Rush Limbaugh's sexist and racist tirades designed to demonize and dehumanize other cultural identities, as evidenced below:[4]

1. "Now I got something for you that's true—1992, Tufts University, Boston. This is 24 years ago or 22 years ago. Three-year study of 5,000 coeds, and they used a benchmark of a bra size of 34 C. They forward that—now wait! It's true. The larger the bra size, the smaller the IQ."
2. "Feminism was established so that unattractive women could have easier access to mainstream society."
3. "There are more American Indians alive today than there were when Columbus arrived or at any other time in history. Does that sound like a record of genocide?"
4. "Taxpaying citizens are not being given access to these welfare and health services that they deserve and desire. But if you're an illegal immigrant and cross the border, you get everything you want."

In addition to deconstructing the cultural conditions that foster Limbaugh's sexist and racist tirades, we need also to understand those ideological elements that informs our policy makers and those individuals who shape public opinion by supporting and rewarding Limbaugh's unapologetic deconstruction of other cultural subjects. For example, Ted Koppel considers him "very smart. He does his homework. He is well informed." George Will considers him the "fourth branch of government" and former Secretary of Education, William Bennett—the virtues man—describes Limbaugh as "possibly our greatest living American."[5] What remains incomprehensible is why highly educated individuals like Ted Koppel, George Will and William Bennett cannot see through Limbaugh's obvious distortions of history and falsification of reality. We want to argue that the inability to perceive distortions and falsifications of reality is partly, but not totally due, to the hegemonic forces that promote an acritical education via the fragmentation of bodies of knowledge which makes it very difficult for students to link historical events so as to gain a more critical understanding of reality.

Against cruel and racist cultural conditions, we can begin to understand that it is not a coincidence that Patrick Buchanan reiterated in his first presidential campaign platform that his fellow Americans should "wage a cultural revolution in the nineties as sweeping as the political revolution of the eighties."[6] During the launching of his 1996 Presidential candidacy, Buchanan unabashedly identified one of the pillars of his cultural war by arguing for the end to illegal immigration "even if it means putting the National Guard all along our southern frontier."[7] In fact, this cultural revolution is indeed moving forward with rapid speed, from the onslaught on cultural diversity and multicultural education to Patrick Buchanan's call to our national and patriotic sense to build a large wall to keep the "illegals" in Mexico. It is the same national and patriotic sense that allowed President Clinton—not to be outdone by the extreme right—to announce in his state of the union address that:

> All Americans, not only in the states most heavily affected, but in every place in this country, are rightly disturbed by the large numbers of illegal aliens entering our country. The jobs they hold might otherwise be held by citizens or legal immigrants. The public services they use impose burdens on our taxpayers. That's why our administration has moved aggressively to secure our borders more by hiring a record number of new border guards, by deporting twice as many criminal aliens as ever before, by cracking down on illegal hiring, by barring welfare benefits to illegal aliens.

> In the budget I will present to you, we will try to do more to speed the deportation of illegal aliens who are arrested for crimes, to better identify illegal aliens in the workplace as recommended by the commission headed by former Congresswoman Barbara Jordan.[8]

An analysis of the far-right Republican attack on immigrants and cultural groups and our liberal Democratic President's remarks during his State of the Union address confirm what has been for decades the United State's best kept secret: that there is no critical ideological difference between the Republican and Democratic parties. Ideologically speaking, in the United States we have a one-party system of government represented by two branches with only cosmetic differences cloaked under the umbrella of Republicans and Democrats.

If Patrick Buchanan vicious attack on immigrants were to be interpreted in ways other than racism, how could we explain his unfortunate testament: "I think god made all people good, but if we had to take a million immigrants in—say Zulus next year or Englishmen [why not Englishwomen?]—and put them in Virginia, what group would be easier to assimilate and would cause less problems for the people of Virginia?"[9]

We believe that it is the same racist sentiment that enabled President Clinton to abandon the nomination of Lani Guinier to head the Justice Department's Civil Rights Division just because she accurately demonstrated in her writings that the working-class poor, African Americans, and members of other minority cultural groups do not have representation in the present two-party system, where the white-male-dominated, capitalist ideology works aggressively against the interests of these groups. It is the same racist ideology that is forcing President Clinton to join the chorus in calling for an end to affirmative action policies, even though the benefactors of the real affirmative action since the birth of this country have been white males who continue to dominate all sectors of institutional and economic life in this society. For example, according to employment data on Boston Banks from the Equal Employment Opportunity Commission "[f]rom 1990–1993, the industry added 4,116 jobs. While the percentage of white male officers and managers rose by 10 percent, the percentage of African-American officers and managers dropped by 25 percent. While the percentage of white female clerical workers went up 10 percent, the percentage of African-American clerical workers dropped 15 percent."[10]

Like multicultural education, affirmative action is also a code word that licenses the new racism that assuages the white working- and middle-class' fear as they steadily lose ground to the real affirmative action programs designed to further enrich the upper class and big business:

> When the Fed raises the interest rates, it helps big business at the expense of individual home owners. When politicians resist raising the minimum wage, it helps big business send off the working poor. When politicians want liability caps, they defend Big Oil, Ma Bell and her offspring and Detroit gas guzzlers over potential victims of defective products and pollution. As the Gingrich revolution slashes school lunches for the poor, corporations get $111 billion in tax breaks, according to Labor secretary Robert Reich.[11]

We also know, that even within the context of the present affirmative action policy, the real benefactors have been white women. Their convenient silence on the present assault on affirmative action, a program from which they have benefited greatly, makes them complicit with the reproduction of the racist "myth that black people take jobs from white people . . . [which leads] one to conclude that African-Americans are not considered Americans. White men lose jobs to other white men who do not say, 'they gave my job to an inferior white man!' White male competency is assumed. African-Americans, regardless of achievement, are forever on trial."[12] In other words, Henry Louis Gates Jr.'s prominence as a scholar did not lessen the racism he had to face at Duke University when he taught there. Cornell West's status as a renowned public intellectual did little for him as he watched nine taxis go by and refuse to pick him up as a passenger in the streets of New York just because of the color of his skin. bell hooks eminence as a major feminist scholar does not lessen the pain of racism coupled with the sexism she endures. Having written eight highly acclaimed feminist books still does not provide her access to the media and magazines as enjoyed by white feminists such as Naomi Wolf. bell hooks recently complained:

> I have written eight feminist books. None of the magazines that have talked about your book, Naomi, have ever talked about my books at all. Now, that's not because there aren't ideas in my books that have universal appeal. It's because the issue that you raised in *The Beauty Myth* is still about beauty. We have to acknowledge that all of us do not have equal access.[13]

bell hooks' statement denudes the myth created by the anti-affirmative action discourse that "pretends that we live in a color-blind society where individuals are treated according to [t]he American ethic [that] has always held that individual effort and achievement are valued and rewarded."[14] The separation of the individual from the group collective consciousness is part of the dominant white ideology's mechanism to fragment the reality so as to make it easier for individuals to accept living within a lie that proposes a raceless and colorblind society. The real issue behind the present assault on multiculturalism and affirmative action is to never fall prey to a pedagogy of big lies. The fundamental challenge is to accept Derrick Bell's call for a "continuing quest for new directions in our struggle for racial justice, a struggle we must continue even if . . . racism is an integral, permanent and indestructible component of this society."[15]

In this chapter, we would like to accept Derrick Bell's challenge by pointing out that the real issue is not Western Civilization versus multiculturalism or affirmative action versus individual effort and merit. The hidden issue that informs the pernicious debate on cultural diversity and its ramifications, such as affirmative action, is cultural dominance and racism. In fact, it is an oxymoron to speak of our American "common culture" and democracy in view of the quasi–apartheid conditions that have relegated American Indians to reservations, created ghettoes, and supported the affirmative action of red lining and policies of Robin Hood in reverse. How can we honestly accept the mythical reality of "our common culture" when its major proponents are simultaneously engaged in a permanent process of putting other cultural identities on trail as demonstrated by Boston University president, John Silber who, during his campaign for governor of Massachusetts in 1990, asked: "Why has Massachusetts suddenly become so popular for people who are accustomed to living in a tropical climate? Amazing. There has got to be a welfare magnet going on here, and right now I am making a study to find out what that magnet is . . . Why should Lowell be the Cambodian capital of America?"[16] If John Silber had conducted his study as promised, he would soon realize his dance with bigotry since the majority of welfare recipients in Lowell are not Cambodians, but white Americans. He would also learn that the Asian community in Lowell represent a real economic force filling the gap for the flight of jobs and capital leaving Lowell struggling with a similar decay to that experienced by other old industrial cities. It is the same dance with bigotry that now informs our politicians in their quest for higher offices, including the presidency. David Duke, a Republican candidate in the Presidential primaries in 1990 minced no words when he stated, "America is being invaded by hordes of dusty Third World peoples, and with each passing hour our economic wellbeing, cultural heritage, freedom and racial roots are being battered into oblivion."[17] These racist sentiments are not lost in the proliferation of radio talk shows like Rush Limbaugh's whose major purpose is to exacerbate the racist fabric of our society as demonstrated by a broadcast by a local talk show in Brockton, Massachusetts, when a caller remarked: "Why should we be supporting these bilinguals? We should take care of our own first. The problem with Brockton is the Haitians, the Hispanics, the Capeverdeans that are ruining our neighborhood."[18] The demonization of the other cultural subjects is unabashedly exemplified by David Duke: "It's them! They're what's wrong with America! They're taking your job, soaking up your tax dollars, living off food stamps, drinking cheap wine and making babies at our expense."[19] Although these examples point to racism at the level of language, we would like to point out that it is no less insidious since it hides the institutional racism which bears on the lived-experience of those who are victimized by institutionalized racism. For example, while Pete Wilson, the governor of California and other politicians make speeches based on a language that demonizes the so-called "illegal" immigrants, the actual lived-experience of racism became immeasurably worse with the institutionalization of racism against immigrants with the passage of Proposition 187 in California.

The cultural condition that led to the passage of this law, which was designed to control the flow of illegal immigrants to California has had the effect of licensing institutional discrimination whereby both legal and illegal immigrants materially experience the loss of their dignity, the denial of human citizenship and, in many cases, outright violent and criminal acts committed by those institutions responsible for implementing the law. According to Human Rights Watch/Americas, "[t]he politically changed drive to curb illegal immigration may be coming at a serious price: beatings, shootings, rapes and death of aliens at the hand of the U.S. Border Patrol.[20]

As the anti-immigrant sentiment grows strong, the Immigration and Naturalization Service plans to increase its force from 4,200 against to 7,000 by 1998 with very little safeguards that the new hires will abate the human rights abuses perpetrated along the United States and Mexican borders. As Allyson Collins of Human Rights Watch/Americas notes, the "anti-immigrant sentiment dims the hope of safeguarding aliens as the United States fortifies its border: these are very unpopular victims."[21] Not only is there no guarantee that the Immigration and Naturalization Service, an agency with a record of hiring agents with past criminal records, will protect the rights of human beings who have already been dehumanized as "aliens" or "illegals," but what is troublesome is the degree to which this dehumanization process has been met by an unsettling silence even among liberals. This is not entirely surprising given the liberals' paradoxical posture with respect to race issues. On the one hand, liberals progressively idealize "principles of liberty, equality, and fraternity [while insisting] upon the moral irrelevance of race . . . Race is irrelevant, but all is race."[22] On the other hand, some liberals accept the notion of difference and call for ways in which difference is tolerated. For example, there is a rapid growth of textbooks designed to teach racial and multicultural tolerance. What these texts do is hide the asymmetrical distribution of power and cultural capital through a form of paternalism that promises to the "other" a dose of tolerance. In other words, the message is that "since we coexist and must find ways to get along, I will tolerate you." Missing from this posture, is the ethical position that calls for mutual respect and even racial and cultural solidarity. As Susan Mendus succinctly argues, tolerance "presupposes that its object is morally repugnant, that really needs to be reformed, that is, altered."[23] Accordingly, racial and cultural tolerance may be viewed as a process through which the different other is permitted to be with the idea or, at least the hope, that through tolerance the intolerant features that characterize the other will be eliminated or repressed. Thus, as David Goldberg pointedly argues:

> liberals are moved to overcome the racial differences they tolerate and have been so instrumental in fabricating by diluting them, by bleaching them out through assimilation or integration. The liberal would assume away the difference in otherness, maintaining thereby the dominance of a presumed sameness, the universally imposed similarity in identity. The paradox is perpetrated: the commitment to tolerance turns only on modernity's "natural inclination" to intolerance; acceptance of otherness presupposes as it at once necessitates "delegitimization of the other"[24]

Racial tolerance as proposed by some white liberals not only constitutes a veil behind which they hide a new form of racism, it also puts them in a very compromising racial position which is readily understood by the victims of racism as observed by Carol Swain, an African-American professor at Princeton University: * "white liberals are among the most racist people I know; they're so patronizing towards blacks."[25]

Against this landscape of racism, it becomes difficult to argue that these positions are taken only by fringe individuals such as David Duke. As hard as we may want to stretch the truth we cannot forget that he has been elected to public office in Louisiana. Nor can we argue that John Silber, the President of Boston University is on the fringe. He is as mainstream as those Republicans who signed on with the Contract with America, which proposes to cut lunch programs for poor children, take away cash assistance to unwed mothers with dependent children, cut fuel assistance to the elderly, abolish the food stamp program and crack down on illegal immigrants while denying social benefits to legal immigrants. In short, the racism and high level of xenophobia we are witnessing

* All of this provides a healthy counterbalance against Michael Apple's "war" on White Republican hegemony. - Both sides are guilty

in our society today are not isolated acts of individuals on the fringe. Rather, these individuals are representative of an orchestrated effort by all segments of the dominant society to wage a war on the poor and on people who, by virtue of their race, ethnicity, language and class are reduced, at best, to half citizens and, at worse, to a national enemy who is responsible for all the ills of our society.

It is against this mean-spirited and racist backdrop that we want to analyze the controversy over multiculturalism and the role that language plays in the process. We will refrain from discussing the way Puerto Ricans dance salza, how Chicanos celebrate *Cinco de Mayo,* how Haitians believe in Voodooism, or the significance of *lambada.* Although the knowledge of these cultural traits is useful, we do not think this knowledge will prepare us to deal with the tensions and contradictions generated by the coexistence of multicultural groups in a racist society. Instead, we will argue that multicultural analyses should not be limited to the study of the "other" making the white cultural group invisible and beyond study. What is important for us to understand is not necessarily how cultural differences are structured along specific behavior patterns. What is important is the understanding of the antagonism and tensions engendered by the presence of cultural differences that coexist asymmetrically in terms of power relations.

Since culture is so intertwined with language and represents a sizable dimension of its reality, and since language is rarely studied as part of our multicultural understanding, we will focus our analysis on the role of language in the dehumanization of other cultural subjects. In other words, not only do we often take for granted that the study of multiculturalism should be done in English only, we rarely question the role of the dominant language through which we study other cultures in the devaluation of the very cultural group under study. Put simply, we understand little of how the English language can provide members of the cultures we study with the experience of subordination and alienation. That is, we need to understand how English masks the web of ideological manipulation that makes the white cultural group invisible and outside the realm of study. For example, this invisibility is partially constructed by the profiling of nonwhite people as people of color. This suggest that white is not a color even though colorless white is a semantic impossibility. Hence, language not only produces cultural and social inequalities by is also used by the dominant white ideology to distort and falsify realities.

It is against this xenophobic backdrop that we want to analyze how language plays an important role in the demonization of people who, by virtue of their race, ethnicity, language, and class are not treated with the dignity and respect they deserve. Using language as a society's mirror, we can begin to understand society's pathological need to demonize the "other" so as to always have an enemy to blame for all its ills. During the '50s, the '60s, and the '70s we had Communism as a justification for all the evils that needed to be confronted. With the fall of the Berlin Wall, President Bush replaced Communism with the War on Drugs (remember that?). Failing to convince society that drugs were the root cause of all societal problems, the administration shifted its attention on another enemy: Terrorism. With the decrease of terrorism worldwide, we now have found a lasting enemy: Illegal immigration. This enemy was readily perceived by Richard Estrada whose grandfather immigrated to El Paso, Texas, in 1916. Estrada recently declared: "Illegal immigration threatens our national security."[26] He substantiated his claim by stating that Americans in Los Angeles cannot find jobs because of immigrants. Therefore, we need to militarize the border so as to protect the spirit of Proposition 187 and take our country back. That is, taking our country back means keeping Mexicans (like Native Americans) from their own land. We say "their own land" because many Mexicans and Native Americans did not immigrate to the United States. Mexicans inhabited the land until the U.S. government—under the doctrine of Manifest Destiny—legitimized the expropriation of almost half of Mexico through the United States provoked Mexican-American War. This expropriation was justified through the idea that if you fight for it and you win, you deserve the land. Could it be that this same principle was in the back of Saddam Hussein's mind when he invaded Kuwait? The attempt to reduce war for land expropriation to being the "ultima ratio" is eloquently captured in Carl Sandburg's poem "The People Yes":

"Get off this estate."
"What for?"

"Because it's mine."
"Where did you get it?"
"From my father."
"Where did he get it?"
"From his father."

"And where did he get it?"
"He fought for it."
"Well, I'll fight you for it."[27]

Language and the Construction of Racism

Given the sophistication of the use of language in the social construction of the other so as to dehumanize other cultural subjects, we feel that educators not only need to become cultural brokers to help crate a psychologically harmless pedagogical space for all students, but they also need to make sure that they do not teach a form of literacy that provides learners with a permanent experience of subordination. We need to understand that language is the only effective tool for us to deconstruct the web of ideological manipulation that makes the white cultural group invisible and outside the realm of study. Educators, particularly those working with multilingual and multicultural students, need to understand how discourses are very often anchored in "shock words, terms or expressions produced by themselves, [which] due to their strong connotations, provoke a reaction no matter what sentence within which they are inserted."[28] In other words, these terms, expressions, and words have a positive association, almost independent of their meanings. For example, in the present discussion of welfare reform, the word "reform" provokes a positive effect that forces most white middle-class individuals to leave its meaning in different contexts unexamined. Who in the white middle class would oppose reforming a social safety net they believe to be benefitting only individuals who are lazy and bent on living off those who work very hard to pay taxes? Who in the white middle class would oppose reforming what Patrick Buchanan characterizes as a "social catastrophe" and blames "Great Society programs not only for financial losses but also for the drop in high school test scores, drug problems and 'a generation of children and youth with no fathers, no faith and no dreams other than the lure of the streets.'"[29] Thus, welfare reform for the poor represents a positive shock word for the vast majority of white middle-class individuals who felt put upon by paying high taxes, in their view, to support lazy individuals who are poor because they do not want to work. When one points out that a higher percentage of their taxes goes to support welfare for the rich, the cry is uniform, immediate and aggressive: there is no room in the United States for incitement of class warfare. By changing the context of welfare reform from the poor to the rich, the shock word value and impact changes accordingly, from positive to negative effect. For example, when the call is to reform welfare for the rich, the reaction is as swift as it is disingenuous. Let's examine some positions taken by politicians and policy makers with respect to class warfare:[30]

- Alfonse M. D'Amato, Republican Senator from New York, set the tone: "There is something that I think is very dangerous taking place in this nation. Let me tell you what it is. It is class warfare under the theory of 'let's get the rich guy, the richest 1 percent' so we set them up, target them. Those are the people we are going to get."

- Senator William S. Cohen, Republican from Maine, put it this way: "We are talking about taxing the rich. Once again, we are engaging in classic class warfare."

- Senator Bob Dole, Republican from Kansas: "I do not know how long we can continue that kind of class warfare."

- Senator Slade Gordon, Republican from Washington: "While reducing the budget deficit may be the most important issue before this Congress, the President and his allies in congress are offering this country what amounts to class warfare . . . I object to these higher taxes."

- Robert K. Dornan, Republican from California, said that "to sell this program of higher taxes, Clinton and his liberal allies here in the House have turned to the standard liberal theme of class warfare, though they have couched it in terms of 'progressivity,' 'fairness,' and 'equality.'"

- Representative Jim Bunning, Republican from Kentucky, labeled the legislation "a historic class warfare scheme."

- Gerald B. H. Solomon, Republican from New York, observed that "as young Russians cover Marx's statue in Moscow with flippant slogans such as 'workers of the world, forgive me,' America is awash in the Marx-Leninesque rhetoric of class warfare."

These politicians are correct in stating that we have an ongoing class warfare in the United States. However, it is a class warfare against the middle class and the poor and not the rich as those quoted above claim. Since the early '60s, there has been a continuous change in the tax code that enriches the upper class while eroding the economic base of the middle and lower classes. This transference of wealth from the poor, lower class and the middle class to the upper class, has resulted in the creation of an enormous gap between a small *èlite* and a growing sea of poverty. For example, 2 percent of the U.S. upper class controls 48 percent of the nation's wealth while 51 percent of African-American children live in poverty. Upon a close examination of the present tax code, we soon realize how the policy makers have insistently waged class warfare that benefits large corporations:

- Chase Manhattan Corporation. Based in New York, Chase is the parent company of Chase Manhattan Bank, the global banking institution. For the years 1991 and 1992, Chase reported income before taxes of $1.5 billion. The company paid $25 million in income taxes, for a net tax rate of 1.7 percent. The official corporate tax rate in those years was 34 percent.

- Ogden Corporation. A diversified supplier of aviation, building and waste management services, Ogden reported income before taxes of $217 million. The company paid less than $200,000 in taxes (that is, less than .5 percent).

While the very rich corporations paid a minuscule percentage of their reported income in taxes, individuals with incomes between $13,000 and $15,000 paid taxes at a rate of 7.2 percent or four times the Chase rate.[31]

As we can see, the power of ideology is so insidious that the unanalyzed positive association of shock words such as "welfare reform" is often accepted by the very people who are in a position to be adversely affected by such reform. Thus, many working-class white people are led away by the illusion that the shock word, "welfare reform" creates, without realizing that they are, perhaps, one paycheck away from benefitting from the very social safety net they want reformed or destroyed. In an age of institutional downsizing (which is an euphemism for corporate greed and maximization of profit) the economic stability of both the white middle and working class is fast disappearing, thus creating an even more urgent need to horizontalize the economic oppression that is eating away their once more or less secure economic status.

Unfortunately, the very ideology that anchors its discourse on positive effect shock words also prevents us from having access to the subtext that often contains the opposite meaning of the illusory "reality" created by positive shock words. It is for this very reason that conservative politicians who propose "welfare reform" as a panacea for all the economic ills of our society will not tolerate a counterresponse that points to the false assumption inherent in the welfare reform proposal. For welfare reform to be equally exercised, we would have to include also welfare reform for the rich who are mostly responsible for exacerbating the already huge gap between the poor and the rich. Since we know that discussion concerning welfare reform for the rich is beyond question, the only way we can rationalize our support for welfare reform is to stay at the level of the positive effect of the shock word that often obfuscates the true reality.

Shock words, terms, and expressions do not only produce positive effects. According to Oliver Reboul, shock words can also "produce by themselves negative effects that disqualify those who use these shock words."[32] Thus, the use of terms such as "welfare for the rich," "oppression," "radical," and "activist" often provokes a negative effect that prevents a thorough analysis of the reality encoded by these terms. In other words, if "oppression" is not allowed as part of the debate, there will be no need to identify its perpetrator "oppressor." This is why, when Donaldo Macedo asked a colleague whom he considered to be politically progressive to read a manuscript of a book he was coauthoring with Paulo Freire she asked him, a bit irritably: "Why do you and Paulo insist on using this Marxist jargon? Many readers who may enjoy reading Paulo may be put off by the jargon." Donald Macedo was at first taken aback but proceeded to calmly explain to her that the equation of Marxism with jargon did not fully capture the richness of Paulo Freire's analysis. In fact, Paulo's language was the only means through which he could have done justice to the complexity of the various concepts dealing with oppression. For one thing, he reminded her, "Imagine that instead of writing *The Pedagogy of the Oppressed,* Paulo Freire had written the *Pedagogy of the Disenfranchised.*" The first title utilizes a discourse that names the oppressor whereas the second fails to do so. If you have oppressed, you must have oppressor. What would be the counterpart of disenfranchised? *The Pedagogy of the Disenfranchised* dislodges the agent of the action while leaving in doubt who bears the responsibility for such actions. This leaves the ground wide open for blaming the victim of disenfranchisement for his or her own disenfranchisement. This example is a clear case in which the object of oppression can be also understood as the subject of oppression. Language such as this distorts reality. It is for this reason that conservatives, as well as liberals, prefer some form of conviviality with a discourse that does not name it, a discourse of euphemism based on shock words.

It is also why the dominant discourse uses the presence of taboo words such as "class" and "oppression" to dismiss the counterdiscourse that challenges the falsification of reality. Thus, to call for the reform of welfare for the rich is immediately dismissed as "class welfare," a taboo concept since we have been inculcated with myths and beliefs that in the United States we live in a classless society. In fact, the ideological power of this myth is so powerful that the policy makers, the media, and the educators, constantly refer to categories such as "working class," and the need to protect the interest of the "middle class" that is overburdened by taxes, all the while denying the existence of class differences in the United States. If in fact we live in a classless society why do we constantly refer to the existence of the working class versus the middle class. However, what is always omitted from the dominant discourse is the existence of the term upper class. As a substitute, the dominant discourse goes through great lengths to create euphemisms such as "rich," "well to do," and "affluent," just to name a few terms. By closing the link between working class, middle class, and upper class, it would be impossible to sustain the myth that we live in a classless society. Therefore, it is important that the dominant discourse suppress the usage of upper class and, in so doing, denies its existence. As a shock work that produces a negative effect, "class" is regarded as such a taboo word that during the 1988 presidential campaign, George Bush berated his Democratic opponent Michael Dukakis by saying:

> I am not going to let that liberal Governor divide this nation . . . I think that's for European democracies or something else. It isn't for the United States of America. We're not going to be divided by class . . . We are the land of big dreams, of big opportunities, of fair play, and this attempt to divide America by class is going to fail because American people realize that we are a very special country, for anybody given the opportunity can make it and fulfill the American dream.[33]

By forbidding the use of the term "upper class," the dominant discourse engages in the social construction of a mythical classless society as was aggressively argued above by George Bush. Thus, the dominant discourse so acts in order to prevent the understanding of the mechanisms used as obstacles to the development of spaces for dialectal relationships. We are reminded of a deal of a college of arts and sciences at a public university who, when pressured by the central administration to get the college more involved in education and teacher preparation, asked the chair in the English department to appoint a liaison with the graduate school of education. However, he cautioned her to avoid nominating someone who was radical. Thus, "radicalism" is a shock word that triggers a negative effect and all those involved in work that is *a priori* considered by the dominant discourse as radical are dismissed as political and therefore not scientific and prevented from taking part in the discussion, particularly if the overall agenda is to maintain the status quo. In like manner, denouncing racism with strong conviction is often considered radicalism. A moderate position is to acknowledge that racism exists but not to advocate doing anything about it, which would not change the very structures that produce racism. In fact, to denounce racism with conviction becomes a worse social crime than the racist acts themselves. In the political sphere, politicians use taboo words as effective means to control the population, manufacture consent and dismiss any challenge presented by a counterdiscourse. Other taboo shock words such as "socialism," "communism," and "Marxism" have the same effect and are often successfully used for ideological control.

Let's consider the negative effect of the shock word "migrant." We have often wondered why we designate the migration of Hispanics to other geographical areas seeking better economic opportunities as "migrants" and, in contrast, we call the English migrants who came to Plymouth, Massachusetts, "settlers." The same is true for white South Africans. They are not referred to as migrant workers. They are called "settlers." The same is also true of the mass migration to the West during the Gold Rush. These fortune seekers became known as "settlers." We also wonder why today we continue to call the Hispanic community which has been here for many centuries "migrant" and fail to use the same term to categorize the large migration of Massachusetts workers to Florida and elsewhere during the last recession. Thus, we can begin to see that the term " migrant" is not used to describe migration of groups of people moving from place to place. "Migrant" is used to label and typecast Hispanic ethnically and racially while using this typecast to denigrate and devalue the Hispanic culture. "Migrant" not only relegates Hispanics to a lower status in our society but it also robs them of their citizenship as human beings who participate and contribute immensely to our society. Paradoxically, by uncritically adopting the dominant discourse, we unknowingly become participants in our own oppression. The denigration of Hispanic culture so as to paralyze it is consistent with the internal colonial effort to perpetuate exploitation. According to Amilcar Cabral, "The colonizer not only creates a system to repress the cultural life of the colonized people; he also provokes and develops the cultural alienation of a part of the population, either by the so-called assimilation of indigenous people, or by creating a social gap between the indigenous people elites and by the popular masses."[34] Unlike past colonial powers that relied on armed forces to perpetuate their domination and exploitation, the internal colonialism in the United States relies heavily on ideological manipulation through cultural repression, cultural alienation, and a racist cultural assimilation perpetrated through myths and a pedagogy of big lies. What the dominant class fails to recognize is that cultural assimilation does not necessarily translate into human freedom. How can we honestly speak of human freedom in a society that promotes the following poem:

Ode to the New California

I come for visit, get treated regal,
So I stay, who care illegal.

Cross the border poor and broke,
Take the bus, see customs bloke.

Welfare say come down no more,
We send cash right to your door.

Welfare checks they make you wealthy,
Medi-Cal it keep you healthy.

By and by, I got plenty money,
Thank, American working dummy.

Write to friends in mother land,
Tell them come as fast as can.

They come in rags and Chebby trucks,
I buy big house with welfare bucks.

Fourteen families all move in,
Neighbor's patience growing thin.

Finally, white guy moves away,
I buy his house and then I say,

Send for family, they just trash,
But they draw more welfare cash.

Everything is much good,
Soon we own the neighborhood.

We have hobby, it's called "breeding,"
Welfare pay for baby feeding.

Kids need dentist? Wife need pills?
We get free, we got no bills.

We think America damn good place,
Too damn good for white man's race.

If they no like us, they can go,
Got lots of room in Mexico.[35]

This poem was distributed to California Republican legislators by State Assemblyman, William J. Knight. When the legislators' Latino/Latina caucus complained that the poem was racist, Knight explained without apologizing that what he had distributed was "clever," and "funny." He added that the poem was not intended to "offend anyone." This insensitive attitude that borders on racism is not unlike the justification that Leni Reifensstahl, the most renowned Nazi film maker of Nazi propaganda gave when she argued, and continues to argue, that her role in the making of the most well-known Nazi propaganda film, *Triumph of the Will* was strictly artistic and had nothing to do with politics. Her inability to understand the moral and social consequences of her art in promoting hate and racism is part of a process through which she was able to disarticulate her art from the sociocultural and political context that generated heart an in the first place. This disarticulation represents, in our view, a sinister silence that provides the oxygen which, in the case of Leni Riefenstahl, was partly responsible for the Holocaust in which over 6 million Jews were exterminated.

How can we honestly speak of human freedom in a society that generates and yet ignores ghettos, reservations, human misery and savage inequalities. How can we honestly speak of human freedom when the state of California passes Proposition 187 which robs millions of children of their human citizenship. The term "illegal" not only criminalizes, but also demonizes young children. The law proposes to:

1. Refuse citizenship to children born on U.S. soil to illegal parents.

2. End legal requirement that the state provide emergency health care to illegal immigrants.

3. Deny public education to children of illegal immigrants.

4. Create tamper-proof identification cards for legal immigrants so they can receive benefits.

As cultural brokers we need to have the courage and ethical integrity to denounce any and all attempts to actively dehumanize the very students from whom we make our living as teachers. And in response to Patrick Buchanan's call for an "all-out cultural war," all we can say is that we have had enough cultural wars; what we need is cultural peace. The real challenge for educators is how schools can be brokers in this peace process. In other words, how can educators forge cultural unity through diversity.

We want to end this chapter by proposing a pedagogy of hope that is informed by tolerance, respect, and solidarity. A pedagogy that rejects the social construction of images that dehumanize the "other"; a pedagogy of hope that points out that in our construction of the "other" we become intimately tied with the "other"; a pedagogy that teaches us that by dehumanizing the other we become dehumanized ourselves. In short, we need a pedagogy of hope that guides us toward the critical road of truth, not myths, not lies, toward the reappropriation of our endangered dignity, toward the reclaiming of our humanity. A pedagogy of hope will point us towards a world that is more harmonious, less discriminatory, more just, less dehumanizing, and more humane. A pedagogy of hope will reject Patrick Buchanan and John Silber's policy of hatred, bigotry, and division while celebrating diversity within unity.

A pedagogy of hope will also point out to President Clinton and others that they could learn a great deal from those beings who by

A pedagogy of hope – celebrating diversity within unity.

virtue of their place of birth, race, and ethnicity have been reduced to the non-status of "aliens" as evidenced by Carlos Fuentes' words of wisdom:

> We will be able to embrace the other, enlarging our human possibility. People and their cultures perish in isolation, but they are born or reborn in contact with other men and women, with men and women of another culture, another creed, another race. If we do not recognize our humanity in others, we shall not recognize it in ourselves.[36]

Notes

1. Cited in Henry Giroux, *Border Crossings: Cultural Workers and the Politics of Education* (New York: Routledge, 1992), p. 230.

2. Giroux, Henry A., "Transgression of Difference," Series Introduction to *Culture and Difference: Critical Perspectives on Bicultural Experience,* (CT: Bergin and Garvey Publishers).

3. Fiske, John, *Power Plays, Power Works* (London: Venso Press, 1994), p. 13.

4. Randall, S. Naureckus, J., & Cohen, J., *The Way Things Out to Be: Rush Limbaugh's Reign of Error* (New York: The New York Press, 1995), pp. 47–54.

5. *Ibid.,* p. 10.

6. Cited in Henry Giroux, *Border Crossings: Cultural Workers and the Politics of Education* (New York: Routledge, 1992), p. 230.

7. Rezendes, M. "Declaring 'Cultural War.' Buchanan Opens '96 Run, *The Boston Globe,* 3/21/95, p. 1.

8. Clinton, W., The State of the Union, "Clinton Speech Envisions Local Empowerment," For the Record, *Congressional Quarterly,* Jan. 28, 1995, p. 303.

9. Pertman, Admu, "Buchanan Announces Presidential Candidacy." *The Boston Globe,* Dec. 15, 1991, p. 13.

10. Jackson, Derrick, *The Boston Globe,* 4/22/95, p. 13.

11. *Ibid.*

12. *Ibid.*

13. hooks, bell; Gloria Steinem; Uruashi Vaid; and Naomi Wolf, "Get Real About Feminism: The Myths, the Backlash, the Movement," Ms. Magazine, Sept./Oct. 1993, p. 39.

14. Jackson, Derrick, *The Boston Globe,* 4/22/95, p. 13.

15. Bell, Derrick D., *Faces at the Bottom of the Well: The Penance of Racism.* (New York: Basic Books, 1992), p. xiii.

16. *The Boston Globe,* January 26, 1990.

17. *The Boston Globe,* October 24, 1991.

18. Talk radio show, Brockton Massachusetts.

19. *The Boston Globe,* October 24, 1991.

20. "Trouble on the Mexican Border," *U.S. News and World Report,* April 24, 1995, p. 10.

21. *Ibid.*

22. Goldberg, David T., *Racist Culture* (Oxford UK & Cambridge USA: Blackwell Publishers, 1993), p. 6.

23. *Ibid.,* p. 7.

24. *Ibid.*

25. Swain, Carol, *New York Times,* Sept. 19, 1993, p. 158.

26. Estrada, Richard, Conference given at Harvard University, February 1995.

27. Sandburg, Carl, *The People, Yes* (New York: Harcourt, Brace & World, 1964), p. 75.

28. Reboul, Oliver, *Lenguage e Ideologia* (Mexico: Fondo de Cultura Economica, 1986), p. 116.

29. Pertman, Admu, "Buchanan Announces Presidential Candidacy." *The Boston Globe,* Dec. 15, 1991, p. 1.

30. Bartlett, Donald I., & James B. Steele. *America: Who Really Pays the Taxes?* (New York: Simon & Schuster, 1994), p. 93.

31. *Ibid.,* pp. 144–145.

32. Reboul, Oliver, *Lenguage e Ideologia,* (Mexico: Fondo de Cultura Economica, 1986), p. 117.

33. *The Washington Post,* October 30, 1988.

34. Cabral, Amilcar, *Return to the Source: Selected Speeches of Amilcar Cabral,* (New York: Monthly Review Press, 1992), p. 13.

35. From "I Love America!," a poem distributed in May, 1995 to California Legislators by State Assemblyman William J. Knight.

36. Fuentes, Carlos, "The Mirror of the Other," *The Nation,* March 30, 1992, p. 411.

David M. Smith

13

Aspects of the Cultural Politics of Alaskan Education

The Scene

Rural Alaskan schooling has been a major arena of cultural politics since the Europeans came to stay. Earliest schools established by missionaries who, through comity arrangements, divided the territory among them, were designed to force assimilation through systematic deligitimization of social customs, languages, and rituals. Later, to avoid risk of tainting their education with any native influences, it became common practice to move the children from their villages to the lower 48 states during their school years (Jackson, 1886; Darnell, 1970).[1]

In the 1970s this practice was successfully challenged in the courts, ushering in a new era in the cultural politics of rural Alaskan education. The state was now required to provide access to elementary and secondary schooling for all students in every village (Cotton, 1984 p. 30). This development followed the Alaska Native Claims Settlement Act (ANCSA) of 1971 which massively impacted virtually every dimension of native life.

Spurred by the oil industry's desire to gain clear right to the petroleum resources of the state, ANSCA settled the longstanding dispute with the federal government over native land claims. A major feature of the settlement was the ceding of subsurface and surface rights to large tracts of land to newly created and capitalized native corporations with the stipulation that for 20 years neither lands nor stock could be sold or transferred to nonnatives.

Part of the rationale for this approach was Congress' hope that ANSCA would put the levers of corporate power into the hands of Alaskan natives, giving them some "buffered" time to get established and to educate a generation in its transition from subsistence to corporate-based economies. Significantly the act allowed both sides to see in it the promise of realizing their mutually contradictory dreams. From the standpoint of the federal and state governments this solution was seen as a means to spurring assimilation by the Center.[2] However, many Alaskan natives saw the ANSCA settlement as a means to gain control of their own destinies and thus to protect their subsistence lifeways. (See particularly Berger 1985 for a discussion of these issues.)

While from the native perspective few of the promises of ANSCA have been realized, its implementation has coincided with a time of unprecedented prosperity in the state. In the short term, this in effect allowed both the assimilationists and the native power advocates to pursue their programs. Teacher and school administrator salaries rose dramatically attracting people from outside who, blithely unaware of Alaskan native issues, came for a year or two, bringing their uncritical assimilationist perspective to the bush. The University of Alaska used its wealth not to educate and train Alaskan natives for faculty positions,[3] but to bring in faculty from the outside, again scholars who were largely unaware of Alaskan issues.

This was only one part of the story. Even as these hegemonic developments were proceeding apace, they were being countered on several fronts. The Bush caucus in the state legislature was able to force the creation of a number of educational programs at both the K–12 level and in higher education. A number of people both in the schools and in the university, were working to develop programs that addressed the educational needs of Alaskan natives from a perspective of cultural awareness.

Notable among these was the innovative Cross-Cultural Educational Development Program, a university program leading to a Bachelor of Education degree, delivered to the villages and offered in close cooperation with community leadership (C. Barnhardt, 1994). These programs gained a great deal of acceptance and success despite attempts by the dominant political powers, even in these times of great prosperity, to marginalize the efforts. For example, native presence in schools was largely restricted to aides and bilingual coordinators. Virtually no Alaska natives held or presently hold standing faculty positions in the university. Native programs in the university have been housed in units that are vulnerable, have been subjected to serious criticism by the center, and are frequently restructured.

Since the adoption of ANSCA, Alaska has seen two other important changes that have set the stage for the present cultural-political struggle in Alaska education. First, we are witnessing a resurgence of attempts to preserve, and to recapture some of the past vitality of native cultures and lifeways. The pervasive working assumptions that native cultures were indeed dying along with the languages and that assimilation was inevitable are challenged by revisionist scholars. Whereas the past was characterized by exploitation and ethnocide, we know recognize that these processes have always coexisted with powerful currents of resistance. This movement is fueled by those believing that the cultural resurgence of the present can lead in the future to a revitalized native presence in a more pluralistic society (Bruner, 1986, p. 143).

Second, the state has experienced a severe financial crisis associated with lower oil prices and diminished oil production. The result has been a predictable heightening of political tensions, moves to reduce funding to programs seen as marginal, and the promotion of major development schemes. These constitute threats to native interests, ranging from an increase in overt racist behavior, through the undermining of native educational programs, to direct threats to subsistence life styles.

As a consequence, the cultural politics of Alaskan education has currently moved from a persistent simmer to a full boil. One cannot but believe we are at a critical juncture where the success of the center's hegemonic agenda threatens to prevail in maintaining the present social inequities.

This paper examines some of the issues of public education currently demanding our attention in Alaska using a lens suggested in part by ethnography and in part by critical pedagogy. With respect to the former, I take up the focus on the relational, as opposed to the educationist emphasis on the technistic reality of schooling (cf. Smith, 1992 for further discussion of these views). As for critical pedagogy, I use it as suggested by Kranpol to contextualize within the sociopolitical perspective of critical pedagogical theory some of the experiences in everyday schooling of Alaskan natives (1992, p. 18).

The Lens

Critical Ethnography of Schooling

While discussing Joel Spring's book *The Sorting Machine* (1989) in one of my recent seminars, students began to examine the ways in which the sorting function of schooling disadvantage minorities—an obvious reality that still has to be rediscovered every semester by our graduate students. One remarked, as one always does, "But we have to take into account the realities of existence. People do need to get jobs and for this they do need marketable skills." My response was, "But whose reality do we need to recognize, that which (sometimes traced to Durkheim) would have us believe the social order is a given and that it is the task of schooling to adapt us to that order, or the reality of Freire, who suggests the social order is a construct which we take an active role in shaping?" (cf. Hanson, 1975).

This incident, some variation of which we have probably all experienced in our graduate teaching, serves as a useful point of departure for the remarks that follow. The first view is that embodied in the prevalent centristist view of American schooling, and the later, supporting a critical pedagogy, is that underlying the approach on which this paper rests.

Ethnography views schooling as cultural activity and thus seeks to explicate the inevitable multiple realities experienced by its participants. It sees school simultaneously as a factory dedicated to production and an arena where individual human beings work to be, to find their places in the ever changing web of relationships that constitutes society. This web is defined not just by production demands of the institution but also by the identities individuals bring with them and are costantly developing. These realities taken together, the technistic and the relational, are crucial to understanding the cultural political struggle being waged in the educational arena.

1. The Technistic Reality. This reality drives most school related practice, including the recruitment and training of teachers and administrators, curricular decisions, government support decisions, and community responses. Among other things, it assumes the validity of a set of basic skills, defined by the center, that can be objectively tested using methods consistent across cultural, social, gender, and class boundaries.

I call this a *technistic* reality because it reflects the conventional wisdom that the primary role of education is to shape individuals to meet our various occupational needs. In other words, schooling is the designated factory for industrial society. It is designed to efficiently and artfully fill the production slots in our economy while at the same time convincing individuals to accept their roles in it as just and deserved.

This reality, demonstrated though observation of virtually all school practices and the pervasive hand wringing over the state of schooling, can be captured in a set of simple equations as follows:

Education = Schooling: Assessment, inculcation and enhancement of center defined skills.

School: A set of bounded interactions and ritual activities organized around skill inculcation and assessment, designed to mark the passage to human (i.e., productive) status.

Teaching: Techniques for doing schooling.

Teacher: Technician carrying out the decisions of society as translated by management/administration—deskilled and proletarianized (Apple, 1986).

Learning: Appropriate displays of behavior as judged by teacher or curriculum.

Children: Potential repositories of competence, potentially human (productive).

Administration: Management of technicians, quality control and public relations.

Research: Asking what makes things work as they are and applied research, how to make things work more efficiently.

This view of schooling has obvious implications for teacher preparation, for curriculum, and for research. For example, teacher preparation becomes largely an exercise in learning techniques or methods. Curriculum is designed to inculcate what the center has defined as basic skills and to evaluate out those who fail to exhibit the behaviors adduced as evidence of acquisition. Research becomes an enterprise defined as different from schooling (which is done by practitioners), under the control of and appropriate only to the work of credentialed experts (who are defined as intellectuals). *Ergo,* research is intellectual work, conducted under conditions that insure strict adherence to the cannon of scientism as opposed to teaching which consists solely of technical application.

2. The Relational Reality. From an ethnographic perspective, seeing education as schooling and schools as arenas for the inculcation of skills needed for the well being of society (and the concomitant acceptance by individuals of their assigned statuses) is to see only one reality and not the one that accounts for many school related phenomena. Schools are also places where human beings interact for significant stretches of their lives. Since these human beings are gendered, differentially abled, exhibiting differing racial, ethnic and class identities, schools become arenas for negotiation and struggle.

In this reality the equations look quite different:

Education: An unbounded process of becoming aware of one's social and cultural identity, that is, of the possibilities and limits imposed by one's place in the social arrangements.

Schooling: The process of negotiating one's response to and participation in the special demands imposed by a set of institutional structures and expectations.

School: An arena for this negotiation.

Learning: A human *sine qua non,* a coming to terms with the arrangements one has been able to negotiate. (NOTE: Learning precedes teaching in this reality since teaching is predicated upon the ineluctability of learning.)

Teaching: An intrusion into the learning process either in legitimizing the struggle or in delegitimizing it.

Teacher: One of the students' concerns, a representative of the social order the student must contend with and part of the social arrangement students are negotiating a role in.

Administration: A range of possibilities from the establishment of working conditions and practices supporting the intellectual and social work of learning and teaching, buffering these activities from countervailing pressures to serving as impediments to this work by legitimizing only the skill–centered activities.

Research: The attempt to explicate what's going on and what this means to participants in the enterprise.

This reality also has implications for teacher education, curriculum, and the teacher/researcher dichotomy. For example, in the process of being trained in technique, prospective teachers internalize a set of messages about their powerlessness, their untrustworthiness to serve as serious decision makers and of their worth in the economic system. Curriculum, while officially skill centered, also serves as a symbol of the center's presence with which one must find a way to contend. The only cultural tools a student has for this struggle are those she or he brings to the classroom from home, which for students coming from non-school oriented contexts are of a nature to insure an unequal outcome. By negotiating tools I refer to discourse patterns, the use of non-standard speech, styles of interaction and presentations of self, and so on (see Micheals, Heath, Rist, Phillips). Research, which takes account of this reality, is not qualitatively different from the intellectual work of teachers and students; indeed, it becomes a collaborative enterprise.

3. Critical Pedagogy. The notion of critical pedagogy underlying this discussion is taken to be an approach to teaching—learning that has as its end the development of a critical awareness of these two realities (Freire, 1973, 1985). Both of the realities taken together, constitute the social arrangements students must contend with. On the one hand they are going to be dehumanized to skill repositories, largely silenced, and treated as only potentially competent to play a productive role in society. On the other hand they are, as fully functioning and self-legitimized human beings, active and serious negotiants in the development of the social order that ultimately defines them. However the rules of engagement have been established by the dominant society.

A critical pedagogy entails not only a critical recognition of these realities, but explores possibilities for reconfiguring the arrangements. In other words, it makes one of the central concerns of schooling a critique, deconstruction and reconstruction of the social arrangements defining the classroom and the larger social context of students' existence. This is accomplished both explicitly as curriculum and implicitly in the kinds of learning-teaching relationships established. In this view, schooling is recognized for what it inevitably is, an important arena for cultural politics.

Culture here must be seen not simply as a set of values, expectations and rules for social interaction that have developed to foster a group's survival and that are then transmitted to individual members. It is rather a mutually constituted set of arrangements constantly being negotiated, challenged and affirmed, and that typically results in silencing (Fine and Weis, 1993, p. 1) of fringe voices, and the ascription of ranked statuses based on ethnicity, gender and class.

For our society historical processes have mandated that schools become significant arenas for negotiating these arrangements. However in the official canon this aspect of schooling has become a submerged reality. So long as this reality of schooling is not legitimized, the process of negotiation inevitably works to the disadvantage of members of subordinate or fringe cultures. That is, so long as schooling is treated as primary a technistic enterprise, concerned with development of marketable skills which can be objectively measured and with transmission of cultural values as givens, so long as we see the struggle for voice and attempts to resist the hegemonic agenda as disruptive, antisocial and self-destructive, schooling will continue to serve the ends of inequality and minority disempowerment.

One further observation is in order at this point. While a critical pedagogy serves to provide a critique of the hegemonic agenda of schooling embodied in the technistic reality, it does not celebrate as unproblematic the subcultures of the disenfranchised. This would be patronizing and ultimately as disempowering as a failure to give members of these groups voice in the construction of social arrangements.

In summary, I view critical pedagogy as a process of legitimating the relational reality of schooling and recognizing its primacy in accounting for school practices, those considered legitimate and desirable, and those considered pernicious. As an explicit goal of the learning-teaching enterprise it seeks to foster classroom relationships that encourage students to safely surface and explore the meaning of their experiencing of schooling (cf. Green, 1988). It recognizes students, wherever they are located on the social scene as whole, fully functioning, problem-experiencing human beings. A concern of this pedagogy is the explorations of the boundaries defining the fringes and the center, not with the end of appropriating behaviors that will move individuals to the center, but with the end of reconstructing the social order and redrawing the boundaries themselves.

Thus, we come full turn to the concern of my graduate student. While the futile goal of skill-centered, technistic pedagogy is the preparation of students to meet the requirements for occupying the center, that of a critical pedagogy, takes as its work the deconstruction of these boundaries themselves.

This conception of pedagogy has important implications for all aspects of schooling including research, classroom practices, community relationships, and curriculum. I briefly raise some of the current developments in the cultural politics of Alaskan education and explore how a critical pedagogy might inform these issues.

Cultural Politics of Alaskan Education

First I sketch the schooling scene in rural Alaska as popularly depicted. Finally I isolate and discuss a few of the issues of cultural politics as a critical pedagogy might address them.

Education in Rural Alaska

The schooling scene in rural Alaska today is usually described as one of pervasive failure and dismay. The standardized test scores in general, and in some districts in particular, lag behind national averages. Students drop out of high school in large numbers. Those who finish are seen as poorly educated. Graduates who do make it to the university frequently leave during the first or second semester.

In the villages, and particularly in the cities where villagers often hang out, alcoholism is recognized as a major problem—a problem being addressed with resolve by native communities themselves today. Suicide has become a leading cause of death among the young, especially young men. This added to the high incidence of accidental—often alcohol-related—death that touches every family in every village in rural Alaska, means that "young death" is an every day, ever-present factor in the lives of school children.[4]

We must add to this familiar litany the continuing threat to traditional meaning-affirming subsistence lifestyles occasioned by the incursion of industrial society. This incursion not only deligitimizes traditional culture and rapes the countryside, at the same time it serves to deny access to the social and economic structures of the center. Most of the new jobs that have been created are filled by whites—frequently men who are married to native women, further complicating the lives of native men. The lethal irony of this situation, of course, is that the primary rationale for a technistic approach to schooling is preparation for jobs.

Schools are the major representatives of modern industrial society in the villages. Curriculum and hiring are determined by a central bureaucracy located outside the village and inaccessible by the community. Superintendents, almost without exception, are nonnative and have earned their credentials outside of Alaska. Only a handful of principals and a slightly larger number of credentialed teachers are Alaskan natives. The majority of rural educators are therefore, for all intents and purposes, itinerant technicians sent into the area by an alien enterprise, charged to implement a program drawn up by directors living and working in places as remote as Orange County, California, or East Lansing, Michigan. They are paid agents of the center, missionaries of the center's hegemonic agenda.

The stage is set for creating the expectation of failure the kids not only have experienced in the villages but which waits them in the university. They come to the university viewed as seriously unprepared, especially in literacy, numeracy, and science. These deficiencies are adduced by the institution as the explanation for any poor performance in entry level classes and for perceived high attrition rates, that is, a number of students leave the university and go back to the village before their first year is completed.[5]

Issues of Cultural Politics in Alaska

In this section I briefly mention several specific developments that illustrate the issues raised in examining the cultural politics of Alaskan native education.

1. Remedial or Bridging Programs. The university has responded to the perceived problem of unpreparedness by creating developmental courses, even a developmental studies department, and the establishment of bridging programs.

These responses are, of course, consistent with a technistic view of education and continue the sorting and reproduction work started in the village schools. In the first instance, they implicitly locate the perceived failure in the students themselves and thus suggest solutions designed to change them, the students. Participating in these remedial or bridging programs serves to confirm the deservedness of the failure label both to the students and the institution. This ubiquitous yoking of native students and expected failure is in itself part of a larger political discourse that stereotypes natives as problems for the university. Since it is virtually impossible to escape the effects of the failure label, especially when it is internalized, this rap will precede one's every move and will be self-fullfilled in virtually every academic encounter.

From a relational perspective, however, these solutions are problematic in that developmental and bridging programs, while designed to give select members of the fringes those attributes which will facilitate their move to the center, serve to reify and harden the boundaries. These boundaries which arbitrarily carve up the social space determine who is object and who is subject in the social discourse.

These approaches may indeed result in the movement of a few individuals to the center giving an illusion of progress. However, they make it harder than ever to change the boundaries themselves and ultimately contribute to increasing inequality. By allowing a few to escape the confines of fringe or subaltern status, without attacking the boundary problem itself the message conveyed to those left behind is, "We must be responsible for our own limitations, the boundaries are breechable."

Ogbu (1978) and others have shown that this is an illusion. When the boundaries are breached in any number, as is now happening in Alaska, a new set of forces is unleased to reinforce the status quo. "You made it through the gates but you don't really deserve your new status."[6]

To summarize, a technistic pedagogy attempts to move individuals from the fringes to the center without disturbing the boundary arrangements, thereby controlling the numbers of individuals who can move while maintaining the inequitable social arrangements. A critical pedagogy raises the whole issue of boundaries and the processes of boundary maintenance to a conscious level, then examines and critiques these arrangements opening possibilities for addressing them at both an individual level, that is, by making clear to individuals the consequences of daily choices, and the system level, by raising an awareness of these deeper realities to policymakers.

2. The ITBS. The use of standardized tests to assess basic skill achievement in rural, primarily native schools is of ongoing concern to educators sensitive to the cultural political dimensions of schooling practices. It has been widely assumed by the center majority that native students are being poorly prepared by village schools for productive careers. This assumption has gained some credence since the inception of a statewide testing program was mandated by the state legislature in 1988. The test used in this assessment is the Iowa Test of Basic Skills. According to an Alaska Educational Association (AK-ERA) White Paper examining the issues of test bias, the results of testing since its inception "shows notable performance differences between students in urban and rural areas, native and nonnative students, and bilingual and non–bilingual students" (Kleinfeld, *et al.* 1991, p. 1). In light of this, the use of the ITBS as an appropriate instrument for collecting comparative data has been met with understandable unease on the part of thoughtful educators and native peoples alike.

To help alleviate this unease, ostensibly to see if there were any biases in the test, and to explain the rationale for the testing program to the public, AK-ERA underwrote an examination of the ITBS that was published as the White Paper alluded to above. The investigation included a special item bias study conducted by H. D. Hoover (*ibid.*, p. 7).

The White Paper makes a reasoned and compelling case for the fairness of the instrument, discussing what it purportedly measures (general knowledge and basic academic skills, p. 4), what it does not measure (intelligence, creativity, drive to achieve, concern for others, or other important human characteristics, p. 4) and, cautioning against misuse of the results. The end result is to generally assure the reader that the testing program, while modest, is benign, unbiased, necessary as an objective measure of where our children stand relative to the achievement of other children nationwide, and indicative of how well individual schools are doing.

I have indicated that the White Paper makes a reasoned and compelling case for the fairness of the instrument and ultimately for the reasonableness of the testing program. This, of course, is only true if we accept as unproblematic the epistemological assumptions underlying technistic approaches to schooling (e.g., that we need to know objectively where children stand relative to others) and the center's hegemonic agenda.

This agenda is made explicit in the paper. First, we are told that the rationale for the testing program rests in the state's desire to see if it is getting a reasonable return on the capital it is investing ($488 million per year and $4,600 per student) in the production of adequately skilled students (pp. 1–2). Second, we are assured that it is important to provide educators and parents with diagnostic information so students with special needs can be identified, that is, that students be sorted out and efficiently dealt with (p. 9). Third, we need to provide accountability information for the public and legislators, that is, assure the proletarianization (Apple, 1986) and control of teachers (p. 9).

A critical pedagogy would surface as problematic each of these functions and assumptions exploring the extent to which they dehumanize the participants in the schooling process, promote ethnocide, foster inequality, reify the social boundaries, and assure the center's control over people's lives. It would also critique the center's right to define what constitutes and what counts as having acquired basic skills.

3. Control of Curriculum. This leads us to a third arena in the cultural political struggle in Alaskan native education, the control of curriculum. Space permits only a cursory sketch of this issue which is central to the enterprise of schooling and raises at least three concerns appropriate for critical examination. These are, the discounting of native ways of thinking, the imposition of the center's disciplinary boundaries, and the construction of what Ongtooguk, following the lead of Anyon, calls the creation of "a veil of silence" over native history and lifeways (Ongtooguk, 1993; Anyon 1979).

As indicated above, the center has defined what counts as basic skills and, through the imposition of a standardized testing program, specifically designed to measure the general knowledge and academic skills used in determining a persons economic value, presumes to dictate a particular world view. Kawagly (1995) rightly contends that insistence upon accepting and operating within this epistemological framework disadvantages and delegitimizes native peoples.

In order to be successful in school, native students must accept a way of thinking that from their point of view is destructive of the very reality which assures their survival and the vitality of their lifeways. This requires the submersion of spirituality to an instrumental secularism as a way of relating to and understanding the natural world. Their myths are treated as folklore and the center's myths are taught as unassailable truth. A holistic view of the natural order is forcefully replaced by an analytic, reductionist model. They must accept the notion that their legitimacy, their humanness, is not assured by their place in an extended family—one that extends both historically and horizontally—but by their productive potential in the center's economic arrangement.

Barnhardt (1992) relates an incident in which he was meeting with the elders in an Athabascan village while a government wildlife biologist attempted to explain research that was being done to predict the pike population and particularly to explain a sudden drop in this population so that informed fishing regulations could be formulated. Tiny radio transmitters had been implanted in the gut of a number of the fish so their movements could be traced. The elders thought the entire operation as both amusing and offensive since the placement of transmitters rendered the fish unusable for food and because the entire operation was ultimately geared to reducing the supply of pike available for subsistence use.[7]

In the discussion that ensued, the elders were able to answer all of the concerns of the biologist calling exclusively upon local knowledge. They knew where the pike spawned and what factors influenced their population fluctuations. This knowledge reflected an understanding of the natural factors of flooding and erosion, the role of beaver with their dam building and deforestation, and the importance of controlling harvests by making use of other food sources when necessary.

In order for the scientists to have understood the issue would have required study by fishery biologists, mammalogists, engineers, and social scientists. These specializations represent the center's disciplinary arrangements reflected in school curricula. Given the realities of life in rural Alaska, is it any wonder that attempts to develop and impose a center defined and dominated curriculum meets with limited success? A critical pedagogy would not simply ask how to make scientists of native students, but what kind of science is appropriate.

One of the most disturbing aspects of the center's curriculum is the way in which it treats native history and lifeways as nonexistent or at least not worthy of a central place. This kind of silencing is especially pernicious. It is clearly at the root of so much of the misplaced concern with the lack of self-esteem native students are supposed to exhibit. As Demmert (1991) has pointed out, the issue is not one of self-esteem but of the esteem in which students are held. It starts with the pervasive silencing of their stories and histories.

A critical pedagogy would examine the reasons for insisting on only presenting the center's story. It would also, as Harold Napeoleon (1991) reminds us, not treat native history as totally unproblematic. It would have as its goal the creation of a new story for each student, one that is neither a recitation of failure and self-hate, nor an unmodulated glorification of a reconstructed history. It would take into account the complex realities of the present.

In this sketch, I have rather arbitrarily focused attention on three of the cultural political battles presently being engaged in Alaskan native education. I have said little about the appropriateness of the center's notions of teacher preparation, an interest being explored by Lipka (1991). I also have not touched upon the problematicity of conventional center models of educational leadership. These are based on the industry model of management (Callahan, 1962), and reflect a model of the mythic ideal nuclear family with a highly skilled authoritarian father, an unskilled nurturing mother and carefully disciplined children. Finally, I have not discussed classroom practice or research. All of these are emerging as arenas in the cultural political struggles of Alaskan ,ative education (cf. Lipka, 1989, 1994).

Conclusion

This paper is intended to sketch the outlines of a critical pedagogy, a pedagogy that does not see the goal of education to be the facilitation of the movement of fringe groups to the center. It addresses the social arrangements that exist and the nonproblematicity of the center imposed and enforced boundaries.

From this perspective, I have explored several issues constituting the current cultural political struggle over Alaskan native education. It is my hope that this suggests a fruitful approach, not just to explicating the issues but to addressing serious inequities.

Notes

1. This history has been amply documented in the literature. Cf. Fienup–Riordan (1991), Darnell (1970), Koponen (1964), Olson (1931).

2. By center I mean the prevailing power structure which defines itself and the fringes. At the same time it constructs the social boundaries and creates the mechanisms for enforcing them.

3. The University of Alaska Fairbanks at present has not a single Alaskan native faculty member with a doctorate and has only two or three tenured native faculty members.

4. This situation gives new meaning to the technistic view that childhood is "down time" or mere preparation for adulthood with death a distant irreality. One can speculate about the need to face death as a constant reality unmasking this fiction, a fiction necessary to justify the many inhumane practices of schooling. Does this not threaten the entire edifice, as seen from the standpoint of a village young person, revealing it for the unsupported shack of tar paper it is?

5. Unfortunately, and seemingly of little concern to the administration, we know little of what this early "drop-out" pattern means. Some come back a few years later, others go on to other universities, others participate in some of the distance education or correspondence programs the university offers. (Cf. Gilmore and Smith, 1990 for a discussion of this issue.)

6. A major confrontation between the native community and the university administration occurred in the fall of 1991 over this issue. A professor charged publicly that undeserving native students were being graduated. Investigation proved the allegations to be unfounded. However, the native community was upset at what they saw as slow and inappropriate response on the part of the institution to the incident. (See Gilmore, Kairaiuak and Smith, 1996 for an analysis of the institutional response to this crisis.)

7. Subsistence itself is an issue that illustrates the conflict between the center's epistemology and that of Alaskan natives. To the center, subsistence only means the taking of game for consumption. For Alaskan natives, it is seen as way of life touching upon ever aspect of existence.

References

Anyon, J. (1979). Ideology and U.S. History Textbooks. *Harvard Educational Review* 49(3):361–86.

Apple, M. (1986). *Teachers and Text: A Political Economy of Class and Gender.* Boston and London: Routledge and Kegan Paul.

Barnhardt, C. (1994). *Life on the Other Side: Alaska Native Education Students and the University of Alaska Fairbanks.* Ph.D. Dissertation. University of British Columbia.

Barnhardt, R. (1992). *Proceedings of the Alaska Native Science Education Colloquia.* Fairbanks: Center for Cross Cultural Studies.

Berger, T. (1985). *Village Voice: A Report of the Alaska Native Review Commission.*

Bruner, E. (1986). Ethnography as Narrative. *The Anthropology of Experience.* Turner, V. and E. Bruner, eds. Urbana and Chicago: University of Illinois Press, 139–55.

Callahan, R. (1962). *Education and the Cult of Efficiency: A Study of the Social Forces that Have Shaped the Administration of the Public Schools.* Chicago: The University of Chicago Press.

Cotton, S. (1984). Alaska's "Molly Hootch Case": High Schools and the Village Voice. *Educational Research Quarterly* 8(4):30–43.

Darnell, F. (1970). *Alaska's Dual Federal–State School System: A History and Descriptive Analysis.* Unpublished Ed.D. Dissertation.

Demmert, D. (1991). Class Lecture. The University of Alaska, Fairbanks.

Fienup–Riordan (1991). *The Real People and the Children of Thunder: The Yup'ik Eskimo Encounter with Moravian Missionaries John and Edith Kilbuck.* Norman and London: University of Oklahoma Press.

Friere, P. (1973). *Education for Critical Consciousness.* New York: Seabury Press.

Friere, P. (1985). *The Politics of Education.* S. Hadley, Mass.: Bergin & Garvey.

Fine, M., & L. Weis (1993). Introduction. Fine, M. & L. Weis (eds.) *Beyond Silenced Voices.* Albany: State University of New York Press, 1–6.

Gilmore, P., & D. Smith (1989). Mario, Gary and Jesse: Contextualizing Dropping Out. *What Anthropology Says about Dropping Out.* H. Trueba, G. & L. Spindler (eds.). Philadelphia, Falmer Press.

Gilmore, P., D. Smith, & L. Kairaiuak (1996). Resistance, Resilience and Hegemony: An Alaska Case of Institutional Struggle with Diversity. *Off White: Readings on Society, Race, and Culture.* M. Fine, *et al.* (eds.). New York: Routledge.

Green, M. (1988). *The Dialectic of Freedom.* New York: Teachers College Press.

Hanson, R. (1975). Friere vs. Durkheim: On Pedagogy and the Functions of Education. *The Academic Discipline and the Structure of Education.* Rose, E. (ed.). Lincoln: University of Nebraska.

Heath, S. (1983). *Ways With Words.* Cambridge: Cambridge University Press.

Jackson, S. (1986). *Report on Education in Alaska.* Washington: Government Printing Office.

Kawagley, A. O. (1995). *A Ypiaq Worldview: A Pathway to Ecology and Spirit.* Prospect Heights: Waveland Press.

Kleinfeld, J., et al. (1991). *Alaska Statewide Assessment Student Testing Program: Are the Tests Biased?* White Paper #1. Anchorage: Alaska Educational Research Association.

Koponen, N. (1964). *The History of Education in Alaska: With Special Reference to the Relationship Between the BIA Schools and the State School System.* Unpublished. Ed.D dissertation, Harvard University.

Kranpol, B. (1992). *Toward a Theory and Practice of Teacher Cultural Politics: Continuing the Post Modern Debate.* Norwood: Ablex Publishing Corporation.

Lipka, J. (1989). A Cautionary Tale of Curriculum Development in Yup'ik Eskimo Communities. *Anthropology and Education Quarterly,* 20(3): 216–231.

Lipka, J. (1991). Toward a Culturally Based Pedagogy: A Case Study of One Yup'ik Eskimo Teacher. *Anthropology and Education Quarterly,* 22(3):203–223.

Lipka, J. (1994). Culturally Negotiated Schooling: Toward a Yup'ik Mathematics. *Journal of American Indian Education.* (Spring 1994):14–30.

Michaels, S. (1981). Sharing Time: Children's Narrative Styles and Differential Access to Literacy. *Language in Society,* 10:423–42.

Napoleon, H. (1991). *Yuuyaraq: The Way of the Human Being.* Fairbanks: University of Alaska, Center for Cross Cultural Studies.

Ogbu, J. (1978). *Minority Education and Caste: The American System in Cross-Cultural Perspective.* New York: Academic Press.

Olson, O. (1931). *History of Higher Education in the Territory of Alaska.* Masters thesis: University of Washington.

Ongtooguk, P. (1993). *Their Silence about Us: The Absence of Alaska Natives in the Curriculum.* The University of Alaska (unpublished manuscript).

Philips, S. (1983). *The Invisible Culture: Communication in the Classroom and Community on the Warm Springs Indian Reservation.* New York: Longman.

Rist, R. (1973). *The Urban School: A Factory for Failure: A Study of Education in American Society.* Cambridge: MIT Press.

Smith, D. (1992). Anthropology of Education and Educational Research. *Anthropology and Education Quarterly,* 23(3):185–98.

Spring, J. (1989). *The Sorting Machine Revisited: National Educational Policy since 1945* (updated edition). New York: Longman.

Yali Zou

14

Dilemmas Faced by Critical Ethnographers in China

Richard A. Schweder has summarized recently (1996) the current debate on ethnography:

> True ethnography aims to represent otherness in such a way that "we," who are outside the relevant situation, can imagine what it is like to be in it . . . A true ethnography is about something called culture. As everyone knows, there are many definitions of *culture*. The definition I was taught as a "mantra" in 1963 in my first undergraduate course in anthropology was "patterns of behavior that are learned and passed on from generation to generation" (Shweder, 1996: 18–19).

The problem in postmodern times is that some people go to the extreme called "solipsism" which is "the view that the only mental life you can ever really know is your own" (Shweder, 1996: 21). Shweder concludes that:

> If "true ethnography is possible, then either solipsism is wrong or ethnographic authority is not really threatened by radical doubts about the existence and character of other minds . . . If true ethnography is possible, then either solipsism must be wrong, or else ethnographic authority is compatible with radical doubt (Shweder, 1996: 24).

While scholars continue to debate even the possibility of ethnographic research, others raise the fundamental ethical question about the oppressive character that can be attributed to ethnographic research, unless such research is "critical," or directed to revealing oppressive situations and in no way treats people "as objects" of our inquiry. De Genova has recently written:

> The practice of ethnography poses an intractable problem: it is the singular means of formal social research that enables a production of the textured knowledge of human perspectives and structures of feeling in the present that emerges only through extended engagement with everyday lives, labors, and struggles of living people, while it is simultaneously an inherently objectifying methodology (1997).

De Genova adds that long before the ethnographer writes a text, the question of who writes, for whom and for what purposes must be faced, that is, the question of the personal identify of the researcher becomes central to the very effort of conducting research (1997).

Critical Ethnography

Since the 1960's the literature on critical ethnography has attempted to theorize about, and operationalize methodologically, the concept of empowerment in order to meet the challenges of studying oppressive social environments. Howard Becker, an influential scholar, in his presidential address to the Society for the Study of Social Problems, raised this question with the social scientists: "Whose side are we on?" Indeed, in his book·*Boy in White* (1961), he strongly urged sociologists to take the side of the underdog. He argued that sociologists cannot conduct objective research because they cannot help but be biased. Roger Simon and Donald Dippo, in their article "On Critical Ethnographic Work" (1986), point out that critical ethnography requires three fundamental conditions:

1. A particular "problematic" that defines data and analytic procedures in a way consistent with a pedagogical political project.

2. The engagement of such work within a public sphere that allows it to become a starting point for social critique and transformation.

3. The inclusion of a reflexive inquiry that would identify the limits of its own knowledge claims.

In *Doing Critical Ethnography,* Jim Thomas (1993) claims that this ethnography is a means of invoking social consciousness for societal change. Henry Giroux, in his book *Theory and Resistance in Education* (1983), maintains that critical ethnographic work requires entering the public sphere. Such a sphere is a place of public critique of social practice that leads people to an understanding of the grounds of their own actions in the historically and socially situated context of their lives; and Concha Delgado–Gaitan (1993) in a recent article, "Researching Change and Changing the Researcher," suggests that researchers can be agents of change while they conduct rigorous research. Critical ethnography can be perceived as very powerful methodological instrument, even at times risky and painful. Carspecken, for example, suggests that the goals of researchers hide psychological self-identity baggage and paradoxical traps:

> Society at present structures too many identity claims on comparisons with other groups of people: "I am a worthy human being because I am not one of them." Researchers carry this baggage as much as anyone. But any identity that depends on negating the worth of others is ultimately limited and ultimately falls short of human potentiality . . . This is why many people enjoying a privileged position in society feel threatened by the plight of the poor. They do not want to know too many of the details. They want to explain social inequality by blaming the victims or in any other way that leaves their accustomed identities intact. They are afraid of being wounded (Carspecken, 1996: 1704–171).

The reason for perceiving critical ethnography as a threat is, in the ultimate analysis, because ethnographic work is not only a mental exercise but a moral commitment to action.

Since 1980, the amount of debate on the role of critical ethnography for empowerment in fieldwork research has dramatically increased. The central questions that are yet to be answered satisfactorily are: As researchers, how do we deal with our personal values and biases in the research process? What is the role of the researcher? Should the researcher adopt a political agenda with specific actions and in specific social contexts? Is it ethical for researchers to engage in political action? What are the consequences of taking action, both for the research agenda itself and the researchers? What is the social and political impact of our research and the writing of it? How intrusive is the research process culturally?

Researchers today face difficult questions and confront their own values in their daily investigative activities. As a researcher, I have also faced serious dilemmas that I would like to share with you. The dilemmas that I and other colleagues faced while conducting critical ethnographic research in China will help illustrate the crossroads faced by ethnographers today, especially ethnographers doing work in ethnic communities. We defined our study as a critical ethnography, because it was organized around the assumptions that Chinese society has witnessed oppression, in part by the fact that it has been dominated by the Han hegemonic culture and authority which has been imposed upon ethnic minority groups for centuries. The purposes of the study were: (1) to explore the process by which Miao ethnic minority students became empowered—essentially the relationship between ethnic identity and power—and (2) to identify their role in Chinese modern society as well as in the Miao communities. As a researcher, I hoped that the study of this process could inspire other minority groups to invest in their own education while at the same time retaining their cultural heritage.

In order to conduct the study, I had to discuss with the students under study my understanding of the nature of empowerment and, by implication, its desirability. I felt that they were proud of being Miao and of being selected for training at the university level. Using Richard Quantz' (1992) definition "critical ethnography is recognized as having conscious political intentions that are oriented toward emancipatory and democratic goals," I sought the means to better the lives of the Miao oppressed minority by sharing with them what we knew about other ethnic groups and the empowerment process they sought through the strengthening of their ethnic identities.

Ethnic Groups in China

The challenge of understanding any of the many ethnic groups, or "nationalities," in China is compounded by the series of rapid demographic, social, economic, and political changes that have taken place in the last half century. Since the People's Republic of China was established, demographic changes have been dramatic. China had a relatively modest population between 50 and 100 million between the first and the eighteenth centuries. During the Qing dynasty (in the 1770s) the population was about 100 million. By 1840 it has increased to 400 million, and when China became the People's Republic of China on October 1, 1949, it was 500 million (Poston & Yaukey, 1992: 1). By 1990 the population had jumped to 1.13 billion.

The ethnic, social, linguistic and economic diversity of Chinese people is overwhelming and complicated. In 1951, China officially recognized 56 ethnic groups in China. Among them the Han was considered the dominant group, both numerically and politically. The other 55 groups, the so-called minority groups or nationalities, had, according to the 1990 national census, a population of 91,200,314 million people that was 8 percent of the total population of China (1.13 billion). Since 1982, when the Chinese census showed a population of 1,008,175,288, a figure considered extremely conservative by experts (Crespigny, 1992: 285), the policy of one child per family was adopted. The 55 ethnic minority groups, however, were exempted from it. (For a detailed listing of these groups and their geographic distribution see Trueba and Zou, 1994: 61–70). In 1990 the five largest ethnic minority groups accounted for over 48 million people: (1) The Zhuang in the south central part of China (with 15,489,630); (2) the Manchu in the northeast (with 9,821,180); (3) the Hui in the northwest (with 8,692,978); (4) the Miao in the southwest (with 7,398,035); and (5) the Uygur (with 7,214,431) in the northwest. In addition to the 55 recognized ethnic groups there are about 1 million persons who belong to other, smaller groups, that have not yet been given the status of "nationality" by the government and so do not enjoy the privileges given to the other groups.

In China, 68 percent of the territory is areas primarily occupied by minority groups. China's borders with Russia, Mongolia, Korea, Pakistan, India, Vietnam, Laos, and Burma run through areas primarily occupied by minorities. These areas are relatively isolated. The privileges given to minority-dominated geographical areas (which constitute "autonomous regions") were granted by the government in an effort to keep them affiliated, while at the same time retaining Han hegemony. Autonomous regions were offered administrative, legal and resource control, under specific parameters; in fact, the central government retained supervision and control of major resource allocations. There are other minority groups, for example the Manchu of northeastern China, that were never isolated and who played a major role in enriching Han cultural traditions (Crespigny 1992: 276–290; Schwarz, 1984).

Soon after October 1, 1949, the Chinese Government, recognizing the practical and strategic importance of ethnic minority groups, sent its military arm (the People's Liberation Army or PLA) to minority-dominated regions, and formally appointed political chiefs who were sympathetic with the Han and with the central government. Thus the political organization of China resulted in 24 provinces (predominantly composed of Han Chinese) and five autonomous regions populated primarily by ethnic minorities: Tibet and Xinjiang in the northwest, Ningxia in the north central, Inner Mongolian in the north, and Guagnxi Zhuang in the southwest (Ma, 1985: 186–193). These five regions were presumed to have some common cultural elements, or at least some political linkages. In theory, the autonomous regions were supposed to enjoy regional autonomy, possess a national identity, have the power to elect their administrative head and use native languages for official purposes (Ma, 1985: 28–29). In practice, the Han culture represented by military and political central government personnel, continued to exercise strict control. The reason was simply that more than two-thirds of China's territory and perhaps its richest mineral and agricultural resources existed in the vast autonomous regions.

The Miao, with a population of almost 7.4 million are not only the fourth largest ethnic group, but one with a unique history of rebellion and struggles for autonomy from the Han people. They live primarily in three provinces: Guizhou (about 3.6 million), Hunan (1.6 million), and Yunnan (900,000). Other Miao people live in the Sichuan province, in the Guangxi Zhuang autonomous region, and the Hubei province, not counting the hundreds of thousands who fled China to live in Indochina, and subsequently became refugees in the United States (now called Hmong), Canada, Europe, Australia, France, and other countries (see Trueba, Jacobs, and Kirton, 1990; Pan, 1993; and Trueba and Zou, 1994: 74–82).

The Miao migration is divided into various linguistic and sociocultural subgroups. A number of migrations have occurred since the seventeenth century and are documented. The Miao were portrayed as tough fighters in their struggle against the Qing Dynasty in 1735, 1795, and 1799. These rebellions were followed by massacres and oppression that lasted centuries (Liu 1991: 22–23). In the last three decades, many of the Miao in Guizhou have been among the poorest groups in China (see Trueba and Zou, 1994: 76). The geographic, linguistic, and cultural isolation of the Miao has been a factor on their low economic level. Not until recently have their languages become the object of study at the university level. The Miao languages belong to the Miao–Yao group of the Chinese-Tibetan family, and are divided into three linguistic groups: (1) West Hunan, East Guizhou, and Sichuan/Yunan. These languages are not mutually intelligible but share certain syntactic and lexical forms. The current Miao written language is the result of decisions made by a Government group of experts and linguists whose task was to reform and adapt the old Miao script system, and to create a Latin Alphabetic script, which was a welcome initiative by all Miao since the turn of the century. It is believed that the impact of Western missionaries resulted in the use of the Latin alphabet.

The Insider vs. Outsider Dilemma

After a long period of preparation in the United States, in 1992, Dr. Henry Trueba and I began an ethnographic research project in China that focused on Miao university students. We did the study both in Beijing, at the Central University for Nationalities, in the heart of the capital of China, and at the Guizhou Institute for Nationalities located in the south central part of China. We selected 14 Miao students for our study. Seven from the Central University for Nationalities in Beijing and seven from the Guizhou Institute for Nationalities in Guizhou province. The Central University for Nationalities affiliated directly to the State Educational Commission of China was established in 1951. It has 2,300 faculty and staff and enrollment of more than 7,000 students from all 56 ethnic groups. The Guizhou Institute for Nationalities was founded in 1951 under the leadership of the Educational Commission of Guizhou province. It has 2,500 students from 18 different ethnic groups. These 14 students we studied were all originally from rural areas. Their parents were mostly peasants, although a few were teachers, government officials, and village heads. All of their families had very low incomes. We realized that the children of the poorest Miao peasants who eventually became university students and faculty, obtained high prestige as members of mainstream Chinese society and were recognized as leaders in their own villages.

As a Chinese, after receiving 5 years of professional training in an American university, I was invited by my main professor (Henry T. Trueba) to conduct a research project on the Miao of China. Professor Trueba's works on the Hmong people of California inspired me to search for the ancestors of the Hmong in China. Dr. Trueba and the other professors at the University of California considered me as a native Chinese, and therefore, in their eyes I was an insider of the Chinese culture and had the authority to interpret it. On the one hand, they were right, I had spent 40 years in China and knew the country fairly well (I thought); I had grown up in the Chinese middle class, and I knew well mainstream ideology and lifestyle as a member of the Han people (the mainstream population of China that comprises 92 percent, about 1.2 billion people). On the other hand, I was educated in the United States, I understood Western philosophy, spoke English and was dressed like other Americans. All this gave me enough credentials to pass for American in the eyes of the Chinese. Furthermore, I was armed with cultural ecological theories, ethnographic research methods and, most importantly, I was funded by an American University to do my research (the University of Wisconsin, Madison).

Before entering the research field my professor and I reviewed the literature, developed the research design, articulated specific questions to be answered by the research, and planned carefully the implementation of the design through strategic gradual steps. In conducting the research, however, we had to wake up to the reality of our own social identities and cultural roles in China, at least as defined by the Miao people with whom we were working. Consequently, I became aware of my dual identity, and that I was caught in a difficult position. I was both a Chinese in the opinion of the Americans, and an American in the opinion of the Chinese. But I knew I was neither, or perhaps I was both. That became a serious problem as I continued to reflect on my own identity, although during the research I did not have enough time to think seriously about it.

As I mentioned earlier, since I saw myself as a Chinese who lived in China most of my life, I was placed in the category of "insider" with regards to the Chinese culture. However, because I had come from the Han group, which is viewed as the mainstream cultural group and the "oppressor" or controlling group, I could not really claim to have the same way of thinking as those who are ethnically, socially, and economically different, as in the case of the Miao. They have constructed another set of values and perceptions of what is considered to be a "subculture" of the Chinese society, and different from my own culture. Therefore, all I could do was to describe my understanding of what I heard, what I saw, and what I felt in a way of thinking that I socially constructed in settings dominated by the Han people. Furthermore, I constructed these perceptual frames also from the perspective of Western academia. Indeed, the two cultures, the Han culture and Western academia, filtered my views. After five years of intensive study and training in the United States, and with an American institution grant I went back to China to conduct empowerment research with the Miao students with whom I was unfamiliar. Therefore, my dual ideological identity placed me in an asymmetrical power relationship with the Miao students. They viewed me as "superior" and in a position of power.

Let me give you an example. When we went to the Central University for Nationalities of Beijing we lived in the dormitory on the campus to be in close proximity to the students. Next to our rooms was the foreign affairs office. All of our activities were under the officials' surveillance; they were responsible for approving who could come and see us, where we could go, and in what rooms we could meet. At the same time, however, the officials were eager to provide us with information after we told them we planned to write a book telling Americans about minorities in China. All the information the officials offered to us was official government policy and some government propaganda materials. We asked the foreign office for permission to meet with Miao students. After some negotiations, we got the chance to interview and discuss our research project with Miao students. Before we met them, we prepared a set of questions ranging from their personal background to their opinions about the government policies toward minorities.

The first meeting consisted of 15 students and two professors. We started asking them questions about their experiences and their journeys from their home village to the university. At first they kept silent, and they seemed to be anxious about the kinds of answers they could give to our questions. We felt a little embarrassed and didn't know what we were supposed to do. Then their professor told us, "Don't feel bad. They didn't prepare for these questions, so they do not know how to answer them." After the meeting we learned that the foreign affairs officials had already prepared the students on what they should say to the Americans. At this time, only three years after the democracy rallies in Tiananmen Square, the Chinese government considered the United States an unfriendly power which has a nefarious impact on order, stability, and the Chinese habit of obedience to authority. Additionally, public expression of one's ideas was closely guarded. Students could not freely say what they wanted to say. In addition, when we arrived in Beijing the Chinese Communist Party Congress had just come to a close. The central theme of the conference was opposition to Chinese intellectual bourgeois liberalism, and the government was worried that students would once again stage demonstrations against the Chinese government. Therefore, the government kept a close watch on the students.

We remembered that on the day the conference ended, we went to Tiananmen Square and there saw many military soldiers, policemen, and plainclothes public security personnel watching people's activities. So when we asked questions to the unprepared students they hesitated in answering. The students didn't know what they could tell foreigners especially from the United States and what might get them in trouble. The professor started to enlighten the students and told them in front of us, "You should not worry, you can say what you experienced. For example, you can tell them how the government cares about minority people, and gives minorities preferential treatment, so you have a chance to enter college." Then students started to recall their hardships both in the village and school. For example, Mr. Wang, a 23-year-old student from the Guizhou province, told us that his Han classmates laughed at his poor clothing and quite often he didn't have money to buy food. (Trueba and Zou, 1994: 88–91). As he talked about the hardships that he experienced and his family's difficult life he cried. His story touched both us as researchers and the professors. Then Professor Wu started telling his own story, the story of his sacrifices and sufferings as a poor Miao student. After the interview Dr. Trueba called the student to the side and gave him 100 Chinese dollars and encouraged him to study hard in order to help his people change the Miao economic situation. Here we can see the different power relations involved in the student's life—many layers of oppressions. While the Chinese official ideology contains the behavior of students, the university authority defines and sanctions it; and the professors have also a powerful influence on them.

Another day, a young Miao university professor invited us to observe his class. When he came to our dormitory to meet us, the gatekeeper (a government officer) stopped him and asked him whether he had requested permission from the foreign affairs office in advance for such arrangements. When we came down to the door, we explained to the officer that we had asked the professor to come to discuss one of his courses and his pedagogy in the classroom. Similar red tape and bureaucratic inquiries occurred in situations when phone calls came from the outside, when unexpected students or other visitors attempted to talk to us, or when we attempted to change our schedule.

In China, a discussion of oppression cannot be public because it would be considered antigovernment and subject the participants to incarceration and other sanctions. For the Chinese students, however, the official ideology determines the norms of appropriate behavior. Therefore, obeying the social norms from the stand point of the government is a sign of good citizenship. As we began to ask students politically sensitive questions, we realized that there was an element of risk and uncertainty associated with critical ethnographic research in a specific context or situation, especially in the context of university students who are often penalized the most for their use of freedom of speech. As researchers, we had to keep in mind that our first responsibility was to the people and cultures we studied. Consequently, we had to accept the constraints of the cultural setting in which we functioned. In the end, we kept asking ourselves, how can we, as researchers in a foreign land, pursue our research agenda and still be responsible for the safety of the people we study?

The Researchers and the "Subject/Objects" of the Research

Another dilemma is: How do researchers deal with their dominant cultural identity while working with ethnic minority people? In critical ethnographic research sometimes we unconsciously recreate a context for dominance and tend to impose our values. As we began our research at the Central University for Nationalities, we identified the group of Miao students and professors, organized the schedule for individual and group interviews, and proceeded to ask our questions regarding their rationale for leaving their villages and becoming university students and professors. We wanted to know how strongly they felt as "Miao" and what the role of this ethnic identity was in their motivation to achieve academically. We unconsciously conducted our research without reflecting on the automatic assumption about the "subjects" of our research as if they were "objects." This happened until we started to build rapport and understand individual stories of poverty, struggle and oppression that had characterized the lives of many of those students. At that moment we turned around our methodology and began to investigate ways in which we could assist them, and gradually my professor and I were adopted as "honorary" members of their clan. When we went southwest 2,000 miles away from Beijing to the Province of Guizhou, we interviewed another group of Miao university students. We realized this group of Miao students was different from the one in Beijing. We were interviewed first at length before we could even get to the points we were investigating. They demonstrated to us that they felt competent, they described the Miao as a cosmological ethnic/racial group scattered throughout the entire world, and they interrogated us about the treatment of the Miao (Hmong) in the United States. They also gave us their long-term view of economic and industrial plan to move upwardly the entire Miao group around the world and wanted to know if we were ready to invest in such effort. The Guizhou students were from the same low income, rural background as the students from Beijing. The Guizhou students, however, constituted a strong ethnic majority in that province, and consequently spoke from a position of power. In contrast, the Beijing Miao students were considered of a lower status in comparison with the others in the Capital, political and economic center. The experience in Guizhou made us aware that we had mistaken the first group of Miao as objects, not as subjects and persons. We became humble. During our research project, we discussed with the Miao students their plans for the future. Instead of answering our questions they asked us what we thought they could do to help their own people in the future. Actually, they changed roles and became the researchers, and used us as consultants; they were looking up to us for guidance and practical advice. And they were doing it with a global perspective and ambition, as they talked about the Miao being a cosmic group, an international force, and having a bright destiny. We told them some success stories of minorities in the United States and how the Miao could use their knowledge to develop natural resources in their areas. Similarly we discussed how they could and communicate with the outside world to attract investments from the Western world, and how they could actively participate in public events in order to make the Miao group more visible. They followed our thoughts and developed many new ideas. Mr. Tao Wencen, an 18-year-old student, said that after he graduates he will organize county cooperatives and business firms, and later he will use the capital accumulated from the cooperatives to establish a Miao city with hotels, restaurants, and other tourist facilities. Mr. Xiaoping Tao said, "I want to help Miao people become literate; collect and edit Miao folklore and publish a book; write a book on the history of my Miao village." Mr. Xiong Jianliang wanted to become a village leader and use his intelligence to develop his village (Trueba and Zou, 1994: 99–100).

We accepted our newly found role as interviewees and participated in the discourse with equal generosity, expressing our position and ideals. We could not maintain a position of objective neutrality or nonparticipant observers. We were already become advocates for the Miao people we had met, and we began to plan ways of assisting them further in any way we could. Here we switched from traditional ethnography to advocacy research and critical ethnography. We did not realize that until we finished the first cycle of research in our first two visits in China. From this point on, we began to ask questions about the transition from rural Miao to members of mainstream society in the capital city. We were interested in knowing how they were ridiculed when they moved from Miao speaking schools to Mandarin speaking schools. The Han students laughed at them because they viewed them as ignorant and smelly peasant who could not speak Mandarin.

During our research we encountered some dilemmas that stemmed from the asymmetrical power relations between ourselves and the students. The question here is not how different our positions were, but how did we participate in these relations and to what extend we offered help to the people we studied. In his *On Critical Ethnography,* Richard Quantz subscribes to the view that critical ethnography is not a value-free effort, indeed no research is value free; all research should, consequently, advocate the universal values of freedom and the pursuit of happiness (R. Quants, 1992: 447–506).

The question I want to raise is whose definition of freedom and emancipation should be used, that of the researchers or that of the people under study? In the research process we quite often received requests from students for advice or comment on their situation. Our responses were obviously colored by our values of what is best from the perspective of American society. But being Chinese, I personally felt that students had the right to discover "freedom and emancipation" on their own. We presented our ideas and comments candidly. There was no question that our ideas contained cultural values that could influence the students. However, because students asked us directly what our opinion was on certain issues, we felt obligated to respond freely. Obviously we were not neutral in stating our opinions. By implication we were taking a political position *vis-à-vis* American values.

One of the dangers of this critical approach may be that it leads to the establishment of a power hierarchy and leads one to adopt an overly cynical view of the world. We are often not aware of when we conduct this kind of research, there is potential danger to use our superior position to impose our ideology to the people we study. In the underlying assumptions of empowerment theory, Jennifer Gore (1992; Delgado–Gaitan and Trueba, 1991; Delgado–Gaitan, 1996) criticized the fact that researchers consider themselves to be change agents and think they can offer what the oppressed people need. This automatically puts researchers in a dominant position. That is precisely what we became aware of during our research in China. Power differentials between us, the researchers, and those we study do exist and will continue to exist. Researchers must be constantly aware of how these differences in power can tailor the responses of persons under study, and color or distort the researchers' perceptions and interpretations of the findings. Here is another dilemma: To what extent can researchers advocate, and actively pursue the emancipation of others without being questioned regarding their motives, and without being perceived as arrogant, superior, patronizing, and judgmental? The delicate balance of power between two asymmetrical positions depends on who controls the discourse and who makes decisions. Researchers who become change agents must make sure to release the control of the discourse and decision making to the people under study. After completing our project we became convinced that our presence constituted positive intervention precisely because we did not push our ideas. We presented our suggestions humbly and let the students control the discourse and decide whether they wanted to followup or not. When I visited China this past summer, I had a wonderful talk with the students I studied, and confirmed my feelings about the beneficial impact of our work. More recently, some of the students have become professors, scientists and social activists; the others are actively working in fields related to Miao language and culture.

Thinking through the ways in which our activities could be interpreted, we could have been perceived, on the one hand, to push Miao students in a positive direction towards a strong self-identity and with new ideas about possible options available to them. Yet, we did not do the walking for the students, or the talking, or the thinking. After we presented our ideas, the students took over and interviewed us with the goal of accomplishing their own purposes. Therefore, in reviewing the moral dilemma associated with helping individuals, and choosing sides, we need to understand the specific political social context of a given research project. We must make serious efforts to be open, but not imposing or patronizing, even on issues related to possible "oppression" especially if the inferences about "oppression" and the concepts are ours.

The post-Cold War period is likely going to be increasingly characterized by conflict and hostility between Western nations and the Asian nations bent on challenging Western hegemony. As Western researchers we need to be sensitive to our own values and ideologies and be aware of these impact on recreating our interpretations of other cultures.

Conclusion

At the beginning of this chapter I mentioned the three fundamental requirements of critical ethnography stated by Simon and Dippo (1986), the challenges alluded to by Carspecken (1996), and Delgado–Gaitan (1996) associated with critical ethnography and empowerment. I believe that we have fulfilled all three requirements. (You may want to read our book and be the judge, Trueba and Zou, 1994).

1. We consider this study to be a critical ethnography because it dealt with the issue of empowerment through education. We examined the inner motivations of why Miao university students pursued academic careers, and found out that it was precisely because they remained committed to their ethnic identity that they could endure many sacrifices in order to get their education and enter mainstream society.

We believe that the foundations for empowerment are a solid self-identity and a clear concept of one's own ethnic community. Through the process of conscious awareness of the nature of an ethnic community, one can understand better students' motivation to achieve academically. Our study constitutes an example of critical pedagogy precisely because it documented how students used their ethnic identity as their main strength in the struggle for emancipation from their poverty and isolation. We conducted this study in such a way that we respected the political position of students and did not force in them any ideological frameworks.

2. Furthermore, we focused on the process of transformation, not the transformation Westerners want to produce in other countries, but the transformation that the Miao minority people themselves engineered and implemented on their own by engaging in education and becoming university students first, and later university professors. The intellectual, moral, and cultural transformation from Miao village children to respected university professors with a high national status, is clearly affecting the overall pride of the Miao people. The focus was not on the problems (as we saw them) of the Chinese society that had neglected peasants, including Miao peasant groups, but rather on the strategies used by Miao peasants to gain an understanding of their own potential to move up within the Chinese society. We focused on how their strategies helped them get out from under what they perceived as a social, economic and political oppression suffered at the hands of the Han mainstream society for many centuries. Therefore, this is a study of change in process, a study of the beginning of important changes in Chinese society. These changes affect the existing stratification of ethnic minority groups in China by first educating Miao people and then placing them at the top of the society as university professors.

3. Finally, the study focused on the reflexive inquiry that characterized Miao thinking about their own culture, their lives,

> and the changes from village life to life in a large metropolis such as Beijing. Miao professors enlarged the students' world views, and they became consciously aware of the psychological and personal changes that characterized their intellectual growth and their collective pride as Miao "intellectuals." This reflexive nature of Miao empowerment is also demonstrated in the written discourse of many new young professors who are now highly respected by their colleagues from the Han and other groups. The critical consciousness they are reaching, allows them to articulate in clear terms their own ethnohistory as a group look down upon for centuries, and becomes a source of strength and pride in their own cultural identity around the world, including the Miao living outside of China.

In brief, we believe that critical ethnography is not only possible but extremely important in the social sciences in order to document process and change from the standpoint of the individuals without power. Also, in order to avoid any hegemonic and colonialist attitudes of researchers, or their characteristic "directives" and "authoritarianism," researchers have to become learners of other peoples' cultures and values. We had to learn as researchers from the Miao professors and students how to relinquish control of the discourse and other substantive matters to the Miao people. The content of the research, the discourse during our research, and the flow of information during the research was balanced by an ongoing dialogue about process. We discovered that the Miao students were prepared to be information for us, and to treat us as potential investors, while retaining great pride in their traditional culture and current progress in education. We were happy to offer information and to learn, but were not eager to sell them our views, or advocate our kind of society. At times we explained some of the problems that racial minorities face in America. Indeed, in the end, the reason for the success of the Miao students and faculty was, in their own words, the pride of being Miao and of belonging to such a wonderful international community.

One of the important inferences we made from this study was that the process of empowerment is grounded in two equally powerful pivotal principles: (1) the principle of firm ethnic identification that recognized the place one occupies in the larger society and the affiliation with a given value system, and (2) the principle of psychological integrity whereby one draws on his/her cultural values in order to gain the necessary strength for empowering him/herself. Both of these principles are clearly related to the insightful work and interpretation of critical pedagogy by Peter McLaren and his colleagues (McLaren and Lankshear, 1994). If learning is ultimately a political act, then learning for empowerment is the most direct effort to have control over one's life and to enjoy the civil and human rights other people enjoy. This was the case of the Miao students in China.

Critical ethnography, also called "ethnography for empowerment" (see Delgado–Gaitan and Trueba, 1991, and Delgado–Gaitan, 1996) has consistently pursued equity issues in racial, ethnic and language minority groups (see M. Suarez–Orozco, 1991; C. Suarez–Orozco and M. Suarez–Orozco, 1995; Trueba, Rodriguez, Zou and Cintron, 1993, and a number of chapters in this volume). Critical ethnography is a research approach inspired by the philosophy and principles underlying critical pedagogy as it has been eloquently articulated by Freire (1973, 1993) and his followers (Giroux and McLaren, 1986; Giroux, 1992; McLaren and Leonard, 1993; McLaren and da Silva, 1993; McLaren, 1989, 1995). Critical ethnography, however, can not be a totally neutral nor blind to the historical, social, political, and economic trends coloring data gathered and subjects under research.

References

Becker, H. S. (1963). *Outsiders: Studies in the Sociology of Deviance.* New York: Free Press.

———. (ed.) (1964). *The Outsider: Perspectives on Deviance.* New York: Free Press.

———. (ed.) (1967). Whose Side Are We On? *Social Problems* 14(3):239–247.

Carspecken, P. F. (1996). *Critical Ethnography in Educational Research: A Theoretical and Practical Guide.* New York: Routledge.

Crespigny, R. de (1992). *China in This Century.* New York, NY: Oxford University Press.

Delgado–Gaitan, C. (1993). Researching Change and Changing the Researcher. *Harvard Educational Review* 63(4):389–411.

———. (1996). *Protean Literacy: Extending Discourse on Empowerment.* London: Falmer Press.

Delgado–Gaitan, C. & H. Trueba (1991). *Crossing Cultural Borders: Education for Immigrant Families in America.* London: Falmer Press.

De Genova, N. (1997). *The Production of Language and the Language of Oppression: Mexican Labor and the Politics of ESL in Chicago Factories.* Paper presented to Spencer Foundation Winter Forum (UCLA), Feb. 14, 1997. Unpublished manuscript.

Freire, P. (1973). *Pedagogy of the Oppressed.* New York: Seabury.

———. (1993). *Pedagogia da Esperança: Um Reencontrol com a Pedagogia do Oprimido.* Sâo Paulo, Brazil: Editora Paz e Terra, S.A.

Giroux, H. (1983). Theories of Reproduction and Resistance in the New Sociology of Education: A Critical Analysis. *Harvard Educational Review,* 53(3):257–293.

———. (1992). Educational Leadership and the Crisis of Democratic Government. *Educational Researcher,* 21(4):4–11.

Giroux, H. & P. McLaren (1986). Teacher Education and the Politics of Engagement: The Case for Democratic Schooling. *Harvard Educational Review,* 26(3):213–238.

Jessor, R., A. Colby, & R. A. Shweder (eds.) (1996). *Ethnography and Human Development: Context and Meaning in Social Inquiry.* Chicago & London: The University of Chicago Press.

Liu, J. W. (1991). "The Argument on the Miao Minority's Migration Across Country and the Theory of National Vertical Distribution," in T. Li, D. Pan, and Z. Yang (eds.) *Miao Study,* II, (pp. 19–29).

Ma, Y. (ed.) (1985). *Questions and Answers About China's National Minorities.* Beijing, China: New World Press.

McLaren, P. (1989). *Life in Schools.* New York: Longman.

———. (1995). *Critical Pedagogy and Predatory Culture.* New York and London: Routledge.

McLaren, P. & P. Leonard (1993). *Paulo Freire: A Critical Encounter.* New York and London: Routledge.

McLaren, P. & C. Lankshear (ed.) (1994). *Politics of Liberation: Paths from Freire.* London and New York: Routledge.

McLaren, P., & T. T. Da Silva (1993). Decentering Pedagogy: Criticla Literacy, Resistance and the Politics of Memory. In P. McLaren & P. Leonard (eds.) *Paulo Freire: A Critical Encounter* (pp. 47–89). New York and London: Routledge.

Pan, D. (1993). *The History and Culture of the Miao Nationality.* Unpublished manuscript, Guiyang, China, Guizhou Institute for Nationalities. Translation by Yali Zou.

Poston, D. L., Jr., & D. Yaukey (eds.) (1992). *The Population of Modern China.* Series title: *The Plenum Series on Demographic Methods and Population Analysis.* New York: Plenum Press.

Quantz, R. (1992). On Critical Ethnography (With some Postmodern Considerations). In *The Handbook of Qualitative Research in Education,* M. LeCompte, W. Millroy, & J. Preissle (eds.), (Pp. 447–506). San Diego: Academic Press.

Schwarz, H. G. (1984). *The Minorities of Northern China: A Survey.* Center for East Asian Studies, Bellingham, WA: Western Washington.

Simon, R. & D. Dippo (1986). On Critical Ethnographic Work. *Anthropology and Education Quarterly,* 17:196.

Suárez–Orozco, C. & M. Suárez–Orozco (1995). *Transformations: Immigration, Family Life and Achievement Motivation Among Latino Adolescents.* Stanford, CA: Stanford University Press.

Suárez–Orozco, M. M. (1991). Migration, Minority Status, and Education: European Dilemmas and Responses in the 1990s, *Anthropology and Education Quarterly,* 22(2):99–120.

Thomas, J. (1993). *Doing Critical Ethnography.* London: Sage Publications, Inc.

Trueba, H. T., L. Jacobs, & E., Kirton (1990). *Cultural Conflict and Adaptation: The Case of the Hmong Children in American Society,* London, England: Falmer Press.

Trueba, H. T., C. Rodríguez, Y. Zou, & J. Cintrón (1993). *Healing Multicultural America: Mexican Immigrants Rise to Power in Rural California.* London, England: Falmer Press.

Trueba, H, & Y. Zou (1994). *Power in Education: The Case of Miao University Students and Its Significance for American Culture.* London, England: Falmer Press.

Villenas, Sofia, The Colonizer/Colonized Chicana Ethnographer: Identity, Marginalization, and Co–optation in the Field. *Harvard Educational Review,* 66(4) (Winter 1996):711–731.

Peter McLaren*

15
Afterword
¡Ya Basta!

In the United States we are living at a time of undeclared war. Each day we negotiate our way through mine-sown terrains of confrontation and uncertainty surrounding the meaning and purpose of identity. American democracy faces Janus-like in two simultaneous directions: into a horizon of hope and coexistence and into the burning eyes of klansman in a sheet soiled with blood. While on the one hand, this current historical juncture is witnessing an unprecedented growth of white supremacist organizations living on the fringes of social life, on the other hand, establishment conservatives are stridently asserting nativistic and populist sentiments that barely distinguish them ideologically from their counterparts in racialist far right groups and citizen militias: The Ku Klux Klan, Posse Comitatus, The Order, White Aryan Resistance, Christian Identity, National Alliance, Aryan Nations, American Front, Gun Owners of America, United Citizens of Justice, and militia groups have organizations in most, if not all, of the 50 states.

Young white males and females who may find these racist groups unappealing can still find solace in politicians such as Pete Wilson and Bob Dole whose anti-immigrant and Latinophobia policies and practices deflect their racializing sentiments through flag waving, jingoism, and triumphalist acts of self-aggrandizement designed to appeal to frightened white voters who feel growing numbers of

*Portions of this chapter were published in the *Educational Foundations* journal.

Spanish-speaking immigrants will soon outnumber them. Politicians have become white warriors in blue suits and red ties dedicated to taking back the country from the infidel. Recently, amid headlines of black churches in the south being razed by arson, a Los Angeles newspaper ran a photograph of Bob Dole at a Southland political rally. The magnetic allure of Dole's head, its skin a translucent blue, tensile, its shiny yellow tongue as if dipped in kerosene, seemingly wagging, appeared in metonymic relationship to his message: Anglos are under siege from an alien nation—Mexico—and its time civilized white folks wrestled back the land from the barbarians.

Guillermo Gómez–Peña writes:

> This identity crisis translates into an immense nostalgia for an (imaginary) era in which people of color didn't exist, or at least when we were invisible and silent. The political expression of this nostalgia is chilling: "Let's take our country back." The far right, like Pete Wilson, Newt Gingrich, Jesse Helms, and Pat Buchanan, along with many Democrats, are in agreement on the following: This country must be saved from chaos and collapse into Third-Worldization; "illegal" immigrants must be deported; the poor should be put in jail (three strikes, you're out); welfare, affirmative action, and bilingual education programs must be dismantled; and the cultural funding infrastructure that has been infiltrated by "liberals with leftist tendencies" (the National Endowment for the Arts and the Humanities and the Corporation for Public Broadcasting) must be decimated. In the euphemistic Contract with America, ethnic "minorities," independent artists and intellectuals, the homeless, the elderly, children, especially immigrants from the South, are all under close watch (1996, p. 173).

On the day of General Colin L. Powell's address to the 1996 Republican Convention in San Diego, former Education Secretary and current director of Empower America, William J. Bennett, published a commentary in the *Los Angeles Times* "Civil Rights in the GOP's Mission" (Aug. 12, 1996, B5). Evoking the figure of Dr. Martin Luther King, Jr., Bennett called for the end of racial discrimination through the abolition of affirmative action. Bewailing the civil rights leaders of the past 30 years (with the exception of Dr. King, of course, whose symbolic power he seeks to conscript into his own agenda) whom he argued are a group of malcontents who have wielded a "racial branding iron," have "diminished the moral authority of the civil rights movement," have "fanned the flames of racial resentment," and have "helped Balkanize America," Bennett calls for the government to eliminate "race-based preferences" for people of color. He putatively wants Africa Americans, Latino/as, and other ethnic minority groups to be judged by the "content of their character." He cites African Americans such as Ward Connerly, chairman of the Civil Rights Initiative and General Powell as continuing "the great civil rights tradition of Dr. King."

However, Bennett's vision is perniciously short-sighted and malificent and effectively domesticates King's place in the civil rights struggle. And his logic is disturbingly flawed. It is similar to the conservative school board that abolishes school breakfast programs for hungry children because such programs are "antifamily." Since the children eat at school and not with their parents and siblings at home, they are apparently offending the values that made this country great. Supposedly, it is better to go hungry with your family than to be fed at school. Bennett"s arguments are similarly confused. First, he appears to work under an assumption that U.S. society has reached a point of relative economic justice and affirmative action is no longer necessary. Second, he appears to either be unable or unwilling to fathom the nearly intractable reality of white privilege and uncontested hegemony in the arena of the economy. Third, he fails to realize that racist white people are going to be suspicious of African-Americans and Latinos/Latinas whether they are assisted by affirmative action initiatives or not. And fourthly, his vision is propelled by a nostalgic view of a United States as a middle-class suburban neighborhood in which people of color do not have so much "attitude" and where whites are the uncontested caretakers of this prelapsarian nation of consensus and harmony. To be colorblind in Bennett's restricted use of the term is to be naive at best and ignorant at worst. Because not to see color in Bennett's view really amounts in ideological terms to be blind to the disproportionate advantage enjoyed by white people in nearly all sectors of society. It is akin to conservative politicians who bemoan critics of tax breaks for the rich (welfare for the rich) for engaging in "class warfare." One does not have to be an economist to realize that since the Reagan administration, money has been transferred from the ranks of the poor into the coffers of the rich in record proportions. Yet conservative politicians resent people who label these practices as "unjust." After all, if rich (mainly white) people can work the system to their advantage, then all the power to them. Bennett has turned the logic of Martin Luther King upside down. He has replaced social analysis with homilies about "character." That a former Secretary of Education would take a position like this is especially telling, given the state of critical self-reflection among politicians in this country. Politicians of Bennett's ilk want to increase the role of charitable institutions in this country. If people of color are to be helped, then it should be done by private individuals or organizations and not the government. But wealthy private organizations have benefited from the hegemony of white privilege in the government and the marketplace. Unbridled capitalism in our present post-Fordist service economy is ruthlessly uncharitable to the poverty stricken. Nevertheless, transferring the challenge of economic justice from the government into the hands of philanthropists who feel "pity" for the poor is not the solution. Bennett misses the crucial point that not to have affirmative action for people of color in the present social structure amounts to a hidden affirmative action for white people. Bennett's position tacitly seeks the incorporation of racialized groups into the corporate ethics of consumption where white privilege increasingly holds sway. His ethics of racial tolerance can therefore work as a means of social control of populations of color. His motivated amnesia with respect to the history of capitalism causes him to ignore the macrostructures of inequality and injustice and the classbound hierarchies and institutionalized racism of United States society and to act as if United States society already obtains on the issue of economic equality across diverse ethnic populations. There is a false assumption at work in Bennett's logic that views culture as essentially self-equilibrating, as providing similar sets of shared experiences to all social groups. The culture of diversity heralded by Bennett is a decidedly homogenized one, cut off from the contingencies of state power and economic practices.

If Bennett is so intent on character building and fears that African Americans are now being viewed by white people as bearing the "stigma of questionable competence" because of affirmative action, why doesn't he place greater emphasis on improving the character of white people, by encouraging them not to stigmatize, demonize and peripheralize people of color not only in the boardrooms but also in all walks of life.

It is precisely Bennett's stubborn unwillingness to recognize the asymmetrical allocation of resources and power that overwhelmingly favor white people as much now as during King's era, that effectively truncates Bennett's vision, fashioning it into a form of soundbyte histrionics.

The essays that comprise this volume speak directly to the current crisis of democracy that has deported hopes and dreams of growing numbers of minority populations across United States into an abyss of emptiness and despair. The crisis has exposed the infrastructure of American democracy to be made of Styrofoam, trembling spray-painted pillars of a Greek temple in an off-Broadway play. Democracy has been cut at the joints by events that are currently transpiring both locally and throughout the globe.

Commenting on the aftermath of the Los Angeles uprising and the analytic inversion of recent racial ideology and politics in the post-Civil Rights era in the United States (and seemingly forecasting the recent landmark welfare legislation of 1996) Omi and Winant write:

> Thus have we come, so it seems, full circle. Poverty and discrimination, seen in the past as problems requiring state action, are now seen as the *results* of state activity. What was once the solution (activist social policies) has now become the problem (dependence), and what was once the problem (the lash of poverty) has now become the solution (market forces) (1993, p. 99).

The crisis of democracy is linked to a general *problématique* which related to the future of democratic life and the formation of citizenship. The duration of the present crisis can be seen in the globalization of the economy, the racialization of special reconfigurations resulting from global flows of populations; a far-ranging geopoltical realignment; the destabilization of the influence and authority of the nation state, a lack of democratic principles being extended to the economic sphere, deindustrialization, deregulated markets, incoherences in public narratives of nationalism, growing transnational business organizations, large scale diasporic migrations of oppressed peoples (including significant migrations within large cities such as New York and Los Angeles), international economic ruptures and instabilities, a decline of the two-parent single-earner family, a shift in the process of capitalist accumulation worldwide from a national/multinational axis to a national/transnational one, and an exercise of unaccountable power by corporations. Linked to the shift toward a post-industrial, a post-Fordist, service economy premised on outsourcing and flexible specialization are transformations in the sphere of identity construction. New regimes of subjectivity can be traced to technological transformations and access to new forms of information. Yet economic exchange across national borders has done little to improve the lives of the secondary sector proletariat who still struggles to survive the current ideological climate of neoliberal politics and bourgeois individualism. The narcissistic, acquisitive self is the vanishing point at the center of consumer capitalism while it also serves as the periphery of our boundedness as polis, as community. The capitalist self is the embodiment of commodity fetishism and the logic of exchange. The cultural logic of late capitalism has delimited collective agency precisely by regulating what it purports to liberate, by harnessing that which it proposes to release. Late capitalism brings the private self into existence at the cost of the disappearance of the social, the vanishing of the real. It signals a crisis of the subject, ushering in a pragmatics of subjection. It reveals a virus lodged deeply within the public spheres of this nation chronically riven with an imbalance of justice.

Computer technology has made intentional acts of destruction even more destructive in this era of late capitalism. Financial transactions that can eliminate the *ejido* plots of the Chiapan peasantry are now made more "user-friendly" through computer banking; military assaults on "fanatics" and "terrorists" hunkered down in the sands of distant lands can now be washed away like bugs on a car windshield, as consecrated blips disappearing on a computer screen; demasculinized machineries of physical destruction (the "cruise" missle that is always "cruisin' for a "bruisin' ") used by Western phallomilitary warriors to liquefy non-Christianized bodies have become the high-tech wonders of the century. Charred flesh, pulverized bones, and puréed organs splattered over your uniform are—unlike earlier, more muscularized wars—now considered unnecessary embarrassments that can largely be eliminated through killing at long distances.

Ethnic Identity and Power brings together a number of crucial themes in the current debates over democratic social life: the politics of ethnic identity and capitalist social relations (Trueba, Lima and Lima, Macedo and Barthelomé); the rise of white supremacist movements (Spinder and Spinder); critical teaching and educational reform in the U.S. and Mexico (Wager, Calvo Pontón, Gutierrez and McLaren); Chicano struggle and *Zapatista* and Ñähñu resistance movements (DeVillar, Rodríguez, DeVillar and Franco); bilingual education (Constantino and Faltis); affirmative action (Shakelford and Shakelford); Mexican workers in rural California (Trueba); critical ethnography (González and Trueba, Eldering, Zou, Smith); and immigration (Suárez–Orozco). The theme of ethnic identity and the politics of diversity and difference underwrite all of the essays in this volume. While the authors collectively call for a greater tolerance for and inclusion of ethnic groups among dominant Anglo constituencies, some authors suggest that tolerance without the elimination of capitalist relations of exploitation is not enough (e.g. Macedo and Bartolomé, Gutierrez and McLaren).

What is most impressive about this project by Yali Zou and Enrique Trueba is its attempt to give lived texture to the abstract taxonomy of theory as it attempts to be employed to understand the political meaning of difference. In this volume personal accounts and narratives join forces with a commitment to eliminate racism and the demonization of the other, progressive ethnographic approaches, and a determination to force democracy to live up to its name. Yet this struggle is a daunting one. While some postmodernists adventitiously asset that identities can be fluidly recomposed, rearranged, and reinvented in these new "pluralistic" times, I maintain that this is a short-sighted and dangerous argument. However, my assertion that the contents of particular cultural differences is not as important as how such differences are embedded in and related to the larger social totality of economic, social, and political differences may strike some readers as extreme. Yet I think it is fundamentally necessary to stress this point.

We are not autonomous citizens that can simply choose whatever ethnic combinations that we desire in order to reassemble our identity. While the borders of ethnicity overlap and shade into one another, it is dishonest to assert that pluralized, hybridized identities are options available to all citizens. This is because class, race and gender stratification and objective constraints and historical determinations restrict the choices of some groups over others. The division of labor linked to political organization and the politics of marketplace regulate choices and often overdetermine their outcome (San Juan, 1996).

Rather than stressing the importance of diversity and inclusion, as do most multiculturalists, I think the stress should be on the social and political construction of white supremacy and the dispensation of white hegemony. Whiteness needs to be identified as a cultural disposition and ideology linked to specific political, social, and historical arrangements.

One of the themes I would like to emphasize is the need to incorporate, yet move beyond, discussions of diversity and exclusion when discussing the politics of ethnicity. The discourse of diversity and inclusion is often predicated on hidden assumptions of assimilation and consensus that serve as supports for liberal democratic assumptions of identity.

Neo-liberal democracy, performing under the banner of diversity yet actually in the service of capital accumulation, often reconfirms the racist stereotypes already prescribed by Euro-American nationalist myths of supremacy—stereotypes it is ostensibly committed to challenge. In the pluralizing move to become a society of diverse voices, liberal democracy has often succumbed to a recolonization of multiculturalism by failing to challenge ideological assumptions surrounding difference that are installed in its current anti-affirmative action and welfare "reform" initiatives. In this sense people of color are still placed under the threshold of candidacy for inclusion into the universal right to self-determination, and interpolated as exiles from United States citizenship.

In any volume on the topic of ethnic identity, using the term "race" as an explanatory concept is extremely problematic, especially in connection with the standard race relations (e.g., black vs. white) paradigm. As Miles and Torres (1996) point out, the idea of race necessarily affects a sociological reification in which complex social process are reduced to the consequences of thing called race. For instance, "race" does not determine school performance and life chances. What fall under the banner of "race" are often the complex processes of parental class position, active and passive racialized stereotyping, and exclusion in the class room. As Miles and Torres remark: "it is not 'race' that determines academic performance; rather, academic performance is determined by an interplay of social processes, one of which is premised on the articulation of racism to effect and legitimate exclusion" (1996, p. 32).

In this view, "race" becomes an artifice that endeavors to naturalize itself through a sociological legitimacy based on the sanctified discourse of empiricism and based upon an imputation of inferiority characteristic of racism. Miles and Torres reject the race relations problematic as the locus for the analysis of racism but they do not reject the concept of racism. In doing so, they are better able to recognize the existence of a plurality of historically specific racisms by employing the term "racialized formation." Race is an ideological construction, and the meaning associated with the term has evolved considerably over time (Miles, 1982, 193). Of course, it cannot be denied that people use the idea of race triumphalistically to celebrate group affiliation and also use race to classify, demonize, exclude, and marginalize others and act in ways consistent with such patterns of classification. I am trying to sound a caution with respect to how we uncritically employ race as an explanatory concept or construct. For instance, exclusion by skin color or phenotype is not a natural phenomenon, it is a socially and historically produced practice, culturally constructed process in which people learn over time to attribute certain meanings to certain distinctions which result in historically constituted forms of collective identity and patterns of social inequality. Such cultural marked distinctions become significations attached to the sign "race." Mike and Torres note: "People do not see 'race': rather, they observe certain combinations of real and sometimes imagined somatic and cultural characteristics which they attribute meaning to with the idea of 'race' (p. 40)." I am not suggesting—for it would be ludicrous as well as disingenuous—that we can merely "signify" race out of existence since as a cultural marker it historically has bequeathed privilege to bearers of light skin and pain and suffering (not to mention slavery and genocide) to dark-skinned populations. I am arguing that "race" is a term used to "mark" distinctions attributed to something natural and essential. But as Miles and Torres remind us:

> A difference of skin colour is not essential to the process of marking: other somatic features can be and are signified in order to racialize. Indeed, in some historical circumstances, the absence of somatic difference has been central to the powerful impact of racism: the racialized "enemy within" can be identified as a threatening presence even more effectively if the group is not "obviously different" because "they" can be imagined to be everywhere (pp. 40–41).

It is not the concept of race that is a problem but the dominant and narrow idea of race that has become naturalized and incorporated as a central category in everyday parlance that is a problem. Race, in this sense, becomes a racialized category. Racial groups are not monolithic categories of existence and the process of racialization needs to be seen in the context of social relations of production. Miles and Torres are, I believe, correct in asking educators and social scientists to qualify their use of the term, move away from the ideological notion of race relations, and begin to explore with more exigency the complex relationship of racialized social practices, exploitation, and resistance.

I am thinking of how the U.S. Census Bureau has suggested how "whites" comprise a distinct race even though the concept of race has definitely been shown to not denote any clear definition of biological stock. Latinos, for instance, have been invented by the 1930 Census Bureau as "white" or "ethnic" ("persons of Spanish mother tongue") to a "black" or "racial" ("other nonwhite") category in the 1940 census. In the 1950 and 1960 census, Latinos became white again ("white persons of Spanish surname") while in 1970 they became white *and* bilingual ("white persons of Spanish surname and Spanish mother tongue"). In 1980 Mexican Americans, Puerto Ricans, and other Central and Latin Americans with diverse national origin were classified as "non-white Hispanic" (Moore and Pachon, 1985). Here the term "white" is fabricated as a race which then becomes a marker against which other groups are affirmed or oppressed.

We must not fail to acknowledge—perhaps we cannot acknowledge this enough—that racism must be understood in relationship to capitalist social formations and shifts within the world economic system. Capitalism is now more virulently mobile than ever and the nation-state has grown considerable weaker as a political structure. Exploitation of the worker is easier when international capital can move across national boundaries so unencumbered by the state. Robert Miles has noted (with respect to Europe) that "the increased expression of, and articulation between, nationalism and racism can be explained by this conjunctural ensemble of economic, political and ideological relations (1994, p. 216).

We must remember the historically specific forms that racism takes. For instance, Balibar (1991) comments upon the racialization of mechanized manual labor. This modifies the body and creates "*body-men* whose body is a machine body, that is fragmented and dominated, and used to perform one isolable function or gesture, being both destroyed in its integrity *and* fetishized, atrophied and hypertrophied in its 'useful' organs" (1991, p. 211).

Balibar also notes that there is "a constant relation of reciprocal determination between 'class racism' and 'ethnic racism' and *these two determinations are not independent*" (1991, p. 214). He further expands this idea by arguing:

> It is crucially important to note that, in the historical field where *both* an unbridgable gap between state and nation and endlessly re-emerging class antagonisms are to be found, nationalism necessarily take the form of racism, at times in competition with other forms (linguistic nationalism, for example) and at times in combination with them, and that it thus becomes a perpetual headlontg flight forward. Even when racism becomes latent, or present only in a minority of individual consciousness, it is already that internal excess of nationalism which betrays, in both senses of the word, its articulation to the class struggle (pp. 214–215).

Another theme which develops from this volume is the role of the educator as researcher, intellectual, and social agents. Given the reorganization and disorganization of capitalism over the last several decades, the public trust in the role of the intellectual has diminished dramatically. Zygmunt Bauman (1992) has chronicled the changes and challenges to the role of the intellectual throughout the last century. According to Bauman, Western societies have witnessed changes in the mode of governance that can be witnessed in various historical projects: that of "civilizing" the masses by "training" them in education sites and by means of other ideological state apparatuses according to the discourses of the ruling elites; ensuring obedience from the masses through panoptic systems (such as the rule of law) which ensure social efficiency by scientific management; employing techniques of seduction and of social control and integration into a larger ethics of consumerism; new technological revolutions in communication and the specialization and professionalization of the middle classes have facilitated the politics of seduction. Since ideas are no longer as necessary as they once were to bolster hegemonic practices of social control or techniques of seduction, intellectuals have become largely marginal to the dominant public sphere. Yet such a marginalization needs to be contested for the sake of educating the public about issues such as race, class, gender, multiculturalism, and political economy. We need to work hard within the visible public spheres of this nation—as have many of the authors in this volume—to reposition the debates over affirmative action, immigration, and the politics of difference within a more complex theoretical framework. Such a framework will help analyze and expose the simplistic, misguided and ethically repugnant systems of intelligibility endorsed by conservative policymakers. Such discourses fuel the peripheralizing assault on minorities and immigrants. Critical educators need to do everything in their power to make sure that these discourses are chopped off at the knees.

A theme that I would like to highlight is that of a tension between theory and experience in discussing issues of race, class, and gender in the context of colonialism and imperialism. There is a general resistance to theory in much ethnographic work, some of which is understandable and probably methodologically healthy; yet other aspects of this resistance is manifesting itself in a call for actionable knowledge and insurgent research that takes social life and subjectivity as largely transparent and self-evident. Such knowledge is often not reliable enough for us to undertake actions as revolutionary actors in history. Reliable knowledge recognizes the everyday commerce that transpires between consciousness and the objective determinations of a world riven with capitalist social relations, cultural logics, and subject positions. Experience is important in any praxis of liberation. But speaking from one's experience or location as, for instance, a subalterm subject, offers no guarantee that one's voice is indeed one's own. The voices that we acquire are not necessarily our own but are rather "constituted" voices.

Our voices are crisscrossed with vectors of power and positionality related to the contextual specificities of where we place ourselves as subjects and where we find ourselves as agents. Himani Bannerji puts it thus:

> We need a reflexive and relational social analysis which incorporates in it a theory of agency and direct representation based on our experience. As such I can directly express what happens to me. But my experience would only be the starting point of my politics. For a further politicization my experience must be recounted within a broader socio-historical and cultural framework that signals the larger social organization and forms which contain and shape our lives. My expressive attempt at description can hold in itself the seeds of an explanation and analysis. We need to go beyond expressive self-referentiality and connect with others in time and space. For this reason, an adequate description of the smallest racist incident leaves room for reference or contextualization to slavery, colonization, imperialism, exploitation of surplus value and construction of the labour market through gender, "race" and ethnicity; nation states to organize and facilitate these processes and practices, and concomitant reifying forms of consciousness (1995, p. 84).

Bannerji's comments prove instructive in arguing for a dialectical theory of agency. Such a dialectical theory uses experience as a *starting point* for the organization of social inquiry. Experience in this view becomes a set of disjunctive social relations within the larger social order. The social agent speaks simultaneously from her lived experience and from a position in the world that shapes both her oppression and resistances. She speaks, therefore, as both a knower-subject and social-object within the larger patriarchal capitalist division of labor. Bannerji argues for an integrative and reflexive analysis that "allows anyone to speak for/from the experience of individuals and groups while leaving room to speak "socially" from other locations, along the lines of the relations that (in) form our/my own experience (p. 84)."

Consequently, social analysis must begin from subjectivity and should not, in Bannerji's view, reify itself into a fixed category of identity. Furthermore, there needs to be a *coherence* of feeling and being and for this reason Bannerji argues against modernism's homogeneity of subjectivity and postmodernism's fragmentation of subjectivity.

Experiences are the concrete instantations of objective social forces. However, hyper-theory witnesses the ontological being completely absorbed by the epistemological (Williams, 1979, p. 166–167). While experience for Raymond Williams was a way of challenging the formal densities of orthodox and systematic theoretical articulations, it also functioned as "an independent principle of ethicopolitical legitimation" (Radhakrishnan, 1996, p. 144). Radhakrishnan detects an important weakness in William's position: Williams fails to recognize the "constituted" nature of experience.

I do not have sufficient space to devote to the issue of essentialized identities, a topic which I have discussed elsewhere in detail (McLaren, 1995; McLaren, forthcoming), especially in the context of *mestizaje* identity. Suffice it to say that I do think that this volume should be seen as speaking to a concept of identity which is essentially de-essentialized (Rattansi, 1994). An emphasis on de-essentialized identities are especially important at a time in history when opportunities present themselves to forge new forms of solidarity. Gomez–Peña reports:

> The myths that once grounded our identity have become bankrupt. Sixties-era pan Latin Americanism, *la mexicanidad* (unique, monumentals, undying), and Chicanismo (with thorns and a capital C) have all been eclipsed by processes of cultural borderization and social fragmentations. Like it or not, we are now denationalized, de-Mexicanized, trans-Chicanized, and pseuedo-internationalized. And worse, in fear of falling into a new century we refuse to assume this new identity, roaming

> around instead in a Bermuda Triangle. We live in economic uncertainty, terrorized by the holocaust of AIDS, divided (better yet, trapped) by multiple borders, disconnected from ourselves and others by strange mass cultures and new technologies that appeal to our most mediocre desires for instant transformation and psychological expansion (1996, p. 172).

Following Rattansi, the concept of identity is understood within a Foucauldian framework that includes, among other characteristics, the following: "the deflation of a rationalist/Cartesian pretension to unproblematic self-knowledge"; "a critique of the conception of a linear connection to subjects to the external world, in which reality is made transparent from a uniquely privileged vantage point through the application of rationality and empirical disciplines"; a critique of human nature as consisting of a timeless, unchanging or defining ensemble of narratives; an emphasis on alterity and the processual character of identity construction and transformation; an emphasis on identity as an axis consisting of many sites of articulation and multiple discourses and practices of enunciation and positioning; an emphasis on the microphysics of power as an operative feature of identity of construction; and finally, an emphasis on the concept of the social that does not view social structures and cultural practices as totalizing, pre-given structures but rather as "practices of regulation, resistances and representation" (1994, pp. 29–30).

Gómez–Peña recently warned against the new politics of essentialism with respect to the construction of identity:

> In reaction to the transculture imposed from above, a new essentialist culture is emerging, one that advocates national, ethnic, and gender separatism in the quest for cultural autonomy, "bio-regional identity" and "traditional values." This tendency to overstate difference, and the unwillingness to change, or exchange, is a product of communities in turmoil who, as an antidote to the present confusion, have chosen to retreat to the fictional womb of their own separate histories. Even our so-called "progressive" communities are retrenching to a fundamentalist stance (1996, p. 11).

Since not all hybridities are equal, we must attach to the term an ideological tacit nominal qualifier (Radhakrishnan, 1996). In making such a claim, Ragagopalan Radhakrishnan provides us with an important distinction. He maintains that we must discern between metropolitan versions of hybridity and postcolonial hybridity. Whereas the former is a *ludic* form of capricious self-styling, the latter is a critical identitarian mode. Metropolitan hybridity, notes Radhakrishnan, is "characterized by an intransitive and immanent sense of *jouissance* while postcolonial hybridity is marked by a "frustrating search for constituency and a legitimate political identity" (1996, p. 159). Metropolitan hybridity is not "subjectless" or neutral but is a form of identitarian thinking informed by the cultural logic of the dominant West Postcolonial hybridity seeks authenticity in a "third space that is complicitous neither with the deracinating imperatives of Westernization nor with the theories of a static, natural, and single-minded autochthony" (p. 162).

Critical multiculturalism as a point of intersection with critical pedagogy supports the struggle for a postcolonial hybridity. Gómez–Peña captures the concept of post colonial hybridity when he conceptually maps what he calls the "New World Border":

> a great trans—and intercontinental border zone, a place in which no centers remain. It's all margins, meaning there are no "others," or better said, the only true "others" are those who resist fusion, *mestizaje,* and cross-cultural dialogue. In this utopian cartography, hybridity is the dominant culture; Spanish, Franglé, and Gingoñol are *linguas francas;* and monoculture is a culture of resistance practiced by a stubborn or scared minority (1996, p. 7).

Si Se Puede

While this volume does not investigate the many and various racist discourses of the postmodern metropole that position the racialized subject within practices of inferiorization and transgression, nor speculates upon the complex possibilities of racialized networks of alliance and cooperation, we are never the less provided many illuminating narratives contextually specific to the politics of inferiorization, exploitation, exclusion, and discrimination that take place in the United States, Mexico, the Netherlands, and Canada. The plight of indigenous Chiapans and other groups of rural workers constitute the centerpiece of this volume, as we are invited to reconsider the role of a capitalist reconstituted peasantry throughout the globe.

The question of ethnic social practices and the politics of universal justice is the urgent question of the new millennium. How are educators to approach this question with a politics both progressively critical and optimistic? William E. Connolly calls for an *ethos* of critical responsiveness in pointing out the inherent paradoxical and relational character of the *code* of universal justice. He notes:

> As a movement struggles to cross the magic threshold of enactment, it may introduce a new right onto the register of justice. It thereby exposes retrospectively *absences* in a practice of justice recently through by happy universalists to be complete. If and as the new movement becomes consolidated into a positive identity, it too becomes sedimented into settlements of the newly configural pluralism. And its presumptions, too, may now constitute a barrier to the next drive to pluralization (1995, p. 185).

Unlike the *codification* of justice, an *ethos* of critical responsiveness is not grounded in transcendental or ontological principles. In fact, an ethos of critical responsiveness *exceeds* justice by recognizing that there is never any justice without absence. Consequently, an ethos of critical responsiveness becomes *uncodifiable* in calling into question the complete closure of any grand narrative or universal principle through proclamation, divine fiat or rational consensus. While the practice of justice is ethically indispensable, it must exist in *dissonant independence* with an ethos of critical responsiveness.

Connolly notes that the ethos of critical responsiveness maintains that diversity is never irreducible to basic proclamations, rules, commands, or laws. Rather, diversity is always contingent and relational and to think of it as solid ground is to do it an injustice (Giroux, 1993). Consequently, "the ethos and the code coexist in an asymmetrical relation of strife and interdependence" (1995, p. 187). The point is that identities should never be naturalized or transcendentalized since there is always a fleeting, fugitive and contingent quality to identity. Connolly notes that "the cultivation of critical responsiveness grows out of the appreciation that no culturally constituted constellation of identities ever deserves to define itself simply as natural, complete, or inclusive" (1995, p. 188).

Throughout this volume, hope erupts in the empty space of alterity by splitting itself off from optimism and attaching itself to social struggle. In other words, the hope contained in this volume is not the hope brought on by a naive sense of teleology or a tie-dyed positive thinking about the future but by a commitment to struggle against white Anglo patriarchal capitalism.

We need to fatally unsettle the equation between whiteness and rationality; in fact, we need to decanonize all civilizing narratives, and the construction of the Latinos/a as the Other of reason and enlightenment. The inferiorizing and marginalizing practice of white supremacy, coupled with its inflection into the corporate thrust of multinational capitalism, constitutes one of the great challenges of the new millennium. The collusive relationship among white supremacy, patriarchy, and capitalism need to be faced head-on by criticalist educators working in the interstices of the dominant culture. The answers will not be simple, but I am sure they will be forthcoming. I harbor no illusion that we need to move in the direction of creating a romanticized image of *mestizaje* identity, crossing borders unproblematically with the cry: "we are all *mestiza;* none of us are pure; authenticity is a modernist illusion so let's all get together to celebrate our hybridity!" Such a view is to reinforce systematically the hegemony of white institutions and structures of domination cemented by the social relations of capitalist exploitation. Certainly we need "new, more open, non-absolutist forms of cultural politics within and between the minority communities and their articulation with the politics of the 'center'" (Rattansi, 1994). But our struggle for such "new ethnicities" cannot be undertaken outside of an oppositional politics that recognizes white supremacy and its marriage to neoliberalism as one of the greatest obstacles to democracy and social justice.

Questions of ethnic identity necessarily lead to concerns with schooling, the state, and social justice. Critical pedagogy is aimed at contesting the metropolitan gaze of the bourgeois state upon its disenfranchized, peripheralized, and subaltern others, unsettling, interrupting, and decanonizing those dominant pedagogies whose assumptions are grounded in the civilizational narratives of empire and the tropes of the Western unconscious. Such dominant pedagogies attempt to sequester and dispossess the voices of the marginalized to stabilize and domesticate them through the power of existing discursive regimes and reigning discourses of the state. This volume sets out to contest such an attempt at domestication. In this volume the voices of the subaltern subject is accorded the dignity of constructing her own voice and sounding it along the mean streets of capitalist gangsterism and in the precincts of the privileged. Rummaging through the rag and bone shop of the national soul, the oppressed are the only hope we have to piece together the social conscience of a country lost in greed, hatred, and avarice. It is our job to become their instruments of hope. *Ethnic Identity and Power* can be such an instrument for developing criticalist pedagogical approaches in classrooms.

References

Balibar, E., & I. Wallerstein (1993). *Race, Nation, Class: Ambiguous Identities.* London and New York: Verso.

Bannerji, H. (1995). *Thinking Through.* Toronto, Canada: Women's Press.

Bennett, W. J. (1996). "Civil Rights in the GOP Mission." *Los Angeles Times,* Monday, August 13, 1996. B5.

Connolly, W. (1995). *The Ethos of Pluralization.* Minneapolis and London: University of Minnesota Press.

Feagin, J. R., & V. Hernan (1995). *White Racism.* London and New York: Routledge.

Frankenberg, R. (1993). *White Women, Race Matters.* Minneapolis: University of Minnesota Press.

*Sections of this Afterword will appear in Peter McLaren, *Pedagogies of Dissent,* Boulder, Colorado; Westview Press, forthcoming.

Gatens, M. (1996). *Imaginary Bodies.* London and New York: Routledge.
Giroux, H. (1993). *Border Crossings.* London and New York: Routledge.
Gomez-Peña, G. (1996). *The New World Border.* San Francisco: City Lights Bookstore.
Ignatiev, N. (1995). *How the Irish Became White.* London and New York: Routledge.
Kahn, J. S. (1995). *Culture, Multiculture, Postculture.* London. Thousand Oaks. New Delhi: Sage Publications.
Lipsitz, G. (1995, September). "The Possessive Investment in Whiteness: Racialized Social Democracy and the 'White' Problem in American Studies." *American Quarterly.* 47(3): pp. 369– 387.
Luhrmann, T. M. (1996). *The Good Parsi.* Cambridge, Massachusetts and London, England: Harvard University Press.
Martin–Barbero, J. (1993). *Communication, Culture and Hegemony.* London. New York. New Delhi: Sage Publications.
Miles, R. (1982). *Racism and Migrant Labour: A Critical Text.* London: Routledge.
Miles, R. (1993). *Racism After "Race Relations."* London: Routledge.
Miles, R. (1994). "Explaining Racism in Contemporary Europe" in Ali Rattansi and Sallie Westwood (eds.), *Racism, Modernity and Identity.* Cambridge, MA and Cambridge, UK: Polity Press.
Miles, R., & R. Torres (1996). "Does 'Race' Matter? Transatlantic Perspectives on Racism after 'Race Relations' in Vered Amit-Talai and Caroline Knowles (eds.), *Re-Situating Identities.* Toronto, Canada: Broadview Press.
Omi, M., & H. Winant (1993). "The Los Angeles 'Race Riot' and Contemporary U.S. Politics" in Robert Goding–Williams (ed.), *Reading Rodney King.* London and New York: Routledge.
Radhakrishnan, R. (1996). *Diasporic Mediations.* Minneapolis and London: University of Minnesota Press.
Rattansi, A. (1994). " 'Western' Racism, Ethnicities and Identities in 'Postmodern' Frame" in Ali Rattansi and Sallie Westwood (eds.), *Racism, Modernity and Identity.* Cambridge, MA and Cambridge, UK: Polity Press.
Ridgeway, J. (1995). *Blood in the Face.* New York: Thunder's Mouth Press.
Roediger, D. (1993). *The Wages of Whiteness.* London and New York: Verso.
Roediger, D. (1994). *Towards the Abolition of Whiteness.* London and New York: Verso.
Rugoff, R. (1995). *Circus Americanus.* London and New York: Verso.
San Juan, Jr., E. (1995). *Hegemony and Strategies of Transgression.* Albany, New York: State University of New York Press.

Sarup, M. (1996). *Identity, Culture and the Postmodern World.* Athens, Georgia: The University of Georgia Press.

Shohat, E., and R. Stam (1994). *Unthinking Eurocentrism.* London and New York: Routledge.

Sleeter, C. E. (1996). "White Silence, White Solidarity" in Noel Ignatiev and John Gavey (eds.), *Race Traitor.* London and New York: Routledge.

Tsing, A. L. (1993). *In the Realm of the Diamond Queen.* Princeton, New Jersey: Princeton University Press.

Visweswaran, K. (1994). *Fictions of Feminist Ethnography.* Minneapolis and London: Univesity of Minnesota Press.

Williams, R. (1974). *Politics and Letters.* London: Verso.

Yudice, G. (1995). "Neither Impugning nor Disavowing Whiteness Does a Viable Politics Make: The Limits of Identity Politics" in Christopher Newfield and Ronald Strickland (eds.), *After Political Correctness.* Boulder, San Francisco, Oxford: Westview Press.

Contributors

Beatriz Calvo obtained her M.A., and is finishing her Ph.D. at the *Universidad Iberoamericana* in Mexico City in sociology. She has worked as a researcher at the *Centro de Investigaciones y Estudios Superiores en Antropología* in Mexico City, and is currently teaching and doing research at the *Universidad Autónoma de Cuidad Juárez,* Chihuahua, Mexico. Her areas of specialization are qualitative research methods, educational enthography, basic education and teacher education. She has written several books and many journal articles, book chapters and essays.

Robert A. DeVillar spent his early elementary school years in the United States, his upper elementary through high school years in Seville, Spain, and earned his B. A. (Latin American studies, social sciences) from the University of the Americas, Mexico City. He received a master's degree in ethnic studies from San Jose University, and earned another masters and a Ph.D. degree from Stanford University in Bilingual/Cross-Cultural Education, respectively. His research emphasis include equity issues of minority groups within democratic settings and implications of electronic technologies for enhancing first and second language development, pro-social behaviors among integrated groups, and academic results and school completion rates for language, and other minority groups. As an associate dean, University of California, Davis, DeVillar directs the UC Educational Research Center and co-directs a joint doctoral program in educational leadership in Fresno. His chapters in this volume stem from his year's Fulbright experience in Mexico.

Lotty Eldering is professor of intercultural pedagogics at Leiden University, the Netherlands. She studied cultural anthropology and received her Ph.D. at the University of Amsterdam with a dissertation on "Moroccan Families in the Netherlands." She has also published many articles and books on children of other immigrant groups and their education at home and at school. From 1987 to 1992 she carried out, with her researchers, the evaluation of a state-funded home intervention program (HIPPY) for ethnic minority mothers and children. Her current research projects concern, more specifically, involvement with ethnic minority children at risk. Besides her academic work, she has been a member of several committees advising the Dutch ministers of education and of social welfare on the policy for realizing equity of chances for ethnic minority children.

Christian Faltis (Ph.D., Stanford University) is a professor of bilingual education at Arizona State University, Tempe, Arizona. He is also the editor of *TESOL Journal.* In 1986, he was a Fulbright Scholar at the National Autonomous University of Honduras, Tegucigalpa, Honduras. He has authored over 40 articles and chapters on bilingual education topics. He has written or edited eight books and has two new books in the making: *Understanding and Caring for Bilingual Education in Elementary and Secondary School* (Allyn & Bacon) and *Teenagers, Bilingualism, and ESL in the Secondary School* (Teachers College Press). His book, *Joinfostering: Adapting Teaching Strategies for the Multilingual Classroom* was published as a second edition in 1996 (Merrill). His research interests are secondary bilingual education, critical case study research, and literacy.

Peter McLaren is professor at the graduate school of education and informational studies at the University of California, Los Angeles. Professor McLaren is the author and editor of numerous books on critical pedagogy, cultural studies, critical literacy, critical ethnography, and social theory. His work has been translated into Spanish, Portuguese, Catalan, Hebrew, Polish, German, French and Japanese. He lectures worldwide. Professor McLaren is also a faculty advisor to UCLA's Chicano Research Center.

Victor M. Franco Pellotier is a research professor at the Center for Research and Advanced Study in Social Anthropology (CIESAS) in Mexico City. Franco received his undergraduate degree in linguistics, a master's in anthropological sciences and is completing his doctoral studies in linguistics at the Autonomous Metropolitan University (UAM). His research interests focus upon with sociolinguistics, communications, discourse analysis, and symbolic anthropology. Franco's research in the Otomi region of the Mezquital Valley in the state of Hidalgo (Mexico) spans more than a decade; however, his recent sociolinguistic research (in collaboration with R. A. DeVillar) has centered upon the use of indigenous-produced and enacted videos of members of the îəhpu community to use as a catalyst for internal discussion and action relative to their linguistic and cultural revaluation processes. Franco's research and publications also address the Amuzgo indigenous community in Oaxaca, particularly in terms of nor conflict among familial relations, and usage of kinship terminology and attitudes toward it.

Cirenio Rodríguez obtained his Ph.D. in Policy and Organizational Analysis from the University of California at Santa Barbara. He is currently a professor in the educational administration and policy studies at California State University where he also serves as associate vice president for academic affairs. Dr. Rodríguez has written on effective schools, politics of education and culture and education and chicanos in education. He serves as an elected member of a local school board and worked as the executive director of a community-based Chicano activist organization. He is also active in the National Association of Chicana/Chicano Studies.

James F. Shackelford has B.S. and M.S. degrees in ceramic engineering from the University of Washington and a Ph.D. in Materials Science and Engineering from the University of California at Berkeley. He is currently a Professor in the Department of Chemical Engineering and Materials Sciences and Associate Dean for the Undergraduate Studies in the College of Engineering at the University of California, Davis. He teaches and conducts research in the areas of materials science, and the structure of materials, nondestructive.

Penelope L. Shackelford has a B.A. degree in philosophy and music from the St. Joseph College for Women in Orange, California, and an M.A. in the arts and consciousness from John F. Kennedy University in Orinda, California. She has taught in private and public schools in California and Canada and has been the owner/director of an art gallery. She is currently the associate art editor for *Multicultural Education Magazine.* She is also an art critic and features writer for the Davis Enterprise. She is a member of the Northern California Council of the National Museum of Women in the Arts, a member of the National Association for Multicultural Education, and a board member of EducArt Projects.

David M. Smith is professor of anthropology and linguistics at the University of Alaska-Fairbanks and formerly professor of education. He moved to Alaska in 1986 from the University of Pennsylvania where he had served as associate professor of education and director of the Center for Urban Ethnography. While at Pennsylvania he founded, and for eight years directed, the Penn Ethnography and Education Research Forum. He has also served as president of the Council for Anthropology and Education. His research on the social-cultural dimensions of literacy and the cultural politics of education and had been conducted in Africa, inner-city and suburban Philadelphia and Alaska.

George Spindler holds a Ph.D. from the University of California in Los Angeles. He is Professor Emeritus at Stanford University where he has taught since 1950. He is the founder of Educational Anthropology and has published and edited several hundred volumes dealing with this field, such as *Anthropology and Education* (1955), *Education and Culture* (1963), *Education and Culture Process* (1974, 1987), *Doing the Ethnography of Schooling* (1981, 1987), *Interpretive Ethnography of Education* (1987), and *Patchways to Cultural Awareness: Cultural Therapy with Teachers and Students* (1994). His *Series in Case Studies in Cultural Anthropology* (edited with Louise Spindler, published by Harcourt Brace Jovanovich College Publishers) cover all areas of the world. **Louise Spindler**, the first woman to get a Ph.D. in Anthropology at Stanford University, was an extraordinary woman who conducted fieldwork and co-authored many books with George Spindler. She passed away on January 23, 1997, and this book is dedicated to her.

Marcelo M. Suárez–Orozco is a psychological anthropologist and professor of education in both the human development and psychology and learning and teaching areas of the Harvard Graduate School of Education. He is author of many books published in Europe, Latin America, and the United States. His books include *Central American Refugees and U.S. High Schools* (1989); *Status Inequality* (with George A. DeVos, 1990); *The Making of Psychological Anthropology II* (coedited with George and Louise Spindler, 1994); and (with Carola Suárez–Orozco) *Transformations: Immigration, Family Life, and Achievement Motivation Among Latino Adolescents* (1995). He has taught at the University of California and at various European universities, including the Catholic University of Leuven and the University of Barcelona. In 1995, he was elected directeur d'estudes associe, École des Hautes Études En Sciences Sociales, Paris, and in 1996 he delivered the Norbert Elais Lecture at the Amsterdam School for Social Sciences. Suárez–Orozco was educated in public schools in Latin America and received his Ph.D. in anthropology from the University of California, Berkeley, in 1986. While a fellow at the Center for Advanced Study in the Behavioral Sciences at Stanford (1992–93), he became a volleyball fanatic. Students interested in a psychocultural exegesis of soccer in post-World Cup America may wish to refer to his first published essay, "A Psychoanalytic Study of Argentine Soccer."

Enrique T. Trueba received his Ph.D. from Pittsburgh University. He is a visiting professor in human development and psychology at Harvard University. A former dean of the School of Education at Madison, Wisconsin, and former vice president for academic affairs at the University of Houston, he has continued his research on the socio-cultural context of adaptation and the relationship between language and culture in the process of knowledge acquisition. His most recent books include *Cultural Conflict and Adaptation: The Case of the Hmong Children in American Society* (with L. Jacobs and E. Kirton, 1990, being translated into Chinese); *Crossing Cultural Borders: Education for Immigrant Families in America* (with

C. Delgado–Gaitan, 1991); *Myth Or Reality: Adaptive Strategies of Asian Americans in California* (with L. Cheng and K. Ima, 1993); *Healing Multicultural America: Mexican Immigrants Rise to Power in Rural California* (with C. Rodríguez, Y. Zou, and J. Cintrón, 1993); *Language and Culture in Learning: Teaching Spanish to Native Speakers of Spanish* (with B. Merino and F. Samaniego, 1993); *Power in Education: The Case of Miao University Students and It's Significance for American Culture* (with Y. Zou, 1994); and *Ethnic Identity and Power: Cultural Contexts of Political Action in School and Society* (in press, with Y. Zou). He is currently completing a volume on Mexican immigrant women in California.

Jon Wagner is professor in the division of Education at the University of California, Davis, where he teaches courses on school change and educational reform, qualitative research methods, the social and philosophical foundations of education, and the writing and rhetoric of educational research. He is author of *Misfits and Missionaries,* an ethnographic study of a school for black, high school dropouts, and editor of *Images of Information,* an examination of the used of still photography in social science research and teaching. His policy interests focus on the design of cooperative, university-school research projects. His research interests focus on issues of school change, school organization and achievement; university-school collaboration; and the culture and social organization of educational research.

Dr. Yali Zou received her M.A. and Ph.D. at the University of California, Davis. She is an associate professor in the department of Educational Leadership and Cultural Studies of the University of Houston and the director of Asian American Studies Center at the University of Houston. She is co-author of *Healing Multicultural America: Mexican Immigrants Rise to Power in Rural California* (with H. Trueba, C. Rodriguez, and J. Cintron), and *Power in Education: The Case of Miao University Students and its Significance for American Culture* (with H. Trueba). Now she is completing a book entitled *Chinese Culture in America.* She has received several teaching excellence awards and has been named an Honorary Professor of the Central University for Nationalities in Beijing. She is also an Honorary President of the Beijing International Business Institute.

Index

ability groups. *See* tracking
academic achievement, 78, 81, 114
academic failure, 83, 337
academic failure of oppressed groups, 13, 15
academic performance, 96–97
academic performance and race, 419
academic standards, 78
academic success, 14–15, 17–18, 82–83, 99–102, 134
academics first, 77, 78–79, 83–85, 93, 106
Academy of Ñähñu Culture (ACÑ), 237, 239–240, 249
acculturation, 198–199, 212, 234
achievement exams, 116
Ada, Alma Flor, 113
adaptation to disruptive cultural change, 27, 29–32
adaptive strategies, 47
adequate pedagogies, 14, 21
advocacy research, 4
affirmative action, 7, 133–154, 349, 350, 414–415, 417, 422
affirmative action, call for abolition of, 412–414
African American
population, 52
students, 81, 91
teachers, 117, 121, 122–123
African Americans, 5, 57, 329, 348, 349, 353, 358, 413, 414–415. *See also* blacks
Africans, 328
Afrocentric curriculum, attacks on, 37–38
Aid to Families with Dependent Children (AFDC), 149
Alaska Native Claims Settlement Act (ANCSA), 369–372
Alaska's educational system, 13, 369–387
alcoholism in Alaska, 378
aliens, as shock word, 366
alternate identity of indigenous groups, 210
American cultural dialogue, 27–29
American Friends Service Comittee (AFSC), 311
American Front, 411
American Indians, 74, 221, 222, 227, 231, 350, 355. *See also* Native Americans; Indians
American values, 28
Americas Watch, 197
Amnesty International, 197
Anglo teachers, 117

Anglos, 412
angry white males, 287
anthropology, 3, 14, 15
anti-democratic actions, 197
anti-immigrant sentiments, 13, 18, 35, 45–46, 137–141, 283–315, 346–348, 351–366, 411–429
anti-immigration groups, 4
anti-immigration script, 289, 292–295
Apple, Michael, 114
applied pedagogy, 3
arson of black churches, 412
art, 3
art, Mexican, 189
Aryan Nations, 411
Asian Americans, 295–296
Asian students, 81
Asians, 59–60, 74, 135, 138, 141, 153, 351
assimilation, forced, 369
Association of Mexican American Educators (AMAE), 51

Bakhtin, Michael, 114
Bakke case, 145
Bakke, Allan, 145
Balibar, E., 421
Balkanization of America, 413
Bannerji, Himani, 423–424
Bartolomé, Lilia I., 13, 345–366, 417
Bartra, Roger, 189–190
Bauman, Zygmunt, 422
Becker, Howard, 390
Bennett, William, 32, 33, 37, 347, 412–416
Berber language, 265
biases, 4
bicultural education, 212
biculturalism, 30, 336
bigotry, 345–366
bilingual
  classrooms, 113
  education, 113–129, 212, 336–338, 417
  teachers, 119
bilingualism, 17
Black English, 124
Blacks, 74, 135, 136, 140–142, 420. *See also* African Americans
border bandits, 309–315
border patrol, 293–295, 303–306, 311
bourgeois individualism, 416
bourgeois revolution, 329
Bowles, S., and Gintis, H., 19
bowling patterns, 286
Brazil, 2, 323
Brazilian education, 339–342
Bronenbrenner, U., 259–264
Brown Berets, 50
Buchanan, Patrick, 35, 292, 347, 357, 365, 412
burden of identity, 327
Bureau of Alcohol, Tobacco, and Firearms (ATF), 34
Bush, George, 361

California Proposition 187. *See* Proposition 187 (California)
California Proposition 209. *See* Proposition 209 (California)
California, education system 67–109
Calvo, Beatriz, 7, 159–184, 417, 433
Camacho, Manuel, 231
Canada, 427
capitalism, 326, 414, 416, 421, 422, 428
capitalist
  accumulation, 330
  exploitation, 417
  ideology, 348
  social relations, 345–366, 417
Caribbeans, 44
Carspecken, P. F., 19, 20, 391, 404–405
Casablanca, Morocco, 265
Castañeda, Jorge G., 231–232
caste-like immigrants, 15
Castroism, 229

Central America, 333
Central University for Nationalities, Beijing, 395–400
changing demographics in U.S., 44, 416
Chiapas, Mexico, 8–9, 188, 192, 195–198, 201, 205, 209–210, 214–216, 223–234, 416, 427
Chicago schools, 336–338
Chicanas, 43, 47. *See also* Mexicans
Chicano struggle, 417
Chicanos, 5, 47–48. *See also* Mexicans
Chihuahua, Mexico, 231
child labor, 3
children's books, 128–129
China, 2, 13, 59–60, 389–407
Chinese
  language, 45
  society, 392
  teachers, 117
Christian Identity, 411
Ciudad Juárez, Mexico, 8
Civil Practice Act of 1950, 45
Civil Rights, 413
  Act, 133
  movement, 51
class, 419
  division, 329
  racism, 421
  society, 328
  stratification, 418
  warfare, 357–366, 414
class-bound hierarchies, 415
classroom discourse, 120–123
classroom materials, 120, 124–125
Clinton, President Bill, 36, 287, 292–293, 347–348, 365–366
cocacolonization, 213
coffee, 196
Coffey, Ruth, 292
Cold War, 285
collaborative
  decision-making, 73, 75, 77, 89
  education, 67
  teaching, 5, 6, 67–109
college enrollment, Hispanics, 141–142
Colombians, 53–55, 333
colonialism, 2, 327, 422
colorblindness, 413
commercial media, 223
communications, 3
communism, 229, 355, 362
concepts of the self, 4
conceptualization of identity, 324
conflict between minority and majority, 210
Connolly, William E., 427–428
conscientization of oppression, 19
conspiracy theories, 284
Constantino, Rebecca, 6, 13, 113–129, 417
contained underlife, 115
continuing education for Mexican teachers, 170–172
cooperative learning, 78, 85–87
counterscript, 115–116
crime, 283
criollo, 231
crisis of identity, 331
critical ethnographers, 389–407
critical ethnography and empowerment, 392, 397, 405–407
critical ethnography, 13, 14, 18, 19–22, 259–280, 371–377, 390–393, 402–407, 417
critical multiculturalism, 426
critical pedagogy, 4, 10, 13–15, 18, 48, 113, 371–377, 380, 382, 384, 405, 415, 429, 426
critical teaching, 67–109
critical theory, 3, 4
Cross-Cultural Educational Development Program (University of Alaska), 370–371
Cuba, 333
Cubans, 44, 53–55
cultural adaptation, 14–15
cultural ancestry, 199
cultural conflict, 20
cultural determinism, 15
cultural discrimination, 331–338

cultural diversity, 68, 73, 321–342
cultural filiation, 323
cultural healing, 22
cultural hegemony, 20
cultural malaise, 283–315
cultural pluralism, 335–336
cultural politics of Alaskan education, 369–385
cultural politics, 27–41
cultural preservation, 199
cultural psychology, 3
cultural self-determination, 234
cultural stereotypes, 201
cultural therapy, 13, 21–22, 27, 38–41
cultural war, 13, 345–366
cultural-ecological model, 259–264
cultural-ecological perspective, 259
culturally meaningful teaching strategies, 16–17
culture of discontent, 284
culture, notion of, 205–206
curriculum control in Alaskan schools, 382–384
curriculum reform, 14
cynicism, 284

De Genova, N., 390
de-essentialized identity, 424–425
deconstructing language, 345–366
deIndianization, 210
Delgado-Gaitan, Concha, 391, 404–405
democracy rallies in China, 398–399
democracy, 48, 204
democracy, crisis of, 415–416
democracy, in Mexican education, 160–161
democracy, notion of, 208
Democratic National Convention (CND), 214
Democratic Revolutionary Party (PRD), 195–196
democratization in Mexico, 7, 159–184
demographic changes (China), 393
demographic projections, 154
demographics (China), 393–394
demographics of Latino immigrants, 51–61
demonization of others, 354–356
detracking, 5, 67, 80–82. *See also* tracking
developing world, job loss to, 284
developmental niche, 262–264
deviant practices, 211
DeVillar, Robert, 8–9, 187–216, 221–255, 417, 433
dialectical theory of agency, 423–424
Díaz, Porfirio, 202
dis-location, sense of, 284, 288–315
discourse patterns, 375
discrimination, 415
disruptive underlife, 115
disindianización, 210
disposable labor force, 285
diverse students, 6
diversity of Latinos, 51–52
division of labor, 418
Dole, Bob, 32, 411–412
domestic problems, U.S., 283
dominant culture, 334–335
dominant intergroup dynamics, 200–216
dominant script, 115, 116, 125
Dominican Republicans, 53–55
Donald, Dippo, 390–391, 404–405
doubling, 323
downsizing, 285–288, 303
drop-out rate (Alaska), 379, 385
drop-out rates, 136
Duke University, racism at, 349
Duke, David, 351, 353

Ebonics, 124
ecological environment, 260
economic decline, 283–284
economic diversity in China, 393

education in rural Alaska, 378–385
education statistics for Latinos, 57
Educational Commission of Guizhou Province, China, 396
educational diversity of Latinos, 51–61
educational ethnography, 3
educational reform, 105
educational reform in Mexico, 159–184, 417
educational reform in the U.S., 417
effective teaching strategies, 14, 16, 72
El Cardonal, Mexico, 240
El Salvadorians, 53–55
Eldering, Lotty, 10, 259–280, 417, 434
elite-acculturated adaptation, 30
empirical research, 4
empowerment, 20–21, 49
empowerment and academic achievement, 6
empowerment and critical ethnography, 392, 397, 405–407
empowerment and education, 339–342
empowerment of students, 6, 20–21, 67–109
empowerment theory, 403
enculturation, 199
endangered self, 21, 46–47
enduring self, 21, 46
engineering education, 133–154
English as a second language, 19
English as official language of U.S., 37
English fluency, 79
English proficiency tests, 113–114
English-only movement, 37
Equal Employment Opportunity Commission, 348–349
equal educational opportunities, 67
equity, 14
Eskimos. *See* Native Alaskans
essentialized identities, 14
ethnic clubs, student, 86, 91
ethnic diversity, 73–75
ethnic diversity in China, 393
ethnic diversity of Latinos, 51–61
ethnic identity, 4, 18, 345–366, 417
ethnic identity and power, 1
ethnic leadership, 48, 62–63
ethnic minorities, definition of, 261
ethnic racism, 421
ethnic violence, 13
ethnographic documentary, 235
ethnography, 389–390
ethos of critical responsiveness, 427–428
Europe, 2, 11
European Americans, 32
Evaluation Retreats, 76
exclusion in classroom, 419
exosystem, 260
experience, as concrete instances of objective social forces, 423–424

Faltis, Christian, 6, 13, 113–129, 417, 434
farm workers, 136
fatalism, 284
Federal Bureau of Investigation (FBI), 34
feelings of academic failure, in Latino students, 337
Fernandes, Florestan, 339–342
Festival of Films in Langage of Limited Diffusion, 224
Fez, Morocco, 265
Fictitious Mexico, 210
Filipinos, 60, 74, 140
Fiske, John, 346

France, education of culturally diverse children in, 334–335
Franco Pellotier, Victor M., 9, 221–255, 417, 435
Freemen, 34
Freire, Paulo, 1, 2, 10, 15, 18, 19, 48–49, 360, 372, 376, 407
French colonialism, 264
fringe right, 36
Fuentes, Carlos, 366
funk, 287
future, dimension of the, 342

Gaceta de Solidaridad (Solidarity Gazette), 193–194
gang activity, Latino, 44
Gate, Henry Louis, Jr., 349
gender inequities, 3
gender stratification, 418
genocide, 3
geographic origin, 199
Germanies, 285
"ghettoization" of students, 81
ghost workers, 45, 301–302
Gingrich, Newt, 32, 33, 37, 412
Giroux, Henry, 114, 116, 391
global immigration trends, 1
global marketing, 213
global upheaval, 283–315
globalization, 283–315
Godínez, General Miguel A., 231
Goldberg, David, 353
Gómez-Peña, Guillermo, 412, 424–426
Gore, Jennifer, 403
grade level, 116–117
Guadalupe Hidalgo Treatry, 44–45
Guagnxi Xhuang autonomous region, China, 394, 395
Guanajuato, Mexico, 222
Guatemala, 196
Guatemalans, 53–55
Guerrero, Mexico, 197, 231
Guinier, Lani, 348
Guizhou Institute for Nationalities, 396, 400–402
Guizhou province, China, 395
Gun Owners of America, 411
gun control, 36

Haitians, 53–55
Hakim, Peter, 197
Han hegemonic culture, 392, 394–397
Harker, Roger, 38–39
health statistics, 135–136
hegemonic discourse, 6, 13
heightened tensions in Alaska, 371
Helms, Jesse, 412
Henderson, Judge Thelton E., 140, 144
Henry, Jules, 19
heterogeneous grouping, 5, 67, 73, 75, 104. *See also* detracking
Hidalgo, Mexico, 9, 188, 225, 233
hierarchy, color-bound, 221
high risk students, 80
Hispanic culture, 362–363
Hispanics, 74, 135, 136, 138, 139, 140, 153–154
Hispanics, concept of, 333
historical determinants, 418
Hmong people, 395–396, 401
Hñähñu language, 239–255
Hñähñu literacy, 251–252
home language and culture, 18–19
home, concept of, 286–289, 303
homelessness, 346
homophobia, 3
hooks, bell, 349–350
hope, concept of, 1, 428
Hui ethnic minority (China), 393
Human Rights Watch/Americas, 352
Hunan province, China, 395
Hussein, Saddam, 355
hybridity, 426, 428

IDEA Kit, 113
identity, 321–342
identity formation, 259
identity, struggle for, 221–257
illlegal immigrants, 364–365
immigrants and crime, 306–315
immigrants, 137, 139, 283–315
immigrants, Mexican, 45
Immigration and Naturalization Service (INS), 137, 292, 305–306, 311–313, 352
immigration as theater of collective anxieties, 289
immigration mythmaking, 289–292
immigration policy, 137
immigration, 417, 422
imperialism, 206, 422
Indian education in Mexico, 8–9
Indians, 29–32, 35, 45. *See also* American Indians; Native Americans
indigena, 222
indigenous images and identity in Mexico, 187–216
individualism, 416
Indochina, 395
inequality, 283
infant mortality rates, 136
infotainment, 224
Inner Mongolia autonomous region, China, 394
Institutional Revolutionary Party (PRI), 190, 193–196, 222
institutionalized racism, 14, 351, 415
integration of minority, 339
integration, 198
Inter-American Dialogue, 197
inter-ethnic communication, 73
interaction styles, 375
intercultural, notion of, 208, 210
interdisciplinary curricula, 73, 75
interdisciplinary teaching, 5, 67–109
internal migrations, 1
intolerance, 138, 335
intracultural, notion of, 208, 211
Iowa Test of Basic Skills (ITBS), 380–382
Islam, 267–269
Ixmiquilpan, Mexico, 240

Jamaicans, 53–55
Japanese, 60
job insecurity, 283–284
Johnson, Lyndon, 134
Josephy, Alvin M., 215
Juárez, Chihuahua, Mexico, case study of, 161–184
Juárez, Victor Manual, 215
judicial system, 284
justice in Mexican educational system, 160

Kenitra, Morocco, 265
King, Martin Luther, Jr., 412–415
King, Rodney, 95
Koppel, Ted, 346–347
Koreans, 60
Krauze, Enrique, 190, 209
Ku Klux Klan, 411

Language Assessment Scales, 113
language and culture, 12
language and learning, 113–129
language as racism, 345–366
language, native, 199, 201
late capitalism, 416
Latin America, 44
Latin American immigrants, 51
Latinas, 44, 321. *See also* Hispanics; Mexicans
Latino
  celebrations, 50
  children, education of, 336–338
  ethnic identities, new, 43–63
  families, strenghth of, 58–59
  farm workers, 56
  leadership, 62–63
  organizations, 50
  populations, diversity of, 47
  socioeconomic diversity, 51–61
  teachers, 117, 121

Latinocentric curriculum, attacks on, 37–38
Latinophobia, 411
Latinos Unidos para Mejor Educación, 50
Latinos, 5, 14, 44, 47, 49, 50–63, 321, 329, 332–334, 413, 420, 428. *See also* Hispanics; Mexicans
levels of education, of various Latino groups, 53–55
Lima, Elvira S. and Marcelo G., 12, 13, 321–342, 417
Limbaugh, Rush, 32, 346–347, 351
Limited English Proficient (LEP), 73
linguistic diversity, 5, 68, 73
linguistic diversity in China, 393
linguistic hegemony, 126–128
linguistically diverse students, 6
linguistically meaningful teaching strategies, 16–17
Los Angeles, 117
Los Angeles police, 95
Los Angeles uprisings, 415
low academic expectations, 79
low-income families, 73
low-performing students, 80
lower wages, 285

Macedo, Donaldo, 13, 62, 345–366, 417
macrostructures of inequality, 415
macrosystem, 260
Manchu ethnic minority (China), 393
Mandarin language, 402
Manifest Destiny, 45, 355
maquiladoras, 164–165, 167, 182, 203–204
Marcos, Subcomandante (Zapatistas), 225, 227, 229–230
marginality, 198
marginalization, 210, 422
Marrakech, Morocco, 265
Marxism, 229, 360, 362
Marxism/Leninism, 229
Mayan Indians, 8
McLaren, Peter, 13–14, 19, 407, 411–429, 434
McVeigh, Timothy, 35
Mead, Margaret, 19
mechanized racism, 421
media, Mexican, 221–257
mediation, 323
Mehan, Bud, 109
Mendus, Susan, 353
Menominee Indians, 29–32, 35
Mesmin, Claude, 334
mesosystem, 260
mestizaje identity, 209, 424, 428
mestizo, 44, 59, 221–222, 231
Mexican American Political Action, 50
Mexican American students, 81
Mexican Americans, 333. *See also* Hispanics; Latinos
Mexican
  Constitution, 227
  culture, 49–50
  economy, 9
  educational system, 7, 9, 159–184
  government, 212, 222–223, 230–232
  identity, 187–216, 221–257
  immigrants, 51
  media, 187–216
  peasants, 196
  Revolution, 8, 189, 195
  self-expression, 221–257
  television, 9
  War of 1848, 202
  women, 18, 19, 165
  workers, 46, 417
  working families, 17–18
Mexicans, 53–63, 333, 355. *See also* Hispanics; Latinos
México imaginario, 210

Mexico, 2, 5, 44–63, 412, 427
Mezquital Valley, Mexico, 240–250
Miao ethnic minority (China), 392–407
Michoacán, Mexico, 222, 231
microsystem, 260
middle class students, 81
migrant, as shock word, 362–366
Miles, Robert, 419–420, 421
militarization of the U.S.'s southern border, 305
militia groups, 34, 36, 37
minorities in China, 393
minority culture deficit, 197
mixed ability grouping, 81
modernization of education, Mexico, 159–184
Moll, L., 16
Montana Militia, 34
moral codevelopment, 77, 93–96, 98, 99–102
moral leadership, 73, 105, 107
Morin, Edgar, 235
Moroccan children in Holland, 5, 10–11, 259–280
Moroccans, 264
Movimiento Estudiantil Chicano de Aztlán (MECHA), 50, 51
multicultural education, 349, 350
multicultural education, attacks on, 37–38
multiculturalism, 14, 325, 329, 349, 350, 354
multilingual education, 336–338, 356
muralists, Mexican, 189

Ñähñu
  alphabet, 242–243
  family life, 244–246
  immigration, 252–253
  Indians, 9–10
  resistance movement, 188, 214–215, 225–226, 233–234, 236–255, 417
  shepherding, 243–244
  video documentary, 250–255
nation, notion of, 208
National Action Council for Minorities in Engineering (NACME), 149
National Alliance, 411
National Association of Bilingual Education (NABE), 6, 113
National Commission for Democracy (NCD), 201–202
National cultural unity, concept of, 187–189
National Democratic Convention, 229
National Farm Support Program (PROCAMPO), 194
National Indigenous Institute (INI), of Mexico, 188, 226
National Program of Solidarity (Pronasol), 193–194
National Rifle Association (NRA), 34, 36, 37
National Science Foundation (NSF), 151
nationalism and racism, 421
nationalism in Mexico, 160
Native Alaskans, 13
Native Americans, 29–32, 35, 135, 141, 215, 221, 222, 227, 231, 329, 355. *See also* American Indians; Indians
native land claims, (Alaska), 369–372
native-oriented adaptation, 30
Nazis, 364
Neo-Vygotskians, 12
neoliberalism, 203–204, 416, 418, 428
Netherlands, 10–11, 259–280, 427
Netherlands, demographics, 264
New Republicanism, 37
New World Order, 36
new educational federalism, in Mexico, 159–184
Nicaraguans, 53–55, 333

Ningxia autonomous region, China, 394
Noël, Lise, 213
non-standard speech, use of, 375
non-white Hispanics, 420
North America, 2
North American Free Trade Agreement (NAFTA), 8–9, 165, 190–191, 195, 202, 210, 223
nostalgia, 4
Nuevo Leon, Mexico, 209

Oaxaca, Mexico, 197, 231
objectivity, 3, 213
offical knowledge, 114
official rhetoric versus reality, in educational reform in Mexico, 159–184
Ogbu, John, 15, 17, 380
oil producation and prices (Alaska), 371
Oklahoma City bombing, 35, 37
Olympics, in Mexico City, 228
oppositional self-identity, 17
optimism, American, 285
Orozco, José Clemente (muralist), 189
otherness, concept of, 299, 323
Otomí, 188, 214–215, 225–226

Pacific Islanders, 74, 135
paranoia, 11, 284, 292–295, 297
parental belief systems, 262
patriarchy, 428
Patriots, The (militia group), 34, 35
Paz, Octavio, 189, 192–193
pedagogical initiatives, 6
pedagogy, 321
pedagogy and politics, 5, 87–90
pedagogy of hope, 365–366
The Pedagogy of Hope (Freire), 2
pedagogy of the excluded, 321–342
The Pedagogy of the Oppressed (Freire), 360
pedophilia, 3
People's Liberation Army of China (PLA), 394
phenotype, 419
pigmentocracy, 221
political action, 48–49, 59, 61
politics of discrimination, 427
politics of diversity, theme of, 417, 422
politics of ethnic identity, 325–327, 345–366, 417
politics of exclusion, 427
politics of exploitation, 427
politics of inferiorization, 427
poor people, 348–349
Popkewitz, Tom, 105
population figures (China), 393
population growth, Mexico, 196
population, African American, 52
population, Latino, 51–52
population, U.S., 135
Posada, José Guadalupe, 189
Posse Comitatus, 411
post-industrial democracies, 283–315
post-nationality, 285, 300
poverty, 44, 283, 358, 415
  Mexico, 209
  Latinos, 53, 56
  rates, U.S., 135–137
Powell, Colin, L., 412
power of language, 345–366
power, 67–109
praxis, 20
preservation of native culture and life (Alaska), 371
pro-democratic struggle, 213
pro-immigration script, 289–292
Pronasol (National Program of Solidarity), 193
Proposition 187 (California), 139, 296, 300, 308–309, 351–352, 355, 364–365
Proposition 209 (California), 7, 140–141, 144–146, 152
pseudo-xenophilia, 290

psychology, 14
public education in Mexico, 159–184
public media, 223
Puebla, Mexico, 231
Puerto Ricans, 44, 51, 52, 333
Putman, Robert D., 286

Quantz, Richard, 392, 402–403
quota system, 134

race, 14, 328
race as ideological construct, 419–420
race, concept of, 14, 221, 418–419, 420
race relations paradigm, 418
race stratification, 418
racial identity, 345–366
racial tolerance, 353, 414
racialized stereotyping, 419–420
racism, 2, 3, 13, 94, 127, 138, 141, 197, 328–331, 334, 345–366
racism, concept of, 419–420
racist groups, 411
Radhakrishnan, Ragagopalan, 424, 426
radical militias, 4
radical right, 14
Ramos, Samuel, 189
reaffirmation, 31–41
realism, 235, 253–24
reflective practice, 69
refugees, 283–315
Regents of the University of California, SP-1 and SP-2, 144–146, 147, 152, 153
resistance, ethical-moral, 116
relational reality, 380, 474–476
religion, 199
remedial or bridging programs in Alaskan education, 379–380
remedial students, 80
remediation, 211–212
reproduction of the social order, 20
Republican backlash, 34
Republican Contract with America, 353
research conflicts, 13
researchers as agents of change, 403–404
resistance in teaching, 114–116, 120–123
resistance to theory, 422–423
resistance zone, 115–116
resistance, sociopolitical, 116
restrictive acculturation, 199
Riefenstahl, Leni, 364
Rif mountain region (Morocco), 265
Rivera, Diego, 189
Rodríguez, Cecilia, 201, 205, 214
Rodríguez, Cirenio, 5, 13, 43–63, 417, 435
role of language in dehumanization, 354–355
role of principal in Mexican educational system, 172–174
rote memorization, 124
Rouch, Jean, 235
Ruiz, Bishop Samuel, 197
rural communities, 136
rural poverty, 136–137

salaries, Mexican teachers', 175–177
Salinas de Gortari, President Carlos, 16–166, 193–195, 204, 211, 228, 231
Salvadoreans, 333
San Luís Potosí, Mexico, 222
Sandburg, Carl, 355–356
Sandel, Michael, 284
scaffolding, 15–16, 21
Scholastic Aptitude Test (SAT), 123
Schonhausen/Roseville project, 39–40
school reform, 70, 76, 105
school socialization, 5, 67–109
Schweder, Richard, 389–390

segregation, 45, 133
selective acculturative, 200–201, 211
self-determination, Indian, 231
sexism, 13, 46
Shackelford, James F., 7, 133–154, 417, 435
Shackelford, Penelope L., 7, 133–154, 417, 436
Sichuan province, China, 395
Silber, John, 351, 353, 365
Simon, Roger, 390–391, 404–405
Siqueiros, David Alfaro (muralist), 189
situated self, 21, 46
skill and drill classroom activities, XX, XXX
skin color, 199, 419–420
slavery, 3, 328
Smith, David M., 13, 369–385, 417, 436
social control, 422
social diversity in China, 393
social heteroglossia, 114, 116, 121
social justice, 68, 107
social participation, in Mexican education, 160
social reproduction theory, 68, 109
socialism, 229
socialization, 199, 201
socioeconomic diversity of Latinos, 51–61
sociology, 3, 14
Solidarity Gazette *(Gaceta de Solidaridad),* 193–194, 211
solidarity, in Mexico, 160
Sonora, Mexico, 231
South America, 333
Soviet Union, collapse of, 285
Spanish language, 6, 118, 121, 122, 124
Spanish literacy, 127–128
special needs students, 80
Spindler, George and Louise, 4, 13, 19, 21, 27–41, 46, 417, 436–437
staff development, 69
standardized achievement measures, 107
standardized tests, use in Alaskan schools, 380–382
State Educational Commission of China, 396
stereotypes, 334, 418
Stone, Oliver, 225
Stop Immigration Now (SIN!), 292
student
  empowerment, 72–73
  engagement, 77, 90–93, 99–102, 106
  ethnicity, 72
  recruitment, 133
  retention, 133
students, 67
Suárez-Orozco, Marcelo M., 5, 11–12, 13, 283–315, 417, 437
subjectivity, 424
subordinate intergroup dynamics, 200–216
suicide and death in Alaska, 378
Surinamese, 264
Swain, Carol, 353
symbolic violence, 345

Tabasco, Mexico, 231
Taibo, Paco Ignacio, 195–196
talented and gifted students, 81
Tamaulipas, Mexico, 222
Tanger, Morocco, 265
teacher learning, 68, 70
teacher preparation, 69
teacher-student collaboration, 16
teachers as learners, 69
teaching strategies, 14–17
technistic reality, 373–374, 377, 379–380
technologies, new, 285
technology, 416–417
terrorism, 355, 416
terrorists, 294
Tetouan, Morocco, 265

Texaco scandal, 141
The Order, 411
Third-World poverty, 139
Thomas, Jim, 391
Tiananmen Square, Beijing, China, 398–399
Tibet autonomous region, China, 394
Tlatelolco massacre, 227–228
tolerance, call for, 417
Torres, R. 419–420
Torres-Guzmán, María, 113
tracking, 75, 81, 104
transculture, 424–426
transgenerationality, 199
transnational alliances, 59–60
transnational economic and social formations, 283
Trueba, Enrique (Henry) T., 5, 7, 13, 43–63, 49–50, 133–154, 395–407, 417, 437–438
types of adaptation, 27

U.S. Census Bureau's definitions of race, 420
underemployment rates, 137
underepresented students, 134, 148
undergraduate admission, 141–143
underlife, 115
undocumented immigrants, 46
United Citizens of Justice, 411
United Farm Workers Union, 51
United States, 44
University of Alaska, 370–371
University of California, Davis, 7, 42–152, 396
  Business Education Science Team (BEST), 148
  California Alliance for Minority Participation (CAMP), 150
  Center for Women in Engineering, 151–152
  Engineering Summer Residency Program (ESRP), 146–147
  Mathematics, Engineering, and Science Achievement (MESA), 147–148, 149, 151
  Mentorships and Opportunities for Research in Engineering (MORE), 150–151
  MESA Engineering Program (MEP), 148–149, 152
  National Consortium for Graduate Degrees for Minorities in Engineering, 152
University of California Regents, SP-1 and SP-2, 144–146, 147, 152, 153
University of Wisconsin, Madison, 396
Uygar ethnic minority (China), 393

vacuum of legitimacy, 284
value-free research, myth of, 402–403
Vasconcelos, José, 189
video industry, 224
video ethnography, 234–236
Villenas, Sofia, 43–44
violence against immigrants, 283
violence, 13, 44, 46
violent crime rates, 135
Vygotsky, L. S., 12, 15–17, 20–21

Waco incident, 34
Wagner, Jon, 5–6, 67–109, 417, 438
Weaver, Randall, 34–35
welfare benefits, 138
welfare reform, 357, 359
West, Cornell, 349
White Aryan Resistance, 411
white
  ethniclass, 27–41
  hegemony, 418
  male-dominated society, 348–349
  males, 35, 348
  race, 420

white (*continued*)
supremacism, 14, 411, 418, 428
supremacist movements, rise of, 417
supremacist organizations, 411
whiteness, 328, 418
whites, 30, 32, 37, 45, 74, 135, 141–142, 329, 354, 414–415
Will, George, 346–347
Williams, Raymond, 424
Willis, Paul, 19
Wilson, Governor Pete, 34, 140, 300–302, 304, 351–352, 411, 412
Wolf, Naomi, 350
women, 136, 140
working poor, 135
World Trade Center bombing, 293–294, 306
writers, Mexican, 189

xenophobia in Europe, 314
xenophobia, 2, 3, 137–138, 353–355
Xinjiang autonomous region, China, 394

Yucatán, Mexico, 222
Yugoslavia, former, 285
Yunnan province, China, 395

Zacatecas, Mexico, 222
Zapata, Emiliano, 229
Zapatista Army of National Liberation (EZLN), 223, 227
Zapatista National Liberation Front (EZLN), 191–192, 201–202
Zapatista resistance movement, 8–9, 188, 195, 201–205, 210, 223–234, 417
Zapatista video documentary, 228–229
Zedillo, President Ernesto, 203
Zhuang ethnic minority (China), 393
zone of proximal development, 16–17
Zou, Yali, 13, 389–407, 417, 438